Instructor's Manual

to accompany

Negotiation
Readings, Exercises, And Cases

Third Edition

Roy J. Lewicki
Ohio State University

David M. Saunders
McGill University

John W. Minton
Pfeiffer College

Prepared by
Laura Turek

Boston   Burr Ridge, IL   Dubuque, IA   Madison, WI   New York   San Francisco   St. Louis
Bangkok   Bogotá   Caracas   Lisbon   London   Madrid
Mexico City   Milan   New Delhi   Seoul   Singapore   Sydney   Taipei   Toronto

Irwin/McGraw-Hill

A Division of The McGraw·Hill Companies

Instructor's Manual to accompany
NEGOTIATION: READINGS, EXERCISES, AND CASES

Copyright ©1999 by The McGraw-Hill Companies, Inc. All rights reserved.
Previous editions copyright 1985 and 1993 by Richard D. Irwin, Inc.
Printed in the United States of America.
The contents of, or parts thereof, may be reproduced for use with
NEGOTIATION
Readings, Exercises, and Cases
Roy J. Lewicki, David M. Saunders, and John W. Minton
provided such reproductions bear copyright notice and may not be reproduced in
any form for any other purpose without permission of the publisher.

1 2 3 4 5 6 7 8 9 0 QSR/QSR 9 3 2 1 0 9 8

ISBN 0-07-059346-9

http://www.mhhe.com

TABLE OF CONTENTS

		Page
Introduction		1
Cautionary Notes on Teaching Negotiation Skills		4
Challenges of Teaching Negotiation (article)		6
Structuring the Negotiation Course		18
Additional Resource Materials		23
Special Guidelines for Using Role Playing Instruments		24
Sample Course Outlines		28
Exercise 1	Disarmament Exercise	37
Exercise 2	Pemberton's Dilemma	49
Exercise 3	The Used Car	52
Exercise 4	Knight Engines - Excalibur Engine Parts	57
Exercise 5	Universal Computer (I)	64
Exercise 6	Universal Computer (II)	69
Exercise 7	Twin Lakes Mining	74
Exercise 8	Salary Negotiations	85
Exercise 9	Newton School Dispute	95
Exercise 10	Bestbooks / Paige Turner	106
Exercise 11	Elmwood Hospital Dispute	113
Exercise 12	The Power Game	124
Exercise 13	Coalition Bargaining	137
Exercise 14	Jordan Electronics Company	148
Exercise 15	Third Party Conflict Resolution	156

Exercise 16	The Connecticut Valley School	178
Exercise 17	Alpha-Beta	192
Exercise 18	The New House Negotiation	217
Exercise 19	Eurotechnologies, Inc.	227
Exercise 20	The Pakistani Prunes	235
Exercise 21	Planning for Negotiations	244
Exercise 22	Sanibel Island	246
Exercise 23	The Playground Negotiation	254
Exercise 24	Collecting NOs	277
Exercise 25	500 English Sentences	282
Exercise 26	Sick Leave	291
Exercise 27	Town of Tamarack	300
Case 1	Capital Mortgage Insurance Corporation	314
Case 2	Pacific Oil Company	321
Case 3	A Power Play for Howard	332
Case 4	Creating The GM-Toyota Joint Venture	334
Case 5	Collective Bargaining at Magic Carpet Airlines	343
Case 6	Vanessa Abrams	354
Case 7	500 English Sentences	358
Case 8	Sick Leave	361
Questionnaire 1	Personal Bargaining Inventory	364
Questionnaire 2	The SINS Scale	368
Questionnaire 3	The Influence Tactics Inventory	377
Questionnaire 4	The Trust Scale	381

INTRODUCTION

Welcome to the third edition of the Instructor's Manual for *Negotiation: Readings, Exercises and Cases*. The first editions of this book, published in 1985 and 1993, have been very well received. Courses in negotiation and dispute resolution have become popular fixtures in schools and colleges of business, public policy, urban affairs, etc. In addition, the academic study of negotiation and dispute resolution has enjoyed a significant "boom" in the past several years, leading to a rapid growth in research studies, "applied" articles for managers and practitioners, and new role plays, simulations and other teaching technology. As a result, we had a very rich pool of resource material from which to compile this edition. We hope you find these materials useful, and that they enhance your teaching effectiveness in this exciting, interesting and challenging area!

All of the revisions in *Negotiation: Readings, Exercises and Cases* (and this Instructor's Manual) are paralleled by revisions in the companion textbook, *Negotiation* (1999, Third Edition), also available from McGraw-Hill/ Irwin. Either book may be used separately, or they may be used together in a course. See the following section for changes we have made to this volume, and to the companion text.

Organization of the *Readings, Exercises and Cases Book*, and Changes from the Second Edition

As you will note, the Reader is divided into four major sections. The first section is the Readings section. Readings from newspapers, magazines, and applied management journals have been selected because of their emphasis on conflict, the negotiation process, or the psychological and sociological dynamics that are related to negotiation (e.g. persuasion, communication, power, etc.). Either as stand alone assignments or combined with the textbook, the readings offer a rich variety of perspectives, insights, and case examples of negotiation and conflict management processes in social interaction. Since there has been so much published in this field since the second edition, almost 50% of this material is new, and we hope you agree that the collection is very rich and diverse!

The earlier editions divided these readings into fourteen sections. In the third edition, we have reorganized the material into four parts. The first part, Fundamentals of Negotiation, examines some critical aspects common to all negotiations and has four sections: (1) The Nature of Negotiation; (2) Prenegotiation Planning; (3) Strategy and Tactics of Distributive Bargaining; and (4) Strategy and Tactics of Integrative Negotiation. The second part, Fundamental Subprocesses of Negotiation, examines three critical subprocesses of negotiation: (1) Communication and Cognitive Biases; (2) Finding Negotiation Leverage; and (3) Ethics in Negotiation. The third part, Individual, Group and Cultural Contexts of Negotiation, examines the broader contexts of negotiation in four sections: (1) Social Context; (2) Team and Group Negotiations; (3) Individual Differences; and (4) Global Negotiations. Finally, the fourth part of the readings portion of the book, Managing Difficult Negotiation Situations, is divided into two sections: (1) Individual Approaches; and (2) Third-Party Approaches.

The second section of the Reader contains 27 experiential exercises and simulations, an increase of 50% over the second edition. Most of these activities have been developed specifically for use in courses, workshops and seminars on negotiation and dispute resolution. Some we developed ourselves, but many others were developed by our friends and colleagues, and are used here with their permission. As a package, the 27 exercises cover almost every topic and content area that an instructor could want to cover in a regular academic course: simple games, simple single issue negotiations, multi-issue negotiations, dual and multiparty negotiations, distributive scenarios, integrative scenarios, simulations emphasizing differences in power and international differences, and scenarios permitting third party intervention. Many of the exercises are new, and most of the old ones have been updated with more current financial information, etc. The individual role information for the role plays continues to be placed in the Instructor's Manual for 3 reasons. Our primary reason for doing so is the inability to preserve the confidentiality of role information when the roles for all sides were reproduced in the Appendix of the Reader. This has become an increasing problem as faculty are using role plays as graded class exercises, etc. Second, with the increased "resale" of textbooks, we were finding that students often bought used books which had the role information torn out or marked up. Finally, students frequently forget to bring their books to class, and so the instructor must have at least several photocopies of individual role information available anyway. As a result, we felt that the instructor could keep greater control over confidential role information if it were only published in the IM, and copies reproduced for each class. We realize that this creates somewhat of a logistical and financial burden for some instructors, and we address some of these problems later on in this section.

The third section of the book contains 8 case studies of negotiation, a 50% increase over the second edition. From our perspective, the purpose of a good negotiation case is to help the student see the unfolding of a negotiation from start to finish, both to permit examination of key strategic and tactical steps and to add richness to their own role plays and real negotiations. Interestingly, this is the area where there has been the least development of new teaching materials, particularly cases which can be used to highlight the interactive and evolving dynamics of the negotiation process. We have included three old "stand-bys" from the previous edition, Capital Mortgage Company, Pacific Oil (plus the accompanying technical note), and General Motors-Toyota; we did not change the numbers or the dates in these cases. Five additional cases have been added: two were highly successful cases that have been perfected over the past several years (Vanessa Abrams, Magic Carpet Airlines) and three appear for the first time in print as cases in this volume (A Power Play for Howard, 500 English Sentences, Sick Leave).

The fourth section of the book contains four self-assessment questionnaires. Three of these questionnaires--Personal Bargaining Inventory, the Ethics Questionnaires, and the Influence Tactics Questionnaire --were included as exercises in the previous edition. The fourth questionnaire, Interpersonal Trust, was developed expressly for this volume. Scoring and Interpretation materials are provided in this Instructor's Manual.

Finally, the Appendix of the Reader contains only the additional case material from the Capital Mortgage and Pacific Oil cases. As we indicated above, all of the individual role information for the exercises is reproduced with each exercise in this Instructor's Manual.

Using This Manual

This manual contains many elements that we hope will assist you in teaching your course:

1. An introduction to some techniques and methods for teaching a course that uses the elements we provide in these books. If you are not familiar with using role plays or teaching cases, we suggest that you consult these materials, the resources cited, and the special sections at the end of the introduction on Special Guidelines for Using Role Plays and Instruments.
2. An article prepared by Roy Lewicki, and published in *The Negotiation Journal* that comments on some of the unique challenges and difficulties of teaching courses on negotiation and dispute resolution. For the instructor inexperienced in teaching in this field, this reading is strongly suggested.
3. Guidelines for structuring a course on managerial negotiation. There is no one way to teach this course. In fact, we never fail to be impressed by the new and creative ways that instructors find to use and adapt experiential materials (and accompanying cases, graded exercises and papers, etc.). We have included sample course outlines, as well as, cross-listed the sections of the readings with the exercises and cases, so that instructors may pick and choose topical headings with appropriate cases and role play scenarios.
4. A list of additional resources for course outlines, role play materials, etc.
5. Special guidelines for instructors who are using role playing for the first time, or for those who would like to review the pedagogical foundations of this approach. These guidelines were initially published in Hall, D. T., Bowen, D. D., Lewicki, R. J., & Hall, F. S. (1988). *Instructor's Manual to Accompany Experiences in Management and Organizational Behavior*. Third Edition. New York: John Wiley.
6. Teaching notes for each of the 27 exercises, eight cases and four questionnaires.

Finally, as we noted in the earlier editions, we have not attempted to create a pool of examination questions. As we point out, examinations are not a common method of student evaluation in courses of this nature. Instead, we suggest several alternative options for evaluating students in the opening notes to this manual.

Enjoy! And please contact us with your questions, concerns, and suggestions for future editions.

Feedback to the Authors

We hope the materials in these volumes serve you well. We would be pleased to receive any feedback, suggestions and corrections that you have, or to answer any questions that come up as you use these materials. Please don't hesitate to contact us, and let us know how these materials work in your own organization or university.

Roy J. Lewicki	David M. Saunders	John W. Minton
College of Business	Faculty of Management	School of Business
The Ohio State University	McGill University	Pfeiffer University
1775 College Road	1001 Sherbrooke W.	4701 Park Road
Columbus, OH 43221	Montreal, QC H3A IG5 Canada	Charlotte, NC 28209
614-292-0258	514-398-4028	704-521-9116, ext. 236
lewickir@cob.ohio-state.edu	saunders@management.mcgill.ca	mintonjw@boone.net

CAUTIONARY NOTES ON TEACHING NEGOTIATING SKILLS

The purpose of this section is to share some insights and observations about teaching courses on negotiation. We have learned--through many interesting but tension-filled experiences--that when instructors let students "experiment" with conflict and power through role plays, simulations and questionnaires, things do not always proceed as calmly and predictably as we might like. For some instructors, these experiences are the spice of exciting classroom instruction; for others, they are the unpredictability that one may find a bit threatening and intimidating, since the learning event may occasionally appear out of control. Therefore, in order to help the instructor understand these dynamics, and lead students to learn the most from them, we will attempt to provide some insights and cautionary notes in this section.

Our Assumptions About You, The Instructor

In preparing this Instructor's Manual, we debated about the amount of background and preparatory materials that we should include on both experiential learning and case teaching. We decided to make an assumption: that instructors who would adopt this book were already fundamentally familiar with the mechanics of conducting experiential exercises, self-assessment questionnaires, role plays, and case teaching. We would therefore limit our commentary to the more specific dynamics of conducting learning experiences about negotiation, power and conflict. Short overview notes on the general approach to using role playing and instruments in the classroom are reproduced following this introduction.

For those of you about whom we made the INCORRECT assessment--that you are not familiar with the mechanics of experiential exercises or case teaching--we recommend that you consult any one of a variety of sources on this subject. We have found that the best overviews to conducting experiential exercises may be found in the Instructor's Manuals of several leading Organizational Behavior texts. We specifically recommend the introductory sections of the following Instructor's Manuals:

Hall, D. T., Bowen, D. D., Lewicki, R. J., & Hall, F. S. (1996). *Instructor's Manual to Accompany Experiences in Management and Organizational Behavior.* Fourth Edition. New York: John Wiley.

Cohen, A. R., Fink, S. L., Gadon, H., & Willits, R. D. (1996). *Instructor's Manual to Accompany Effective Behavior in Organizations.* Seventh Edition. Homewood, IL: Richard D. Irwin.

For case teaching, the Cohen et al. manual also provides an excellent discussion. Harvard Business School Case Services has several good books and pamphlets on case teaching and the case method.

Finally, we wish to recommend to you *The Journal of Management Education*. Published since 1975 (formerly as *Exchange*), this Journal publishes many articles on methods, strategies and issues in experiential, case and traditional pedagogy in the organizational behavior field. If a colleague or your local library does not now subscribe, contact Sage Publications.

In this section, we reprint an article written by the senior author, which appeared in *The Negotiation Journal*. The article explains some of the ways that teaching negotiation is different from other experiential-based courses, uses a well known model of experiential learning to explain the various vehicles for learning in the course, discusses some general problems in structuring a negotiation course, and describes some of the unique challenges that are created for instructors in these courses. For those who do not have extensive teaching experience in this area, we hope the article creates an appropriate groundwork for understanding the course specifics that we describe later in this Introduction.

TEACHING IDEAS
CHALLENGES OF TEACHING NEGOTIATION

Roy J. Lewicki[1]

Courses in negotiation have become a growing industry. Eleven years ago, when I first taught a negotiation course to students in a graduate school of business, there were perhaps two or three other comparable courses in the United States. Reading and case materials at that time were drawn largely from labor relations, social psychology, and international diplomacy. Simulation materials were adapted from game theory, collective bargaining and psychological experiments. Only one or two practitioner-oriented trade books were available in the marketplace.

Today, many new negotiation courses are started each year in business schools, law schools, public policy schools, schools of international relations, and undergraduate curricula. Case studies and simulations are being systematically developed to analyze and enact negotiation in each of these environments and contexts. Research emphasis has largely moved from the development of new theoretical bases to applications and the analysis of negotiations in situational context. Practitioner oriented books on negotiation abound, and comprehensive textbooks are beginning to appear. Finally, seminars for executives and practitioners are available from almost every reputable training organization and consulting firm.

Despite this dramatic proliferation of negotiation courses, seminars and resource materials, there has been little explicit discussion of how negotiation should be taught. My purpose in this article is to initiate such a discussion by exploring some of the central problems, issues and dilemmas of teaching negotiation. While some of these problems are not unique to teaching negotiation skills (and related courses in power and conflict management), others specifically arise because of the nature of the subject matter and the pedagogical style necessary to create a rich and challenging learning environment

How Teaching Negotiation is Different

Some elements of teaching negotiation are very different from teaching more traditional courses. The following examples of such differences contribute both to the excitement and to some of the challenges of teaching in this field:

1. Negotiation is a relatively new course area, and, until recently, each instructor largely reinvented the wheel each time he/she designed a negotiation course. While this newness offers the opportunity for creativity, it also results in much idiosyncrasy in both what is taught and how it is taught. A few who were involved in the early teaching ventures learned of one another's existence and compared notes. It is only recently, however, that sets of course outlines have been available for instructors to review and compare (Neale and Northcraft, 1985).

---

[1] Reprinted from *The Negotiation Journal*, January 1986, pp.15-27

2. Because of the newness of the field and the lack of open discussion about teaching negotiation, there has been little systematic dialogue and research on how the subject should be taught. Each instructor has developed a personal teaching model based on quasi-random experimentation and intuitive judgment. These models and their implications have not been tested.

3. As noted in the introduction the study of negotiation is truly interdisciplinary. Negotiation has been studied in a variety of different contexts, and both researchers and instructors have liberally borrowed models and theories from one context and applied them to another. Yet the appropriateness of the cross-context translation and application has seldom been tested. For example, researchers in third party dispute resolution have often noted that third parties operated in different environments and contexts e.g., labor relations, the courts, community disputes, corporate organizations and international diplomacy. Moreover, research findings derived in one context were readily applied to another as though the contexts were identical. Yet until recently, no effort was made to test this transferability and determine how much contextual factors actually affected third party behavior and effectiveness (Lewicki, Sheppard, and Bazerman, forthcoming). The same manner of unbridled cross-field application has occurred in most of the negotiation research, and in teaching the subject.

4. While negotiation can be taught as a purely academic course (and usually is taught this way in social science departments or in a doctoral seminar), the movement in negotiation training has been toward combining skill development and intellectual training. This has occurred because the greatest demand for negotiation courses is in professional schools of business and law, where there is a stronger emphasis on pragmatic education. In addition, students enter the course with varying degrees of behavioral expertise. While most students have not been exposed to negotiation theory and models, many have negotiated for a long time, some in a professional capacity. To the degree, then, that a negotiation course emphasizes skill development, students may have to unlearn old, unproductive behaviors as well as learn new behaviors.

A Model for Teaching Negotiation Skills

There are several key assumptions about the teaching and learning of negotiation that, though they may seem obvious, should be stated explicitly.

First, negotiation is a *comprehensible social process*. Negotiation is not a mystical process in a black box; it can be analyzed, understood, and modeled. Second, negotiation is a *learnable and teachable skill*. Negotiators are made, not born, and skills can be improved and relearned throughout life. Finally, change and improvement in negotiating behavior require a *combination of intellectual training and behavioral skill development*. Thus, the most effective approaches to teaching negotiation will integrate intellectual analysis and skill development in a complete pedagogical package.

To demonstrate how skill development and theory may be integrated together in teaching negotiation, I will employ a simple, broad-based model of experiential learning (Figure 1). This model, derived from the work of Kolb, Rubin and McIntyre (1983), proposes that learning occurs in four interrelated steps:

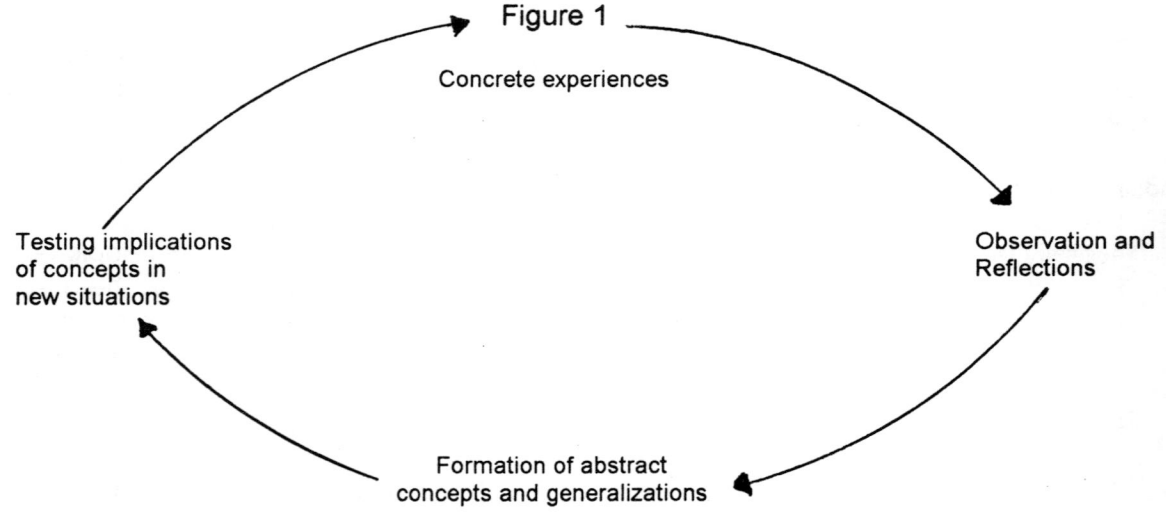

Figure 1

- The development (or external introduction) of concepts, principles and generalizations, leading to
- Predictions, hypotheses, or testing of the implications of these new concepts, leading to
- Actual behavior and concrete experiences, leading to
- Observations, reactions and reflections on that behavior, leading back to further concepts, principles and generalizations (theory).

Students can begin anywhere in this cycle to change their behavior or their understanding of it. For instance, athletes who want to improve their tennis swing might begin this process by becoming more aware of their current swing (actual behavior and reflection). This then leads to an effort to define why the swing is poor (reflection and principles), followed by an intention to change the wrist position while swinging (principles and intentions), then a change in the way the racket is swung (behavior). Similarly watching a videotape of a professional tennis player or reading a book about tennis would be an infusion of principles, leading to intentions to behave differently; actually taking a lesson would be an introduction of principles and some "practice" (new behavior, reflection, intention to behave differently, and more new behavior).

This model is useful in several ways. First, it applies to many different situations where skills are learned and developed, and allows us to break down the skill development process into its component parts. Second, since the learning model has several component parts, it is most useful to structure the learning process to bolster each of the elements. Finally, there are several competing theories as to the optimal place to "enter" this learning circle. I will note some of these competing theories in the discussion that follows.

Structuring The Course

While it is possible that some doctoral-level instructors may wish to teach only theory and research, instructors at other levels generally want to structure a course that is designed to improve the student's negotiating behavior. In particular, courses designed for executives or MBA students should offer a blend of theory and skill practice, since these students are primarily interested in improving their negotiating behavior. Courses structured in this way are more likely to help the student recognize the relation between theoretical principles and actual behavior, thereby preparing the student to negotiate more effectively. Finally, experiential components add a dimension that makes the course more interesting, enjoyable, exciting, and relevant to both student and instructor.

There are many ways to structure a negotiation course -- in terms of the topics covered, intellectual and experiential materials used, etc.[2] Since I am not proposing that there is one definitive way to teach this topic, the following ideas are intended as suggestions only. However, an ideal course structure should emphasize each of the four stages in the experiential model, and I shall make specific recommendations regarding course design elements that may be used for each stage.

Theory and Concepts. Most academic courses emphasize theory and scholarly research. Negotiation is no exception. There is a large volume of material available on the negotiation process, written from many different perspectives (e.g., psychology, economics, communications, sociology, law, and political science). Instructors seem to prefer all varieties of textbooks, research books and articles, or mass market publications written largely for practitioners. The following topics are addressed in most negotiation courses through lectures or assigned readings;
- The dynamics of interpersonal and intergroup conflict,
- An overview of the negotiation process;
- The economic structure of negotiation, and some exposure to game-theoretic models;
- The basics of competitive, distributive, win-lose negotiation;
- The basics of collaborative, integrative, win-win negotiation;
- Interpersonal, intragroup, and intergroup negotiation;
- The use of power, and negotiating in unequal power relations,
- Approaches for resolving unproductive negotiations, including the use of third parties.

Intentions/Predictions. Intentions and predictions are ways that the negotiator translates theory and concepts into practice. Whether it be a desire to try a different strategy in negotiation, or apply a concept from the reading, students should be specifically encouraged to engage in planning and goal setting prior to negotiations. This may be accomplished in the following ways:
- Requiring students to engage in a planning process prior to simulated negotiations, or to real-world experiences. Planning may include preparation of information and arguments, setting negotiation goals and objectives, predicting the opponent's objectives and personal style, and selecting a strategy to achieve the goals.
- Requiring students to "experiment" with new behaviors. Instructors often make a point to encourage students to simply try out different negotiating styles and approaches. Students may be encouraged to try more cooperative or competitive behavior, be more or less talkative, or assume positions of power contrary to their normal experience. The assumption is that the class provides a safe environment in which to try new behavior

---
[2] For a sample of negotiation course outlines from leading instructors, see Neale and Northcraft, 1985.

and gain feedback from others, but without endangering the substance of an agreement or the long-term relationship between the parties that is at stake in real negotiations.

Students may also be specifically encouraged to practice the prescribed behaviors of a particular model, such as different ways to achieve integrative agreements (Pruitt, 1983) or different ways to act as a third party in resolving a dispute (Sheppard, 1984; Brett, 1983). Finally, students might learn new behaviors by imitating a model who negotiates correctly (according to some prescriptive theory or framework). This process is analogous to watching the tennis pro's technique with a backhand swing, or watching a videotape, and then trying it yourself. While behavioral modeling has been used a great deal as a way to master complex skills, remarkably little if any training in negotiation has used either live or videotape models as a way to teach negotiation skills.

Actual Behavior. The primary vehicle for introducing actual negotiating behavior in class is through role playing and simulations. Some instructors use role plays and simulations at the beginning of a course, to acquaint students with the behavioral dynamics before the conceptual material is addressed; others use them in the middle or later parts of the course, to illustrate key principles or demonstrate the complexity of a large intergroup negotiation; still others use them throughout the course, beginning with simple scenarios (games and one issue negotiations), and building toward more complex negotiations as the course progresses.

At this time, while there is a great deal of case material available, it is not centralized in any one location. Much can be derived from books of resource materials (e.g., Lewicki and Litterer, 1985), commercially distributed scenarios (e.g., Bass, Bass and Shapira, 1982), dispute resolution organizations (e.g., American Arbitration Association or National Institute for Dispute Resolution -- Brett et al., 1985) or case clearinghouses (Program on Negotiation Case Clearinghouse or Harvard Business School Case Services). New materials with a wide variety of applications are constantly being developed and are usually shared among instructors teaching in this field.

Role plays and simulations may be conducted during class time, or they may be set up at the end of a class, to be completed by the students on their own. I suggest instructors use several of each kind. In-class activities allow the instructor to describe the simulation and instructions clearly, monitor student behavior closely, and debrief events "on the spot." However, simulation effectiveness may be constrained if the classroom facility does not have sufficient "break out" space for groups to meet and work independently, or if the allotted time is inadequate. In contrast, simulations apart from classes allow students to prepare at their leisure, control (and manipulate) the time and place of negotiation, meet as often as is necessary, use breaks and recesses strategically, etc. A twenty-minute in-class simulation between very competitive students may consume three or four hours outside of class.

Grading. Several instructors have experimented with grading students on their negotiating behavior. Some use simulations that allow various settlement packages to be scored with point schemes (e.g., Edwards and White, 1977), and assign grades based on the number of points won. With other simulations, grades can be determined on the basis of who negotiated the better package for each party in the dispute, or who invented the most integrative solutions. Unfortunately, there appear to be very few efforts to evaluate students on the effectiveness of their behavior rather than on outcomes.

Grading on the basis of actual negotiating outcomes is viewed as realistic by some students, particularly those who already negotiate well, but as troublesome by those who expect to have their performance judged by more traditional academic methods

Reaction and Reflection. Negotiation instructors who use simulations must also devote ample class time to debriefing students about these experiences. There are several objectives for the debriefing process:
- To compare and evaluate the different outcomes achieved by different subgroups;
- To compare and evaluate the different planning and strategizing processes that led to these outcomes;
- To help students compare and evaluate the differences between their intended actions and what may have actually occurred;
- To use the simulation to highlight key conceptual and theoretical points;
- To create the opportunity for students to note deficiencies in their own behavior, or the negotiation process, and to define -- implicitly or explicitly -- new or different ways to behave.

There are many ways to achieve the reaction and reflection objectives through course structure and design. First, students may discuss the simulation after it has occurred, or they may complete some form of standard "debriefing" questionnaire. Second, simulations may be videotaped, and students may be asked to watch and critique their behavior. Third, students may be asked to prepare a formal written analysis of the simulation, applying theories and concepts to the situation or setting explicit goals for future behavior. Instructors frequently use these application papers or journals to encourage students to monitor their own behavior and apply theory as appropriate. Finally, students may also be required to complete a comprehensive assessment of their own "negotiating style." Data for this assessment can be generated from reflection on their behavior in the simulations, feedback from other students and by completing one or more personality self-assessment questionnaires on dimensions related to negotiation -- such as conflict management style, assertiveness, ethics, etc.

Negotiation case studies are another major learning vehicle in the reaction and reflection phase. Cases expose students to the negotiating behavior of others, encouraging examination of behavior in the context in which it occurs. Theories, concepts and models are also provided to enrich intellectual comprehension. Cases are discussed in class or may be given as examinations to test successful analysis and application of theory. Films and videotapes are also good case material, allowing students the opportunity to observe nonverbal behavior and strategic nuances as well as negotiation techniques. Unfortunately, few if any quality case-oriented films and videotapes are available for instructional use.

Differences Among Learning Populations. Whether the instructional module is two hours, one day, three days or an entire semester, the instructional design should include all four elements of the experiential learning module. This cycle may be completed once in a short program, or multiple times in a longer program or course. Measurement may be formal, as in graded examinations and papers, or informal, as by simply noting behavior. Moreover, students should be encouraged to continue to keep a personal journal to monitor their negotiating behavior and compare goals set prior to actual negotiations with the results of the process. As in any skill development program, consistent monitoring and practice of new and different behavior is more likely to lead to behavior change and enhanced effectiveness.

In addition, different student populations should probably receive varying exposure to different components of the learning module. As noted elsewhere (Lewicki, 1979), university students are more comfortable with theory and abstraction, and more able to work with conceptual models that may not have ready application. In contrast, executives and practitioners are generally immersed in the behavioral dynamics of the process, but are less facile with the complex theoretical abstractions. Instructors working with these latter groups will find it more useful to limit conceptual input to "friendly theories": those that are less abstract, or immediately tied to in-class simulations, case analyses, or elaborate, relevant examples.

Unique Problems In Teaching Negotiation

I believe that teaching negotiation and conflict management creates several unique challenges and problems that instructors do not typically encounter in other courses. I will now describe some of these challenges.

1. *The Volatility and Unpredictability of Classroom Dynamics.* Most negotiation instructors are intellectually aware of the dynamics of conflict. Competitiveness and conflict lead to heightened emotions, distortion of perception and judgment, misattribution of the causes of behavior, heightened cohesiveness in one's own group, and the enhanced likelihood of behaving unproductively and unethically. However, it is one thing to understand these dynamics intellectually and recognize them in others, and another to experience and manage them.

Because of these dynamics, courses in conflict, power, and negotiation often energize and motivate students, making classes exciting. Events occur that students remember long after the course is over and the intellectual content is forgotten There is, however, a negative side to these dynamics: students will often be angry at one another and sometimes at the instructor. They will say things they don't mean, and do things for which they do not understand the consequences They will get carried away by the moment yet be surprised or even remorseful later.

The instructor, who cannot run away from such situations, must be comfortable around others who are in conflict. Sometimes an instructor is unwittingly entrapped in these dynamics, becoming "part of the problem" rather than an uninvolved observer. Because classroom events are not always predictable and plannable, an instructor of a course dealing with negotiation and conflict management should be prepared to address, manage, and integrate spontaneous classroom events with the learning objectives of the course.

2. *Multiple Instructor Roles.* In a traditional academic course, the instructor has clear-cut role responsibilities: to structure a coherent course outline, lecture, facilitate discussion, and evaluate student performance. However, by virtue of the variety of educational experiences described earlier, as well as the unpredictability of conflict dynamics, instructors in negotiation courses are placed in multiple (and often conflicting) roles. Instructors must continue to act as formal educators, but also have enhanced responsibilities as classroom managers, referees, mediators and counselors. While these roles and accompanying responsibilities may appear to be distinct and explicit, in practice they are frequently vague or in direct conflict. Following are some guidelines for each role:

Educator/Evaluator. The instructor's responsibilities are, as just outlined, to structure the course, to be an expert in the conceptual foundations of conflict and negotiation, to convey that expertise through lectures or readings, to facilitate classroom discussion, and to evaluate student learning and performance.

Classroom Manager. The instructor's job is to orchestrate the learning experience. Role plays need to be planned with regard to preparation and distribution of materials, securing adequate facilities, time scheduling, and organizing students into groups. Before an exercise is concluded, students should discuss the exercise and abstract key points. Simulations are useless activities without this analysis. Finally, applications should be drawn to the major conceptual points.

Regulator/Referee. The instructor's responsibilities are to define the boundaries for appropriate and inappropriate behavior in the classroom and in simulations. The instructor will frequently become the policeman, prosecutor, judge and jury in setting and enforcing rules. Some of those rules are academic, while others are procedural and relate to the simulation. The instructor must decide which rules to make, how to enforce them, and what to do when they are broken.

Mediator/Counselor. Finally, as noted earlier, students often become angry and entrapped in the conflict dynamics. Negotiations may have deadlocked, or ended in betrayal. Yet for the educational process to proceed, students must be able to detach themselves sufficiently to assess events and behavior and move on to other activities. The instructor's job is to help the class achieve this balance, and frequently requires intervention as a mediator or counselor.

Role conflict for the instructor *consistently* occurs among these various role responsibilities. These conflicts arise when student and instructor disagree on the appropriate role to be taken, or when an instructor must assume several different roles and each prescribes a different behavior. Management of these conflicts can significantly enhance or detract from the instructor's enjoyment of a course, student learning in a course, and student satisfaction with the course. Examples of such conflict are:

- Students try to anticipate the instructor's implicit models for effective negotiating behavior. As a result, they are afraid to be spontaneous, take risks or try new behaviors because they believe the instructor will use grades to punish them (conflict between the Evaluator and Educator roles).
- Instructors must decide whether to allow students to behave destructively, and to discover the consequences for themselves, as opposed to stopping that behavior and depriving the student of the learning experience. Similarly, instructors must decide when to stop a simulation to curtail escalating conflict (Educator and Referee roles).
- Instructors often require students to analyze their behavior through self-assessment papers and journals. Some of the least experienced and most destructive student negotiators are blind to their own behavior and the consequences it has for others. Instructors need to critique this behavior in their feedback on the paper; yet the student must believe that the academic grade awarded on the papers reflects the quality of analysis, not the behavior itself. In short, academic assessments must be seen as independent of judgments about the effectiveness of negotiating behavior (Evaluator and Counselor role).

Resolution of Instructor Role Conflict. The examples just noted are only a few of the role conflicts the instructor will experience. Each conflict offers the instructor a dilemma and a choice point for effective course management. Based on my experience, there are several key principles that may be used to guide the instructor's resolution of these choice dilemmas:

- Be explicit with students about the instructor's multiple role responsibilities, and the inevitability of role conflict -- whether real or perceived. These possible role conflicts should be discussed on the first day of class, when students may hear the problem but not understand it. They may then be repeated as the need arises in the course.

- Be explicit with students in advance about the formal criteria for grading in the course, and how the criteria will be applied. This is a principle of good teaching in any classroom, but it is even more critical in a negotiation course. Explicit and independent criteria help students believe that the grading process is independent of their behavior or an instructor's "whimsical judgment."

- Be clear that students should do as they please, but that they are responsible for the consequences of their behavior. In a course that requires extensive role playing and simulation, students frequently use instructors as a target for both dependence and counterdependence. These projections help to confound the instructor roles. For example, on the one hand, students fear that if they misbehave in a simulation (e.g., act exploitatively or unethically), their grade will be affected. So they act inhibited, or ask the instructor's "permission" to behave in ways they ordinarily would not. On the other hand, students also believe that the instructor will stop, control, or regulate undesirable behavior; hence they behave more competitively or outrageously than they might otherwise. The instructor should make it clear that students not only make their own choices about their behavior, but also must live with the consequences of that behavior. If they choose to behave competitively or unethically and engender anger or mistrust among their classmates, these are realistic consequences that cannot be avoided.

3. *Regulating Classroom Dynamics*. There are a number of other procedural rules that are necessary and useful for instructors to stipulate, such as the following :

- All behavior, including behavior in simulations and role plays, is "real." Students sometimes try to argue (usually ex post facto) that role playing and simulations are not "real" because there are no actual outcomes and people play artificial roles. These arguments are often used to avoid taking responsibility for their behavior or its consequences, or to deny the impact of that behavior on others. Moreover, they argue that they certainly would have behaved differently had this been a "real" situation. Instructors will recognize this behavior as defensive and myopic, yet often feel frustrated in their inability to persuade the student that this is a limited and perhaps distorted view. Instead of becoming entangled in such arguments, it is usually easier to have students accept the initial premise that all behavior in the course is "real," that they make choices about the way they behave, that behavior has consequences and they must be willing to live with them. The stakes may be different outside the classroom, but the behavior is no less real.

- It is imperative that the confidential information provided in most role playing scenarios will in fact be treated as confidential. Instructors should routinely insist that students not read the opposite side's information, or excuse themselves from the exercise if they are aware of the other side's confidential information.

- Small groups negotiating within the context of a larger course should view behavior as independent and autonomous from other small groups. This is an extension of the previous procedural rule on confidentiality, but applies to discussing the role play with other students in the course before they have completed the exercise. Gaining confidential information from other groups that may have already completed negotiations, etc. will be viewed in the same light as reviewing the other side's confidential briefing documents.
- The behavior of individuals and groups within the boundaries of the course should be held in strict confidence. Courses in negotiation typically occur within a larger academic context, in which students may know one another very well. Behavioral dynamics in the course may frequently become the subject of discussion and gossip outside the course, perhaps embarrassing students who are not proud of their behavior. Students should be encouraged to respect the rights of others and to refrain from out-of-class discussions.

4.   *Unethical Conduct.* Violations of confidentiality are only one form of ethical violation. Students may "bluff" about their position, or tell an outright lie. They may spy on another's planning session, or steal the other's documents. They may try to bribe or influence a referee. Instructors should treat these events as important dynamics that need review and attention. Moreover, while instructors frequently set aside one or more classes to discuss ethics specifically, I believe that the best discussions occur "on the spot," as perceived ethical violations occur and are challenged. I suggest the following strategies for discussing ethical issues:

- Make note of the issues raised and bring them up in the debriefing of an activity (particularly if students do not raise them).
- Do not take a normative position as the instructor. Instead, work to elicit the perceptions and perspectives of the actor, those affected by the action, and observers.
- Use the discussion to develop an agreement on the implied ethical "rule" that may have been violated (e.g., "Lying is bad"). Test out whether everyone agrees that this is the rule, whether the rule applies in this case, and whether the rule has been actually violated. The odds are that the class will not be unanimous on this point.
- Use the rule and its perceived violation to highlight how people disagree about the rules that govern competitive social behavior. Also, point out how the distorted perceptions that accompany conflict enhance the debate about perceived ethical violations and their appropriateness.

5.   *Extreme Emotionalism, Revenge and Violence.* Students, and even experienced instructors laugh nervously when this is mentioned. However, "truth in packaging" requires that I admit that occasional episodes of extreme emotion, revenge, and violence do occur.

Students don't believe that anyone would ever get that upset over a "silly" simulation; many inexperienced instructors don't believe it either. Yet people become very upset when betrayed, duped or ignored. Heated words and accusations can lead to long-standing feuds, revenge, and even physical confrontation. The following steps are recommended to prepare for this possibility:

- A "no violence" rule should be announced at the beginning of the course. Students may laugh it off, but the point should be made clear.

- Instructors should instantly terminate a simulation or role play when passions become extreme. Announce that the exercise is over, separate the parties, allow individuals to calm down, and/or call a break. When passions cool, reconvene that group and have people come to grips with what occurred. I strongly recommended that students be encouraged to "ventilate" by talking about how they feel, but not by hurling accusations at the other side and resuming the fight. I decidedly do not recommend that the instructor dismiss the class and ask people to "cool off and come back next week." This only allows students to continue the dispute outside the classroom, and to protract the feud in the broader academic culture by spreading rumors, building alliances and allowing the feud to surface in other courses.

6. *Negotiating Rules and Procedures With Students*. There are usually one or more students who will attempt to use the substantive topics of the course as a rationale for testing the instructor. If, as the instructor may maintain, many things in the world are negotiable, then why not the course requirements, rules and procedures? These students will either explicitly attempt to renegotiate the rules -- due dates, content of assignments, exemption from assignments -- or defy the rules and then attempt to negotiate the consequences. Other students will explicitly state that the best way to evaluate students in the course is by grading their negotiating effectiveness with other students or with the instructor. Finally, others will attempt to renegotiate grades and evaluations.

Some instructors are comfortable simply saying "no" to these students, enforcing the preset rules and procedures. Others are torn by the compelling persuasiveness of the arguments, or perhaps their desire to reward the innovative and enterprising student who creatively challenges the system. Once again, there are no hard and fast answers, but my recommendation is to stick with the explicit rules.

The fairness and equity of the grading system is at stake in this discussion. If the instructor plans to evaluate academic performance based on examinations or papers, then students believe this system will be consistently applied to all. If some students can successfully renegotiate their academic obligations with an instructor, the instructor's fairness is called into question. An instructor cannot reward such entrepreneurial initiative by one student without conveying the impression that the rules are not systematically and uniformly applied. Such negative perceptions are ultimately detrimental to an instructor's evaluation and adjudged effectiveness by the class majority. The instructor will lose credibility and respect in the eyes of the students.

Future Agenda

In this article, I have attempted to review the status of knowledge about the teaching of negotiation. As I have pointed out, while academic courses and seminars on negotiation have grown dramatically in the past few years, little has been written about the process, and even less research has been done. Instead, each instructor has developed an individual approach to the topic.

My hope is that this article will stimulate further dialogue on the subject. Given the importance of negotiation skills to professionals in all fields, and the accelerating growth of negotiation courses within professional schools, closer attention should be paid to the pedagogical styles and tools that are used to teach this subject. I hope that commentary will be received not only from other academicians, but from practitioners who negotiate every day. This discussion can only help to improve the effectiveness of teaching negotiation skills.

REFERENCES

Bass R., Bass B.M., and Shapira, Z. *Nuclear Site Negotiation*. La Jolla, Calif.: University Associates, 1982.

Brett, J.M., "Mediator-advisors: A New Third Party Role." In *Negotiating In Organizations*, ed.. Max Bazerman and Roy J. Lewicki. Beverly Hills: Sage Publications, 1983.

Brett, J.M., Greenhalgh, L. Kolb, D., Lewicki, R.J. and Sheppard, B.H.. *The Manager as Negotiator and Dispute Resolver*. Washington, D.C.: National Institute for Dispute Resolution, 1985.

Edwards, J.T., and White, J.J. *The Lawyer as Negotiator*. St. Paul, Minn.: West Publishing Co., 1977.

Kolb, D., Rubin, I.M., and McIntyre, J.M. *Organizational Psychology*. 4th Ed. Englewood Cliffs, N.J.: Prentice Hall. 1983.

Lewicki, R.J. "Organizational Behavior for Executives." *Exchange: The Organizational Behavior Teaching Journal* 4 (1979): 34-39.

Lewicki, R. and Litterer, J. Negotiation: *Readings, Exercises and Cases*. Homewood, Ill.: Richard D. Irwin, 1985.

Lewicki, R.J., Sheppard, B.H., and Bazerman, M. *Research on Negotiation in Organizations*. Greenwich, Conn.: JAI Publishing Co., forthcoming.

Neale, M., and Northcraft, G. *Bargaining and Dispute Resolution Curricula: A Sourcebook*. Durham, N.C.: Eno River Press, 1985.

Pruitt, D.G. "Achieving Integrative Agreements." In *Negotiating in Organizations*. ed. Max Bazerman and Roy J. Lewicki. Beverly Hills: Sage Publications, 1983.

Sheppard, B.H. "Third Party Intervention: A Procedural Framework" In *Research in Organizational Behavior*, 6th ed. B.M. Staw and L.L. Cummings. Greenwich, Conn.: JAI Publishing, 1984

STRUCTURING THE NEGOTIATION COURSE

In talking with many instructors about the ways that they design and teach courses in negotiation, we know that there are as many different course designs as there are instructors! As a result, we only offer here some general guidelines to instructors about the factors which should be taken into consideration in designing and structuring a course. Many of these guidelines and suggestions were identified in the previous Negotiation Journal article; we will briefly review them here.

1. ***Class Size***. Instructors differ on their ability to manage various groups in experiential learning activities. Good experiential learning requires a classroom of moderate size -- i.e. big enough to conduct multiple role plays that will produce different results, small enough to orchestrate the experience in a limited time. We recommend a minimum class size of 12-16, and a maximum class size of 36-40. However, some of us have taught these activities to groups of 60 or more. In these settings, tight orchestration of activities is a must!

2. ***Facilities***. Role playing with multiple teams negotiating simultaneously requires that each team have a room or place to meet, and that additional space is available for one or both teams to caucus. Thus, it is most desirable to have several break-out rooms available near the classroom for negotiation and caucusing. It will be almost impossible to conduct this class in a fixed-seat auditorium with no options for break-out space. Some instructors prefer to teach this course at night when they can have access to lots of empty classrooms that are full during the daytime. Others assign role plays to be done outside of class. If in any doubt, move the class to a place where extra rooms or flexible seating are available.

3. ***Class Hours***. It is also extremely difficult to teach this class in a number of short class periods. 50-60 minute classes do not allow students to prepare for and carry out an exercise; spanning the exercises over two days frequently takes the "life" out of them. We recommend that you schedule this class for AT LEAST 75 minutes. Longer class times are generally preferred (90-100 minutes), and some instructors even prefer one 3-4 hour class period once a week. While the fatigue factor is high, the longer class allows for maximum flexibility in carrying out role plays, discussing them, and integrating them with conceptual material.

4. ***Sequencing of Content***. This is a matter of choice among instructors. The issue boils down to one question: is it more advantageous for students to read theory and hear lectures about a topic (e.g. integrative bargaining) before experiencing it in a role play, or is it better to do the role play first? Instructors differ on this question, and we suggest that you experiment with both formats.

5. ***Assignment Evaluation and Grading***. Instructors have used a variety of different learning vehicles in courses on negotiation. We make the following suggestions:

- **Examinations**. We recommend essay or case-analysis examinations. Essay exams may be used to test understanding and application of concepts presented in the text and in class. Case-analysis examinations should assess the negotiation and conflict dynamics of a selected case, and perhaps application of theories and approaches. We do not recommend short answer, multiple choice examinations.

- **Term papers**. We have frequently given students a number of options for a term paper assignment:
    - Researching and analyzing a negotiation as reported in the media -- e.g. a labor-management dispute, disarmament talks, international negotiations, major business deals, etc. There is an unlimited number of topics to be taken from history, politics, labor relations, business and international affairs.
    - Researching and analyzing a negotiator -- e.g. Kissinger, a labor leader, or someone the student can get information on. Actual interviews with car dealers, real estate salespeople, insurance adjusters, etc. often provide interesting experiences.
    - Preparing a paper that summarizes a stream of research in one of the many areas of negotiation -- e.g. the effectiveness of threats, face saving, strategies of deterrence, effectiveness of third parties, etc. Topics can be generated from the research-oriented textbooks and journals.
    - Writing a "personal case," based on a student's own negotiating experience. Students should write a case that describes their experience, and then analyze that case. Because students are frequently still "myopic" about their own effectiveness or ineffectiveness as negotiators, we frequently encourage students not to select this option unless they can get someone's view other than their own about the events and how they transpired.
    - Actually negotiating for something of personal value, and then writing a paper on it. Instead of describing a past experience, students can also be asked to plan and execute an actual negotiation during the span of the course, and then write a paper on it. The paper can entail the actual planning for the negotiation, the execution of the negotiation, report of results, post-hoc interviews and analysis, integrating theory, models, etc. Students have done some wonderful projects: negotiating a grade change with a faculty member, resolving a conflict with a roommate, parent, spouse or friend, negotiating a new job assignment, salary or working conditions with an employer, buying automobiles, furniture and sporting goods, etc.
    - Writing a role play. Finally, students may combine personal negotiating experience with historical research to write a role play scenario rather than a case or description. These role plays can be tried in the classroom and used in future classes.

- **Personal Application Papers or Diary**. These assignments encourage students to reflect upon a simulation or role play, and to abstract the key learning points out of that event. We generally either require students to keep a weekly journal that is periodically collected and reviewed, or assign 4-5 application papers in a term. Here is a sample from one of our course outlines:

    "The purpose of the paper is to encourage a reflection and analysis process on the 'learning by experience' simulations; the paper also gives the instructor a sense of your individual progress, and your strengths and weaknesses as a negotiator. Your task in this paper is to describe your reactions, perceptions, impressions or significant insights gained from participation in or reflection on the simulation. You may talk about yourself, or the behavior of other people, and may want to address some or all of the following points:

1. Briefly, what happened in the simulation, role play (or 'real-life negotiation') -- that is, provide a brief overview of the key events.
2. What did you learn about yourself from this experience?
3. What did you learn about the behavior of others from this experience?
4. How does this experience compare to others that you have had in similar or comparable circumstances?
5. What did you learn about bargaining or conflict from this situation?
6. How do the concepts in lectures or readings enrich your understanding of the process of negotiation, its outcome or your own negotiation style?
7. What would you do the same or do differently in the future, or how would you like to behave in order to perform more effectively?

> Each paper will be read, commented on, graded, and returned to you. The purpose of the grades is to encourage thoughtful analysis and understanding of the simulations, and to encourage use of theory and research presented in readings, and lectures. A good short paper is one which tries to step back from a simulated bargaining situation, identifies key events and processes, uses readings or lecture material to help structure the analysis, and is well written. All of these guidelines are just that -- guidelines. Outstanding papers have frequently been written in the past that do not closely conform to this format."

Whether the short papers are used or not, students may also be asked to write a summary self-evaluation paper at the end of the course. These papers are usually 5-8 pages in length, and ask students to address the following points:

1. Do I enjoy bargaining? Do I enjoy being in situations of conflict, and/or do I enjoy attempting to persuade others to my point of view? Why?
2. Do others see me as a good bargainer? Am I seen as strong or weak? Am I perceived as one who gives in easily, or holds out too long, or knows when to make conciliations and tradeoffs?
3. How do I see myself in relation to the question in (2) above?
4. How effective am I at persuading others? How effective are my verbal skills to argue my points?
5. At what time do I feel most competent in bargaining? Least competent?
6. How do I respond when I hold the power in a situation? How do I respond when I have little or no power in a situation?
7. Overall, what are my major strengths and weaknesses as a negotiator, and what kind of learning goals must I set for myself for the future?

We have had good experience with personal learning papers and journals, and summary papers on personal learning and development. Many students like them -- but some don't, and it shows in the amount of time and effort they give to the activity. Two cautionary notes about using diaries, journals and learning summaries:

- They are time consuming to read. Evaluation for each student takes significantly longer than grading an exam. In addition, individual feedback to students -- written or verbal -- is also very time consuming.
- Grading and evaluation of journals, by necessity, becomes a reasonably subjective process. As a result, while the instructor will be able to discriminate differences in the conscientiousness paid by the student to the journal writing task, the detailed nature of entries, and level of student insight and personal learning that may be occurring, it may be very difficult to explain and justify such differences (and the related grade) to students. If you, and/or your students, have a strong need for objectivity in grading, using journals can create a problem.

- **Graded negotiation**. Lastly, we have often graded students on the outcomes of several negotiations. One clear consequence of this practice is that it raises the competitiveness of the simulations considerably; but it also forces students to evaluate their positions carefully and take the process seriously. An example of one format for using graded negotiations is as follows:

Graded Negotiations. Three role plays will be conducted outside of class. By virtue of a point scheme assigned to particular variations in settlements, negotiators will be evaluated on the settlements they achieve. The procedure will basically operate as follows:

1. Roles will be assigned and the negotiations explained at the end of a particular class period. Students will be assigned to one or two person teams, and opponents specified.
2. Students will have an entire week to arrange a negotiation with their opponent and arrive at a settlement.
3. Results of negotiation are due in writing to the instructor by a specified deadline. Failure to meet the deadline will result in a penalty.
4. Teams will be assigned grade-points based on the quality of their solution as compared to all other teams playing that same position.
5. All members of a team will be assigned the same grade points for the exercise unless appealed to the instructor. Appeals must be specified in writing no later than 24 hours after the negotiation results are submitted.

There will be three role plays, and they are weighted in their contribution to the final grade. Role Plays 1 and 2 will be worth x% apiece, and Role Play #3 will be worth y%."

If an instructor is going to use graded negotiations, we suggest the following rules of thumb:

- Graded negotiations should comprise no more than 1/3 of the total course grade.
- There should be several graded negotiations.
- Agreements arrived at by the students should be submitted to you in their handwriting and signed by both sides, so that there is no disagreement as to what was agreed to.
- In purely distributive negotiations, students receiving the best package on each side should be given the best grades. Thus, in a buyer-seller negotiation, the best buyer outcome and the best seller outcome get the top grade, and others are graded relative to the top in each group.

- In simulations which emphasize integrative negotiations, students should be graded based on the best cooperative, innovative joint agreement that is derived. Student judges may be used as an aid to determine what are the "best" solutions. STUDENTS SHOULD BE TOLD WHETHER THEY WILL HAVE A NEGOTIATION GRADED BY DISTRIBUTIVE OR INTEGRATIVE CRITERIA.

- Unless you set up explicit criteria to do so, students should not be judged on their behavior in the negotiations, but on the results they achieve. If you think you are able to judge "better" or "worse" negotiator performance, we would be pleased to learn of the scheme you develop or use to do this.

- In evaluating negotiation outcomes and assigning grades -- particularly integrative negotiations -- we have frequently been challenged by students as to the validity of our evaluation criteria. Be prepared to defend the criteria you use if you employ this method. We have also found it helpful to delegate a small group of students to be an "appeals panel" for hearing grade grievances on graded negotiations, and/or to develop the criteria for evaluating the results of each scenario. Thus, for example, a small group of students could be asked not to do the role play, but instead to develop the criteria by which others' solutions will be judged.

- We have recently experimented with combining the graded negotiation and an analysis paper on the negotiation. Thus, part of the grade is assigned based on the actual outcome achieved in the graded role play, while another part of the grade is based on the quality of an analysis paper on the event. This combines two types of assignments into one, and creates the opportunity for students with good negotiating skills but poor writing/analysis skills (and vice versa) to perform well.

In summary, grading negotiations can be a creative alternative to reading papers and correcting exams. However, the more competitive the classroom environment, the more the instructor may become enmeshed in numerous "grading hassles" with students about criteria used, how good their solutions were, etc. Be prepared for this as a logical offshoot of any efforts to grade students on their performance. Take appeals only in writing, and consider them when you are not under direct pressure from a student's own persuasive negotiating ability.

Additional Resource Materials

The following sources may be consulted for additional resource materials that can be used in teaching this course:

- **Sample Course Outlines**. See Neale, M. and Northcraft, G. Bargaining and Dispute Resolution Curricula: A Sourcebook. Durham, N.C.: Eno River Press, 1985.

- **Role Play Materials**.
  a. Contact the National Institute for Dispute Resolution, 1901 L Street N.W., Suite 600, Washington, D.C. 20036, for their complete catalogue of books, videotapes, articles, etc. on dispute resolution in the public and private sectors. Two slightly dated but excellent volumes of role plays and comprehensive teaching notes are two volumes of *The Manager as Negotiator and Dispute Resolver*, one for O.B. and Management courses by J. Brett, L. Greenhalgh, D. Kolb, R. Lewicki and B. Sheppard, and the other for Economics and Decision Analysis courses by D. Lax, W. Samuelson, J. Sebenius, R. Weber and T. Weeks.

  b. Contact the Clearinghouse at the Harvard Negotiation Program (Harvard Law School, 500 Pound Hall, Cambridge, Mass 02138) for their catalogue of role play and videotape materials. These are not free, but sample copies may be purchased as well as copies for an academic course. *The Negotiation Journal*, also published by the Harvard Negotiation Project and Plenum Press, often features articles on negotiation pedagogy, and reviews leading text and resource books in the field.

  c. Contact the Dispute Resolution Research Center at the Kellogg Graduate School of Management, Northwestern University, Evanston, IL. (708-491-8068) for their collection of exercises on disk, *Negotiation and Decision Making Exercises*. These disks contain many excellent role play scenarios, many of which are "scoreable" so as to be able to calculate and rank order outcomes more precisely. The Northwestern Center also has an excellent reprint series of research articles on negotiation.

- **Videotapes**

  To our knowledge, there are very few videotapes on actual negotiations that are publicly available. The National Institute for Dispute Resolution has a few videotapes available. The videotape that accompanies the Detection Technologies role play (similar to Eurotechnologies, Exercise 19) may be particularly useful. The American Arbitration Association has some excellent videotapes available for teaching about arbitration and mediation. Contact the AAA. Finally, the Harvard Program has produced several videotapes as well. Please contact us if you know about others.

SPECIAL GUIDELINES FOR USING ROLE PLAYING AND INSTRUMENTS

The following guidelines will be useful to instructors who have not had extensive experience with role playing activities, or have not used self diagnostic questionnaires and personality scales in the classroom.

Special Guidelines for Using Role Playing[3]

Role playing is probably one of the oldest (comparatively speaking) techniques for making behavioral science materials "come alive" in the classroom. The advantages are well known and have been spelled out more fully in a variety of sources (Miles, 1959; Thelen, 1964; Maier, 1965, 1975). We will only briefly list them here:

1. Role playing provides a real world context for exploring behavioral principles, as opposed to discussing them as abstract theory or as principles devoid of the organizational nitty-gritty.
2. It allows for spontaneity and involvement in the material, and requires more of a personal commitment from the student than reading and discussing a case.
3. It permits the examination of behavior, as opposed to theoretical analysis or speculation. What people actually do is, of course, often quite different from what they say they would do or others should do. Role playing enables us to look at what people actually do.
4. At the same time, it gives people the opportunity to experiment with new ways of behaving without necessarily facing the real-world consequences of that experimentation.
5. Finally, the involvement bred by role playing increases diagnostic skills for understanding the nature of the situation, the complexity of human behavior (as opposed to being able to articulate "simple common sense"), and to test out possible solutions.

The role-playing scenarios in this book specify times, description of the roles, and discussion. However, many other behavioral science cases can easily be adapted for role-playing use in the classroom. We offer the following guidelines for using a role-playing activity:

1. Plan how to you are going to use it. Consider the use of the role play in the broad context of both the content and other learning devices to be used.
2. Decide whether you are going to preselect people for certain roles from the class, involve the class in this "casting" process, or merely ask for volunteers. There are usually good reasons for doing your casting in a particular way. You may want to select certain "types" of people to play certain "types" of roles -- you ought to share these criteria with the class after the exercise. On the other hand, you may want to have the class help you select

---

[3] Reprinted from *Instructors Manual to Accompany Experiences in Management and Organizational Behavior*, 2nd Edition. New York: John Wiley and Sons, 1982. Used with permission.

people, you may want to select at random, or you may want to select individuals who make significant points in a class discussion.

3. Decide whether you want to "replicate" the role playing by having everyone take on a role and conducting a number of role plays simultaneously, or use the role play as a demonstration in front of the class. While the former breeds the greatest degree of involvement, the latter is more common, gives you more control over the learning process, and allows for other options.

4. Allow warm-up time for the role players. Make sure they understand their own role and what expectations are placed on then by the scenario they will enact. (Often, however, you may want to ask individuals to play a role impromptu, as they are discussing a case.)

5. Decide whether you want to share knowledge of what the other role players will be presenting, or whether each role player should see only his own "script." This latter alternative is usually used when the nature of the role play deals with people's hidden thoughts, feelings, or attitudes, or when people are in competition or conflict with one another.

6. Know when you want to "cut" --at your own discretion, or fix the time limits and adhere to them.

Alternative uses of role playing are becoming more common, supplementing the technology of videotape. Here are some ideas:

1. Interrupt a role play and allow people to step out-of-role and discuss what they have been doing -- then return to the action.

2. Interrupt a role play and use other members of the class as "consultants." Each role player meets with his consultants before he returns to continue the role play.

3. Complete a role play, videotaping the entire sequence. After some discussion of the role play, introduction of theory or concepts, etc., replay the videotape, stopping it at critical points. The initial action can often be done before class.

4. Interrupt a role play and let other members of the class substitute for one or more of the role players, then continue the action. This technique might be used when you want to explore different ways of handling a problem (e.g., role playing a supervisor managing a difficult motivation situation with employees).

5. Try "instant replay" with live action or videotape. After stopping a role play and critiquing it, repeat the same scene with the same (or different) actors. This is often a very useful process when asking people to master specific skills (e.g., giving feedback, listening, interviewing, etc.).

6. Experiment with "alter-ego," a variation on the "substitute" principle. People in the audience can act as a particular role player's alter-ego, saying what they think the role player is thinking or feeling but not verbalizing. This is often a good way to get feelings and thoughts on the table that would otherwise go unspoken.

Finally, you should plan for a thorough discussion of the role play -- the people, the types of behavior shown, and the important concepts. Don't forget to explore how "easy" or "difficult" it was for people to play particular roles, or to "get in" and "get out" of a role. This is usually important information, and often relates to the subject matter of the role play and the learning environment in the classroom.

Special Guidelines for Using Instruments

There are several activities in EMOB that use psychological tests or questionnaires – "Analysis of Personal Power" (no. 32), "Organizational Climate Questionnaire" (no. 41), etc. A number of others are commonly available to measure personality, motivation and leadership. There are a number of advantages to using instruments in teaching organizational behavior:

- They are a simple way to teach concepts and theory, since the participant must respond to questions that measure the attitudes or behavior relevant to that theory.

- They produce involvement and interest in the theory as it personally applies to the participants, rather than as abstractions.

- They provide useful information for the participant about himself that he can integrate with other aspects of his self-image.

- Similarly, they provide information that helps the participant distinguish himself from others in the immediate environment, as well as from commonly established norms, information that can be confirmed by other kinds of attitudinal and behavioral data.

- When administered more than once over time, they help to measure the degree and direction of change.

Instructors often experience certain disadvantages with instrumentation, however. These disadvantages can, to a large degree, be anticipated and diminished by your awareness of the following:

- Some participants may fear that their scores will be made public, and that others will find out damaging information about them. This concern for privacy is a real and legitimate one, and should be honored.

- Therefore, only ask people to share their scores in small groups, and with people whom they feel they can trust. Don't require individuals to reveal their scores in large groups unless they are willing. Respect the wishes of any individual who does not want to share his scores at all. Finally, we have often found it useful as instructors and group leaders to share our own scores or responses, thus beginning a "self-disclosure cycle" that helps participants to share their scores. Sharing of your own scores will also facilitate discussion and interpretation of the instrument, as we describe below.

- Some participants may feel that such instruments cannot measure anything "meaningful." These attitudes are usually related to a general distrust of behavioral science, a fear of disclosure of personal information, and stereotyped images of psychologists that lead to suspicion and denigration of most attempts to make the study of human behavior "scientific." Therefore, show the relationship of the instrument and scores to real-world examples that would exemplify these scores. For example, with the FIRO-B instrument, show how the person's self-description of himself on the items can relate to behavior that he would demonstrate in interpersonal settings. Also show the relationship of the instrument to the "theory of human behavior" that is being used. Point out those items that cluster together for various aspects of the theory, and how the scores indicate the strength of the individual's dispositions.

- You should also be prepared to help the individual explore "contradictory" data -- that is, information about himself from the instrument which he finds contrary to his own view of his behavior. This may be done by discovering whether the individual felt he was honest in answering the questionnaire (checking the validity of the responses), and/or asking him to describe his scores to close friends to see whether or not they agree with his self-description (checking the validity of his self-perception).

- Also, be prepared to discuss the problems of reliability and margin for error in any set of questionnaire responses. We have usually found it useful to state that any set of questionnaire responses is only one set of data about oneself, and that the data must be explored to see if it is reliable (i.e., to see if the same pattern emerges on additional administrations of the instrument) and valid (fits with the way an individual, or other individuals, perceive his behavior).

- Finally, do not try to use instruments which are too heavily "value-laden" -- that is, instruments for which there is a strong social-desirability component, or where one set of scores (and behavior) is perceived as much more socially valuable than others. Nevertheless, individuals may interpret certain sets of answers in this way. It is important that you stress two things in your discussion of the instrument: First, point out what YOU may feel to be the "socially desirable" set of responses, and indicate how you feel that this has been built into the instrument. Second, legitimize feeling that not everyone is the same, nor can be and that people whose scores deviate from the norm should not be worried about their differences. In using these instruments, we often get the question, "My scores are so-and-so. Am I weird?" In spite of the humor that may surround the question, it is a serious one for many people in the audience, and you should be prepared to handle it effectively.

SAMPLE COURSE OUTLINE

Course Objectives

One objective of the course will be to explore the major concepts and theories of the psychology of bargaining and negotiation, and the dynamics of interpersonal and intergroup conflict and its resolution. A second objective will be to help students develop the sophistication to analyze bargaining and conflict relationships, and to learn (through class discussion and self-assessment) about their own individual "bargaining styles."

My interest is to have students in the course who are committed to both goals. That is, I would prefer to accept students who are committed to the intellectual analysis of bargaining problems (even, perhaps when the applicability of those ideas is not readily clear). I would also want the student to be committed to actively participating in the simulations, willing to have other constructively critique his/her behavior, and willing to try to learn from the feedback as well as the behavior of others in the course. I believe that a dual commitment to these two goals will provide the motivation to effectively maximize student learning.

My goal for the course is to help the student effectively integrate the experiential and intellectual learning components. I do not consider this an easy task.

The course is designed to be relevant to the broad spectrum of bargaining "problems" that are traditionally faced by the manager. Thus, the content is not be restricted to students interested in human resources or industrial relations. Students pursuing careers in sales, marketing, merger and acquisition, banking, purchasing, real estate, entrepreneurship and other areas that require skill in negotiation and persuasion should find the course useful and relevant.

Format

There will be two weekly meetings of the class. Class time will be devoted to lectures, case discussions, videotape, and role plays. Lectures will provide analytical concepts that will integrate the readings and serve as useful frameworks for a richer understanding of cases and role plays. Cases, videotape and the role plays themselves will provide the "application" aspects of this course. In addition, there will be a weekly group meeting and there will often be "out of class" role plays that must be completed before the next class begins. These will be described in extensive detail.

During the quarter, you will also be placed in a "D-Group." The purpose of the D-Group is to create an opportunity for students to talk with other students, in an organized manner, about events in the course. More will be said about the group below.

Textbooks

Two books have been ordered for this course:

Roy J. Lewicki, David Saunders and John Minton, Essentials of Negotiation. Burr Ridge, IL. Richard D. Irwin, 1997. (T in outline)

Roy J. Lewicki, David Saunders, John Minton and Joseph Litterer, Negotiation: Readings, Exercises, and Cases. Homewood, IL: Richard D. Irwin, 2nd Edition, 1993. (R in outline).

Both books will be used extensively in the course.

Handouts

The role play and simulation activities in this course requires extensive handouts. The number of pages exceeds the number that the College will provide *gratis*. As a result, a materials charge will be assessed all students in the course.

Copies of handouts not received in class can always be obtained from Prof. Lewicki or the course assistant at a location to be announced. Students are responsible for obtaining any materials not received due to missed classes.

Student Work Requirements

Class Preparation and Participation. This course will require that students come prepared to class. There are two forms of preparation: reading and assignments.

a. Reading has been assigned to provide an enriched understanding of activities just completed in class, or to "set the stage" for upcoming activities. The instructor has attempted to select a blend of reading that combines analytical richness with detailed examples and applications. Students will be responsible for completing the reading assignments.

b. Assignments are cases, role plays, and questionnaires that must be completed for class, or in between class periods. It is essential that students be prepared by reading the assigned case or briefing information or completing the required assignment.

Students are expected to be prepared for class, to attend class, and to complete the required role plays outside of class. Therefore, you will be required to make time between some class periods to complete required negotiations. Attendance at class is expected unless the instructor is notified. Missing a role play or simulation is not acceptable except for medical emergency. You are also expected to attend D-Group sessions.

The class participation segment of your grade will be based upon your class attendance, D-Group attendance, preparation for all class activities, and the quality of your contribution to class discussions.

Graded Negotiations and Papers: There will be two graded negotiations in the course. In each graded negotiation, students will be evaluated on the basis of their performance in the role play AND the paper they submit on that role play.

Grading on the role play itself will focus on the actual results achieved by each negotiator. Since the role plays differ, criteria will vary from one scenario to the next, and will be announced prior to the role play.

The accompanying paper should focus on preparation and goal setting for the role play, a description/analysis of the actual negotiating events, and a description/justification of the results achieved. A good paper will address:

- A brief summary of the nature of the negotiating problem;
- The preparation that you did, including your goals/objectives;
- Other people involved, and how their personality/style might affect your preparation or actual events;
- The progression of events in the simulation;
- The solution you achieved, and how you "defend" your solution against your earlier goals/objectives;
- Integration of analytical tools from the readings/lectures;
- What you learned from the exercise.

Papers will be evaluated based on the quality of analysis, and against these asterisked points. Papers should be no more than 6 pages, typewritten, double spaced. Papers will be a completely confidential document between student and instructor. Candor is encouraged. You may turn in your paper by code number only if you prefer. Specify DAY or NIGHT section on your paper.

Group Paper. Groups will be created for the purpose of a "group" negotiation. The negotiation will be conducted outside of class. Groups are then responsible for completing an analysis paper of their efforts as a team. More information will be given in class.

Reputation Index. The Reputation Index will be calculated on your negotiating reputation with your classmates, on the basis of their experience with you over the semester. The Index is a proxy for the long-term effects of reputations created by negotiation activities in organizations, where the negotiations you conduct today affect the ways you are seen by others tomorrow. The index recognizes that those individuals who have reputations as trustworthy and effective negotiators will have an advantage in future negotiations, and those who have reputations as untrustworthy and ineffective will have a disadvantage. The index will be completed near the end of the course.

In addition to your reputation index, students may earn "extra credit" on this factor by contributing to others' learning through helpful feedback, insightful participation and other actions that help others learn.

Final Project. You may do one of three things for the "final project:

1. **"Live" negotiation.** You may write up a "live" negotiation that you have with someone during the term. This should be a real issue of importance to you, such as a salary or job

negotiation, a major purchase, negotiation in a critical relationship (family, romantic, friendship, etc.) or an important work-related decision. The following rules apply:

- You must negotiate for something non-trivial.
- The other parties cannot be associated with this course (e.g. students or faculty member) or be aware that this is a class exercise.
- You should articulate your goals, strategy and expectations prior to the negotiation.
- If they are willing (and available), you should interview the other party(ies) or observers after the negotiation to supplement and corroborate your perceptions.

Evaluation of the papers will be based less on success and more on your ability to apply the key issues and concepts we will be working with, put together some sensible strategy, and generate ideas about how to be more effective in the future.

2. **Learning Summary.** You may prepare a personal learning summary. The purpose of the summary is to integrate what you have personally learned about yourself in the course, about others, about negotiation, and about human behavior (particularly in situations of conflict and personal influence). The Learning Summary will be written to the instructor, and will be a confidential document. Grading will be based on the comprehensiveness of your analysis, integration of relevant course materials, data and feedback from others in the course about your style (a MUST element for this paper) and personal reflection on your strengths and weaknesses.

3. **Term paper.** You may prepare an analysis paper of some actual negotiation that has occurred, such as an international situation, labor problem, hostage negotiation, business deal, etc. You may use either archival data (newspaper reports, documents) or interviews or both. Your paper should both "present" the case and then analyze it, using the theory and tools we will present in the course. Students are encouraged to consult with Prof. Lewicki about their topic in advance.

D-Groups. The purpose of the D-Group is to create an environment in which you can talk about events in the course, your own personal reaction to them, and the ways those events are affecting your view of yourself as a negotiator.

D-groups will be composed of 4-6 members. The group is to meet once a week for one hour. You must find a time to meet when all members can, as a rule, get together. During the meeting, discussion might focus on:

- The content of the course;
- Cases and exercises that may have been done, and your personal reactions to them;
- Personal "negotiations" you have had outside the course, and how you have conducted yourself;
- Issues that are arising for you in the course and their implications for your own learning and development as a negotiator.

You should spend a few minutes preparing for your D-group meeting each week. Preparation might include reviewing your answers to the following questions:

- What happened in the role play simulations this week?
- What strategy/tactics did I use, and what strategy/tactics did my opponent use?
- What did I learn from this activity? what do these activities say about my strengths/weaknesses as a negotiator?
- How do these activities relate to the ways I have negotiated, or will negotiate, "real" situations outside of the course?

Each group will submit a 1 page statement week (due in the Monday class), indicating group name and members in attendance, summarizing the topics of the group discussion, and raising any questions or concerns that should be brought to the attention of the instructor or class. The instructor will review all D-Group input, and will meet with any D-Group if requested.

With the exception of this written summary, and information shared with the instructor, IT IS ASSUMED THAT ALL D-GROUP DISCUSSIONS WILL BE CONFIDENTIAL. Students must be able to assume that information shared within a D-group will not work its way into the gossip network of the MBA or MLHR Programs.

Suggested topics for D-Group discussion:

Week 1	Course expectations, past negotiation experiences
Week 2	Cooperation and competition, Pemberton
Week 3	Distributive negotiation
Week 4	Integrative Negotiation
Week 5	Integrative Negotiation
Week 6	Personality Q, Dealing with Difficult Negotiators
Week 7	Group negotiations, ethics
Week 8	International Negotiation
Week 9	Self-Assessment Summary: General reflections

Summary of Grading Components and Points

	Option A Percent	Option A Points	Option B Percent	Option B Points
Graded Negotiation #1, and accompanying paper	15%	30	20%	40
Graded Negotiation #2, and accompanying paper	15%	30	20%	40
Group Negotiation Paper	20%	40	25%	50
Reputation Index	10%	20	20%	40
Live Negotiation or Summary Paper or Term Paper	25%	50		
Class and D-Group Partic	15%	30	15%	30

Summary of Due Dates:

D-Group Reports	Due in Monday Class beginning January 13
Jan 26	Paper #1 due on First GRP
Feb 9	Paper #2 due on Second GRP
Mar 2	Group Paper Due on group case
Mar 13	Final Paper(s) due

The Honor Code As It Applies to This Course:

The Honor Code of The Graduate School, The Ohio State University, applies to all academic work in this course. More specifically, it will be considered a violation of the Honor Code to engage in the following activities:

1. Misrepresenting the written work of others as your own written work.

2. Reading, viewing or discovering the confidential briefing information held by your opponents in any graded role play scenario, by gaining access to that information from your opponent directly or from others in any section of the course who may be playing your opponent's role. (NOTE: THIS MEANS THAT YOU MAY NOT SHOW YOUR BRIEFING INFORMATION TO YOUR OPPONENT AT ANY TIME, OR READ VERBATIM FROM THAT INFORMATION, AND TO DO SO IS A VIOLATION OF THE HONOR CODE!)

3. Reading, viewing or discovering the confidential briefing information of role play scenarios that may have been used in previous offerings of this course.

Course Outline

Class	Topics	Assignment/preparation Code: **T**=text, **R**=reader, **BRC**=Bring Reader to Class
1	Introduction Course Objectives	None Handout Questionnaire
2	Basics of Cooperation	Prepare Ex 2 Pemberton **BRC** Read T, Ch 1 R, 2-1, 2-3 Hand back Questionnaire
3	Basic Structure of Distributive Negotiation	Read T, Ch 2 Prepare The Used Car **BRC** R, 1-3, 1-4
4	Distributive Negotiation	Prepare Cap. Mort. Co. (A), R 643, **BRC** Read T, Ch 4 R, 3-3, 5-1
5	No Class--MLK day	
6	Distributive Bargaining	Prepare Pacific Oil (A), R 659 **BRC** (Read Petrochemical Contracts, R 679, if necessary) Bring $1-2 to class. Read R, 3-1, 3-2, 6-3
6a	First Graded RP Due at 5 p.m.	
7	Distributive Bargaining Intro to Integrative Barg.	R 1-4, 2-2, 6-2 (applies to class 5) Paper # 1 due
8	Integrative Bargaining	Read T, Ch 3 Read R 4-3 Do RP in class
9	Integrative Bargaining	Read R 5-2, 5-3 & handouts Guest speaker: Jim Camp
10	Integrative Bargaining	Read R 4-2, 4-4 Read T Chapter 6
10a	Second Graded RP due at 5 p.m.	

11	Integrative Negotiation	Read R, 4-1 Paper # 2 due
12	Personality Gender	Complete distributed questionnaires and R, Q 2 **BRC** Read R, 11-3, 11-4
13	Dealing with Difficult Negotiators	Read R, 6-4, 11-2, 11-1 Read T, Ch 5 Short RP to be assigned
Outside Class	Group Decision Making	Prepare and do group exercise Read Ch 8
14	Group-on-Group Negot	Read T, Ch 7 Read R 9-2
15	Ethics	Complete Ethics Inventory Read R, 13-1, 13-2 Read T, Ch. 11
16	Power	Bring $ to Class Read T, Ch 9 Read R, 10-1, 10-2, 9-5
17	Group DM/Negot	Group Paper Due on Jaguar Debrief exercise Read R, 9-1
18	International Negotiation	Prepare Alpha Beta **BRC** Read R 14-3 Read T, Ch 12
19	Third Parties	Prepare Ex 13 **BRC** Read R, 12-1, 12-2, Read T, Ch 10
20	Wrapup AWARDS	Complete course evaluation Negotiation and Career Issues

Example 2

Course Number: MBA 698 Course Name: Managerial Negotiation Ver # 2
Classes: 15 @ 180 min. long (includes 15 min. break)

Date	Subject	Essentials	Readings	Cases	Exercises & Questionnaires
1/29	Overview/Orientation	-----	-----	-----	-----
2/4	Introduction to Negotiation	Ch. 1	1-1, 1-3, 1-4	-----	Q. 1, *Option 2*
2/11	INSTRUCTOR OUT				
2/18	Interdependence	-----	2-1, 2-2, 2-3		Ex. 12
2/26	Distributive Bargaining	Ch. 2	3-1, 3-2, 3-3	#1 [Capital Mortgage (A)]	Ex. 9
3/4	Integrative Bargaining	Ch. 3	4-2, 4-3, 4-4	-----	Ex. 5
3/11	Strategy & Planning	Ch. 4	5-1, 5-2, 5-3		Ex. 8
3/18	Negotiation Breakdowns	Ch. 5	6-1, 6-2, 6-3	# 2 & # 3 [Pacific Oil (A) & Tech. Note]	Ex. 4
3/26	Communication & Persuasion Processes	Ch. 6	7-1, 7-2, 7-3, 7-4, 6-1, 8-3	-----	Q. 4 & Ex. 7
4/2	Social Contexts & Power Processes	Ch. 7 & 8	9-1, 9-2, 9-3, 9-4		Ex. 18
4/9	SPRING BREAK	-----	-----	-----	-----
4/16	Individual Differences	Ch. 9	10-1, 10-2, 10-3, 11-1, 11-2	-----	Ex. 11
4/23	Conflict Resolution & 3rd Party Processes	Ch. 10	12-1, 12-2, 12-3	-----	Ex. 10
4/30	Ethical Considerations	Ch. 11	13-1, 13-2, 13-3	-----	Q. 2 & Q. 3
5/7	International Negotiations	Ch. 12	14-1, 14-3, 14-4	-----	Ex. 16

EXERCISE 1
DISARMAMENT EXERCISE

Objectives

1. To create an experience of conflict, particularly between the advantages of cooperation and the advantages of competition in a mixed-motive dilemma requiring choice.

2. To expand the participants' awareness of the way that choices and decisions are made in a small group, particularly when groups are in conflict.

3. To explore some of the dynamics of trust and suspicion between groups.

4. To practice the skills of bargaining and negotiation.

Group Size   Pairs of groups, 2 to 4 persons in each group.

Time Required   Minimum, 1 1/2 hours, maximum, 3 hours.

Special Materials   Record sheets for each team and for coordinator, 21 3x5 file cards (or equivalent) for each team, marking pens.

Special Physical Requirements   Ideally, a separate room for each team and a third room to be used for negotiating. This may be modified by using corners of a large room with negotiations in the center of the room or an adjacent room.

Recommended Reading Assignments to Accompany the Exercise

Reader: 1.1 (Greenhalgh), 1.2 (Pruitt and Rubin), 1.3 (Savage, Blair and Sorenson)
Text: Chapter 1

What to Expect

In this activity, participants experience conflict, both within their own group and between groups, and also experience the dilemmas that must be faced in implementing a cooperative or competitive strategy toward another group. The issues of trust, trustworthiness, exploitation, suspicion, effective communication and the nature of intergroup relations are all the substance, as well as the process, of the participants' activities in this experiment.

Because of the "raw" nature of the experiment, and the absence of an organizational role-playing scenario, participants may tend to argue that their behavior was "playing a game," and not what they would do in "real life." The designers have encountered this argument frequently with this exercise; the problem is a real one.

Students usually use the argument because they want to deny the consequences of what they may have done. But by drawing on the parallels of this exercise to community and organizational life, by probing what the participant thinks he or she would do if the situation were "for real," and by exploring the dynamics of trust, suspicion, etc., that underlie both "games" and "real-world" experiences, this may be sufficient to assist all but the most adamant individual.

The most interesting aspect of this exercise is that it never happens the same way twice. This adds an element of excitement, but also one of unpredictability. Be prepared for the unexpected-- questions about rules and how they can be modified, strategies that teams use, deceptions and ruses used on the other team and the referee, and also the magnitude of feelings that are engendered in some teams, particularly when they are seriously exploited. This experiment sometimes generates feelings of betrayal and resentment that disrupt relationships and color events which follow. These issues should be addressed directly, and there should be ample opportunity for participants to talk through their feelings.

Advance Preparation

1. Read carefully, several times, the rules for the participants. Make sure that you understand how to score the various moves. In addition, you will have to be prepared to rule on "discretionary modifications" or changes in the rules, as requested by the participants. Thus, make sure you read the "Discretionary Rules" section below.

2. Each team will require 20 3x5 file cards (or equivalents). Use a marking pen to create an "X" clearly marked on one side of the card (blank on the other side). Also, each team will need a card with "A" for "Attack" printed on it. Have extra cards available during the game, as some may get destroyed.

3. If the class or group is larger than 12 people, and you have the physical space, you may wish to run several exercises simultaneously. In order to do this, you will have to train referees (faculty colleagues, students, etc.). Ideally, you should have at least one referee for each pair of teams; if you have more referees available, one referee can serve each team, and they can double as "observers" to make notes about the processes within each team. Referees should be trained so that they are as well prepared as you to run the exercise. If you use referees, it is usually best not to take groups yourself, but to help other teams as necessary.

4. The "optimal" physical setting for this experiment is a series of small rooms, separated from but close to one another. Each team should have its own room in which to display its cards and discuss strategy. In addition, a third room should be used as "neutral" territory for negotiations. If you do not have this much space available, set up the physical arrangements so that teams can hide their cards and talk without being overheard by the other team, and so that negotiators are not heard by either team--unless the teams choose to have it that way.

5. You must decide whether you will want people to play for money or "imaginary money." Money increases the participants' involvement in the game; but as the experimental research on this subject indicates, it is not clear whether it increases the tendencies to compete or to cooperate. However, it does increase tendency not to let the World Bank retain funds because of the team's inability to work together. Using real money is recommended.

Operating Procedures, Hints and Cautions

1. If you are using real money, collect it from each participant. $1.00 or $2.00 per participant is recommended. If you are not using real money, announce that each participant should assume he contributed $2.00 to the treasury.

2. Ask all participants to read the rules of the exercise in the text. Then read the rules aloud to them. Demonstrate with a set of materials how the exercise works. This allows participants to visualize how the exercise will run. The three overheads can be used to explain the point values and outcomes. Ask for questions, and answer them so that participants understand the rules. However, *do not answer questions that seek to define how they should behave in developing or implementing a strategy in the exercise.* Questions such as: "Is it better to attack or not to attack?" "What is the purpose of the game?" "What do we negotiate about?" "What is the optimal strategy?" should be answered by literally rereading appropriate sections of the rules, or by a vague statement such as "It's entirely up to you and your team to decide that."

3. Be sure to read the "Discretionary Rules" below, in order to be able to answer questions as they arise at this point or when the exercise begins.

4. Break the class down into teams. Send each team off to its designated "turf" and have them spend 15 minutes planning a strategy, and selecting a negotiator, spokesperson, and recorder.

5. Begin round 1:

    a) Announce to each team that round 1 is about to begin. Tell them that they have 3 minutes to make the first move.

    b) At the end of about 3 minutes, return to each team. Ask the spokesperson if the team has made its move. Record the move on the "Disarmament Exercise Team Record Sheet."

    c) For each move, you will also have to determine if anyone attacked, if a team requests negotiations, or if it is move 3 when negotiations are mandatory.

    d) Although the rules specify that every decision period should last 3 minutes, you may wish to shorten the time periods by a minute or so as the teams fall into a cooperative pattern.

If one or both teams attacked, the game is over. Announce this to the teams, and then have X-up cards compared. The team that has the greater number of X-cards wins 5 cents per team member per card from the team with the fewer number of X-up cards. If both teams have the same number of X-up cards then the team that attacked pays 2 cents per team member per card to the World Bank, and the team that was attacked pays 1 cent per member per X-up card. If both teams attacked, then both teams pay the 2 cent rate.

If a team (e.g., team A) requests negotiations, go to team B, and inform them that team A has requested negotiations. If team B agrees, bring the negotiators together for a maximum of 5 minutes. If team B refuses, return to team A and inform them of the refusal, and go on to the next move.

If it is round 3 or 6, when negotiations are mandatory, ask both negotiators to come to the negotiating area, give them a maximum of 5 minutes, and then ask them to go back to their teams and begin the next move.

6. If the round is not terminated by an attack, it is over after the 7th move. Compare the X-down (blank) cards, and pay each team 2 cents per member per card (from the World Bank) for each blank card. Subtract 2 cents per member per card for each X-up card.

7. Go on to round 2. Play at least two rounds. The rounds may go very quickly if there are a large number of attacks. If you are going to continue for more than 2 rounds, end the exercise when you feel that the teams have established a rather durable "pattern" of reactions to one another - either cooperative or competitive.

Discretionary Rules

It is critical that you decide how you are going to respond to some of the following "inquiries" that participants often make. Your judgment on these issues will be critical to the possible outcomes of the experience, and are separate from some of the major game modifications that are listed in the text.

Q. Can we negotiate before the first round?
A. No. Not unless the instructor wants to make the game more cooperative by allowing communication before either team has begun to commit itself to a strategy. The more communication allowed, the more likely the game will become cooperative. It is usually required that teams must make a move before they can talk to one another.

Q. Can we destroy our attack cards? or Will you hold our attack cards for us?
A. Various forms of this question come under the heading of "disarmament" by one or both teams as a way to enforce the trust of (or compensate for the lack of trust) between teams. The authors tend to permit destruction of attack cards (e.g. tearing them up) for each round, but to reissue them to each team at the start of the next round. We do not recommend that the referee/World Bank

hold attack cards. The referee/World Bank is part of the game - you have an interest in the money, and are therefore very much a player in this exercise. If players wish to surrender attack cards, suggest that they leave them in an agreed-upon place, but that they will have to monitor or "stand guard" themselves. Obviously, the purpose of any attempt to surrender attack cards is to prohibit attacks, since you must enforce the rule that no team can attack without an attack card. (Teams in the past have been so devious as to destroy their attack cards and then manufacture another one with a 3x5 file card and felt-tip pen. You may want to declare this legal or illegal if it happens, depending upon whether you wish to authorize the attack card you give them as the only authorized card.)

Q. Can we bring our cards into the negotiating room? or Can we play the game publicly? or Can we exchange players to go and check on the other team's cards?

A. These questions explore the issue of inspection, which, like disarmament, seeks to overcome trust problems between the teams. Obviously the more public the exercise, the less likely that either team can act exploitatively. The authors have allowed or disallowed this in various plays of the exercise. It may be useful to allow it in order to help teams overcome a serious trust problem between them; on the other hand, it may also be useful to rule it out, in order to point out the real problem of trust, even in good relations with teams.

Q. Can we send in more than one negotiator? or Can we send the whole team into the negotiating room?

A. Yes, we have usually permitted this, but trust is more difficult to achieve and sustain if the team is represented by only one individual, and there is no way the other party (team) can determine whether a negotiator is lying or not.

Q. What happens to the World Bank?

A. The World Bank is likely to have some money at the end of the experiment. An additional task may be designed for referee/instructors as to how they are to dispose of these funds, or the money may be put aside for use later in the workshop, or it can simply be spent on refreshments. However, the participants should not feel that the money will be returned to them. One impact of this may be to create a coalition between the two teams against the "common enemy," to insure that they get their money back. This may or may not occur, as the temptation to exploit the other team is always there.

Alterations and Variations

A number of variations in the experience are possible. Decide what impact you want to have, as follows:

Increase Collaboration:

To increase the likelihood of collaborative responses, the exercise may be altered in many ways: (1) reduce the number of moves in each round to five; (2) require negotiation after each move; (3) create a penalty for an attack, or decrease the incentive for successful attack; (4) increase the relative payoff for X-down cards at the end of the game; (5) permit negotiation before Round 1; (6) permit full inspection of the status of the other team's X's and blanks; or (7) design features to reduce boredom. A repetitive cooperative pattern may produce boredom, which increases the incentive to behave competitively.

Increase Competition:

To increase the likelihood of competitive responses, the design may be altered as follows: (1) increase the number of moves in each round to 10 (and begin with all cards X-up); (2) make negotiation more difficult and costly (i.e., levy a fee); (3) increase the incentives for an attack (e.g., payoff for X-up cards on an attack) or (4) multiply the payoff by three-fold for move 4, and by five-fold for the final move.

Focus on Negotiation Process:

To increase opportunities to examine the negotiation process, all negotiations may take place in a neutral location in the presence of all parties to the negotiation (i.e., both teams observe). The number of negotiators may also be increased to two from each team.

Additional Discussion Questions

The discussion can be held in each pair of teams, or if there were more than two teams, by bringing all teams together to compare the outcomes from each pair. Then break the group down into team pairs to talk about their separate experiences.

Each team should try to react to the discussion questions, indicating its original strategy, and how this strategy was modified over time. Inputs from referees or observers can be reflected against the team's own perceptions of its own behavior and the other team's behavior.

Videotape is particularly useful for exploring the negotiations. Verbal and nonverbal behavior, offers and counter-offers, threats and promises, and clarifying what people actually said (not what they thought they said) can be explored from move to move and round to round.

Concluding Points

This exercise focuses on the nature of decision making in groups, and the relationship between groups. Within groups, it helps us to examine the factors that determine a group decision—development of strategy, response to the actions of an external group, etc. Between groups, it helps us to examine the factors that will determine whether two groups trust one another and learn to work cooperatively, or whether the two groups are suspicious of one another's intentions and act to protect themselves or take advantage of the other group.

There are a number of issues that are raised by the "Disarmament Exercise." We will only try to capture the essence here:

Trust Between Groups. The nature of trust is complex. It is usually based on the individual group's intention to act trustingly, expectation that the other groups will act trustworthily, and confirmation of these intentions and expectations through actions. Trust between one group and the other group will be affected by what the negotiator said, how each side played the game, and what was expected or observed in the other team's behavior. Effective trust demands mutuality--it takes two to tango in the game of trust. If only one side is trusting, and is not careful, it usually gets betrayed. Once betrayed, trust is usually very difficult to reestablish.

Objectives. There are several possible objectives or goals for a group in this situation: to maximize the team's winnings (independent achievement), to maximize the difference between the two teams (competitive achievement); to maximize the total winnings of both teams, with equal parity for each team (cooperative achievement); or to affect the nature of the relationship between the teams, such as desiring trustworthiness and predictability at all costs, or to create surprise, conflict, struggle, and adventure. obviously, some goals cannot be achieved by one team alone the other team must share the goal (e.g., cooperation); other goals probably require that the other team be deceived in order to maximize your goal (e.g., competition).

Team Dynamics. Similar to other experiences that examine the workings of small groups, this exercise offers the opportunity to study the working relationships between members in small groups. The nature of decision making, and the number of people who were involved in and committed to the team strategy are critical factors. Teams which are divided on their strategy, and fail to resolve internal conflict, often experience great difficulty in making the strategy effective, or in resolving difficult negotiations with the other team.

Intergroup Dynamics. When one team successfully arms and attacks while the other is disarming, the attackers tend to feel victorious and confident, but also sometimes guilty; they also sometimes fear retaliation, and hence are unable to trust the other team's intentions, even if it offers cooperation. Those attacked tend to feel duped, foolish, resentful, and futile, and also cannot trust the attacker in the future for fear of being duped again. When both teams attack, there is frustration, disgust, disillusionment, and an uneasy uncertainty that comes from being stalemated with no understanding of how to "turn things around." Finally, when both teams cooperate, there is friendliness, confidence and a sense of accomplishment, yet always for some there is the lingering sense that they could have gained more had they exploited the other's trust.

Negotiators. The negotiator also faces a "classic" dilemma in this experiment - the demands being made on him by his own group and the demands made on him by the other negotiator. Negotiators frequently suffer conflict between their own beliefs and the mandate of their group; experiencing such conflict, they feel constrained by what their group wants in comparison to what they think is right. Additionally, negotiators are frequently drawn toward reaching an agreement with the other negotiator which they may have difficulty selling to their own team. How does a negotiator persuade his own team that he has obtained for them the best possible settlement, while at the same time persuade the other negotiator that he is strong, credible and will only settle for his own group's plan? These pressures often lead the negotiator to be seen as a "hero" if he is successful for his team, and a "traitor" if he shows a sign of weakness or ineffectiveness. Weak negotiators are often replaced quickly by a team eager to maximize its own advantage.

Perceptions and Rationality. A common reaction to this exercise from many participants - businessmen, community leaders, educators, and students is that the exercise creates only one kind of outcome - that is, there is only one "rational" way to play this game. Interestingly enough, however, they don't agree on what that "rational" way is. The "structure" of this situation is called "mixed-motive," in that there are "good" reasons (in terms of the ways to maximize your team's outcomes) for trusting the other team and turning the X-cards down, and also "good" reasons for trying to deceive the other team, or be suspicious of their intentions, and therefore to turn cards X-up and attacking. The outcomes that each team derives are not due only to the structure of the game. They are very much due to:

- Intentions - trusting, deceptive or suspicious - toward the other team, and how this determined strategy;
- Expectations for how the other team would be likely to behave -trusting, deceptive or suspicious - and how this also affected strategy;
- The extent to which negotiations served to increase or decrease trust or suspiciousness in each team;
- Behavior in the game in terms of attacking, or not attacking, lying and truth-telling, etc.

There is thus no single strategy which is rational behavior. The dilemma of the mixed-motive situation is whether to pursue a problem-solving approach, which is appropriate when a group can define the situation as potentially collaborative, or to assume a win-lose bargaining approach, which is appropriate when the goals and preferences of the two parties are truly in conflict and incompatible. In situations where motives are mixed, there are potential advantages to each party for adopting a competitive position and there are other advantages for behaving cooperatively, but results are determined not just by what one team does, but also by what the other group does. The two parties are thus interdependent.

There are many real-world applications of the problems associated with this kind of interdependence. Two students may study together or help each other learn material for a course because they learn more this way; but each wants to get a superior grade in the course. Two executives must work together because their jobs require it; but they are also candidates for the same promotion. Sales and production departments in companies also face a dilemma: production wants to produce as rapidly and cheaply as possible a current line of products, while sales finds that it needs a different product to sell, or can't sell the current product, or that the supply of products is not available when the demand is high. Their perceptions, "negotiations," and behavior will determine the result for the company. In addition, similar types of negotiations may be conducted within a department (e.g., sales), when more than one strategy is appropriate for selling, and when certain groups or "coalitions" within the department have vested interests for employing one strategy against another.

Finally, the nature of union-management relations parallels many of these processes. Unions want to maximize the benefits for the worker, while management wants to maximize the benefits for production and profit. Can both groups achieve their goals, and in a collaborative manner, or do they resort to "attacking" one another through strikes, lockouts, and refusal or inability to bargain effectively? Much of labor relations indicate that collaboration is not easy to achieve.

Only the common "organizational" applications of this exercise are illustrated here. Obviously, participants will also make references to international relations and nuclear strategies, another appropriate area for exploring the "lessons" of the "Disarmament Exercise."

DISARMAMENT GAME
DISCUSSION ISSUES:

1. PARTY'S INITIAL GOALS
2. CHOICE OF STRATEGY
3. DYNAMICS OF DECISION MAKING WITHIN THE TEAMS
4. SELECTION OF SPOKESPERSON, NEGOTIATORS
5. EFFECTIVENESS OF COMMUNICATION WITHIN TEAM
6. EFFECTIVENESS OF COMMUNICATION BETWEEN TEAMS
7. FACTORS DRIVING ESCALATION
8. FACTORS DRIVING DE-ESCALATION
9. CREATING AND MANAGING TRUST

POINTS

Each Player is worth $2.00

Money is on Deposit at the World Bank:

    $ 1.40   in Country Account

    $ .60   in World Bank Account

PAYOFFS:

After Attack with a Winner:

The country with more weapons receives 5 cents per player for each armed weapon that they have more than the other country. Points come from the other country's account.

After Attack with a Tie:

The country that attacked pays 2 cents per player for each armed weapon to the World Bank account. The country that was attacked pays 1 cent per player for each armed weapon. If both countries attacked, then both play the 2 cent rate.

After No Attack:

Each country receives 2 cents per player for each unarmed weapon from the World Bank. Each country pays 2 cents per player for each armed weapon to the World Bank.

EXERCISE 2
PEMBERTON'S DILEMMA

Objectives

This is a relatively simple exercise that is best used when participants are just beginning to study negotiations. It presents students with a structured win/lose situation that focuses on the following dynamics:

1. Individual motives among members of a negotiating team, and the consequence of differences in these motives.

2. The negotiating dynamics that occur among members of a team as they prepare to negotiate with their competitors.

3. Ways that participants can increase the bargaining mix (the collection of issues at stake and differences in individual perspectives that aid or block awareness of these possibilities).

Group Size   The class is divided into groups of six. Three people are on each management team of Country Market and Corner Store. If there is an odd number of students then some teams can be increased in size or observers can be appointed. Any size class can be handled provided space is available. If larger classes are involved (more than four pairs of negotiating teams), than observers can be used to simplify time keeping and to monitor discussions between the teams.

Time Required   60-90 minutes

Special Materials   None; all materials are in the Reader.

Special Physical Requirements   None.

Recommended Reading Assignments to Accompany the Case:

Readings: 1.1 (Greenhalgh), 1.2 (Pruitt and Rubin)
Text: Chapter 1

What to Expect

The exercise frequently starts slowly and then builds momentum as time periods elapse. Sometimes students will approach the instructor and announce that they are familiar with the prisoner's dilemma and know the "right answer". We suggest that you counsel these students to check their assumptions and to continue with the exercise. Those that "know" that the "tit-for-tat" strategy is usually the best one for building cooperation will soon learn that it is not very effective when there are only 12 periods to the exercise and when 3 of these periods have different payoff values.

Advance Preparation (instructor)

Rehearse the rules yourself so that you can explain them if necessary. This situation is a modification of the "prisoner's dilemma" into an organizational setting. The critical modification involves the increase of profits and losses every fourth weekend (the "long weekends"). This addition changes the dynamics from the traditional prisoner's dilemma and places more pressure on the negotiations immediately before these periods. We do not suggest that the instructor draw attention to these special periods, but allow students to identify them on their own (this yields a payoff for careful negotiation preparation).

Operating Procedure: Hints and Cautions

Follow the instructions in the Reader. Once the students understand the rules of the exercise, allow them sufficient time to work out a team strategy. When they proceed through the 12 periods of the exercise, try to synchronize the teams so that they all proceed at the same general pace. We have found it useful to have students make signs that say "open" and "closed", and to display them to each other on a simultaneous count for each move.

Concluding the Exercise

1. Review the outcomes of the various groups from the profit charts. Write a summary table on the board (see below) and ask the students to write the applicable information on the board.

Summary Table

	Country Market		Corner Store	
	Team Names	Profit/Loss	Team Names	Profit/Loss
1				
2				
3				

2. Compare the winnings. Select pairs with:
   a. both high and positive scores (usually a strongly cooperative pair)
   b. both moderate scores (often a group that learned to cooperate)
   c. both low scores (usually a competitive pair)
   d. groups with large differences between scores (usually a pair where one group took advantage of the other)

3. Many instructors will recognize the basic paradigm of the exercise as the Prisoner's Dilemma. The basic prisoner's dilemma is as follows:

Two men suspected of committing a crime are arrested by the police and placed in separate cells. Each is told that he may either confess to the crime or remain silent. Each is told that if he confesses and his partner does not, the one who confesses turns state's evidence against the other and goes free while the other will go the jail for a long time (e.g., 10 years); if both confess, they both go to jail for a moderate term (e.g. 5 years); but, if neither confesses, then the police will have them found guilty of a lesser charge - - carrying concealed weapons - - and sent to jail for 1 year.

Students should be invited to speculate about what the prisoners should do, and why. Parallels may then be drawn between the organizational exercise and the prisoner's dilemma.

4. Since this exercise is often used at the beginning of a course when students are still getting acquainted with the negotiating process, it is often useful to probe their reaction to the experience. In closing, students can be asked to comment on the following:

a. How adequately did the negotiators handle their own management team's interests in the negotiations?

b. How difficult (or simple) did the teams find it to set objectives and to negotiate the team strategies?

c. How did students feel about the other side, who were also negotiating to maximize their self-interest?

d. How many teams built up trust with the other side? Why did this occur? What happened when trust was broken?

EXERCISE 3
THE USED CAR

Objectives

Although the information in this exercise provides the opportunity for a relatively rich and complex dialogue, the focus is on a single issue: the price. As a result, the negotiation is likely to be competitive and distributive as the parties attempt to negotiate a favorable sale price. Specific objectives include:

1. Strategy planning and preparation for a distributive negotiation,

2. Setting of aspiration points, target prices and resistance points ("bottom lines") for negotiation, and understanding the impact of those defined points on a negotiating strategy,

3. Actual execution of a distributive bargaining strategy,

4. Exploring individual motivations and bargaining styles: specifically, the desire and willingness to "bargain hard" as opposed to maintain a cordial long-term relationship in a distributive bargaining situation.

Group Size This negotiation is usually conducted one-on-one, but can be conducted in pairs (e.g. husband-wife teams).

Time Required 45-60 minutes if the teams prepare in advance, 75 minutes if the teams prepare in class; additional time may be added for discussion and debriefing.

Special Materials Background information is provided in the text book. Additional role information is provided here. Role players should be encouraged to write their agreement down on a "contract" provided in the text. Flip charts or blackboards should be available for comparing contracts during the discussion period.

Physical Requirements Ideally, separate negotiating areas for each role playing group, and smaller areas where they may meet to caucus and plan strategy. A common room for setting up the role play and for discussion.

Recommended Readings Assignments to Accompany This Exercise:

Readings: 1.1 (Greenhalgh) 3.2 (Craver) 2.2 (Scott), 6.4 (Brothers), 7.2 (Dees & Cramton)
Text: Chapter 1 (as an introductory exercise) Chapter 3

Advance Preparation

Generally, none. Students may want to borrow money to purchase the car. Be prepared to tell them a current market percentage/rate for interest.

Operating Procedures

Follow the procedure in the student manual. There are three alternative procedures that can be followed for this exercise, and comparable negotiation simulations:

1. Completely conducted in class: assignment of roles, preparing strategy, actual negotiations, and discussion all occur within class time. This option takes the longest, but allows the instructor the most control over all phases of the role play. This procedure is suggested:

    a) For students who are unfamiliar with role playing and may have questions at all points in the process
    b) When time limits must be tightly exercised
    c) When there is no opportunity for advanced briefing.

2. Materials distributed earlier, prepared outside of class, with negotiation and discussion in class. This option takes a moderate amount of time. The instructor should be available for questions as the students prepare their materials. Generally, it is also useful to have a five-minute question period at the beginning of class, to clarify facts or interpretations before negotiations begin. A fixed time limit should be assigned for the negotiation, and the remainder of class should be used for comparison of settlements, evaluation of stalemates, and discussion of strategy.

3. Materials distributed at a previous session, prepared and *negotiated* outside of class, with discussion afterward in class. This option takes the least amount of class time; it also creates excitement among students, particularly if there are *no* time limits to their deliberations. Students must be able to meet in groups or contact one another between classes for actual negotiation. Settlements can be brought to class, or submitted earlier to the instructor for evaluation prior to class time. (e.g., If class meets at 2 p.m., have all settlements due to the instructor by noon, allowing time to evaluate all post settlements and conduct class discussion most efficiently). This option should not be used a) when the students cannot easily get together between classes, b) when the students may not be sophisticated enough to negotiate without coaching or instructor advice, or c) when the instructor wants to maintain a time limit on negotiations. Students may be less likely to follow time limits on their own.

Concluding the Exercise

Once participants have arrived at a settlement (or agreed not to settle), signed "contracts" should be submitted to the instructor or discussed in the general session.

Instructors conduct these discussions in a number of different ways, but the following major points should be covered:

1. A review of the simulation, stressing the key facts in the general information, and the key facts in the individual briefing sheets. This second part is necessary for participants to understand what the given "facts" were, and whether one or both sides fabricated new information during negotiation.

2. A review of the strategies planned by each side. Parties should be encouraged to disclose how they arrived at their target prices, resistance points, and other aspects of their strategy (e.g., who was going to negotiate, tactics to be used, etc.).

3. A comparison of actual settlements for each of the pairs. If possible, actual settlements should be compared to each side's individual aspiration points, target points and resistance points. (See the following sample chart, which may be duplicated on the blackboard, on overhead transparency or flip-chart paper, and filled in as each group presents its settlement). If you have the settlements in advance, this chart may be prepared and revealed at this time.

	BUYER					**SELLER**	
Additional Issues Won/ Lost in the Negotiation	Bottom Line	Target Price	Actual Settlement	Target Price	Bottom Line	Additional Issues Won/ Lost in the Negot.

Group

1

2

3

etc.

4. A discussion of the way that each group arrived at its settlement, and strategic factors in the group's negotiation.

5. Discussion of the nature of distributive negotiations, the conflict and strategies that are produced by problems of this type, and how the groups responded to this situation.

ROLE INFORMATION FOR THE SELLER OF THE USED CAR

EXERCISE 3: THE USED CAR

You have agreed to buy a new Chrysler from a dealer. The down payment on the new car is $4,700, with steep monthly payments. You are low on ready cash, so if you can't come up with the down payment by selling your old Escort you will have to borrow it at prime plus 5% interest. You are supposed to pick up the Chrysler first thing tomorrow morning, so you want to sell the Escort today.

You advertised the Escort (which is in particularly good condition) in the newspaper, and have had several calls. Your only really good prospect right now is the person with whom you are about to bargain--a stranger. You don't have to sell to this person, but if you don't sell the Escort right away, you will have to pay high interest (on the Chrysler down payment) until you do.

The Chrysler dealer will only give you $4,400 for the Escort (as a trade-in), since it will have to be resold to a Ford dealer. The local Ford dealer is not anxious to buy the car from you since a large shipment of new cars has just arrived; in any case, you probably would not receive more than $4,400.

Before beginning this negotiation, set the following targets for yourself:

1. The price you would like to receive for the Escort _____

2. The price you will initially present to the buyer _____

3. The lowest price you will accept for the car _____

ROLE INFORMATION FOR THE BUYER OF THE USED CAR
EXERCISE 3: THE USED CAR

Your car was stolen and wrecked two weeks ago. You do a lot of traveling in your job, so you need a car that is economical and easy to drive. The Ford Escort that was advertised in the newspaper looks like a good deal, and you would like to buy it right away, if possible.

The insurance company gave you $4,000 for your old car. You have only $700 in savings, money that you have intended to spend on a long-overdue vacation--a recreational opportunity that you really don't want to pass up.

Your credit has been stretched for some time, so if you have to borrow any money, it will have to be at an interest rate of prime plus 5%. Furthermore, you need to buy a permanent replacement for your old car quickly, because you have been renting a new Dodge for business purposes and when the insurance-covered rental benefit runs out (as it will, shortly) the rental costs will become prohibitive. This Escort is the best option you have seen. As an alternative, you can buy immediately a high-mileage 1992 Chevrolet Cavalier for $3,800 (the wholesale value), which gets only 20-22 miles per gallon and will depreciate much faster than the Escort. The seller of the Escort is a complete stranger to you.

Before beginning this negotiation, set the following targets for yourself.

1. The price you would like to pay for the Escort _____

2. The price you will initially offer the seller _____

3. The highest price you will pay for the car _____

EXERCISE 4
KNIGHT ENGINES - EXCALIBUR ENGINE PARTS

Objectives

1. To practice distributive bargaining skills.

2. To help students identify situations where integrative opportunities exist in what first appears to be a purely distributive situation.

3. To explore the effects of variations in bargaining mix on the process and outcome of negotiations.

4. To explore the effects of different information and assumptions on negotiation process and outcome.

Group Size The class is divided into teams of two. If there is an odd number of students, some students could work as a pair or observers could be assigned.

Time Required   60-90 minutes

Special Materials   Copy and distribute roles from this manual.

Special Physical Requirements   None.

Recommended Reading Assignments to Accompany This Exercise:

Readings: 3.1 (Aaronson), 3.2 (Craver), 3.3 (Dawson) 7.1 (Wokutch and Carson); 7.2 (Dees and Crampton) 2.3 (Tannen)
Text: Chapters 3, 7

What to Expect

This exercise allows a broad range of distributive tactics to be practised. There is a large enough settlement range that many different negotiation outcomes can be reached. One critical difference in information between the two roles is that the pistons that Knight Engines want to purchase are in fact in stock at Excalibur. Look for how the students handle this situation. Do the people playing the Knight role ask if the pistons are in stock, or simply assume that they are not? Do the people playing the Excalibur role charge a rush fee, even though the pistons are in stock? How does this information influence the final price negotiated? Both sides need to reach a deal, but for different reasons. Watch to see if one party gives the "dire straits" early, and how this affects the negotiation.

Advance Preparation (instructor)

Familiarize yourself with the two roles. Decide if you want to assign students their role before class, or if you want them to read and prepare for their role during class time (this takes 20-30 minutes).

Operating Procedure: Hints and Cautions

This is a very straightforward exercise to run. Follow the guidelines in the reader and assign students to pairs for about a 30-minute negotiation. If some pairs finish early, ask them to read their partner's role information and to discuss how they approached the negotiation (be sure that they have a solid agreement, preferably written down, before they do this).

Concluding the Exercise

1. Review the outcomes of the negotiation using the Summary Table printed below (ask the students to complete the required information on the board).

Summary Table

Name	Bottom Line	Goals	Opening Offer	**Settlement**	Opening Offer	Goals	Bottom Line	Name
1.								
2.								
3.								
etc.								

   a. Ask the students if they see any pattern to the numbers on the board. In distributive bargaining there should be a positive correlation between the size of the opening offer and the amount obtained (research suggests a correlation of about .30, this is discussed in the Distributive Bargaining chapter of the textbook; when opening offers are too high the other party frequently gets irritated and walks away). There will typically be a lot of variance in all of the columns of information on the board. Ask why that occurred, and probe for deeper reasons (personality factors, higher initial goals, intangible factors, etc.).

   b. Ask the class who "won" the negotiation. This is a provocative question that typically will yield a question of "What do you mean, won?" (turn this back and ask them to define the term when they answer). A mix of long-term and short-term definitions will typically arise, and the potential long term costs of a lopsided victory today may surface.

    c.   If it has not been discussed, ask what influence this negotiation will have on the long term relationship between the parties. Did the two sides accomplish both their long- and short-term goals?

    d.   The term "goals" on the summary table was deliberately chosen over the term "target", which frequently translates into solely monetary terms. What other goals did people have? Were they met? If all of the goals were financial, why did this occur?

2.   What type of distributive ("hard") tactics (inflating positions, use time deadlines, etc.) were used during the negotiation? Did anyone bluff (lie)? What effect did this have during the negotiation?

3.   How did the Excalibur negotiators handle the fact that they already had the required pistons in stock? Did the Knight negotiators ask if they were in stock? How should this situation be handled (a nice tie in to the ethics readings or textbook chapter can be made here).

4.   Note that Excalibur negotiators are evaluated based on total sales (dollars) while the Knight negotiators are evaluated on average price and obtaining a quality control guarantee. What effect did this have on negotiations?

Concluding Points

It is important to stress that distributive tactics always involve risk and need to be used with caution. They are always potentially harmful to relationships, and should not be used when the relationship is important. That said, many negotiators are comfortable with distributive tactics and the rest of us need to know how to defend ourselves. Identifying the tactic is half the battle. Once identified, these tactics lose much of their initial power. The recipient of these tactics has a number of choices to make regarding how to respond (do nothing, respond with their own tactic, terminate negotiations, offer to change to more productive strategies, etc.). There is no one right answer to this dilemma, but it is useful to explore in class the strengths and weaknesses of these counter-tactics and to discuss the contingencies that might aid in their choice (e.g., good versus bad BATNA, revenge, etc.).

Finally, distributive bargaining fits the stereotype that many students have of what negotiations are all about. It is useful to identify this point in class and to legitimize this point of view (one theory of stereotypes is that they do contain a grain of truth). On the other hand, there are many other ways to negotiate effectively that are also covered in the reader and textbook and offer students disturbed by this style various alternatives.

ROLE INFORMATION FOR EXCALIBUR ENGINE PARTS
EXERCISE 4: KNIGHT ENGINES - EXCALIBUR ENGINE PARTS

The Excalibur Engine Parts Company has been involved in the production of advanced engine parts for little over a year. It seems that the demand for their specialized pistons has not been as great as anticipated, and some shareholders are beginning to become concerned about the company's disappointing revenues. It appeared that the situation was about to improve six months ago, when the government of Switzerland placed an order for 20,000 of their Series 2.1 Intensaflux (Class "A") pistons. This contract with Switzerland was considered a real coup, because there are several other more established companies that produce the same type of piston. Unfortunately, the contract in question was not approbated by the Swiss legislature and was therefore considered to be null and void under Swiss law. By the time that Excalibur learned of the contract's imperfections, 10,000 pistons had already been produced and packaged. Since Excalibur had no legal recourse, it was stuck with an extra 10,000 pistons in a market that already had a very dissatisfying demand. Financial analysts were predicting that this latest setback would lead to a major loss in this quarter unless Excalibur's management acted quickly.

As fate would have it, a representative from Knight Engines Inc., contacted Excalibur recently and asked whether it would be possible for them to process a rush order for 8,000 of their Series 2.1 Intensaflux (Class "A") pistons within two weeks. Representatives of Excalibur stated that this might be possible, but that certain conditions would have to be attached to such a rush order. First, in order to get some free advertising, Knight would have to agree to indicate on the chassis that their engines were fitted with Excalibur pistons. Second, a rush fee of at least 5% over the selling price would be charged for the extra costs involved for the processing of such an order.

Excalibur's random testing program ensures the maintenance of the high quality of their products. However, even with their strict standards, tests have revealed that 4 to 5% of pistons manufactured contain some sort of defect. Excalibur does offer an excellent quality-control insurance program that guarantees that all pistons delivered will be free from defects. Under the conditions of this guarantee, all pistons are individually tested before delivery. Due to the extra costs involved, Excalibur charges an extra 10% over the selling price for this service. If this particular guarantee is not purchased, defects in the products delivered are the responsibility of the purchaser. As well, prospective customers are usually asked whether they require additional units, in order to provide for situations where replacements are required urgently.

You are the VP of Sales for Excalibur, and it is your responsibility to negotiate a contract with Knight for the sale of the pistons that they desire. In order to determine the contract price, the following should be kept in mind:

1. The Swiss government was willing to pay $600 per piston before that particular contract was annulled. If the Swiss thought that this was a fair price, shouldn't Knight find it reasonable as well?

2.	The total cost to produce this type of piston at Excalibur is $480 per piston. Excalibur's list price for this type of piston is $560.

3.	You are aware that some of your competitors sell inferior pistons of the same size for as low as $400 per piston. You believe that Excalibur's prices are justified due to the higher standards of quality that are maintained at your plants. However, there is a rumour that Knight will be using your company's pistons in order to build engines that will be sold to the government under government contract. If the government could be made aware of the high quality of your pistons, it might work to your advantage the next time the government requests submissions for the supply of engine parts. Obtaining such contracts would certainly quell the complaints of Excalibur's rather timorous shareholders. This goal could certainly be achieved if Knight were to indicate that their engines were fitted with quality Excalibur parts. It is likely that Knight will not to do this without some sort of concession on the part of Excalibur. Perhaps a cut in the profit margin today would reap greater benefits in the future.

4.	As mentioned before, the market for this type of piston does not seem to be as large as originally projected. If this Knight deal falls through, Excalibur might be forced to sell it's pistons to the only other prospective customer who has shown any interest. Hank's Super Monster Tractors Inc., has offered to take all the Intensaflux pistons off Excalibur's hands for a paltry $100 per piston.

Your success during the negotiation process will be determined by the total score that you achieve. The score is determined by multiplying the number of pistons sold by the price per piston that was negotiated.

ROLE INFORMATION FOR KNIGHT ENGINES
EXERCISE 4: KNIGHT ENGINES - EXCALIBUR ENGINE PARTS

The government has recently invited submissions from the private sector for the supply of one thousand V-16Z (Class A) automobile engines. Although these particular engines only have eight cylinders, they can easily duplicate the speed and performance of a sixteen cylinder engine. Their compact size and durability make them ideal for military operations and it is for this reason that the military has decided to incorporate them into their new line of All Terrain Vehicles (ATV's). For reasons that cannot be exposed without jeopardizing national security, the engines must be delivered within 60 days.

Knight Engines Inc., has been involved in the manufacture of a wide variety of engines for nearly five years. Although Knight has managed to turn a healthy profit every year, sales for it's V-16Z engines has been lagging somewhat. It is for this reason that Knight is quite excited by the government's request for V-16Z engines. Knight has dealt with the government before and their established reputation would certainly be a bonus in their favour if per chance another company were to submit an equally low bid. There is, however, one problem: Although Knight does have the capacity to build one thousand V-16Z automobile engines, they do not have the pistons required to make the Class "A" engines. Their regular piston supplier only manufactures inferior "Class C" pistons, which would be unacceptable to the government. Since one thousand engines are to be produced, eight thousand Class "A" pistons are required. If the Class "A" pistons could be acquired within two weeks, the two-month government deadline could be met.

Knight made inquiries at several companies and only one showed any interest in supplying Knight with all the class "A" pistons that it needs on such short notice. The Excalibur Engine Parts Company stated that it would be possible to process such a rush order but that it would do so only on two conditions: First, that the chassis of any engine constructed with their pistons clearly states that it is fitted with Excalibur brand pistons. Second, that a 5% a mark-up be applied due to the extra costs of processing such an order on short notice.

Although the technical aspect of fitting these pistons into the engines presents no problems, the people in manufacturing are rather concerned about using a new type of piston from a company with which Knight has no previous experience. They stated that on the average, about 3 to 4% of the "Class C" pistons ordered in the past (from other suppliers) contained various structural flaws that rendered them unusable. There is no reason to believe that the "Class A" pistons should fare any differently. It is therefore essential that Excalibur provide some sort of guarantee in order to ensure that Knight does not have to pay for defective pistons. Even with such a guarantee, the inevitable delays for the delivery of a replacement could hinder Knight's ability to complete its engines before the government deadline. In order to cushion against such a problem, it might be advisable to order extra pistons. Ideally, Excalibur would agree to take back all unused pistons as part of a guarantee package.

You are Knight's Director of Purchasing and it is your responsibility to negotiate a contract with Excalibur for their Class "A" pistons, the Series 2.1 Intensaflux pistons. Since the price paid for the piston will raise the overall cost of the engine and therefore affect the bid submitted to the government, it is paramount that the lowest possible price be paid. In order to strike a good deal, you must pay careful attention to the following points:

1. You have never before purchased Class "A" pistons. Your knowledge of the market for other pistons (for instance, the Class "C" pistons sell for $250 each) suggests that they should sell for about $500 per piston. The absolute maximum that could be paid per piston and still enable the submission of a competitive bid would be $600 per piston.

2. There is rumour that Excalibur has been trying to get its foot in the door with respect to government contracts. Many of your colleagues find it somewhat unreasonable that Excalibur should have a free ride on Knight's coattails by having their company name mentioned on all the Knight engines fitted with Excalibur pistons, especially when you consider that they are charging a 5% "rush" fee. Perhaps Excalibur should deduct 5% from their price in return for this advertising service. Still, you do not want to press this issue too far because your company president has told you that it might be in the interests of Knight to develop a good relationship with Excalibur's management since Knight may one day be in a position to acquire this smaller company.

3. A competitor of Excalibur's, Mordred Technologies Inc., has stated emphatically that it would in no way be able to fulfill such a rush order for a similar piston in 2 weeks time. However, they did state that if Knight was willing to wait 4 weeks for shipment, they would gladly supply all the pistons required for $470 per piston. Although a 4 week delivery date would certainly not allow enough time to meet the government deadline, Knight could use these pistons to upgrade some engines in stock and await another government or private contract.

Your success during the negotiation process will be determined by two factors: 1) the average price per piston agreed upon; and, 2) the type of quality-control guarantee obtained.

EXERCISE 5
UNIVERSAL COMPUTER (I)

Objectives

1. To have students prepare and execute a negotiation that involves adjustments between two interdependent managers who are organizational peers.

2. To help students recognize an integrative bargaining opportunity in what first appears to be a competitive, distributive bargaining situation.

3. To help students learn how to construct a joint solution that still provides acceptable individual payoffs.

Group Size The group is broken into teams of two. If there is an odd number of students (or if it is desired for other reasons), an observer can be attached to each dyad. There is no limit on group size to run this exercise.

Time Required 60-90 minutes

Special Materials Roles for the two plant managers should be copied from this manual and assigned.

Special Physical Requirements Space for dyads to meet comfortably, out of earshot of other dyads.

Recommended Reading Assignments to Accompany This Exercise:

Readings: 1.2 (Pruitt and Rubin), 1.3 (Savage, Blair and Sorenson), 2.1 (Kuhn), 2.2 (Scott), 2.3 (Tannen)
Text: Chapters 1,2

What to Expect

This role play encourages participants to arrive at a win-win (integrative) solution to an interdependent problem. The dispute is between two production plants and separate profit centers in a highly integrated computer manufacturing company named Universal Computer. One plant (Crawley) produces computer chips, modules, cable harnesses and terminal boards and sends them to a second plant (Phillips) for assembly into larger components. Poor quality at the Crawley plant has led to major problems for the Phillips plant; Phillips is seeking compensation for defective inventory and ways to improve future quality levels. In addition, if the problem is not solved, the Vice President of Manufacturing will likely intervene, and this will create further problems. An important element in this material is that the two plants are operating under different definitions of 95% quality: Phillips wants 95% on every component shipped and Crawley wants 95% as the plant average.

Advance Preparation

Participants should read the Background Information in the text and their own role prior to class, permitting them to familiarize themselves with the problem and to plan their strategy. They should also prepare their initial offer, and record this on the "Initial Settlement Proposal" form in the text.

Operating Procedure

Step I
Follow the procedure outlined in the Readings, Exercises and Cases book. Remind participants that they should have completed the Initial Settlement Proposal before beginning discussion. At the conclusion of the negotiation, remind them to complete the Final Settlement form.

Most dyads will complete the negotiation in the time available. Those who do not are usually in a competitive mode; if this occurs, typically at least one of the parties refuses to accept any settlement and prefers to allow top management to resolve the dispute.

One thing to guard against is the temptation by some participants to "put some more engineering time on this problem", to "go to the boss with this", or in some other way to avoid making a decision. There are two ways to handle this. One is to require the participants to solve their own problems. (You might threaten that, as top management, you will solve the problem for them and both will be penalized for failing to agree.) The other is to let it happen, and then explore how these individuals view their role, their managerial responsibilities, and their personal capability to handle negotiations. This approach can be helpful if the simulation is used during that portion of the course that focuses on individual variations in personality or motivation related to negotiations.

Step 2
At the end of negotiations, have parties show each other their Initial Settlement Proposal, and compare it with the Final Settlement. They should explore:

1. How they got from their initial positions to the final settlement.
2. How each party feels about the final settlement, given where they started.

Step 3
1. Find out which groups completed the negotiation, and which did not. Probe to see what those who completed negotiation did differently from those who did not. It is sometimes helpful to set up a "debate" between those who think a successful conclusion is possible, and those who do not. This debate usually brings out that some negotiators believe that "success" is getting their individual problems taken care of, while others see "success" as finding a way for both of them to survive.

2. It is helpful to post the initial and final settlements for several dyads an a board or flip chart (post then all if time is available). Then, in discussion, emphasize:

a) the range of final settlements reached

b) those dyads where there was a great difference between the initial and final positions vs. those where there was not much difference. Have participants describe how they arrived at these different starting places, the ease or difficulty they had in reaching an agreement, and the degree of satisfaction they feel with the final agreement.

c) invite participants to describe their initial strategies, and how these strategies worked in practice.

3. Discuss the different operational definitions of quality used by the Phillips and Crawley plants (Phillips wants 95% on every component shipped and Crawley wants 95% as the plant average). How was this handled during the negotiation? What effect did it have on the negotiation?

Concluding the Exercise

One closing activity we have found helpful is to invite participants to describe other situations they have been in that are similar to this one, and in which negotiations were used (or could have been used). Have them describe how the negotiations were handled, or if not used, to suggest why they were not used.

ROLE INFORMATION FOR THE PHILLIPS PLANT MANAGER
EXERCISE 5: UNIVERSAL COMPUTER (I)

Phillips and Crawley are two separate plants and profit centers owned by Universal Computer. The quality problem on the modules coming from the Crawley plant has been the most frustrating problem you have had for some time. Not only has the expense of rework and repairs, overtime and additional inspections increased the cost of operation of your plant, but complaints from customers and occasionally failing to meet production schedules have gotten you a lot of unfavorable attention from higher management. What is particularly frustrating is the fact that the difficulty comes from a single area, and also that there is so little you can do directly about the matter.

You would like the additional expenses resulting from these problem to be transferred to the Crawley plant. The plant manager at the Crawley plant has been very stubborn about this matter and has refused to accept any of the costs. While Crawley has been working on the problem and quality has improved somewhat, you have doubts that it will ever be of a desired level for all modules that you receive from their plant. They have made the argument that expenses incurred because of faulty modules should be borne as a regular business expense the way they are for all products purchased outside. While it is true that Phillips has repaired some poor quality items received from other vendors, this is usually done to avoid interrupting production by sending them back to the supplier. You do not know why the company does not charge the supplier for these costs, but assume that it is because it is difficult to write into a purchasing agreement. In any event, when the materials received from an outside supplier do occasionally get bad enough, a shipment will be rejected and sent back. You do not think it is to the company's benefit to accept these costs on items made in its own plants. If the supplying plant had to absorb the costs, pressure would be created within that plant to reduce, if not eliminate, these expenses.

Because the company does not have this practice, however, you are not sure you can get the other plant to accept the repair expenses for all poor quality modules. You are determined, however, that they will have to absorb the expenses on the cost of repairing faulty items of the twelve types of modules where quality has been found to be below the 95% level. You feel strongly that the plant manager of the Crawley plant is making an inaccurate and unfair interpretation of the way the 95% level of quality is to be applied. You are also troubled by the delays in production (often requiring overtime) when large numbers of rejects occur on the twelve types of modules often found with poor quality. You are not too optimistic about getting the Crawley plant manager to accept overtime costs for production, but you are going to insist that either they accept the faulty parts back to replace or repair them quickly, or that they pay you to put repair staff to work on them, even if overtime is necessary.

Unfortunately, while this dispute has gone on, modules have been rejected in incoming inspection at a rate of about $8000 a week. You have refused to work on these, arguing that they should be handled by the Crawley plant. They have refused to accept any responsibility for them. Before long this will come to the attention of the Vice President of Manufacturing and you feel quite sure that both you and the Crawley plant manager will be called on the carpet for not having solved this problem. You have set up a meeting with the Crawley plant manager at his plant for one last effort to try to settle this matter.

ROLE INFORMATION FOR THE CRAWLEY PLANT MANAGER
EXERCISE 5: UNIVERSAL COMPUTER (I)

Phillips and Crawley are two separate plants and profit centers owned by Universal Computer. You have been quite concerned about the quality problems on some of the modules your plant sends to the Phillips plant. Over the last several months considerable progress has been made and you intend to keep pushing on the matter and expect some further improvement, although it will probably not be as great as that realized before. Some poor quality items are bound to occur with a product as complicated as a module. Given the volume at which these are produced, 100% inspection is impossible and sampling, especially at the 95% level of acceptance, is an accepted practice, even though it means that some faulty items will get through.

You feel that the position taken by the Phillips plant manager that your plant accept the costs of repairing all faulty parts is ridiculous. You have to bear the expense on repairing items from your outside vendors when faulty pieces are not returned to them, and you do not see why the same practice should not apply to within-company vendors too. Of course, if shipments were refused because of poor quality they could be shipped back to your plant -- just as faulty shipments are returned to outside suppliers occasionally. You would like to avoid having the faulty shipments returned to you since you would also have to pick up transportation expenses. If you had to repair a rejected lot of modules it might be cheaper to send a repair person to the Phillips plant.

You are particularly puzzled and troubled that twelve types of modules are found to be below the desired quality level when they arrive at the Phillips plant even though they were apparently at the desired level when they left your plant. It is a company policy that plants are responsible to see that products shipped meet stated quality levels, regardless of whether they go to an outside or a within-company buyer. Overall, all modules shipped to the Phillips plant are above the 95% level, so you think that you are complying with company policy but you are nonetheless concerned about the twelve modules that at times do not measure up to the standard, first because you want to get the plant output to a high standard, and secondly because you fear that if this matter gets to higher management, they may revise the interpretation of how the 95% level of quality is to be applied, making it applicable to each individual type of product line rather than to the overall output of a plant.

If you had to accept any of these expenses, you would like to charge part of them to the department in the plant that makes the faulty modules and part to the final inspection department, to give them feedback on their performance and to put pressure on both of them to improve. In addition, the Phillips plant manager has been urging that you absorb overtime costs that come from delayed production, caused by shortages of modules when a great number of them have to be rejected. You think Phillips is way out of line on this matter and would never accept any arrangement like that. Unfortunately, while this dispute has gone on, modules have been rejected at incoming inspection at the Phillips plant at a rate of about $8000 a week. The plant manager at the Phillips plant is just letting them sit there while trying to get you to accept responsibility for them. Before long, this will come to the attention of the Vice President of Manufacturing, and when it does you feel that both you and the Phillips plant manager will be called on the carpet for not having solved this problem.

The Phillips plant manager has set an appointment with you this afternoon at your plant, on what is said to be one last try to settle the matter.

EXERCISE 6
UNIVERSAL COMPUTER (II)

Objectives

1. To have students prepare and execute a negotiation that involves adjustments between two interdependent managers who are organizational equals.

2. To help students recognize the mixed motives that occur in highly interdependent negotiation situations --- the two plants in this exercise are mutually interdependent and there is potential for integrative bargaining, but this is a price negotiation of a single product which can be highly distributive.

3. To explore the effects of a previous negotiation between the two parties (Universal Computer I) on the process and outcome of this negotiation.

Group Size There is no limit on group size to run this exercise. The same dyads that negotiated Universal Computer (I) should be used for this exercise. (Alternatively, this exercise can be used as stand alone price negotiation.)

Time Required 60-90 minutes

Special Materials Roles for the two plant managers should be copied from this manual and assigned.

Special Physical Requirements Space for dyads to meet comfortably, out of earshot of other dyads.

Recommended Reading Assignments to Accompany This Exercise:

Readings: 1.2 (Pruitt and Rubin), 1.3 (Savage, Blair and Sorenson), 2.1 (Kuhn), 2.2 (Scott), 2.3 (Tannen), 8.2 (Sheppard)
Text: Chapters 1, 2, 8

What to Expect

This negotiation is between the managers of two production plants and separate profit centers in a highly integrated computer manufacturing company named Universal Computer. One plant (Crawley) produces computer chips, modules, cable harnesses and terminal boards and sends them to a second plant (Phillips) for assembly into larger components. This is a mixed motive situation. The two plants are part of a larger parent company and have an interdependent relationship so they should be somewhat cooperative. This is a single issue price negotiation, however, which tends to lead people to compete. In addition, the results of the previous negotiation (Universal Computer I) tend to have a large impact on the negotiation process and outcome of this negotiation.

Advance Preparation

None. This material is designed to work as a second negotiation to follow Universal Computer (I). If it is used as a stand alone price negotiation, no advance preparation is needed (the roles in this manual can be read during class time).

Operating Procedure

Step 1

Assign groups to the same teams as in Universal Computer (I). Give them 20 minutes to prepare for the negotiation and 30 minutes to negotiate. Most groups will complete the negotiation during this time, either with a successful resolution or a breakdown of talks.

Step 2

At the end of negotiations, have the teams write their goals, opening offers, and settlements on the blackboard or flipcharts. Explore which groups reached agreement and which groups didn't, and why. Be sure to discuss:

A) The effect (positive or negative) of the previous negotiation on this one. What were the intangibles at stake? Students will sometimes argue that by negotiating after the results of Universal Computer (I) have been exposed that this is an artificial situation that wouldn't occur in industry (e.g., one wouldn't know the true positions of the other side after a negotiation). In a sense this is true, one seldom knows for sure. But on the other hand, people do learn many things about who they negotiate with and reputations are made over time. What this exercise simulates is how these events can have a strong effect on subsequent negotiations. It is useful to remind students that everyone in the same role for both Universal Computing I and II started with the same written roleplay materials, but the outcome of the negotiations are always different. One of the reasons for these differences in Universal Computer (II) is the effect of Universal Computer (I) on the negotiations.

B) There is a large overlap of bottom lines ($7 versus $11.30) in this exercise so theoretically everyone should reach an agreement. If they didn't, why didn't they? (intangible factors, probably, such as the other's reputation, their experience in the previous negotiation, etc). For groups that reached agreement, what determined the value of the agreement? It is likely that the party which first mentioned a numeric value set an anchor for the negotiation which, in turn, had a large influence on the final agreement. This point can be probed and used to discuss the more general question of who should make the first offer in a negotiation and how to prepare for this before negotiations begin.

C) Asking questions is an important part of any negotiation. Explore the questions that students asked during the negotiation, how they were answered, and the assumptions that people made that may have prevented them from asking other questions (e.g., are the A25 chips in stock?). Also discuss how to evaluate answers to questions posed during negotiations (e.g., the importance of listening skills and monitoring nonverbal behavior).

Concluding the Exercise

A good closing discussion is the topic of how an on-going relationship influences any given negotiation, and vice versa. Ask students to discuss examples of this from personal relationships (e.g., friends, family members) and work settings (e.g., peers, bosses), and to note how they negotiate differently with different people.

ROLE INFORMATION FOR THE PHILLIPS PLANT MANAGER

EXERCISE 6: UNIVERSAL COMPUTER (II)

Phillips and Crawley are two separate plants and profit centers owned by Universal Computer. As Manager of the Phillips Plant, you are charged with negotiating the price of the new A25 computer chips. You will meet with a representative of the Crawley Plant to negotiate the unit price for the A25 chip.

Your accountants have assessed the price of the mother boards in which these computer chips will be located, and determined that you must fully absorb the price of these new chips --- that is, you cannot pass additional costs for the A25 chip along to the customer. In previous negotiations you have felt that Crawley inflates their prices significantly, but you have no way to prove this. The prices of computers chips vary greatly, from pennies to well over $20 per chip. Your best estimate is that the value of the A25 is in the $5-$15 range.

The accountants have determined that you can spend up to $11.30 per A25 chip, and you need one for each mother board where you decide to use it. You have no idea how much Crawley will ask for this chip. It is possible to use other chips instead of the A25, but they are not as good for multi-media applications. At this price, you do not make any "profit" on this particular item in the mother board. A price over $11.30 means that you will be purchasing the chip at a loss; any price under $11.30 means that the difference will be an additional contribution to your overall profit on the sale of the mother board.

You believe that you will require approximately 100,000 chips in the next 12 months. Although Crawley has never agreed to do so, it is not uncommon for other suppliers to discount the price from 10-30 percent for all purchases over 50,000 chips. Thus, you may also wish to encourage Crawley to give you an additional discount for all chips purchased over the first 50,000.

Finally, since you are entering the high season for your mother boards, you need almost immediate delivery of approximately 50,000 chips. Crawley may or may not have these in stock, and it is not uncommon for companies to charge extra for high priority deliveries. You want to ensure that this delivery is guaranteed, and that there are minimal rush charges.

In this negotiation, your primary objective is to purchase the chips at the lowest possible price in order to maximize the contribution to profit made to the mother boards by the A25 chip.

ROLE INFORMATION FOR THE CRAWLEY PLANT MANAGER

EXERCISE 6: UNIVERSAL COMPUTER (II)

Phillips and Crawley are two separate plants and profit centers owned by Universal Computer. As Manager of the Crawley Plant, you are charged with the responsibility of negotiating the price of the new A25 computer chips. You will meet with a representative of the Phillips Plant to negotiate the unit price for the A25 chip.

Your accountants have thoroughly assessed the material and labor costs associated with producing the A25 computer chip. They have determined that each chip costs you $7.00 to produce. Any negotiated price above $7.00 will produce a profit for you, while any negotiated price below that will produce a loss. There will be a 5% cost savings to you if Phillips agrees to purchase more than 50,000 chips in the next 12 months.

You have recently learned that another computer manufacturer has published specifications for a computer using a computer chip similar to the A25. They have contacted you and are willing to purchase between 50,000 and 100,000 chips at a price of $8.00 per chip, and indicated that the price is "not negotiable". Your maximum capacity for producing the A25 chip over the next year is 100,000 units and you have none currently in stock. If everything works the way that it is supposed to, you can produce up to 50,000 A25 chips within a month by delaying the production of other products. In the spirit of your Universal Computer's policy, you would prefer to sell to Phillips if an agreement can be reached, but you may sell outside the company if necessary.

In this negotiation, your objective is to sell the A25 chips at the highest possible price so that you can maximize your profits. You may not sell more than 100,000 chips, and you can only negotiate a one year contract.

EXERCISE 7
TWIN LAKES MINING

NOTE: There are two versions of the Twins Lakes material and they are quite different. Exercise 7 allows a free discussion of the challenges that the Town and Company face and explores the dynamics of trying to negotiate integratively under conditions of very different levels of power. Exercise 27 (Town of Tamarack) is a scorable exercise that has the potential to be either distributive or integrative. We suggest that you choose which material suits your needs in the course and that you *use only Exercise 7 or 27 and not both* because while they have many similarities they are different enough to cause confusion among the students.

Objectives

The Twin Lakes Mining Company role play is a multi-issue negotiation scenario that has the potential to be either distributive or integrative. Some groups will become highly competitive, particularly if they try to assign total responsibility for the pollution and cleanup problems to the other party (the Company to the Town, and vice versa). However, other groups are more likely to assume joint responsibility for the problems, and hence engage in mutual problem solving toward a constructive resolution. In addition, there is a large power imbalance between the two sides which is not immediately obvious. If the Company representatives understand how they can use a bond issue to reduce their current capital outlay, then the *net present value* of the total cost of the cleanup is within the limits that their head office has allowed them to spend. On the other hand, the Town has nothing to spend and can only raise additional revenue through increasing taxes (by State law they must have a balanced budget).

Learning objectives for this simulation include:

1. Strategy planning and preparation for a negotiation with distributive or integrative potential;

2. Development of individual team roles and synchronization of those roles into a team strategy;

3. Practice in negotiating a situation where there is a large power imbalance, and trying to use integrative strategies under these conditions.

Group Size Small groups of 3-4 role participants per side.

Time Required 60-90 minutes of team preparation, and at least 60-90 minutes of negotiation time.

Special Materials Background information is provided in the *Readings, Exercises and Cases* book; role information is included in this manual. Groups may be encouraged to prepare charts, graphs, spreadsheets, etc. to support their presentation.

Physical Requirements Ideally, separate caucus areas and negotiation areas for each set of role-play groups.

Recommended Reading Assignments to Accompany This Exercise:

Readings: 2.1 (Kuhn), 2.2 (Scott), 2.3 (Tannen) 4.1 (Gray), 4.2 (Anderson), 4.3 (Rubin) 6.1 (Boulding), 6.2 (Cohen and Bradford), 6.3 (Keys and Case) 6.4 (Brothers)
Text: Chapters 2, 4, 6

What to Expect

As stated in the introduction, the potential for a distributive or integrative negotiation is possible in this exercise, depending on the motivation of the participants. A critical aspect of the preparation for the Company team is to understand that the *net present value* of their commitments for the cleanup allows them to pay for the complete cleanup within the limits set by their head office (see Exhibit 1) as long as the Town Council cooperates by allowing a bond to be issued in its name. Company teams that understand this typically decide to "see what they can get" from the Town Council, and the subsequent negotiations can become very distributive. Almost never does the Company offer to pay for the complete cleanup, even though they were responsible for the pollution in the first place.

The Town Council position is financially very weak; every extra dollar that they decide to spend they must gather by raising taxes. The Town council has two main sources of power: (1) the moral high ground that the company caused the pollution, not the town; and, (2) the use of the Town name on the bond issue makes it a much more attractive bond (a municipal bond instead of a polluting company's bond is more attractive to investors, tax advantages of municipal bonds, corporate write-offs).

Instructors need to decide how much to intervene in the preparation process of this exercise. About half of the Company teams do *not* identify the importance of the net present value of the bond issue, or downplay the extent to which it changes the numbers. Because the bond issue is over 25 years, it has an enormous effect on the Company's position -- note in Exhibit 1 how the value of the filtration plant changes and how the iron particle recovery value accumulates (also see Exhibit 2 for a definition of net present value). Using the net present value figures the company can afford to pay for the complete cleanup within the limits set by the head office. Using unadjusted numbers, the cleanup appears to be far more expensive and is beyond the company's limits. We normally ensure that the Company teams think about this by giving them enough hints that they figure it out themselves during preparation (e.g., you don't have to figure out the net present values yourself, just ask me specific questions and I will tell you specific answers). Company teams that do not figure this out can become extremely defensive during debriefing.

The challenge for the Town teams during preparation is to understand the main source of their power (Town name on the bond issue). Town Councils frequently will agree to pay for a variety of things and not fully realize that for every dollar they agree to spend during the negotiation they have to raise taxes by a dollar. They need to develop a plan where they can explain this to the Company team they are negotiating with and show the Company why they should negotiate integratively. It is this dynamic that is perhaps the most interesting in the exercise. The Town, from the weaker power position, usually understand the integrative nature of the exercise but the Company, from the stronger power position, frequently wants to bargain distributively. During debriefing this needs to be discussed in a much broader context. In addition, the materials are deliberately written with a distributive tone so that negotiators will not immediately perceive the integrative nature of the situation. This can be examined during the general discussion at the end of the class.

Students will also ask the current interest rate. For ease of calculations we tell them 10% per year and to assume that is constant for the 25 years of the bond. We frequently get questions about how bonds work. Instructors need to be prepared to answer general questions about bonds (e.g., interest is paid yearly, the principal is due in 25 years) but it is best to discourage students from getting too hung up by the details so that they miss the overall point (unless they are preparing a snowjob, which is usually counterproductive).

Advance Preparation

Students should pre-read their roles prior to class, and the team preparation (90 minutes) can be done before or during class (with a 90-minute negotiation period plus debriefing time, this makes for a long class). All participants should read the Background Information in the text, as well as the role information provided here in the Instructor's Manual.

Operating Procedure

Follow the general procedure in the *Readings, Exercises, and Cases* book and comparable exercises (e.g., Exercise 3).

Concluding the Exercise

There are many levels of discussion for this exercise. Generally it is best to discuss the content of the different outcomes first, followed by a discussion of the negotiation process, and concluding with a more general discussion of integrative negotiating when there are large power imbalances. Exhibit 1 should be exposed after the content and process discussion but before the general discussion.

1. Content of Outcomes

Discuss the following points and compare the different groups regarding the:

A) Strategy and tactics planned prior to negotiation.
B) Strategy and tactics actually used as negotiation progressed.
C) Target points and resistance points developed by each group, and their impact on settlement.
D) Actual settlements arrived at by the groups. Did anyone think "outside the box"? (e.g., decide to work together to approach the state and federal agencies for joint solutions).

2. Process of Negotiating

A) How did the negotiation begin? what happened next?
B) Was this negotiation integrative or distributive? why?
C) Which side had more power in the negotiation? how did it feel to have more (less) power? how did this effect your behavior?
D) Was this negotiation frustrating? how?

3. General Discussion

Before proceeding with the questions below be sure to expose the figures in Exhibit 1 and the definition in Exhibit 2 to the class (use an overhead or handout). Typically it is best to move from the specific (i.e., case related) to the more general level of discussion.

A) Once teams have worked through their preparation it should be clear to the Company teams (but not the Town Councils) that they can pay for the complete cleanup within the limits set by the head office in Duluth. Why didn't they? Why didn't they simply say we need the Town's name on the bond, we'll pay for the rest, and let's go do something else? (this has *never* happened in over 100 simulations run by the authors; if it happens in your class please let us know the circumstances!).

B) Given the Company's (frequent) resistance to negotiating integratively, what could the Town Council have done to convince the Company to change negotiating styles? How would (did) the Company teams interpret such overtures?

C) More generally, how can the weaker negotiating party ever convince the more powerful party to negotiate integratively? What incentives (if any) does the stronger party have to negotiate integratively with weaker parties? How can integrative negotiating ever be effective among parties with unequal power? Or can it?

EXHIBIT ONE

Funds Available

Twin Lakes Mining Company	$8 million + $1.3 million annually
Tamarack Town Council	none (every dollar spent must be collected by increasing taxes)

Capital Costs	Today's Dollars	Net Present Value - Bond
Filtration Plant	$10 million	$1.02 million
Plant Improvements	$4 million	not eligible
Paving Roads	$2.4 million	not eligible
TOTAL	**$16.4 million**	**$7.42 mil.**

ANNUAL EXPENSES

Bond Interest $1 million

Road Maintenance $300,000

TOTAL $1.3 million

REVENUE

Iron Particle Recovery $16,000 - $20,000 annually
= $1.6 million dollars (compounded annually over 25 years)

EXHIBIT TWO - THE BOND

Principal: Is due once, 25 years from now.

Net Present Value of the Bond: The value of the principal of the bond 25 years from now, expressed in today's value of money (assuming 10% interest earned on today's investment, no inflation).

Interest: Payable yearly.

Case Example

Principal: $10 million due in 25 years

Net Present Value of the Bond: $1.02 million in today's money

Interest: $1 million per year

ROLE INFORMATION FOR TWIN LAKES MINING COMPANY
EXERCISE 7: TWIN LAKES MINING

You represent members of the top-management group of Twin Lakes Mining Company. Twin Lakes has several mines in northern Minnesota and Canada; the Tamarack operation is second in both productivity and contribution to corporate profit. Among you at the table are the Vice President for Operations of the company, the Plant Manager, several corporate staff members and legal counsel. Only the plant manager lives in Tamarack the remainder are from corporate headquarters in Duluth, Minnesota. Assign roles to individuals in your group before you begin the role-play.

The problems of air and water pollution described in the section "Background Information" have existed for a long time. Officials of the company have met with the Town Council several times to discuss these problems. Although you agree with the community concerns, you frankly think that the town has overstated the problems in order to get you to pay for public improvements. You have agreed to remedy several of the most obvious concerns, but have not had to incur major costs up to this point. Now that the state and federal agencies have mandated a cleanup, things have changed considerably. You will have to make some major improvements in order to keep the plant operating.

You are committed to keep the plant open if possible, but not at all costs. You do not want to spend large sums to maintain this operation. Some of your newer mining operations have revealed rich deposits, but will require large investments to gain access; if the Tamarack project costs too much, you would rather close the mine and invest in other operations. As a result top management in Duluth has set a limit of $8 million capital cost (not including bond issues) and $1.3 million yearly as a ceiling that you will pay on improvements. Naturally, you would like to settle as cheaply as possible; any settlement over the limit will require approval from Duluth. Within this overall guideline, your positions on the issues are as follows:

Water Quality. The Tamarack Town Council has maintained that growth in the community will require a second water source in several years, and that Beaver Brook is the logical choice. Hence, construction of a filtration plant on Beaver Brook would clean up the water from the settlement point and provide drinking water to the town.

The Council has been in touch with the civil engineering department of the nearby university. They have been told that recent technology in water filtration can completely purify the water. In addition, the school has been experimenting with several techniques for recovering the fine iron particles and other minerals from the water that now go over the spillway. Additional revenue from the sale of this recovered iron could amount to $16,000-$20,000 annually.

The town has a very small tax base and cannot possibly afford to build the filtration plant on its own. It has been suggested, however, that the town might float a 25-year bond issue to cover the cost of improvements, with payment of interest and repayment of principal to be made by the company. The proposal would need approval at the annual meeting of the town's citizens (i.e., its "electors"), which the Town Council is not sure of getting. If the electors did approve, the state would require the town to guarantee repayment of the bond issue. The town and the company could then negotiate the details of company payments to the town to cover the town's debt service outlays. Such payments would then become legitimate deductions against the company's "bottom line." The Twin Lakes Company has already suggested that it reimburse the town in the amount of 50% of the interest payments on any bonds issued. Given the current interest rates, all payments on such bonds would be approximately $1 million (not including repayment of the principal).

Air Quality. You have already agreed to make approximately $4 million worth of investments to reduce dust around the plant. (This amount counts against the $8 million cap mentioned earlier.) The major problem with the town is over road dust and road paving. It has been stated that the paving of all the roads will cost $2.4 million. Approximately half of these are company-owned roads, and since you use them for large trucks and other heavy equipment, your preference is to use techniques to reduce the dust (oil spraying, water spraying, coarse gravel) instead of paving. Estimates on the town roads are $1.2 million for paving and $150,000 for maintenance (repair, plowing, and so on). The town would like you to pay all of this: since they are public roads, and used more and more by vacationers in the summer, you insist that this is impossible. Privately, you think you should spend up to $800,000 in paving, and contribute $80,000 to annual maintenance, but the less that you can spend, the better off you will be.

Tax Abatement on Company Land. You have been consistently arguing with the town on the tax rate for company-owned land, and feel that their rates are ridiculous. You believe that the basic problem is that the rate on the company land is very similar to rates on private residential land, when in fact you argue that it should be considerably less. You would like to see the following:

a. A reduction of annual taxes from $400,000 to $200,000 on all company-owned land.
b. A reduction of the right-of-way assessments from $200,000 to $100,000.
c. Suspension of tax revenues for several years while major improvements are being made to the roads and the water plant.

It is dramatically clear that you should not continue to pay these taxes and at the same time incur the major cleanup costs as proposed.

Review this information with your teammates and prepare a strategy for negotiation with the Town Council.

ROLE INFORMATION FOR TAMARACK TOWN COUNCIL
EXERCISE 7: TWIN LAKES MINING

You represent members of the Town Council of Tamarack, Minnesota. Among you, there is the Mayor of Tamarack, the Chair of the Town Council, and several members of the town council. Two council members who work for Twin Lakes have excused themselves from the discussions because of conflict of interest; the rest of you are local business people. Assign roles to individuals in your group before you begin the role-play.

The problems of air and water pollution that were described in the Background Information have existed for a long time. The Town Council has met periodically with the officials of the Twin Lakes Mining Company to discuss these problems. While the discussions have been friendly, and some small cleanup measures have been taken, the meetings have usually ended with the major issues unresolved. The Twin Lakes representatives have always maintained that they did not have the economic resources to spend much money on cleanup activities. Now the federal and state agencies have mandated a cleanup. While you are pleased that the company people are under some pressure to make some changes, you certainly do not want to see the company close its operations. To do so would be economic disaster for the town of Tamarack. Within the Town Council, you have taken the following positions on the three major issues:

Water Quality. Growth of the other small industries in town and the summer home development will require a new water supply in several years. Beaver Brook is the most logical choice for a variety of reasons, but construction of a water filtration plant is essential to using this water source.

You have been in touch with the civil engineering department of the nearby university. They have told you about the most recent technology in filtration plants, and assured you that a plant could remove all impurities and make the water potable. In addition, they have been experimenting with several techniques for recovering the fine iron particles that now go over the spillway from the recovery ponds. Additional revenue from the sale of this recovered iron (and other minerals) could amount to $19,000 annually.

The town has a very small tax base, even though property taxes form a substantial part of the town's general revenues. The only ways to increase revenue from this source would be to expand the tax base by annexation (infeasible both politically and operationally), to raise the tax rate (also politically infeasible), or to increase evaluations through reappraisal (not due for another seven or eight years). It has been suggested that the town might float a 25-year bond issue to cover the cost of improvements. Given current interest rates, annual debt service on such an issue would be about $1 million, not including repayment of principal. Typically, such bonded indebtedness becomes the obligation of the town, with repayment revenue to be raised by special assessments against all properties benefiting from the improvements. The town could then negotiate with the company to have it donate sufficient funds to the town to pay for the company-property related portion of the improvements. The company could then gain tax advantages by claiming these expenditures as a write-off against their annual operating revenues. The Twin Lakes Mining Company has offered to reimburse the town for 50% of any interest paid in bonds, on an annual basis.

The passage of such bond measures, though, is subject to approval at the annual open meeting of town citizens (called, in that setting, the town's "electors"). Such meetings are often poorly attended, and passage of a bond referendum by the electors is by no means guaranteed. Finally, the town lacks sufficient fund reserves to lend itself money via inter-fund transfers (e.g., using water/sewer "profits" to pay for non-water/sewer improvements and repaying the water/sewer fund as assessments are paid off). In addition, the town is required by state law to operate with a balanced annual budget--deficit funding is strictly forbidden.

Road Paving. You have been working with the state, and with several paving contractors on the cost of paving the town-owned roads near the Twin Lakes site. Paving cost estimates are about $1.2 million for the town-owned roads, with yearly maintenance of about $150,000. You have no concern for how the company takes care of any roads that are not publicly owned. As you have discussed this among yourselves, you have determined that if you can get the company to pay for all (or a large part) of the capital cost of paving town roads, you will assume complete responsibility for all future maintenance costs.

Taxation of Company Land. You have agreed to listen to several proposals that may be brought forth by the company for tax relief or tax abatement of land owned by the company, or right-of-ways used for moving ore. Naturally, you wish to maintain the tax package as it is, but you are willing to trade this off for major concessions on the first two issues. However, you have decided that any major program of tax relief (short term or long term) will require approval by public ballot of the town's citizens. You are afraid of any decision that will result in losing significant tax revenue without public support of the position.

Review these positions and develop a plan of action for your team.

EXERCISE 8
SALARY NEGOTIATIONS

Objectives

This is a relatively simple, unstructured simulation. It can be used early in a course, when people are becoming comfortable with the negotiation process and with the experience of taking part in role plays and simulations. Its relative lack of structure allows the dialogue to proceed in many different directions, giving students the opportunity to learn about their own flexibility, imagination, values, and personal negotiating style.

Group Size Any size group can be handled, provided there is enough room for trios to work comfortably.

Role Assignments: Use the following table to assign roles within trios:

Student:	Round 1	Round 2	Round 3
One	1A	2B	Observer
Two	Observer	2A	3B
Three	1B	Observer	3A

For each trio, make one copy each of the roles for positions 1A, 2A, and 3A (the supervisors), positions 1B, 2B, and 3B (the subordinates), and **three** copies of the Observer Reporting Sheet (shown in the text, and reproduced in this Teaching Note for your convenience). Put one set of roles (e.g., 1A, 1B, and an Observer Sheet) in an envelope then seal the envelope. Do this for each of the three rounds, and clip or band together one set of envelopes representing the three rounds (1, 2, and 3). Give the set of three envelopes to the Observer for the first round, and ask him/her to distribute the envelopes for Rounds Two and Three to the assigned Observers for those rounds. *Make sure you tell the Observers to not open their particular envelopes until the beginning of the five-minute preparation period for the round they are assigned to observe!* If done correctly, each trio participant will play "supervisor", "subordinate" and Observer once each.

Time Required 60-120 minutes.

By way of example, the following schedule should be followed to fit this exercise into a ninety minute period:

First Round:
First Observer distributes **sealed** envelopes for Rounds Two and Three, then opens envelope # 1 and distributes contents according to distribution table shown above. With the observer keeping time, the negotiating parties spend 5 minutes reading roles, twenty minutes negotiating, and the trio spends 5 minutes discussing the round.

Second Round:
   Second observer opens envelope # 2, and repeats instructions shown for first round, above.

Third Round:
   Third Observer opens envelope # 3, and repeats instructions shown for first round, above.

Special Materials   None, other than role information provided in this Manual.

Special Physical Requirements   None.

Recommended Reading Assignments to Accompany This Exercise:

Readings: 3.3 (Dawson), 4.1 (Gray), 6.2 (Cohen & Bradford), 5.1 (Neale & Bazerman), 10.2 (Fisher & Davis), and 12.3 (Leritz).
Text: Chapter 3, 4, or 6 or (secondarily) Chapters 5, 10, or 12.

What to Expect:

Participants can get very involved in this exercise, and sometimes there is a tendency to ignore deadlines. Allowing more flexible time constraints may increase the richness of the simulation. On the other hand, keeping tight time constraints will allow for enough material to surface to make a lively discussion during debriefing.

Advance Preparation

None.

Operating Procedure: Hints and Cautions

The general sequence of activities for the exercise is contained in the Reader. There are three sets of employer-employee roles (1A to 3B) at the conclusion of this section in the Instructor's Manual. Begin the exercise with roles 1A/1B, and then proceed to 2A/2B and 3A/3B. Assign roles to participants and give each trio a copy of the individual roles (see example, above).

It is suggested that the instructor collect the Observation Report sheets from the observers at the end of each role play, and post the results in a form similar to the observation report. If time is short, only one or two role plays may be done.

To handle the exercise in a shorter time or with different size groups it is suggested that groups of four be developed, with two role players and two observers. In the second round, the role players can become observers and the observers, role players. This allows everyone to take part in a single role play and reduces the time by one-third.

Concluding the Exercise:

Discussion Points:

Discussion after the role-plays can focus on the discussion questions suggested in the Reader, and then on the data. Two general themes are fruitful for class discussion. One is to probe the objectives sought and the reasons why outcomes were perceived as satisfactory. It is important for participants to learn that what may be a satisfactory outcome for them is not necessarily satisfactory for someone else.

A second point to explore is why some groups do not reach agreement or arrive at outcomes satisfactory to both parties. The instructions to both parties give matching bargaining ranges and a strong preference for a positive settlement.

Another feature to observe is whether or not there is any trend in the number of agreements and satisfactory settlements as the class proceeds from Round 1 to Round 2 to Round 3. It is reasonable to expect that some form of a "learning curve" will occur, but be careful to probe for the effects of intangible factors too.

Concluding Points:

Participants can have many personal reflections on this simulation and it is useful to capture them. One way is to have participants compare their experiences in the role-play with actual experiences that they have had in real salary discussions. Many will also have experience in interviewing for a new job, where salary is usually less negotiable.

Another method is to ask each participant to identify one thing learned from their own role play, from observing others, or from the discussion that followed, that they think might be useful during their next salary negotiation. It is also important to ensure that participants clearly understand the unique features of salary negotiations, including:

- Recognizing the importance of the relationship and the long-term consequences of salary negotiation process and outcome;
- The role of intangible factors in the process;
- The fact that many people (superiors and subordinates) find salary negotiations stressful, and the effects of this on the process; and,
- That salary reviews vary a great deal, and can cover many issues in a broad discussion or be very narrow in focus.

OBSERVATION REPORT

TEAM	AGREEMENT REACHED?	SETTLEMENT	SATISFIED? (yes/no) A B	FUTURE RELATIONS? (good/bad) A B

Round One:

1 _____

2 _____

3 _____

etc. _____

Round Two:

1 _____

2 _____

3 _____

etc. _____

Round Three:

1 _____

2 _____

3 _____

etc. _____

ROLE FOR EMPLOYER POSITION IA
EXERCISE 8: SALARY NEGOTIATIONS

You are Vice President of Finance at Ace Company. During a time of crisis three years ago, you had promoted a member of your office staff to the credit manager position; discounting young age and inexperience because the previous credit manager had quit and you were desperate. In time, the word "Acting" had been removed from the title, and the subject of a raise had come up. You had said, "Let's see how this works out. After all, you are pretty young and inexperienced for this job. I don't have any doubts about you handling the job, but I would like to wait. If you are able to handle it, we'll take care of you."

Since then you have had several negotiations with this person about making up the salary differential from that of the other credit managers. This employee is the lowest-paid credit manager at that level, and earns between $12,000 to $15,000 less than the average credit manager earns. Every time that salary negotiations have come up, you have used your skill to play on the awe that this credit manager still holds for the early promotion as the argument to justify the giving of a lower raise. It's almost been a game with you. Every time you negotiate, you are able to whittle down any grandiose demands to make up the financial spread. You pride yourself on being a hard-nosed negotiator, and see negotiation as a game that needs to be played "for keeps". Regardless of the issues at hand, you enjoy being a "tough nut to crack," and usually play that role to the hilt, just for the pure fun of it.

The credit manager is an excellent worker and you have no intention of firing this good employee; in fact, in higher levels of management, this individual has been described as a rising star. If this credit manager were persistent to the point of making a believable threat about leaving, you would probably give in eventually. As part of the "game," though, you make it necessary for every such concession to be dragged out of you. After all, it's only right that others "sweat" a bit to earn what little they will eventually get.

You previously met with this person a few days ago, and after hard negotiating, you were able to settle on a raise of $2,500 over the base salary of $32,000. In your eyes, you "won" this negotiation by your persistent skills and the special circumstances of this particular manager.

Today is the office party, the day when clerical and office staff receive their "bonus checks" of up to $500. (Managers used to receive checks too, but there was a policy change this year and it was decided that managers would be compensated for their efforts through salary changes.) The credit manager, sporting an unhappy face, is now coming towards you!

Take a few minutes to review these facts and devise a strategy for managing the discussion with your credit manager about a pay raise.

ROLE FOR EMPLOYEE POSITION 1B

EXERCISE 8: SALARY NEGOTIATIONS

You are fairly young for the responsibility that the Ace Company has given you as Credit Manager. You were initially promoted at a moment of crisis to take over this vital management function when the previous Credit Manager moved on, and you have handled the situation well. After a few months, the word "Acting" was removed from your title, and you were confirmed in your new role.

When you were first promoted, you had asked for a raise, but your boss had countered: "Let's see how this works out. After all, you are pretty young and inexperienced for the job. I don't have any doubts about you handling the job, but I would like to wait. If you are able to handle it, we'll take care of you."

It has now been three years since that crisis. Although you have received raises every year, they have been in the same order as when you were a toiler in the ranks. You have still not received the one big jump that would put you in the same financial class as the older, more experienced personnel, those who are holding down jobs no more responsible than yours.

In the past you had made a few tries to obtain this pay raise, but you were still somewhat in awe of the position that you held given your tender age. Your boss is a tough negotiator, and each time you have asked for a raise, demanding big money, your boss has maneuvered the conversation around so that you become very thankful for any small raise and equally thankful that your request has not been held against you. You are beginning to realize that this person is something of a "game-player," and probably enjoys making you (and others) sweat.

This was the status on the day of the annual office party. Traditionally, this was also the day the company distributed small bonus checks to everyone on the payroll. These checks were never too large - $500 was tops. As they were passing out the checks, you realized that there was none for you. After talking with another manager about this mistake, you learned that there was a new policy this year, and only the "rank and file," and not "management," would receive bonuses.

This has moved you to action. You currently make $32,000. A few days ago you had a "tentative" (in your eyes) salary discussion with your boss, and you agreed to a raise of $2,500. But now there are no bonuses, you have finally decided to go in and renegotiate for the "big money." It's about time you got financially even with the rest of the managers at your level.

You are on your way to see your boss. This will be that big jump that you have been after for three years, and will put you even with other managers who earn $12,000 - $15,000 a year more than you do. You are going to be tough this time and not let anything wear you down. As a last resort, you may threaten to leave the organization for "greener grass" elsewhere. This option shouldn't be taken lightly, since you might be taken up on your offer to leave! If you do threaten to leave, then back down and don't without adequate recompense, the situation would probably get worse via strained relations with the boss, or by creating the impression that your threats are only a bluff. Take a few minutes to review these facts and then devise a strategy to approach your boss for this raise.

ROLE FOR EMPLOYER POSITION 2A
EXERCISE 8: SALARY NEGOTIATIONS

You are the Financial Manager of the Western Division of the Modern Finance Company. The company has several regional divisions, each structured in a similar way. Your division has a separate financial analysis group. One of your analysts has been with the Western Division since graduating three years ago. In the past year this analyst has done some exceptional work. The projects have been well thought out, and have been implemented without any major problems. This employee has had normal raises in the past years, and the one last year was from $26,000 to $28,500. This raise was determined by last year's salary negotiation between you and the employee, and you believe that it reflects the increased worth of the employee to the Western Division.

The work of this employee has been so good that on one occasion you showed a sample to Margaret Portuganta, the Financial Manager of the Central Division. Portuganta was quite impressed with the work, and has used the plan in her own division. She has kidded you recently about stealing this analyst away from Western for her own staff. You wonder if there is anything serious behind this talk. You would hate to lose this employee, because your efforts in this employee's development have created an outstanding asset that is now paying off with a substantially larger return than expected.

You are a fairly hard negotiator and have given salary increases of about $2,500 to other analysts in the division. You plan on giving more to this outstanding analyst, but not the world. You don't want to lose the analyst to the Central Division and let Portuganta get all the future benefits. A large raise to keep your star would be in order, but only as a last resort.

Take a few minutes to review these facts and devise a strategy for managing the discussion with your analyst about a pay raise.

ROLE FOR EMPLOYEE POSITION 2B
EXERCISE 8: SALARY NEGOTIATIONS

You are an analyst in the Western Division of the Modern Finance Company. This company has several regional divisions, all of which have a staff of analysts working in positions similar to yours. You have a diligent boss, for whom you have worked since you came to Modern three years ago. You have been doing a great job, and have been complimented by your boss on a number of occasions for outstanding work. As far as salary raises, however, you have had what you consider adequate raises, but nothing truly substantial. You feel that your consistently strong efforts, and the exceptionally good project work which you have done, merits a larger than normal raise.

To strengthen your hand, you have been doing a little "seed planting" with Margaret Portuganta, the Financial Manager in the Central Division. While you don't have a firm commitment from her, Portuganta has given you signals that she would like you to work for her in Central. She has seen several of your projects, and was very impressed with the quality of your analysis and your ability to put the plan into action.

Your boss has shown Portuganta some of your work, and told her that you are an invaluable member of the Western Division.

Since your boss feels that you are a valuable worker (and your work has proved it), isn't it time to get the company to show it with dollars? Your last raise moved you from $26,000 to $28,500, which was about a year ago. It is now time to try for the big jump - a $6,000 raise. You have the leverage on your boss, because you have an implied offer from Portuganta. While you really enjoy working for the Western Division you don't want to limit your options, particularly when it involves money.

Take a few minutes to review these facts and then devise a strategy to approach your boss for this raise.

ROLE FOR EMPLOYER POSITION 3A
EXERCISE 8: SALARY NEGOTIATIONS

You are the Marketing Vice President of the Rapid Leathergoods Company, and have held this position for the past four years. One of the people you have working for you is the Director of Mail Order Sales. This person has been in the position for the past two years. In your discussions with the director, you have informally set the requirements and objectives of the mail order sales position. Over the past two years the director has done an excellent job. This is indicated by the improved response in the campaigns of the MaxFli, Fireball and Thunderhead lines. The thinking that has gone into these programs was developed in an excellent manner and the execution has been quite effective. You are quite pleased with the progress on these lines.

There has been one problem area. One of the objectives for this past year was to get more action in the Top Flite line (Rapid's most expensive line of wallets, purses, key cases, watch straps, and so on). The returns on this year's Top Flite sales have been quite poor. This is not a change from Top Flite's history, because it has never been a really successful line. The current director has been unable to change the results of the Top Flite line in the past quarters, and you have no indication that anything in the program has changed.

It is currently salary review time, and while the director has had excellent results in the other lower priced line, the failure to get Top Flite moving is the reason you expect to give only a nominal raise for this year. If new achievements in the Top Flite line can be demonstrated, then you could see your way clear to a larger raise. The director's current salary is $45,000 base pay. You feel that a raise of $2,700 (6 percent) is a fair raise for this year's efforts (normal raises are usually in the 5 - 10 percent range). You are not constrained in granting a raise of more than that figure, but you want some justifiable evidence why the director should get more. You consider yourself a firm but fair negotiator, and are willing to give a raise above $2,700 if the director can demonstrate worthiness.

Take a few minutes to review these facts and devise discussion with your director about a pay raise.

ROLE FOR EMPLOYEE POSITION 3B

EXERCISE 8: SALARY NEGOTIATIONS

You are the Director of Mail Order Sales for the Rapid Leathergoods Company, and have held that job for two years. On the whole, you believe that you have done a satisfactory job. When you took the job of director you had several talks with your boss (the Marketing Vice President), and were thus able to ascertain the job requirements that seemed important. You were able to work out an informal set of job objectives, and have been able to produce a good record against each of these criteria - with one exception. The exception is a major one, and it looms as the biggest stumbling block to your raise.

One of your objectives was to develop a new way to sell Rapid's Top Flite line (the company's most expensive line of leather wallets, purses, key cases, watch straps, and so on) by mail. It has never been done successfully in the past. You have worked hard on methods of improving the Top Flite line. You had experimented with different mailing lists, tried premiums, money-back guarantees, promotional contests that featured trips to Rapid's leather treatment plants, and still the results were relatively insignificant. But in the past months you have been working hard on Top Flite. One particular appeal, using a new promotion mailing list, has produced better results than most. It's too early to come to a definite conclusion. Further testing will be required, but the signs are good enough to be optimistic.

You know your boss is a hard negotiator at raise time. You also know that failure to achieve a breakthrough on Top Flite will make it easy for your boss to deny you anything but the most nominal raise. But you have not told your boss of the recent results with the new list; you plan to save them to counter any argument raised about your lack of performance in that area.

You plan on asking for a $9,000 raise (normally, your raises have been 5 - 10 percent). Your current compensation has a base salary of $45,000. The projects that you have been working on have been MaxFli, Fireball, and Thunderhead. These projects have been excellent successes and have exceeded their projected growths. The Top Flite program was the only blemish in an otherwise excellent record.

Take a few minutes to review these facts and then devise a strategy to approach your boss for this raise.

EXERCISE 9
NEWTOWN SCHOOL DISPUTE

Objectives

This is a complex case. The bargaining mix contains at least six components and there is the strong likelihood of pressures being brought to bear on the negotiators by constituencies and bystanders. In addition, the bargaining is by teams. Consequently, this simulation is often better used after participants have become familiar with several simpler negotiations. The objectives for this simulation are to acquaint participants with the complexity of large team, multi-issue bargaining and to give them experience in developing strategies to achieve their objectives.

Group Size The complexity of the simulation and the time that must be devoted to it places some outer limits on group size. Negotiating teams for the School Board and the Teachers Association can very from 3 to 8 members (we recommend 4-5). Groups larger than eight begin to break down; groups smaller than three eliminate the challenge of holding the group together during negotiations. If the group is larger than 10, we suggest breaking the group into two or more school districts. If several school negotiations are going to be used, make sure participants know which one they are assigned to. We sometimes differentiate groups as East Newtown Schools, South Newtown Schools, etc.

When there are several districts negotiating (a group larger than 30), keeping tabs on the groups and processing discussion after the simulation become difficult. Don't hesitate to appoint observers (some will usually volunteer). It is very useful to have one observer for each team (i.e. for each Board and Teacher Association team), particularly to report events that occurred during caucuses.

Time Required 90 to 150 minutes

Special Materials The descriptions of the Board of Education and the Teachers Association are in the Appendix.

Special Physical Requirements Enough room for each pair of teams to negotiate and for the individual teams to caucus. We often let students negotiate this one outside of class, and ask them to find their own "turf" in a library, study room, lounge, etc.

Recommended Reading Assignments to Accompany this Exercise:

Reader: 3.1 (Vance), 3.3 Brooks and Brooks), 4.2 (Nierenberg), 6.3 (Johnston), 9.1 (Colosi).

Advance Preparation

At the meeting before this exercise, assign participants to negotiating teams. Assign the appropriate position papers to Board and Teacher Association members and instruct them to meet prior to the next session to prepare their strategy and plans. Review with them the rules against reading the other side's position statement.

Operating Procedure

Follow the steps given in the Participant Manual. If the group is divided into more than one school group, prepare a chart to record the initial proposals and final agreements for each so they can be compared.

Concluding the Exercise

School contract disputes are common enough so most people are familiar with some of the issues and outcomes. We have frequently closed by asking participants to compare the outcome in the exercise with the outcomes of actual school contract negotiations they are familiar with, or recalling ones that may be in the local newspapers. We also ask them if participation in the exercise has helped them understand the actual dynamics better, or helped them to a new understanding of the issues.

BOARD OF EDUCATION'S POSITION
EXERCISE 9: NEWTOWN SCHOOL DISPUTE

You, along with the other members of your team, constitute the whole of the Newtown Board of Education. You are to select one or more of your members to serve as chief negotiators representing your side in contract negotiations with the Newtown Teachers' Association. Members of your team not designated as chief negotiators may function in any capacity that the team decides upon.

As indicated in your "Background Information" sheet, the previous contract with the Teachers' Association has expired. It is now the beginning of the school year and, as a result of various pressures, the teachers have agreed to return to work on a day-to-day basis, with the reservation that they may call a strike at any time as long as the contract is not finalized. Your responsibility as far as the Board is concerned, is to conclude an agreement with the Teachers' Association to avert a strike. However, the teachers are not fully informed of just how important it is to you to conclude an agreement. In order to conclude an agreement (in light of the budget situation described in the Background Information sheet), you feel that you have to minimize concessions, reduce staff, obtain an increase in teachers' work load, and retain your prerogatives to make final decisions wherever possible. The board has been informed privately that if it cannot succeed in preventing a strike and finalizing a contract at minimal cost, the community may withdraw its support of the board and ask for your resignation. All members of the board, however, wish to retain their positions on it. Also, the board has discretionary power to transfer funds among budgetary categories if the need arises.

The issues that remain unsettled fall into six general categories:

1. Reduction in staff
2. Work load
3. Evaluation of teachers
4. Salary
5. Binding arbitration of grievances
6. Benefits

These general categories are ranked in order of importance to the board. The board's position on specific issues within these categories is spelled out below. State law requires that all issues in dispute are negotiable.

1. *Reduction In Staff.* The board wants the following:

1.1 System-wide reduction in staff as deemed necessary by the board. The board wishes to retain as much control as possible over layoffs, but may provide opportunities for the Teachers' Association to make informal recommendations of various kinds.
1.2 Final decisions about layoffs of individual teachers, as well as quotas within schools and/or grade levels, should remain with the board. The board wishes to

retain as much control as possible, but may offer mechanisms enabling the Teachers' Association to voice its views.

1.3 Layoffs to become effective 20 working days after contract is finalized. The board wishes to expedite layoffs as quickly as possible, but has some room to negotiate on this issue.

1.4 Notification of layoff to affected teachers to be made not earlier than 10 working days prior to layoff date. The board wishes to minimize notification period. However, the board feels that there is some room to negotiate on this issue.

1.5 Members of the board are generally resistant to hearing grievances from individual teachers who have been laid off. However, the board is willing to accept an informal review procedure as long as it minimizes time investment and permits retention of final discretionary power by the board.

1.6 Recall: The board is willing to accept a recall list but wishes to limit formal eligibility to one year from the date of layoff. The board also wishes to retain full discretion in recalling individual teachers, particularly those whose one-year recall period has expired, if it wishes to do so.

1.7 Notification and acceptance of recall: The board wants written response within 72 hours of notification of recall in order to expedite recall. Again, the board wants to minimize its efforts and obtain a clear indication of recall acceptances as quickly as possible. However, there is some room to negotiate within the context of this principle.

In general, the board wishes to reduce teaching staff in order to absorb part of the overall budget decrease. It also hopes to partially cover increased costs that would result from finalization of the contract presently being negotiated through such layoffs.

2. *Work Load.* The board wants the following:

2.1 Pupil/teacher ratio: The board wants an increase in the system-wide ratio from its current level of 32, to approximately 35. Although there is some flexibility on this issue, the board feels it important for budgetary reasons to come as close to 35 as possible.

2.2 Workday: The board wants an increase in the length of the present workday from seven hours, five minutes, to a full eight hours. The shorter workday was agreed to in better times when the budget was able to tolerate it. Now, the board feels that it wants the time "returned."

2.3 "Prep" time: The board wants elimination of the 50-minute prep time period given to each teacher each workday (one period per day.) Same reasons as in 2.2.

2.4 "Duty-free" time: In the previous contract, the teachers made a concession to the board that called for a reduction in their 1-hour lunch period, to a 50-minute period. Furthermore, the teachers also agreed to divide this 50-minute period into two parts: 25 minutes for lunch, per se, and 25 minutes of "duty-free" time. The board wants elimination of duty-free time given to each teacher, each workday. This amounts to 25 minutes per day. Same reasons as in 2.2.

2.5 Emergency assignments and general obligations: The board wants discretionary power to assign teachers to activities during the 75 minutes gained from 2.3 and 2.4 above. These activities include emergency substitute fill-in; bus duty; hall duty; disciplinary duty and committee service. Also, the board wants to assign teachers to monitor and chaperon after-school athletic and social activities.

In general, the board wishes to increase teachers' workload so as to regain coverage lost by layoffs and budget cuts while at the same time minimizing costs.

3. *Evaluation of Teachers*. The board wants to hire its own consultant to develop a systematic evaluation procedure. It wishes to use these evaluations as aids in each of the following areas:

a. Determination of pay increases.
b. Assignment of teachers to schools and classes.
c. Granting of tenure.
d. Removal of teachers.

3.1   The board feels that evaluation is a legitimate management activity and that the Teachers' Association should provide only advisory assistance, if and when asked, regarding the design and execution of the evaluations.

3.2   The board does not want these evaluations to be freely available to teachers, due to the confidential nature of the material included and the notes likely to have been made by supervisors. Instead, the board is willing to provide limited access through a procedure in which a teacher's supervisor, principal, or assistant principal outlines the contents to individual teachers. Here, the board wishes to retain discretion as to information revealed to individual teachers.

3.3   The board is seeking "unannounced visitations" to classrooms for purposes of conducting observations as part of the evaluation procedure. The board wishes to be unrestricted in its freedom to conduct these observations, but is prepared to accept scheduled visitations.

4. *Salary*. The board wants the following:

4.1   Retroactivity: No retroactivity of salary increases prior to date of contract finalization. However, if necessary, the board feels it can provide a nominal percentage of full retroactivity, but it would prefer not to do so.

4.2   Cost-of-living increase: The board feels that it can only provide a percentage of the previous years' increase in cost of living, as determined by official government figures. However this limit may be approached in many ways, and the board is willing to entertain suggestions.

4.3   Across-the-board increases in salary schedule: The board feels that it cannot provide such increases unless budgetary resources can be obtained through sacrifices made by the Teachers' Association on other issues in the present negotiation.

5. *Binding Arbitration of Grievances*.

5.1   The board is hesitant to consent to a binding arbitration procedure, as a result of certain groups in the community who are adamantly opposed to erosion of management prerogatives. The board is willing to agree to some form of advisory arbitration.

6. *Benefits.* During this time of severe budgetary curtailment the board wants to minimize expenditures for benefits. This includes their direct costs (such as claims reimbursement), as well as costs for administering such programs that would be incurred by the school system.

6.1 Accumulated sick leave upon severance: The board wishes to minimize such expenditures.

6.2 Bereavement leave: The board is willing to go up to two days' bereavement leave in the case of the death of a member of the teacher's immediate family (spouse or children).

6.3 Civic duty leave: The board is willing to grant salary for jury duty only. The board also wishes to deduct the amount received for jury duty from a teacher's regular daily rate of pay.

6.4 Childbirth leave: The board is seeking the following limits on childbirth leave: up to 6 weeks leave for female employees; not more than 3 weeks leave for male employees (spouse). In addition, the board prefers that childbirth leave be included in teachers' total sick-leave benefits.

TEACHERS' ASSOCIATION POSITION
EXERCISE 9: NEWTOWN SCHOOL DISPUTE

You and your teammates are the bargaining team for the Newtown Teachers' Association. You are to select one or more of your members to serve as chief negotiators representing your side in contract negotiations with the Newtown School District. Members of your team not designated as chief negotiators may function in any capacity that the team decides upon.

As indicated in your "Background Information" sheet, the previous contract with the school district has expired. It is now the opening day of the school year. As a result of various community pressures, the Teachers' Association has agreed to return to work on a day-to-day basis, with the provision that it is free to call a strike at any time as long as the contract is not finalized. In this regard, the bargaining team has considered several options ranging from a system-wide strike to a variety of more limited actions. You represent 95 percent of the teachers in the Newtown system. Information available to you indicates that a majority of the membership prefers to conclude an agreement but is willing, if necessary, to engage in a strike action. The remainder of the membership is split, in that one subgroup wants to avoid any strike, while a second group is pressing to call one immediately. You, along with the other members of your team, prefer to conclude a contract rather than strike, but you are ready to do the latter if necessary. You are aware of increasing community pressure on your association and on the school board to conclude an agreement in order to avert a closing of the schools. The Teachers' Association membership is aware of the budget cuts being imposed on the district. However, it has certain demands that it feels are justified and reasonable in light of the increased cost of living and recent gains received by Teachers' Associations in neighboring communities.

In general, the bargaining team wants to avoid a situation where the Teachers' Association loses benefits that have been gained over the past several years. In this connection, it is felt that the Board of Education is essentially trying to reduce staff and, at the same time, obtain a considerable increase in teachers' work load in order to meet externally imposed budgetary reductions. You feel that the board is attempting to pass the burden of the budget cuts along to teachers rather than apportioning them in an equitable manner. Many members of the association also want salary increases that, at the very least, are sufficient to offset the rise in cost of living. Many teachers are willing to share some responsibility in the cutting of the budget and are willing to make a reasonable contribution to this end. A sizeable portion of the membership is willing to accept an increase in workload, provided that the increases are reasonable and that they have some choice as to how this would be accomplished. However, it is felt that the board is asking teachers to incur most of the costs, make most of the sacrifices and seeking to retain its prerogative to make all decisions in these matters.

The issues that remain to be settled fall into six general categories:

1. Salary
2. Evaluation of teachers
3. Reduction in staff

4. Work load
5. Benefits
6. Binding arbitration of grievances

These general categories are ranked (above) in order of importance to the teachers. The bargaining team's position on specific issues within these categories is spelled out below. State law requires that all issues in dispute are negotiable.

1. *Salary.* The Teachers' Association wants the following:

1.1   Retroactivity: All salary increases retroactive to July 1, the anniversary date of the contract. However, information available to the bargaining team suggests that the membership may be willing to accept a partial retroactivity formula in exchange for concessions on other issues. Possibilities include a reasonable percentage of full retroactivity, differential retroactivity linked to criteria such as years of service and present salary level, or other formulas devised by the bargaining team such that any formula agreed upon yields satisfactory concessions on other priority issues.

1.2   Cost-of-living increase: The membership prefers a cost-of-living increase commensurate with the regional increase in cost of living during the previous year, as determined by official government sources. However, information available to the bargaining team suggests that the membership might be willing to accept either a differential formula or one providing a reasonable percentage of the full increase in cost-of-living in exchange for concessions on other issues.

1.3   Across-the-board increases in salary schedule: In order to equalize salaries with those in surrounding districts, the membership is in favor of a $1150, across-the-board increase. Information available to the bargaining team suggests that this figure is somewhat flexible as long as pronounced inequities at the lower steps of the salary schedule are brought into line with those of surrounding districts.

2.   *Evaluation of Teachers.* The bargaining team has information indicating that the School Board is about to hire a consultant to develop a systematic evaluation procedure to be used by the board in determining individual teachers' salary increases and assignments to specific schools and duties. The board also wants to use these evaluations in making decisions pertaining to the granting of tenure and teacher layoffs. The membership is wary of this approach. Instead, teachers want the following:

2.1   Representation in the design and execution of teacher evaluations with particular reference to the specification of performance criteria and rules concerning the conditions under which such evaluations will be made.

2.2   Access by individual teachers to any and all evaluation data obtained and on file.

2.3   The opportunity to challenge, through a specified procedure, any data or entries felt by individual teachers to be inappropriate, inaccurate or otherwise damaging to them, and to have such entries expunged.

In general, the teachers want an explicit agreement, incorporating their input, spelling out the content of teacher evaluations, the procedures to be followed in obtaining such data and their use by the board In the areas of teacher salary, school assignments, tenure, and staffing.

3. *Reduction in Staff.* The Teachers' Association wants the following:

3.1 Minimal and selective reductions in staff, offset wherever possible by activating early retirements, using teachers to fill administrative positions that are currently vacant and using laid-off teachers to fill vacancies created by teachers on both long and short-term leave.

3.2 Layoffs to be jointly determined on a case-by-case basis by representatives of the Teachers' Association and the Board of Education.

3.3 Layoffs to become effective on the last day of the present school term (January 28).

3.4 Written notification of layoff to affected teachers at least 60 days prior to layoff date.

3.5 Right to dispute layoff of individual teachers by meeting and conferring with the board in order to resolve such differences. Where disputes cannot be resolved in this manner, case to be submitted to an arbitrator whose decision would be binding on both sides. In the event of a reversal of layoff resulting from either procedure, the reinstated teacher would receive full salary for any period on layoff status.

3.6 Laid-off teachers to be placed on a recall list in the order of their layoff dates. Teachers to be carried on this list for a period not to exceed three years. In the case of ties between teachers on the recall list, recall to be determined by length of service prior to layoff date. Tied teachers not recalled through this procedure to be placed at the top of the remaining recall list for next consideration.

3.7 Recall notification shall be in writing and teachers shall have 10 days following receipt of notification to inform the board of their intention to accept or decline recall.

In general, the teachers want to minimize layoffs through placement of teachers in existing administrative vacancies, activation of early retirements and the use of laid-off teachers as substitutes for those on leave. Also, representation in layoff decisions, maximization of forewarning to affected teachers, specified recall procedures and a procedure permitting challenges of board layoff decisions are wanted. Within these overall membership preferences, however, the bargaining team recognizes a need to remain flexible in order to make trade-offs wherever necessary.

4. *Work Load.* The bargaining team has information indicating that the membership, though somewhat divided, wants the following:

4.1 Pupil/teacher ratio (average class size): The present system-wide ratio is approximately 32:1. However, this figure is an average, encompassing some smaller and some larger classes. The membership wants to hold the ratio at its present level, but might be willing to accept an increase in certain types of classes in exchange for concessions on other priority issues.

4.2 Workday: The present workday, as established in previous contracts, is seven hours and five minutes. Although there are strong feelings in the membership against any formal increase, the bargaining team feels that it might agree to certain limited increases, particularly where individual teachers voluntarily agree to assume additional responsibilities on an ad hoc basis. The bargaining team wishes to use this option as a lever to gain concessions on other priority issues.

4.3 "Prep" time: Teachers currently have a 50-minute "prep" time period each workday. Much of the membership feels rather strongly about retaining this period "as is" but the bargaining team feels that it might be able to offer a nominal reduction on a rotational or otherwise "shared" basis. The bargaining team feels that any concession on this issue should yield appropriate concessions in return.

4.4 Duty-free time: In the previous contract, the teachers made a concession to the board which called for a reduction in their 1-hour lunch period, to a 50-minute period. Furthermore, the teachers also agreed to divide this 50-minute period into two parts: 25 minutes for lunch, per se, and 25 minutes of "duty-free" time. The teachers are adamantly opposed to any demands made by the board for additional service during the 25-minute "duty-free" period.

4.5 Emergency assignments and general obligations: The teachers are opposed to giving the board discretionary power to assign teachers to various duties during their daily "prep" time or "duty-free" time periods. Such assignments would include emergency substitute fill-in, bus duty, hall duty, disciplinary duty, committee service, and duties involving the monitoring and/or chaperoning of after-school athletic and social events. The bargaining team feels that it can design schemes filling some of these needs, provided that:

a) Decisions pertaining to such assignments are made jointly by representatives of the Teachers' Association and the board.
b) Such assignments are rotated in order to both minimize and equalize such service.
c) When possible, individual teachers have choice in the duties to which they are assigned.

The bargaining team is willing to make such proposals in exchange for concessions on other priority issues. In general, the teachers are willing to make certain concessions on workload, provided that assignments are not made arbitrarily by the board and that any increases are kept to a minimum and are distributed equitably.

5. *Benefits.* The Teachers' Association wants the following:

5.1 Accumulated sick leave upon severance: In light of the fact that teachers in most surrounding communities receive payment for unused sick leave upon severance, the Newtown membership feels it too is entitled to such benefits. However, the bargaining team believes that various formulas can be devised that might be acceptable to the membership if concessions on other priority issues were forthcoming from the board. These might include a percentage of accumulated sick leave, payments keyed to years of service, reasons for severance, and so on. The bargaining team also sees possibilities of phasing in such benefits over several years.

5.2 Bereavement leave: According to a poll taken by the bargaining team, the membership is seeking up to five days of paid leave in the event of death of an immediate member of a teacher's family, including spouse, children, and parents. Also sought are two-day bereavement leaves in the event of the death of a spouse's parent. However, the results of the poll indicate that these preferences are somewhat flexible.

5.3 Civic duty leave: The membership has indicated that it wants full pay from the school district while serving on jury duty, without deductions for any pay received as a result of such duty. However, the bargaining team's information suggests that the membership could be induced to accept a formula in which any pay received for performing civic duty would be deducted from regular pay, as long as teachers incur no less pay as a result of such service to the community. The bargaining team feels that such an agreement would only be appropriate if the board is willing to meet salary demands satisfactorily.

5.4 Childbirth leave: The membership wants 8 weeks for childbirth leave, for both female and male (spouse) employees. A number of teachers also want childbirth leave benefits to be independent of sick leave taken for other reasons. However, the bargaining team feels that trade-offs might be made on this issue in exchange for salary and/or reduction in staff concessions. The bargaining team feels it can develop proposals tying childbirth leave to specific work load issues so as to reduce the overall costs of such leaves to the system.

6. *Binding Arbitration of Grievances.*

6.1 The teachers are seeking binding arbitration of grievances by an impartial party acceptable to the Teachers' Association, but are willing to temporarily accept advisory arbitration provided that teachers' interests are represented to their satisfaction. The bargaining team wants to use this as a lever for gaining concessions from the board on issues related to work and reduction in staff.

EXERCISE 10
BESTBOOKS / PAIGE TURNER

Objectives

1. To provide an opportunity for participants to negotiate issues that are represented in purely quantitative terms.

2. To examine the effect of competitive, distributive assumptions in a negotiation situation where some issues are distributive, some are integrative, and others are compatible.

3. To practice communication skills (listening, non-verbal behavior, asking questions) in a situation with minimal context.

Group Size Students work in pairs. Any number may be conducted, limited only by the size of the space available.

Time Required 45-90 minutes

Special Materials Copy and distribute role information from this manual.

Special Physical Requirements None.

Recommended Reading Assignments to Accompany This Exercise:

Readings: 5.1 (Neale and Bazerman), 5.2 (Tannen), 5.3 (Tramel and Reynolds), 4.1 (Gray), 4.2 (Anderson), 4.3 (Rubin)
Text: Chapters 5, 4

What to Expect

Negotiators tend to approach this exercise with reasonably competitive orientations. This can be enhanced or downplayed, depending on the context in which the exercise is conducted and the degree to which the instructor emphasizes that comparisons across negotiators will be examined later (i.e., to see who got the most points). The more competitively the negotiators approach the issues, the more likely that they will try to "win" on each of the issues, and this mutually competitive orientation will cause them less-than-optimal compromises on some issues.

In contrast, negotiators who are more open-minded about the situation, and who ask questions about their opponent's preferences and priorities, will soon learn that the issues are not structured in a perfectly opposite manner. If the negotiators learn to share information and priorities sufficiently, they will eventually arrive at a settlement that is integrative. The differences in these strategic approaches and their outcomes is central to distinguishing between distributive and integrative bargaining.

Advance Preparation (instructor)

Familiarize yourself with the content of the payoff schedules. Think about where you want to place this exercise in the sequence of the course. It is a fairly easy exercise and can be placed early in the course; alternatively, the later it is placed, the more likely that intangible factors will arise to interfere with good communication.

Operating Procedure: Hints and Cautions

No special rules are required. Participants should be randomly assigned to roles and should have time to read the roles and to prepare for the negotiation. Some participants will have trouble with this exercise because it looks deceptively simple, and people are sometimes confused by looking for complexity. Participants also have some trouble because there are so few "facts" in the exercise. This exercise is more like "horsetrading", and the parties must limit their concessions to be based on what they find to be a good or bad outcome.

Concluding the Exercise

Ask the students to post their results on the blackboard. Begin the discussion by asking different groups to describe the process they used to go about this negotiation. Focus on several different types of groups:

a) Groups that had very low point totals for both sides. These groups are likely to have used a more distributive, competitive approach to these negotiations.

b) Groups in which one party did very well and the other did poorly. In these groups one negotiator is likely to have acted competitively or deceptively towards the other.

c) Groups in which both parties did well. In these groups, an integrative process was likely to have been initiated by one or both sides.

Additional Discussion Points

The discussion points presented in the Reader provide a foundation for further discussion of this exercise. Many lessons surrounding communication, mistaken assumptions, "leaving money on the table", etc. can surface with this exercise.

Concluding Points

This exercise requires a good summary so that students see the deeper lessons and don't simply perceive it as a game. A brief lecture on communication, some discussion of non-verbal behavior and how to interpret it, or a lecture on some critical differences between integrative and distributive bargaining all work well to close this exercise.

ROLE INFORMATION FOR PAIGE TURNER'S AGENT
EXERCISE 10: BESTBOOKS / PAIGE TURNER

The nation's greatest best-selling author, Paige Turner, is looking to change publishers and is entertaining the idea of signing a contract with Bestbooks. Paige abhors the business side of the literary world and has asked you, an up and coming agent, to hammer out a deal with the representative from Bestbooks. Your experience tells you that the negotiation between you and Bestbooks will hinge on the following 8 points:

1. Royalties (percentage per sale)
2. Contract signing bonus
3. Number of print runs for the book
4. Number of weeks that Paige has to promote the book
5. Number of books
6. Advance
7. Number of countries where the book will be sold
8. Number of bookclubs that will adopt the book

You would like to keep Paige on as a client, and you realize that the best way of doing this would be to get the best possible deal from Bestbooks and thereby establish yourself as a top-notch negotiator. Ideally, a successful negotiation will result in a contract that will be favourable to Paige on each of the 8 above mentioned points. You can evaluate your success in the negotiation process with Bestbooks by using the success table on the following page.

You will notice that the issues differ in point values; consider the issues with the higher points to be more important to Paige. Issues that are concerned with money (royalties, signing bonus, advance, number of print runs of the book, number of countries where the book will be distributed, number of bookclubs that will adopt the book) are quite straightforward: the more the better! Signing bonuses are so common you shouldn't have to negotiate for them (in fact, Paige has already decided how to spend this money -- that is why the advance is also important).

The type of contract that Paige will have with the publisher is also important. Writers have become like sportstars; the value of their contracts tend to go up as they switch from publisher to publisher, although this needs to be weighed against the uncertainty that may also be involved in a switch. Basically, Paige wants to only write 2 books for Bestbooks in order to have the freedom to leverage publishers against each other in the future. Finally, Paige would rather spend time writing new books rather than promoting this book. Paige finds book promotion to be a boring, redundant task --- good books do not need promotion, and Paige is a great writer!

Your goal is to obtain the highest possible score. You will have 30 minutes to negotiate a contract and it is quite probable that Paige would throw one of those famous temper tantrums if no contract would result from the negotiations.

Confidential Success Table for Paige Turner's Agent

	Term in Contract	*Points*
Royalties	15%	6000
	13%	5000
	10%	4000
	7%	3000
	5%	2000
Contract signing bonus	$25,000	5000
	20,000	4000
	15,000	3000
	10,000	2000
	5,000	1000
Number of print runs for the book	5	3500
	4	3000
	3	2500
	2	2000
	1	1500
Number of weeks that Paige has to promote the book	35	100
	30	200
	25	300
	20	400
	15	500
Number of books	6	500
	5	1000
	4	1500
	3	2000
	2	2500
Advance	$ 0	0
	5,000	1500
	10,000	3000
	15,000	4500
	20,000	6000
Number of countries where the book will be distributed	14	4000
	12	3500
	10	3000
	8	2500
	6	2000
Number of bookclubs that will adopt the book	5	5000
	4	4000
	3	3000
	2	2000
	1	1000

ROLE INFORMATION FOR BESTBOOKS REPRESENTATIVE
EXERCISE 10: BESTBOOKS / PAIGE TURNER

The nation's greatest best-selling author, Paige Turner, is looking to change publishers and is entertaining the idea of signing a contract with Bestbooks. Paige abhors the business side of the literary world and has asked an agent to hammer out a deal with you, the senior representative from Bestbooks. Your experience tells you that the negotiation between you and Paige's agent will hinge on the following 8 points:

1. Royalties (percentage per sale)
2. Contract signing bonus
3. Number of print runs for the book
4. Number of weeks that Paige has to promote the book
5. Number of books
6. Advance
7. Number of countries where the book will be sold
8. Number of bookclubs that will adopt the book

The president of Bestbooks has stated that it would be great to have the popular Paige join Bestbooks' list of authors, but cautioned that Paige was to be treated like any other author when negotiating a contract. You realize that a favourable contract for Bestbooks would involve giving as little as possible with respect to the above mentioned 8 points. It is imperative that you negotiate a good deal for Bestbooks; the last senior representative was released for being too generous when signing on new authors. You can evaluate your success during the negotiation process with Paige's lawyer by using the success table on the following page.

You will notice that the issues differ in point values; consider the issues with the higher points to be more important to Bestbooks. Issues that are concerned with selling the book (number of print runs for the book, number of weeks that Paige promotes the book, number of countries where the book will be distributed, number of bookclubs that will adopt the book) are quite straightforward: the more the better! Recently authors have started to act like sportstars and have been trying to leverage publishers against each other by changing publishers frequently. Bestbooks has resigned itself to this trend and would rather sign new, high profile writers than try to sign writers to several books (of course in the unlikely event that you could sign Paige to more, that is fine). As far as the advance is concerned, you don't understand why you should agree to both a signing bonus and an advance. To not give a signing bonus would be an insult, so you prefer to resist an advance. Finally, the strictly monetary issues (royalties, signing bonus) come straight from company profits and with the increased competitiveness in the publishing business you need to be as stingy as you can.

Your goal is to obtain the highest possible score. You will have 30 minutes to negotiate a contract and it is quite probable that the president of Bestbooks would quite unhappy if no contract results from the negotiations.

Confidential Success Table for the Bestbooks Representative

	Term in Contract	*Points*
Royalties	15%	1000
	13%	2000
	10%	3000
	7%	4000
	5%	5000
Contract Signing Bonus	$25,000	0
	20,000	1000
	15,000	2000
	10,000	3000
	5,000	4000
Number of print runs for the book	5	3500
	4	3000
	3	2500
	2	2000
	1	1500
Number of weeks that Paige has to promote the book	35	3000
	30	2500
	25	2000
	20	1500
	15	1000
Number of books	6	500
	5	400
	4	300
	3	200
	2	100
Advance	$ 0	5000
	5,000	4000
	10,000	3000
	15,000	2000
	20,000	1000
Number of countries where the book will be distributed	14	4000
	12	3500
	10	3000
	8	2500
	6	2000
Number of bookclubs that will adopt the book	5	7500
	4	6000
	3	4500
	2	3000
	1	1500

EXERCISE 11
ELMWOOD HOSPITAL DISPUTE

Objectives

The principal objective of this simulation is to demonstrate the dynamics of confrontation and negotiation between groups having different sources and types of power. A minority group in a community (the CCC) is fighting to change the building construction plans of a large, powerful university hospital, away from constructing a new research facility and toward enhancing the hospital's commitment to local community healthcare. It is also fighting to secure a more powerful, respected position in the decision-making process about affairs in that community. Thus, this confrontation raises issues at several levels:

- The substantive issues regarding the hospital's building plans (building the research facility while neglecting local community issues);

- The process by which the hospital did not involve the community in developing these plans;

- The "power" of the community to stop the hospital's planning process until the community feels its needs have been heard and met.

A second objective of this simulation is to explore the process of agenda building in negotiation. The issues in this simulation are much less clearly defined and specified than in other role plays in this volume. These differences offer students an opportunity to understand how to construct an effective agenda for a negotiation, to deal with groups who have different levels of organization, discipline and focus, and to explore the different motivations that the Board and CCC bring to this agenda building process.

Finally, a third objective is to introduce the role of mediation in dispute resolution. Because the differential power levels and diffuse issues often lead to polarized and stereotypic conflict escalation and a failure to communication, a third party may be necessary to bring the parties together, aid in developing the agenda, and equalize power for the purpose of effective communication and dialogue.

Group Size The group is broken into three teams: Members of the Hospital Board and Administration, CCC members, and Mediators. We recommend the following groups:

1. A "subgroup" of 3-4 Board members who have been quickly assembled to respond to the sit-in crisis, plus 1-2 senior Hospital Administrators. If you want to hand pick students for these roles, you might select those who appear to you to be the "budding bureaucrats" in the class, older class members, etc.

2. A CCC of at least 10 members. Do not designate anyone as "leader"; their experience in organizing themselves will be a critical learning event.

3. A group of 2-4 Mediators (Optional--see the Operating Procedure, below).

If the class is very large, appoint several students as your assistants, and brief them in advance as to the issues and dynamics. Then let them run a second parallel simulation during class time, or serve as observers who are permanently assigned to the CCC, etc. If possible, videotape some of the group dynamics and negotiations so that these may be shown and compared during debriefing.

Time Required: 120-180 minutes.

Special Materials: Copy and distribute role play materials.

Special Physical Requirements: Rooms in which the Board can meet, and for the Mediators to caucus. The CCC should be given the "worst" facility to caucus (e.g. a hallway, drafty stairwell, etc.) while the Board should be given "plush" conditions (Boardroom, comfortable seminar room, refreshments, etc.) Eventually, most or all of the CCC will join the Board meeting, so it may be desirable to have negotiations take place in the classroom, or to assign this room to the Board for its meeting.

Recommended Reading Assignments to Accompany this Exercise:

Reader: 5.2 (Tannen) 6.1 (Boulding), 6.4 (Brothers); 8.1(Rubin and Sander).
Text: Chapters 6, 8

For the mediators:

Reader: 13.1 (Colosi), 13.2 (Baruch Bush)
Text: Mediation section of Chapter 13.

What to Expect:

See the Objectives (above). The CCC usually organizes some form of protest or confrontation of the Hospital Board, which only serves to polarize the Board and minimize the likelihood that the effective negotiation of change will really occur.

The CCC, a large group, will likely be very poorly organized, and will attempt to bring many unfocused issues to the table; in contrast, the Hospital Board, a smaller, more focused and "businesslike" group, is likely to either "stonewall" the negotiation completely or offer token concessions and attempt to co-opt the CCC.

The skills of the Mediators greatly influences what kind of a role they take. If they are inexperienced, they often do not understand the importance of maintaining their neutrality and effectiveness, and hence either become co-opted by the Board or the CCC. If they are experienced, they are more aware of what they need to do to maintain neutrality and manage their role more proactively.

Advance Preparation

It is helpful to have students read the Background Information and role descriptions prior to class. Mediators should not only read their role, but be "coached" on mediation skills and tactics by the instructors during their preparation. (This can usually be done when the Board and CCC are preparing their strategy, or could be done as an advanced assignment before class). To help the Mediators, we recommend the Mediation Guide included with Exercise 15 in the student book and IM. Students who will be mediators may also consult Section 13 of the Readings book (see the beginning of the note for suggested readings).

Operating Procedure

1. You need to decide whether you are going to use mediators at all, and whether you are going to introduce them at the beginning of the simulation or only after the Board and CCC groups have had a chance to "struggle" with unassisted negotiation. Thus, the options are as follows:

    a) A negotiation solely between Board and CCC groups, in which they attempt to identify and resolve issues without the services of a mediator. This meeting is likely to occur in an atmosphere and process that is highly unsatisfactory and unproductive. End when some stalemate occurs and go directly to a debriefing;

    b) A negotiation between Board and CCC groups in which the Mediator is introduced from the beginning of the role play as parties who have been assigned to help the groups identify issues, communicate more effectively, and make some progress toward resolution;

    c) A negotiation between Board and CCC groups in which the Mediator is only introduced after the groups have made some effort to work on the issues themselves. This gives the groups a chance to flounder on their own a bit before introducing mediation, but it is also the more time consuming. In addition, the Board and CCC groups may sufficiently polarize during their initial contact so that mediators cannot unfreeze them and a mediated solution may be much more difficult to achieve. Once you have made this critical decision, assign roles and then permit the groups to plan strategy.

2. Groups should have at least 30-40 minutes to plan after reading their roles. Independent negotiations between Board and CCC, if permitted, should last at least 30 minutes. Facilitation by mediators may take another hour. Allow at least 30-60 minutes for debriefing and wrap-up. If time is a factor in this scenario, we suggest doing one or more of the following:

    a) Set time limits and stick to them. This may mean that an agreement is not reached. While this is always a disappointment, it can be less of a difficulty in this simulation. Many of the major objectives of this simulation occur <u>early</u> in the session, i.e. organizing, agenda building, assumptions about own and the other, expressions of power, constituency and bystander influences, and efforts by the mediator to gain credibility and acceptance. The conflict often cools off because the students become deadlocked, frustrated and "check out" until someone rescues them.

    b) Allow the Board and the CCC to hold their strategy session prior to class or at a previous class.

    c) Extend the negotiations over two class sessions. Participants sometimes find ways to create constituency or bystander pressures in the interim between classes.

    d) Do not permit the Board and CCC to meet directly. Involve the mediator from the outset and treat this as a mediation simulation.

3. Don't forget the observers. Effective observers should be pretrained in understanding negotiation processes, agenda building, power dynamics in negotiation, strategies of high power and low power groups, and effective mediation. Have the observers read appropriate articles from the Sections on Planning, Power and Third Parties of this Reader.

Concluding the Exercise

This simulation frequently evokes strong responses from participants. Some enjoy it greatly and have fun. Others find the complex issues and pressures difficult to handle and somewhat remote from negotiation. To draw these out and give some perspective, we have found it helpful to quickly go around the group and ask people to identify one thing that made the simulation pleasant or fun and one thing that made it frustrating or difficult.

Do not hesitate to emphasize the power dynamics that occur between the Board and the CCC. Board members often act aloof, condescending or patronizing toward the CCC, and become angry when the group's leadership cannot control the "rabble" or when it presents ambiguous and unclear demands. Similarly, the CCC often places a strong investment in being disruptive, hostile and unfriendly to Board members.

Finally, try to emphasize what tactics were used by mediators, and how effective these tactics were. Determine how the mediators decided on what they would do, and whether or not they were effective.

To help the instructor, we have attached copies of an overhead transparency that is frequently used in debriefing this exercise.

Instructor References:

Bolman, L., & Deal, T. (1979). "A Simple--but Powerful--Power Simulation" *Exchange: The Organizational Behavior Teaching Journal* 6, (3).

Oshry, B. (1995) *Seeing systems*. San Francisco: Berrett Koehler.

Susskind, L. (1996) *Dealing with an angry public*. New York: Free Press.

Susskind, L. and Cruikshank, J. (1987) *Breaking the impasse: Consensual approaches to resolving public disputes*. New York: Basic Books.

Zartman, I. W. (1997) The structuralist dilemma in negotiation. In Lewicki, R.J., Bies, R. J. and Sheppard, B. H. *Research on Negotiation in Organizations*, Vol. 6, pp. 227-246.

POWER STRATEGIES IN ELMWOOD HOSPITAL DISPUTE

Low Power Strategies:

- Threat of chaos
- Media exposure--"Hold you up to the public light of day" (public persons are accountable)
- "Moral outrage" arguments--we are moral, you are not
- Rhetoric, polemic
- Disruption/disorder, rabble rousing
- Threat of numbers or masses (sitting in)
- Unpredictability of action--"Rationality of irrationality"
- Disorganized--cannot make decisions, get together

High Power Strategies:

- Use titles, formality
- Control who is at the table
- Choice of spokesperson
- "Board room" setting
- Establish and maintain order--rules, regulations, procedure
- Long term control--"We'll be here forever"
- Control/manipulate the negotiation agenda and where the negotiations take place
- Have actual reward/punishment power
- Make it look like we are responsive and changing while stalling, debating, etc.
- Limited authority (need the rest of the board)
- Ultimate legitimate authority
- Depersonalize the low power group--don't deal with them as individuals get to know them, permit them to create an identity.

Mediators:

- Establish their credibility
- Cut through the frustrating, debilitating, well-intentioned rhetoric
- Create a scenario through participation with the low power group; don't do it by fiat!
- Be careful about getting co-opted!

HOSPITAL BOARD & ADMINISTRATION ROLE DESCRIPTIONS
EXERCISE 11: ELMWOOD HOSPITAL DISPUTE

The Director, his aides, and some members of the Board of Trustees are now meeting in a hospital lecture room to decide what to do next. From what the judge said, or, at least, the way you interpret it, he expects you to settle the dispute soon, in joint discussion with the CCC.

From the show of community support outside the hospital, it looks like the CCC could stay here forever. And while you can't make a showing that the occupation is injurious to patients, it has become hard to run the hospital while they're in there. Besides, such a spectacle is eroding your authority. You have got to settle things fast if you're going to have any authority and respect left.

You believe you simply cannot turn that site over to the uses the community wants. Your own uses are just too important. Besides, you've got specific grants and fund-raising drives lined up.

You have to figure out how to get the CCC out of there and buy some time. One possible strategy (if you can't pressure them out) might be to offer them two or three seats on the Board (demand number one), and talk them into dealing with all other issues at the Board level. With bimonthly meetings, difficulties in getting quorums, and so on, you could keep them talking for months--and settle the controversy in a rational, responsible way.

On the other demands, you just don't know where the money is going to come from. You could increase the efficiency of outpatient services if you could get community patients to keep their appointments, but you're not even sure how to do that.

As part of the strategy you develop for the negotiations, you should consider carefully the roles of the persons on your negotiating team and how they will be portrayed. Some suggested administration representatives include:

Hospital Administrator
Representative(s) of the Board of Trustees
Representative(s) of the Hospital's Medical Executive Committee
Someone from Outpatient Services
Hospital Attorney
Community Relations person

Some of the factors you should consider during your strategizing include:

1. The position of the administration on each of the issues.
2. An assessment of the sanctions available to the administration.
3. Possible restrictions on those sanctions.

4. An assessment of the CCC's power.
5. The possible impacts of internal relationships on the administration (i.e., doctors, nurses, trustees, and so on).
6. Some estimate of the maximum concessions the hospital might be willing to make.

At the outset, please designate one of your team to take notes of your deliberations, conclusions and assumptions for discussion and comparison purposes after the exercise is completed.

CONCERNED COMMUNITY COALITION ROLE DESCRIPTION
EXERCISE 11: ELMWOOD HOSPITAL DISPUTE

You almost wish that judge had issued his injunction because you're having trouble sustaining this demonstration. With people's jobs in jeopardy and no negotiations taking place, you're going to start losing people soon and you may be worse off than before. You've got to get some kind of visible victory--some change in behavior. You know you can't get everything at once, but you have to show the community that health care is going to be different--*now*. Maybe these facilities they announced are needed, maybe not- -but not at the expense of your people's needs. You also have to make sure that these needs are always heard and understood.

As a part of the strategy which you develop for the negotiations, you should consider carefully the roles of the people on your team and how they will portray them. The CCC team for the meeting might include:

The Coalition chairman.
The legal representative.
Representative of a leading community organization.
Member of hospital paraprofessional or housekeeping staff.
Representatives of other typical community interest groups.

Some of the factors which should be considered during your strategizing for the meeting include:

1. The goals and demands of the CCC.
2. The priority ordering the demands.
3. The relative power and sanctions presently possessed by the CCC, and the hospital's apparent perception of that power.
4. Possible allies and additional leverage which the CCC might tap.
5. Limitations on the coordination and use of available and potential resources.
6. Some estimate of the probable minimum package the CCC will accept.

At the outset of your strategizing session, please designate one member of your team to perform the additional task of recording your deliberations, assumptions, and conclusions for purposes of discussion and comparison after the exercise is completed.

MEDIATOR ROLE DESCRIPTION
EXERCISE 11: ELMWOOD HOSPITAL DISPUTE

As you can see from the "Background Information" regarding the development of this conflict, you have been appointed by the judge in an attempt to resolve the current impasse between the Hospital Board and Administration and the CCC. As a group, you will have to decide what actions you wish to take in order to carry out the judge's orders, and to facilitate some sort of resolution between the two sides.

The parties have asked for one final opportunity to meet together in a attempt to resolve their differences. If, however, they are unable to make substantial progress by the announced deadline, you have stated that you will enter the conflict and attempt to initiate actions that may help to facilitate resolution of the remaining issues.

In developing your strategy and tactics as mediators, you ought to consider a number of factors related to the effective functioning of third parties:

1. You probably will want to remain *disinterested* with respect to preference for particular solutions, but *interested* with respect to moving the parties toward *some* solution. That is, your major goal is to get the parties to a settlement *they* can live with, not necessarily some solution *you* prefer.

2. You will probably want to control the *process* of conflict and negotiation more than the *substance*. In general, you ought to try to "regulate" the conflict in order to prevent eruptions of unproductive arguments, name calling, demonstrations, or other incidents that are likely to perpetuate the current polarization. Some techniques for controlling the conflict might include:

    a) Separating the parties into different rooms, including perhaps at some point separating chief negotiators from their teams.

    b) Meeting with each side separately to try and clarify their true demands, and to identify (if possible) their true "resistance points," strength of commitment to various issues, areas where concession making is possible, etc.

    c) Carrying offers, communications or other messages between separated teams.

    d) Developing impressions among the mediation team as to (1) areas where teams could make easy concessions or trade concessions, (2) ways to "split up" issues that currently seem difficult to resolve, (3) identifying "settlement points" on issues where there currently seems to be no overlap in the bargaining range, and so forth. In most mediation, these impressions are not mandated on the parties, but are "suggested" or "introduced" to one or both sides as ways to help the parties make concessions they would not normally want to make.

e) Arranging public negotiations between the teams to discuss or review specific proposals, issues, and so on.

f) "Moderating" negotiations between the groups, to control communication and keep it from escalating into unproductive argument, and so forth.

3. You will probably want to work up some brief description of your qualifications to be mediators, so as to communicate prestige, authority, and impartiality to both sides.

4. You may want to think about ways to help negotiators on one or both sides "unhook themselves" from commitments or positions they have already taken publicly, and feel they cannot back down from without losing face.

5. You may want to think about how much you want to use:

a) "Persuasion" of one or both sides to change their positions.
b) "Coercion" (e.g., public pressure) to move people.
c) "Transmission" of information about one team to the other team in order to identify resistance points or settlement areas.
d) "Reconstitution" of the original bargaining relationship in public view.

In summary, the science (and art) of mediation involves systematic efforts at defusing unproductive hostility, separating or combining the parties to maximally facilitate productive exchange of offers and communications, and helping the parties envision settlement ranges and settlements that they can agree to without looking weak or losing face. All of this should be accomplished in such a way that the parties feel comfortable in working with you, believe you have their best interests at heart, and come to feel more generally satisfied that they have arrived at an agreement.

EXERCISE 12
THE POWER GAME

Objectives

1. To explore the dynamics of power at the individual interpersonal, group and system levels.

2. To create an opportunity for students to examine their personal beliefs about power strategies, and the impact of structural dimensions of power on individual and group behavior.

Group Size Any size group--minimally 12.

Time Required 80-90 minutes for running the exercise, and at least equal time for class discussion.

Special Materials Copies of the three briefing Sheets following these instructions.

Special Physical Requirements Three rooms, one for each group (see below) and perhaps additional space (a lounge or large classroom) for large group meetings.

Recommended Reading Assignments to Accompany This Exercise:

Readings: 6.1 (Boulding), 6.2 (Cohen and Bradford), 6.3 (Keys and Case)
Text: Chapter 6.

What to Expect:

This simulation models a three-tiered social system, with upper, middle and lower class groups. The upper class is given a large amount of resources and decision-making authority; the middle class is given some resources and authority, and the lower class is given no resources and little authority. Within a short period of time, each group begins to behave (in its attitudes and disposition toward the other groups) in ways stereotypic to its "position" in the social structure. The simulation provides a rich opportunity to examine the behavior of groups as a result of differentiating power and decision-making authority, as well as the reactions of individuals to their placement in this structure. "Personal power" and personal power strategies also become extremely important.

Advance Preparation

A thorough understanding of the rules and procedures of the simulation is necessary. The instructor should have identified the physical space to conduct the exercise, and have selected other instructors or graduate students to work as "observers" (help record events as they occur). Videotape in some rooms is also useful for later analysis. Finally, the instructor should carefully prepare the debriefing session, in order to generate as many different perceptions of events and their meaning as possible. Instructors may do well to consult similar exercises developed by Bolman and Deal (1979), Oshry (1976) and Peabody (1983) to gain a perspective on the issues that need to be observed and processed later.

Operating Procedure

1. Determine a sum of money to be contributed by each member. This amount is usually $1-2 for students, at least $5 for executives. The money should be collected before any further information is announced; if questioned, you should state that the money will be used for the class exercise, and the way it will be divided will be announced in a few minutes.

2. Determine groups. Three groups must be created: a Top group, a Middle group and a Bottom group. The Top is always small (2-4 members); the Middle group is moderate size (3-6 members), and the Bottom contains the remainder of the class (at least twice as large as the middle group). Several students should also be preselected as observers (we call them "anthropologists" because they are clearly there to observe and not intervene). If you think there are individuals whose behavior and demeanor makes them behave more like a top, middle or bottom, you can put these people into these groups, or you can intentionally put them into a DIFFERENT group.

3. Preassign members to groups. Assignment should be based on some predetermined arbitrary criterion that lends high "status" or "prestige" to the Top group, and low status/prestige to the Bottom group. In the past, the "Top" group has been chosen on the basis of emergent class leadership, perceived stature among fellow students, grade point average, all males, older students, or other indicators of "higher" status. Middles and Lows would be selected from the lower end of the same dimensions. Students may also be selected on the basis of their perceived comfortableness/uncomfortableness with holding power and using it, etc.

4. Determine "territories." Each of the three groups should get a room, or "turf." The Tops should get the best space, e.g. a lounge with plenty of comfortable chairs, a conference or boardroom table, doors that lock, refreshments, etc. The Middles should get a modest meeting space, e.g. seminar room or classroom, and the Bottoms should get the least desirable space, e.g. a corridor, drafty hallway, old classroom with non moveable furniture, etc. We

have even put bottoms in closets and corporate cubicles, a message they "get" quickly.

5. Divide the money by giving 2/3 of the total dollars collected to the Tops, 1/3 of the total dollars to the Middles, and none to the Bottom.

6. Give each group a set of instructions about the exercise and their movement. These instructions are provided in this manual immediately following this exercise. **They must be photocopied prior to class**. Note that these rules specify clearly:

    a) The responsibilities of each group
    b) The communication permitted between groups
    c) The ways that the Top group may change the rules at any time, with or without notice.

7. Assign each group to its turf. State that the simulation will last for <u>exactly one hour</u>, and that at the end of the hour, you will call "time" and the exercise will be over. Before dismissing the groups, introduce any observers whom you have appointed and give them the "legitimacy" to roam around and take notes. If a portable video unit is available, use it to pick up intergroup dynamics in hallways or team rooms—particularly among the Top and Bottom groups.

8. Do not interfere in the simulation in any way once it is occurring, i.e. answer questions about what people are "supposed to do", interpret what is going on, etc. Similarly, resist <u>all</u> impulses to tell people what they can or cannot do unless individuals are in danger of physical harm (e.g. physical confrontation) or valuable property is endangered (e.g. fire alarms, furniture, etc.). Suggest that people consider other, less violent/radical options for expressing their power or powerlessness.

What Happens?

1. The Top Groups usually focuses on several questions: a) what their responsibilities are with respect to helping others learn from the simulation, and how to accomplish this; b) whether they should keep the money, distribute it among the others, or make the other two groups "work" for it, c) whether to share power with the other groups, or hold on to it. These discussions are frequently at a leisurely pace and philosophical level, without awareness of the building level of discontent in the other two groups.

2. The Middle group is frequently torn between their desire to "be buddies" with the Top group, in efforts to conserve power and resources, or to ally with the Bottom group and seize power from the Top. The general drift is toward allying with the Top group, and being co-opted by them; alliance with the Bottom seldom occurs unless strong personal relationships exist across group lines, or their ideas and suggestions are actively rebuffed by the Top group.

3. The Bottom group is typically upset that they have had their money removed from them and "have no power." However, there is a great deal of confusion about how to respond to this situation. Many students choose to "sit out" and criticize the situation without being willing to take any action to change it. (Analogies can later be drawn by the instructor to this "typical" student behavior in social or university settings). Other students are energized to build alliances with the Middle group, to try to approach the Top group, or even to break the rules. The level of frustration rises as they are rebuffed or patronized by both Middle and Top groups. Our experience with business undergraduates and MBAs is that they are slow to get angry enough to take action, but willing to follow through when they get worked up.

4. There is generally a high level of involvement for almost all participants, except those in the Bottom group who choose to "drop out" and view any effort at power as either "worthless" or "inconsistent with their values". Instructors should be attuned to such behavior and be willing to help students confront it during the discussion period.

Alternatives and Variations

1. Some instructors suggest that the groups be required to meet for 15 minutes with only their group, before they can contact another group. Often the Middles and Bottoms, having very little structure, immediately rush to see the Tops and become incorporated into their activities before the Tops have had a chance to debate their role and assignment. As a result, the Tops invite them in and the exercise becomes more of a collaborative decision making task than a real power separation. If you want to enhance the likelihood that the Tops will try to control things, give them time to meet before contact can occur.

2. Similarly, some instructors try to invent rules to prohibit the Tops from abdicating their power early on. While we understand why this rule might be made, we think that the choice to abdicate is one the group ought to have, even if it changes the dynamics of the exercise.

Concluding the Exercise

Instructors will find that there are many things that occur during this one hour, and that a highly emotional group may take several hours to process all of the data generated. Time should be allocated for students to "ventilate" and begin discussion immediately after the exercise. The following procedure is suggested for handling all of the discussion issues:

1. Announce that the exercise is over at the end of one hour. All deliberations should be suspended. Students may be given a short break, or asked to return to a classroom or lounge for discussion.

2. Individually (in writing), or in small groups of 3-4 (still within their status group), students should discuss the following:

- a) What did I learn about power from this experience? Does it remind me of events I have seen in other organizations, or in society?

- b) What did I learn about my own power, and my own reactions to power or powerlessness? (How did I think about what power was?) Was I satisfied with the amount of my power? How did I try to exercise power, deny that I had power, or try to gain more?

3. Following this, discussions in the large class group may focus on the following issues:

    a) How were the three groups constructed? What was the impact on individuals of being in each group?

    b) How much trust/mistrust was there, and what were the in-group/out-group dynamics created by simply putting people in these groups?

    c) How did "structural justice" work in these groups? How did Tops react to power, Middles to the ambivalence of their setting, and Bottoms to powerlessness? Help participants recognize that these reactions are the result of the <u>structural</u> distinctions and groupings, and not the personalities of the people in those groups.

    d) Which groups and individuals were more influential or less influential? How was influence expressed in these groups (e.g. personal deals, negotiation strategies, coercive efforts, etc.).

    e) How do the power dynamics of this situation relate to organizations, universities, economic systems, race relations, etc.?

You may also summarize the discussion by using the overheads from Elmwood Hospital Dispute (Exercise 11) in the previous section.

Finally, it is recommended that the instructor make <u>no</u> assumptions about how the money will be handled. If the money is still in the hands of the Top and/or Middle groups—as it usually is—the instructor is to assume that it will remain there until told otherwise. Somewhere in the debriefing, practice points usually exert considerable pressure on these groups to redistribute the money, or pool it for a class-wide social event. The instructor should guide this discussion and examine it as a significant left-over component of the power game, but not attempt to force any solution on the Top/Middle group that they are not happy with.

For greater insights into discussion and evaluation of this simulation, and comparable power exercises, consult:

Bolman, L., & Deal, T. (1979). "A Simple--but Powerful--Power Simulation" *Exchange: The Organizational Behavior Teaching Journal 6(3)*.

Oshry, B. (1995) *Seeing Systems*. San Francisco: Berrett Koehler.

Zartman, I. W. (1997) The structuralist dilemma in negotiation. In Lewicki, R.J., Bies, R. J. and Sheppard, B. H. *Research on Negotiation in Organizations*, Vol 6, pp. 227-246.

DEBRIEFING THE POWER GAME

- What did you learn about power from this experience? Does it remind you of events you have seen in other organizations, or in society?

- What did you learn about your own power, and your own reactions to power or powerlessness?

- Were you satisfied with the amount of power you had? How did you try to exercise power, deny that you had power, or try to gain more?

TYPICAL POWER STRATEGIES AND REACTIONS

LOW POWER GROUPS:

Exposure	"Tell others" inside and outside the organization about others' inappropriate behavior.
Threat of chaos	"You keep this up and we will raise havoc here!"
Moral outrage	"We have justice on our side"
Confrontation	Sometimes disruptive, sometimes not.
Malingering	Doing the bare minimum, doing exactly what one is told and nothing more.
Giving Up	Psychologically "checking out", giving up, going through the motions.
Getting mad/ Getting even	Various forms of sabotage, revenge, underming, etc.

MIDDLE POWER GROUPS:

- Don't take risks in order to conserve what power you have.

- Don't take risks, in order to keep the favor of the High power group.

- "Mediate" between High and Low groups.

- Get co-opted, bought out by one or both groups.

- Insist that the High group "recognize" the Low group, become Low's "friend in court"

- Paralysis while waiting for one or both groups to act.

- Ambiguity and insecurity about one's position, role.

HIGH POWER GROUPS:

- Use titles, formality, social distance.

- Control who is at the table and the "agenda" of the group.

- May give power away to Middles or Lows if they feel guilty or awkward about exercising power.

- Establish and maintain rules of the game.

- Monopolize or control scarce resources.

- Pretend to challenge and be responsive, while covertly maintaining status-quo

- Stall, delay (use up time).

- Withhold information and control communication.

- Depersonalize and stereotype Low group ("they" aren't like "us").

BRIEFING SHEET FOR GROUP 1--TOP GROUP
EXERCISE 12: POWER GAME

You have been assigned to Group 1, the Top group for this exercise. Your task as a group is twofold:

1. You are responsible for the overall effectiveness of the simulation, and student learning from it. It is your responsibility to discuss, decide and carry out strategies to maximize these objectives. You may use any means you choose to achieve these goals.

2. Your group has been assigned the responsibility for 2/3 of the total dollars collected in this simulation. It is your decision as to how to use this money.

All groups have been informed about rules regarding communication between groups. Members of the Top group are free to enter the space of either of the other groups, and to communicate whatever they wish, whenever they wish. Members of the middle group may enter the space of the Bottom group whenever they wish, but must request permission from the Top group to enter the Top group's space - this permission can be denied by the Top group. Members of the Bottom group may not disturb the Top group in any way unless specifically invited by the Top group. The Bottom group does have permission to request communication from the Middle group by knocking on the door of the room housing the Middle group. The Middle Group may refuse permission. Members of the Top group are given authority to make any changes in the rules that they wish, with or without notice.

BRIEFING SHEET FOR GROUP 2 - MIDDLE GROUP
EXERCISE 12: POWER GAME

You have been assigned to Group 2, the Middle group in this exercise. Your task as a group is twofold:

1. You are responsible for assisting the Top group in maximizing the overall effectiveness of the simulation and student learning from it. It is your responsibility to provide any assistance to them or take any action yourselves that may achieve this end.

2. Your group has been assigned the responsibility for 1/3 of the total dollars collected in this simulation. It is your decision as to how to use this money.

All groups have been informed about rules regarding communication between groups. Members of the Top group are free to enter the space of either of the other groups, and to communicate whatever they wish, whenever they wish. Members of the Middle group may enter the space of the Bottom group whenever they wish, but must request permission from the Top group to enter the Top group's space - this permission can be denied by the Top group. Members of the Bottom group may not disturb the Top group in any way unless specifically invited by the Top group. The Bottom group does have permission to request communication from the Middle group by knocking on the door of the room housing the Middle group - the Middle group may refuse permission. Members of the Top group are given authority to make any changes in the rules that they wish, with or without notice.

BRIEFING. SHEET FOR GROUP 3 - BOTTOM GROUP
EXERCISE 12: POWER GAME

You have been assigned to Group 3, the Bottom group in this exercise. Your task as a group is twofold:

1. To help the Top and Middle groups maximize the overall effectiveness of the simulation, and student learning from it. It is your responsibility to provide any assistance to them, or take any action yourselves to accomplish this end.

2. To identify whatever resources you have for influencing the other two groups.

All groups have been informed about rules regarding communication between groups. Members of the Top group are free to enter the space of either of the other groups and to communicate whatever they wish, whenever they wish. Members of the Middle group may enter the space of the Bottom group whenever they wish, but must request permission from the Top group to enter the Top group space. This permission can be denied by the Top group. Members of the Bottom group may not disturb the Top group in any way unless specifically invited by the Top group. The Bottom group does have permission to request communication from the Middle group by locking on the door of the room housing the Middle group. The Middle group may refuse permission. Members of the Top group are given authority to make any changes in the rules that they wish, with or without notice.

EXERCISE 13
COALITION BARGAINING

Objectives

1. To explore the dynamics of trust between groups in a competitive situation.

2. To experience one's individual reactions to the stress of competition with unequal resources, and the outcomes of winning or losing.

3. To understand how trust, credibility, equity, and resource power are the critical elements for any coalition situation.

4. To understand how groups exert power and influence on other groups.

Group Size: Three teams of four to eight members, approximately the same number *of* members on each team.

Time Required 1 1/2 to 2 hours

Special Materials None. Having change (small bills and coins available) will help.

Special Physical Requirements Optimally, a room with movable chairs (in which to do negotiations) and several small separate rooms nearby for the caucus groups to meet.

Recommended Reading Assignments to Accompany this Exercise:

Readings: 3.3 (Dawson), 8.1 (Rubin and Sander), 8.2 (Sheppard), 9.2 (Vanover)
Text: Chapter 6, 9

What to Expect:

In this activity, three groups of individuals must work together to establish a contract. That contract will determine the amount of money (or points) they receive for the exercise. Since a contract can only be established between any pair of teams, the third team will be excluded--unless it is compensated in some way by the winning pair, or fooled by a false agreement. In addition, certain coalitions may leave money on the table; therefore, the participants are also actively forming a second coalition to insure that the game manager or referee does not get to keep some of the money.

The benefits of this exercise are that it engenders, in a relatively short period of time, strong feelings about and personal recognition of the issues of trust, credibility, equity, power, and the consequences of winning and losing. It also helps the participant to experience how coalitions get formed, and what it takes to maintain them or destroy them. Applications can be drawn from these experiences to the functioning of agreements within and between organizations: determining which individuals are better negotiators and have more credibility, determining what kinds of power can be used, and understanding how the use of some kinds of power can undermine agreements while trust and credibility are essential to the formation of any viable agreement.

There are also several liabilities to the exercise. First, individuals and groups often deceive each other in the process of deal-making; if this occurs, it engenders strong feelings which need to be vented. Even if ventilated effectively, these feelings may carry over into other classes. Second, the organizational "lessons" of this exercise may be very strong at the personal level, but not as strong in the students' ability to apply these to the functioning of real organizations. The instructor may have to help students make this bridge. It may therefore be effective to use this exercise in conjunction with readings and class materials on the creation and management of partnerships, joint ventures, strategic alliances, building interdepartmental and inter-unit cooperation, as well as the individual use of power and negotiation skills.

Advance Preparation

This is an exercise in which the "theory" of coalition formation can be a very useful addition. It is recommended that you assign readings, or prepare a lecture, to follow the discussion (see some suggestions at the end of this note); but if you prefer to assign reading materials before the experience, this will probably not affect the nature of the experience.

Do the following steps before you run this exercise:

1. Read the "rules" in the student manual carefully. You should understand these rules well. You will probably be asked about them by the students, who may also want to change or modify the rules (see the following section).

2. Copy the "ballot" at the back of this section of the IM (optional). You can use this ballot or simply ask students to submit a written ballot on a blank sheet of paper that is comparably worded.

3. If your class period is shorter than 75 minutes, you will need to divide the exercise into two classes. We recommend that the exercise be divided in the following way:

    a) Set up the exercise, read the instructions, and give students the task to prepare their group strategy. Then conduct the actual exercise and debriefing in the next class.

    b) Break the exercise BEFORE students actually come to agreement (e.g. if you have gone two rounds and they have not agreed, break it before agreement actually occurs). Tell the students NOT to discuss the exercise out of class (although if they do, they will probably have discussions that will lead to a quick coalition when class resumes).

c) We do NOT recommend breaking the exercise right after the coalition has been formed and before the Debriefing; this leads to a very stale discussion in the debriefing, because most of the emotion has gone out of it and will be ventilated outside of class.

Operating Procedure, Hints and Cautions

Decide whether you are going to use real money or points. This decision is critical to the outcome of the exercise, since the nature and source of the stakes will affect coalition behavior. We STRONGLY encourage you to use real money, even in small amounts, because students view the exercise much more seriously if you do. If the money comes from the students (instead of your supplying the funds, for example), the students will be more likely to form a coalition which does not let you keep some of the funds. (Thus, there are actually "two'" coalition experiments going on: one among the participants, and another between the participants and you.) Second, points are unlikely to create the same degree of involvement and commitment--although this is not always true.

Decide how you plan to "dispose" of the funds that may be remaining with the referee at the end of the activity. You will be asked about this, and you may want to reveal your decision or not reveal it, depending on the impact that you want to have on coalitions. This includes coalitions that capture less than 100 percent of the funds, or when no coalition is formed. You may want to return it to the students, spend it for a class party, keep it yourself, or conduct another round of the exercise.

You must decide the specific amounts that will be awarded to the winning coalitions. The "Stake" chart on page 519 of the Reader has been left blank because group size will vary, and therefore so will the total amount of the money contributed. The following formula may be used (the exact percentages are not relevant, and we suggest rounding to the nearest dollar):

* The AB coalition should receive 100% of the total resources.

* The AC coalition should receive 85-90% of the total resources, the rest to be kept by the referee.

* The BC coalition should receive 75-80% of the total resources.

Remember to announce the exact dollar amounts for each coalition prior to starting the negotiations!

You may want to divide the entire class into teams, or you may wish to run this as a "fishbowl." If you have an assistant or TA, you can break the class into groups of 15-30 and run multiple iterations. You can also ask some students to do the exercise and make the rest of the class observers (for example, when you do it for money, some don't want to contribute, so that decision automatically creates a group of observers). (Composing teams with the same number of members on each makes dividing up the money significantly simpler!) If you do this, brief the observers about what to look for and then pair several observers up with each team, so they can follow them to the caucus, to negotiations, back to caucus, etc.

Participants in this exercise often create "side bets" as protection. These bets usually take one of two forms: payments to the third team (the one left out of the coalition) to insure that this team will not sabotage the coalition, or as an "insurance" side bet between the two teams which are in the coalition to make sure one does not defect in the final balloting. For example, Alpha and Beta, planning to coalesce, may also make a $10.00 "side bet" which will go to one team if the other defaults during the balloting. As the game administrator, you may be asked to hold the money and enforce that side bet. Some instructors refuse to do this (because they don't want to be involved as an enforcer in someone else's side bet), while others charge a fee (e.g. 20%) of the side bet to act as the enforcer. This is up to you, but we recommend that you either not do it at all or not help the teams enforce their own agreement cost-free. Initiating cooperation is often costly--why protect teams from each other risk-free?

Generally, talking between teams is not permitted in this exercise except in negotiations. While you may be asked about this, it is difficult to monitor groups unless you have additional referees to help. Allowing additional conversations increases the probability that "side-bets" or other arrangements will be created informally.

Alternatives and Variations

1. A variation of this activity, particularly with larger populations, is to eliminate the groups and conduct the exercise in trios. Thus, A, B and C "groups" only have one individual, and individuals negotiate for themselves rather than for groups. This engenders high involvement, can be done in more limited physical space (e.g., assign trios to areas of a classroom, having them conduct negotiations by whispering or moving to another part of the room), and also allows you to compare and contrast a number of *different* settlements of the same coalition problem. It is more difficult to orchestrate, however, particularly when you are using real money, and a lot of the interpersonal negotiating dynamics will not come out in the debriefing.

2. If you are short of time, you may want to set up teams in the preceding class period; have participants read the rules, meet with their team to develop a strategy, and come to the class period prepared to begin negotiations.

3. It is suggested that eight be the maximum number on a team, particularly since time is limited. If you have more that 24 students in the class, it is suggested that you train additional referees, and have them conduct a replication of the exercise in another room.

4. You may change some of the structural aspects of the rules, particularly the total amount of resources, the percentage distribution of resources, the percentage

distribution of resources for each coalition, and the order of discussions. This will tend to increase/decrease the likelihood of certain coalitions forming. Similarly, increasing the number of teams to four, and permitting coalition teams of pairs or triads to gain certain percentages of the resources, will make the problem considerably more complex.

5. Finally, you can tell participants that there will be more than one "round" of coalition formation, each with different distributions of resources. Otherwise, participants in this game may act exploitatively, knowing that only one coalition will ultimately be formed and that they will not have to work with others in the future. Thus, once the exercise is finished, you can do it again in the next class period, using the same teams but, perhaps, changing their team name (A, B or C). Increasing the longevity of the relationship makes people "think twice" about exploitative behavior, and creates significant learnings for those people who destroy their trustworthiness and credibility in the first round.

Concluding the Exercise

Discussion Questions

1. What was the initial strategy developed by your team?

2. How was your team strategy influenced by the "resources" (dollars, points or percentage allocation of payoffs) that your team contributed to a coalition?

3. How was your team strategy influenced by the location of your team in the order of negotiations (e.g. first, second or third)?

4. How did the prior "reputation" of people on your team, or the other team, affect your strategy?

5. How were decisions made in your team about your strategy? About changing your strategy? Were you happy with the way decisions were made?

6. How did you pick your President and negotiators? On what criteria?

7. How did your strategy change after you had a chance to talk to the other teams?

8. In retrospect, did you make the right decision about President and negotiators? Why or why not? Did you ever change negotiators?

9. What did the negotiators do that encouraged or hurt the development of trust between teams?

10. Were there any side-bets, or side-contracts developed between teams? If so, what were they? Were they honored or violated?

11. Did you wish that you could (or did you) talk to other teams at times <u>other than</u> the formal negotiating period? If so, what kinds of things would be (were) discussed?

12. Were you satisfied with the ultimate settlement? Why or why not?

13. What were the most important factors that influenced the ultimate settlement between teams? Do you think you could have influenced this earlier? Why?

Concluding Points:

The following kinds of concerns are very important to people in forming, and maintaining a coalition:

The *trust and reliability* of the *negotiator* and the *teams*. People may want to act credible and trustworthy, or they may be willing to exploit others' good faith in order to get the best short-run deal for their own team. Each kind of behavior usually has consequences for future relations between teams: trust usually breeds further trust, whereas exploitation breeds mistrust, suspicion and strong desires to gain revenge.

The best contract between teams. What kinds of calculations were performed to discover the best possible agreement between teams? Most people will negotiate a coalition that insures that the largest amount of money is won by the coalition (e.g., BC), and that the amount is shared in some fair way between teams. They will probably also want to make sure that the referee does not retain any funds, unless they approve of his use of the money. However, when teams want to make sure that they are part of the winning coalition, these "optimal" goals may be sacrificed for short-run gain.

Concerns for equity or fairness. This may take several forms in a coalition situation. First, certain teams may feel that because they contribute more to a coalition than the other team, they deserve more of a return. For example, a winning coalition, with Team C as a member, receives one of the two largest payoffs. A winning coalition, with Team A as a member, earns one of the two smaller payoffs. Since Team C is a more "desirable" partner for Team A or B to have, Team C may demand a larger share of the payoff. (It is not unknown for such contracts to backfire. Team C may decide to hold out for a large share of the payoff; A and B, angered by this move, will coalesce and win the smallest amount. Team C, if motivated by greed, can lose altogether if it is not careful.)

A second source of concern for equity and fairness may be that all teams feel they must derive some part of the payoff--otherwise the excluded team will work to destroy the coalition between the two other teams. For example, teams A and B know that if they coalesce, some resources will be left to the referee. Since they don't want to do this, B and C may decide to coalesce and share some of the winnings with A. Thus, a concern for fairness may also make the referee a "common enemy," insuring that he does not win because of the inability of the teams to get together. However, the side-contract with A must be carried out.

Coalitions are an active part of most organizational life, particularly when decisions are made by a democratic-voting method rather than through an autocratic chain of command. In these organizations--political, community, volunteer, etc.--coalitions are formed to gain support for an issue, carry a vote, or perhaps block a vote or change from occurring. People in these coalitions will be concerned about how much they can trust the parties they have coalesced with, how much they are putting into the coalition and what they are getting out of it, and the impact of the current situation on their willingness to coalesce with these same people in the future.

Recommended Readings

Berquist, W. , Betwee, J. and Meuel, D. *Building Strategic Relationships*. San Francisco: Jossey Bass, 1995.

Bleeke, J. and Ernst, D. *Collaborating to Compete: Using Strategic Alliances and Acquisitions in the Global Marketplace*. New York, John Wiley, 1993

Faris, P. C. *Building Customer Partnerships*. Amherst, MA: HRD Press, 1995.

Limerick, D. and Cunnington, B. *Managing the New Organization*. San Francisco: Jossey Bass, 1993.

Mintzberg, H. *Power in and around organizations*. Englewood Cliffs, NJ: Prentice Hall, 1983.

Murnighan, K. (1991) *The dynamics of bargaining games*. Englewood Cliffs, NJ: Prentice Hall.

Pfeffer, J. *Managing with Power*. Boston, MA: Harvard University Press, 1992.

Watkins, M. and Rosegrant, S. (1996) Sources of power in coalition bargaining. *Negotiation Journal*, January, 47-68.

COALITION BALLOT

Your Team (Circle One):   A   B   C

Team _____ has established a valid a coalition with Team
(your team)

_____. As a result of this coalition, Team _____ should

receive $_____ and Team _____ should receive

$_____.

Signed: _____.

DISCUSSION QUESTIONS

1. What was the initial strategy developed by your team?

2. How was your team strategy influenced by the "resources" (dollars, points or percentage allocation of payoffs) that your team contributed to a coalition?

3. How was your team strategy influenced by the location of your team in the order of negotiations (e.g. first, second or third)?

4. How did the prior "reputation" of people on your team, or the other team, affect your strategy?

5. How were decisions made in your team about your strategy? About changing your strategy? Were you happy with the way decisions were made?

6. How did you pick your President and negotiators? On what criteria?

7. How did your strategy change after you had a chance to talk to the other teams?

8. In retrospect, did you make the right decision about President and negotiators? Why or why not? Did you ever change negotiators?

9. What did the negotiators do that encouraged or hurt the development of trust between teams?

10. Were there any side-bets, or side-contracts developed between teams? If so, what were they? Were they honored or violated?

11. Did you wish that you could (or did you) talk to other teams at times *other than* the formal negotiating period? If so, what kinds of things would be (were) discussed?

12. Were you satisfied with the ultimate settlement? Why or why not?

13. What were the most important factors that influenced the ultimate settlement between teams? Do you think you could have influenced this earlier? Why?

COALITION BARGAINING
CONCLUDING POINTS

1. Definition of a "best contract"

2. What are sources of power in this situation?

3. What role does trust play? Who was trustworthy or not trustworthy?

4. What role does "fairness" play? How do we decide what is a fair settlement?

5. What are the lessons from this exercise for building and maintaining effective strategic relationships between individuals, groups and organizations?

EXERCISE 14
JORDAN ELECTRONICS COMPANY

Objectives

This exercise simulates a negotiation problem within the context of a group decision making situation. Each of the people attending the meeting represents some group or department within Jordan Electronics, and has a set of preferences and priorities for his or her preferred outcome. As a result, there are likely to be multiple conflicts in the meeting about what objectives are to be attained, and how they are to be pursued. For these reasons, therefore, what initially appears to be a rather simple meeting in fact becomes a complex multi-level negotiation. First, parties have "hidden agendas" that they may openly or covertly try to promote. Second, it is often not clear whether a given negotiator is promoting his or her own individual "hidden agenda," promoting the needs and objectives of the department that he or she represents at the meeting, or working, for the "overall best interest of Jordan Electronics." As a result, there can be a number of different solutions to this problem, usually resulting from the negotiating strategies used by particular role players and the effectiveness with which the Chairperson conducts the meeting.

The objective in this exercise is less to reach a solution than it is to explore the difficulty of negotiation in group decision making situations. The objectives we work toward in this case are:

1. to have participants analyze and understand the complex structure of this problem, and the diversity of individual motives;

2. to have participants recognize the nature of "hidden agendas" and the negative impact they can have on integrative group decision making;

3. to help participants understand that successful settlement of this kind of problem requires both creative problem solving and skilled committee or task force management.

Part of the chairperson's job is to build an agenda that incorporates all of the "valid" concerns of parties while weeding out the trivial and personal concerns. Thus, for example, the Senior Engineer's personal feelings about the situation, or the short-term inconveniences created for manufacturing, are less important than the major questions of price and production which must be considered.

Group Size The group is divided into teams of five. Each member of the team is assigned one of the roles in the case. We often try to assign the "Chairperson" role to the most skilled member of each subgroup. Any size group can be handled, limited by space for them to meet and the time to get reports during debriefing.

If there are extra group members after teams have been assigned they can be used as observers. It is usually not desirable to reduce the size of the teams, since that reduces the complexity of the problem. If one role needs to be dropped then it could be the chairperson's (allowing a "leaderless" discussion to occur) or the VP-Sales (we sometimes hand the private role information of this missing person to the chairperson and tell him or her that this person, e.g. the VP-Sales, will miss the meeting but has sent them the attached "memo").

Time Required 90-120 minutes

Special Materials Copy and distribute role information from this manual

Special Physical Requirements Sufficient space for group to meet as a whole, and also to permit teams to meet.

Recommended Reading Assignments to Accompany This Exercise:

Readings: 2.1 (Kuhn), 2.2 (Scott), 2.3 (Tannen) 10.2 (Fisher and Davis), 9.3 (Zack), 8.2 (Sheppard)
Text: Chapters 2, 8, 9

Advance Preparation

Participants should have read the case and their roles prior to coming to class. If role are distributed in class, allow an extra 20-30 minutes preparation time.

Operating Procedure

Follow the sequence laid out for the participants. Make sure to warn people to follow their role closely in the exercise. Participants should have read the case and their role prior to coming to class. Because of the complexity of the case, we often find it helpful to compose "role clarification groups" for 10-15 minutes before the role play begins. All people with the role VP-Production, etc., would get together and discuss their information to clarify what their character wants, etc. The purpose of this group is not to achieve uniformity in the way people play the role, but to understand the role and perspective from which this character views the problem. The instructor can move from group to group, asking for questions and clarifying points. Then disband the groups and ask them to regroup as Jordan management teams.

Concluding the Exercise

Frequently teams do not reach agreement during this simulation. Step three, therefore, is **very important** since it permits participants to examine what was going on and what actions needed to be taken to reach a settlement. When the discussion on Step 2 is ended, urge participants to probe deeply and frankly in discussing their "bottom line" in Step 3. It is helpful to note on a chalkboard or flip chart the things groups report at this point.

Top management groups in organizations are often viewed from the outside as unified, monolithic entities who act as though they were of a single mind. In fact, these groups are more accurately viewed as coalitions of individuals who often disagree on goals, strategy and company policy, and who often act very much as characters in this role play did.

Members of a coalition have multiple loyalties--their own needs, the needs of the group or department that they represent, and the needs of the overall coalition (organization). It is not uncommon for these loyalties to get confused, muddled, or substituted for one another in group decision making.

While every individual and group in an organization would like to have his or her objectives maximized and concerns protected, most people will find that their objectives are not optimally pursued and their concerns are not fully protected.

In these environments, decisions are not always made according to the laws of what is most rational, or what is best for all. Instead, decisions are often made depending on who has the most power or "clout," or who can argue best for his/her point of view.

Organizations do achieve settlements to problems like this, but by their very nature, these solutions are often compromises and tradeoffs. They are not "neat" and clean, and there will always be costs, risks and "losers" along with the benefits, advantages and successes.

ROLE FOR VICE PRESIDENT-FINANCE
EXERCISE 14: JORDAN ELECTRONICS

The President spoke with you shortly before leaving for surgery. As usual, the President did not want to get involved in working out this problem, but wanted results and quickly. "I want the new model of the JAC 36, and I want it soon. The more up-to-date it is, the better. Above all, I want it to sell." Other than that, you were given no instructions about what was wanted or how you were to proceed. You were asked to chair the meeting, and to get the group to come to a consensus on these decisions: (1) Should the new model of the JAC be manufactured? (2) If it is to be manufactured, at what price should it be sold? and, (3) If the new model is not to be manufactured, what should be done next?

In thinking about the meeting, you are not sure how to proceed. You believe the best thing would be for each person at the meeting to report briefly on his or her position on the new model and the group's proposals for decisions (1) and (2). Decision (3) should only be considered if there is a negative conclusion to (1). After hearing the report, you should try to see if there is an obvious and easy solution. Otherwise you will help the group search for compromises and trade-offs.

Although you are not sure what direction Jordan should take, you do know that it is imperative that something be done to reverse the continuing trend of decreasing annual revenues. Jordan is still a market leader, but you wonder how long it can maintain its position while the competition's financial statements are looking stronger and stronger every year.

As well, you are beginning to receive complaints from shareholders who are arguing that the yearly dividend is insufficient. One reason dividends are kept low is due to the ploughing back of profits into the company to support its rather ambitious R & D program. Your greatest fear, however, is that any program to manufacture a new JAC 36 will require additional financing. Any new assets would have to be financed through debt, and you are sure that your already nervous bankers would complain about how Jordan is becoming over leveraged. Interest charges are actively eating into Jordan's profits, and you sometimes worry about the company's liquidity position over the long term. Yet, something must be done in order to rectify the somewhat stagnant position of Jordan. Hopefully, any decision taken will be one which will produce the lowest financial burden possible.

Given the President's instructions, you feel personally responsible for having the committee reach a consensus before the meeting breaks up. The worst thing that could happen is for the President to return and find the issue still unsettled; you would probably be held responsible for that.

ROLE FOR VICE PRESIDENT-MANUFACTURING
EXERCISE 14: JORDAN ELECTRONICS

The President spoke to you before leaving for surgery. As usual, the President did not want to get himself too involved in solving this problem, but wanted results, and quickly. "I want the new Jac 36 soon, and the more up-to-date it is, the better. Above all, I want it sell." You agreed to do everything you could to get the JAC 36 costs into line and to begin production as soon as possible.

You have been Vice President - Manufacturing for a little over a year, having previously been superintendent of the major Jordan manufacturing plant. You are annoyed with the President's decision to go ahead with a redesign of the JAC 36. Adding the voice-activated command feature is turning out to be trickier than it first seemed, and adding the optical coupling is going to require considerable reworking of several production positions, adding some extra tests, and retraining several workers. Production costs are always hard to estimate when a lot of new features have to be handled.

About a month ago, you had your first performance review with the President since becoming VP - Manufacturing. One big negative factor in your review was cost overruns in manufacturing; if you don't bring these into line you could lose your job. With the cost of labor and materials skyrocketing these days, you might as well use a dartboard to make estimates. In estimating costs on the JAC 36, you have decided it is better to be safe than sorry; hence you have padded your estimates by 5-10 percent margins of error. This way, if you keep costs down you will really look good; on the other hand, if the likely (but unforeseeable) problems occur, you will be covered. At least the President has decided not to go for the portable unit using the new advanced microprocessor; that would have made costs really difficult to estimate.

The Senior Electrical Engineer is probably going to be the biggest problem in the upcoming meeting. This person has a frustrating way of thinking, will continually push you to defend your costs, and is generally aggressive in criticizing your operation. Your last cost estimate would set the selling price at $20,000. If really pressured, you probably could reduce the cost estimate but at the expense of reducing your own cushion in the budget. You would be willing to do this only as a last resort. The higher the selling price you get the group to agree to, the more security you have against unanticipated cost overruns.

ROLE FOR VICE PRESIDENT-SALES
EXERCISE 14: JORDAN ELECTRONICS

The President spoke to you before leaving for surgery. As usual the President did not want to get too involved with solving the problem, yet wanted results - and quickly. "I want the new model of the JAC 36 as much as you do, and the more up-to-date, the better. Above all, I want it to sell." You were encouraged to get a strong and realistic sense of the market and to present that information at the New Products Committee meeting. You agreed to do everything you could to get the thing into production and to hold costs down.

You like your job at Jordan Electronics. It has been a comfortable job because in the past R&D has given you what you have wanted in the way of products and modifications. Being responsive to the market has proved successful for Jordan in the past and made your job easier because you always had what the customer wants. It is most important that you encourage the others to maintain this strategy in the future.

The market is beginning to change, however, and it is not as predictable as it was. The latest market research studies bring that out. The recent marketing studies do not match your "gut feeling" about the future of the JAC 36. First, you were surprised at the data suggesting a strong market for the old JAC 36. Your own sales figures show that while Jordan's sales have remained level for the past 18 months the total size of the market has increased dramatically, so that Jordan actually has a smaller market share. A new design is clearly necessary. Second, all the potential customers who your staff surveyed indicated that they want the easier operation of the voice-activated command features and the advantages of the optical coupling, concerns not detected by the "official" market research. Finally, you also think that the indifference of the market toward a portable JAC 36 is incorrect, since most of your salespeople come back each week with request after request for a portable model.

You have learned to trust your own instincts and believe what you hear from your salesforce more than what market research tells you. You have the following priorities for the meeting:

1. Time is critical. The sales force had been clamouring for a new JAC 36 for some time. They find that customers are beginning to ridicule Jordan for not keeping up with the competition, and this is beginning to effect the morale of the staff.

2. You think Jordan needs to produce both a bench-mounted and a portable JAC 36. The portable design is clearly the wave of the future. If you had a nonportable unit, you could probably hold off most of the market for a while until a portable one could be developed. You don't want R & D to know that, however --- they are always screaming for more time, and the more they have the more they take.

3. Price is an issue. The VP-Manufacturing's estimate for the nonportable unit was $20,000. You know that is too high. It could probably sell for $18,000; the portable unit could probably sell for $1,500 more, or $19,500.

ROLE FOR SENIOR ELECTRICAL ENGINEER
EXERCISE 14: JORDAN ELECTRONICS

The President spoke to you before leaving for the hospital. As usual, the President did not want to get too involved in solving the present problem, yet wanted results and quickly. "I want the new model of the JAC 36, and I want it soon. Above all, I want it to sell." You agreed to do everything you could to get the new model of the JAC 36 into production at a reasonable price.

You have worked for Jordan Electronics for almost 25 years. In the years that you have worked together, the President has always shown confidence in your problem-solving ability. It does anger you that some people who joined the company after you now have better jobs. When the company was small, you (along with everyone else) did a fair amount of selling, and for a long time, you were effectively in charge of production.

You finally worked out all the bugs in the redesign of the JAC 36. It took a while to add features and yet not add to the size or cost of the unit. Of course, they are really going to have to be on their toes in purchasing and in the factory if the costs are going to come on target. Thank goodness they decided not to go ahead with the portable unit! Some people seem to think that the only problem with a portable unit is the adaptation of the advanced microprocessor; but there is a great deal involved in making the cabinet shockproof, ensuring that the unit is dust and moisture tight, and in other refinements not obvious to the nonprofessional engineer. Actually, you would feel better if you had more training in the design and manufacture of the new advanced microprocessor. Sooner or later, the President is going to want a portable unit. Now that you will have a little breather from the JAC redesign, perhaps you can get the company to send you to an engineering seminar this summer to learn more about this new microprocessor.

You know that the new design has really added very little to the cost of the JAC 36. Working with the VP-Manufacturing over the last several months, you also know that manufacturing is a pretty sloppy operation. You are pretty sure that if there are going to be cost problems, they will be in this area. If you dug into them, you probably could cut $500 off these costs in a day or so. Moreover, if you had the time (probably two to three months), you bet you could further redesign the gadget and knock an additional $300 - $400 off the cost of the product by eliminating some frills and by selecting lower-cost materials.

Most of all, you are loyal to the President and want to do as much as possible for the good of the company.

ROLE FOR DIRECTOR - RESEARCH AND DEVELOPMENT
EXERCISE 14: JORDAN ELECTRONICS

The President spoke to you before leaving for the hospital. As usual the President did not want to get too involved with solving the problem, yet wanted results - and quickly. "I want the JAC 36 as soon as possible. The more up-to-date it is, the better. Above all, I want it to sell." You have agreed to do everything you could to get the new model into production and at a reasonable price.

You pride yourself on running a tight R & D operation, one that continues to work at the frontier of scientific knowledge and one that makes continuous contributions to Jordan's products. You are annoyed with the President's decision to go ahead with a simple redesign of the old JAC 36. You believe the real future of the industry lies with the portability of such units. Redesigning the old machine is a waste of your department's time and energy. Moreover, the VP-Sales continues to be a pain. Sales are the people that pushed the President to adopt the simple redesign and said that the portable model was of secondary importance. Now sales says that the portable JAC 36 is what they need to make a really big splash. You can understand that the sales picture changes, but you do wish they would make up their minds about what they really need.

Fortunately, your department's reputation for quality and innovation is still on a solid base. On the way into your office today you stopped in to see your electronic designer, and were told that the team has solved two of the major technical snags that have stymied the development of the portable JAC 36. There is a good chance that all the bugs will be worked out in four to five weeks. With some cooperation from the Senior Electrical Engineer, a portable design should be feasible in the very near future.

Consequently, you are very reluctant to devote any more of your department's time to redesigning the old JAC 36 by adding a few frivolous features. Although the voice-activated command entry device might be a novel addition, you cannot foresee the scientific community becoming too excited by this feature. As well, optical coupling is usually only required for microprocessors used in super computers that generate fantastic amounts of heat. The old JAC 36 generates the same amount of heat as an ordinary television set. Your people are very interested in the new microprocessor developed by the Japanese and are anxious to begin development of a new portable unit. As a result, you have decided to do the following things at the meeting:

1. Tell the VP-Sales and the others that you are close to a breakthrough in the design of the portable JAC 36.

2. Persuade the stubborn Senior Electrical Engineer that the portable model is the best alternative and that more extensive work should begin on this immediately.

3. Dissuade the others from continuing with the addition of those frivolous features so that your department's time and energy can be focused on the development of a really new product.

EXERCISE 15
THIRD PARTY CONFLICT RESOLUTION

Objectives

There are three objectives to this exercise:

1. To understand the criteria that third parties use when they intervene into a dispute and help others resolve it.

2. To illustrate how different criteria can lead to different assumptions about strategies that the third party needs to pursue to resolve the dispute.

3. To practice mediation as a third party resolution strategy.

Group Size

Part I, the case discussion, can be done as a large class. You might assign students to "buzz groups" of 3-5 members for 15 minutes, to discuss the case among themselves, before bringing the class together.

Part II, the role-play, should be done in groups of 3 or 4. Groups of 3 will have each participant play one of the two disputants (Brenda Bennett and Harold Stokes) and the third party (Sam Pinder). In groups of 4, assign the fourth member to be an observer and report back during the debriefing.

Time Required

Part I:

- Case Reading: 5 minutes to read the case. You may assign the case as homework if desired.
- Case Discussion: 15-20 minutes in buzz groups, 20-30 minutes in class discussion.
- Presentation of Third Party Framework: 15-20 minutes

Parts II and III:

- Reading: 15-20 minutes to read the Mediation Guide (may be assigned as homework)
- Review: 15-20 minutes to walk through Mediation Guide steps and discuss with class.
- Prepare Roles: 10-15 minutes to read roles, prepare to play roles or to be mediator. Observers may be trained in this time frame.
- Mediation: 35-45 minutes.
- Debriefing: 30-60 minutes

Special Materials Copy and distribute role play information from this manual.

Special Physical Requirements: None, if you are only doing Part I. If you are doing Parts II and III, you will need breakout spaces for the 3-4 person groups to execute the mediation role play.

Recommended Reading Assignments to Accompany This Exercise

This exercise matches up well with text Chapters 5 and/or 13. It is primarily compatible with articles 5.2 (Tannen), 5.3 (Tramel & Reynolds), and/or any of the articles in Section 13 (Colosi, Elangovan, or Bush). It may also be used with articles 5.1 (Neale & Bazerman), 10.2 (Fisher & Davis), and/or 10.3 (Greenhalgh & Gilkey).

What to Expect

There are two parts to this exercise. During the case discussion in Part I, the instructor can help students surface the assumptions that they make about conflict and their primary objectives when they intervene into someone else's dispute. These assumptions and objectives shape the strategies used by third parties. As the instructor leads the case discussion, these assumptions and objectives will emerge and can be crystallized by the subsequent short lecture. In Part II, students can practice mediation as a technique for helping others resolve their disputes effectively.

As with most exercises involving conflict and conflict resolution, class participation and discussion is lively and involving.

Advanced Preparation:

It is helpful to have students read the Seatcor case in advance, and to read/prepare their individual roles. Students playing mediators should have time to review Part II (the Mediation Steps) in detail, and prepare for their job.

Operating Procedures:

Part I:

Case Overview:

The Seatcor Case was generated from interviews with actual managers about problems they faced in managing conflict. The focus of the case is a manager (a Senior Vice President) who has a problem handling his subordinate (Joe) and his subordinate's subordinate (Charles). The SVP must decide how to enlist Joe's support to involve Charles in the five-year plan. There are a number of factors that make direct action on this problem difficult for the SVP:

1. Since Charles was hired largely at the SVP's recommendation, the SVP must recognize that Joe may be resisting the SVP's intervention in the situation.

2. Not only did the SVP push to hire Charles, but also Charles and the SVP have been meeting for lunch without Joe. This violation of the "chain of command" may also threaten Joe, assuming he knows about the meetings.

3. The SVP has some reservations about Joe's management ability and style, but probably has not talked directly to Joe about these. The SVP may or may not want to confront these problems directly.

As a result, the SVP must decide whether he/she wants to talk to Joe or Charles directly, and, if so, what he wants to say to them. The SVP must also decide whether he wants to try to resolve the dispute by telling the parties directly how to resolve their problem, or by trying to bring Joe and Charles together to problem solve about their relationship and the evolution of the five-year plan.

As the instructor will realize, there is no single "answer" or solution to this case. Instead, the objective of the case is to generate various action plans that will allow the instructor to discuss the different assumptions made by students in the SVP role. It is suggested that the instructor follow this format:

1. After the class has read the case, the instructor should ask students to put themselves in the role of the Senior Vice President of Operations and to contribute their views on what they would do about the problem (Joe not involving Charles in the five-year plan). Require students to be specific about exactly what they would say or do to Joe or Charles (or others). Each "action plan" may be listed on the blackboard or on separate sheets of paper. Do not critique the ideas yet or allow students to critique them--at this point, you are most interested in "brainstorming" as many options as possible. Try to get at least five to six different approaches out.

2. During the generation of action plans, the instructor may decide to ask students to role play dialogues between the SVP and either Joe or Charles. This works best when you think the students are trying to use a strategy that will fall apart in implementation. For example, if the students feel that the SVP should order Joe to involve Charles, ask the students to play the SVP and you (the instructor) play Joe. Be resistant and recalcitrant and point out to the SVP that you are only doing it because you have to; you never liked or wanted Charles in the first place. Role playing is useful as a vehicle to:

    a) Engage the students in the "live dynamics" of the case;

    b) Force students to deal with the behaviors and feelings of actors in the case;

    c) Generate data on "what if" scenarios that permit richer discussion of various complex action plans.

3. Go back to each action plan generated. Press the person who suggested it to tell you:

    a) The objective of their strategy--i.e., what are they trying to do by taking this approach? (See the four criteria of efficiency, effectiveness, satisfaction, and fairness listed in "Concluding the Exercise.")

- b) How much they are trying to directly influence exactly what Joe or Charles should do to resolve their dispute.

- c) How much they are trying to directly influence how Joe and Charles interact to resolve their own dispute.

4. Near each strategy listed on the blackboard, or on a chart separate from the strategies, identify each strategy by indicating:

    a) Objectives (see "Options", below).

    b) Amount of third party control over outcome (high or low).

    c) Amount of third party control over the process by which the parties resolve the conflict (high or low).

5. Have the class evaluate each strategy in terms of how realistic, practical, and effective it seems to be. Encourage debate and discussion. You may take a "vote" at the end of the discussion if you wish, asking students to indicate their most preferred strategy.

6. The instructor should then move to Part I of the "Concluding the Exercise" section (below), to summarize the primary objectives third parties have in resolving disputes, and how these objectives are met by different strategies.

As an alternative to the process outlined above, the instructor may wish to rent a copy of "Conflict on the Line" (CRM/McGraw-Hill films), a case study of a manager's intervention into a subordinate conflict. "Conflict on the Line" can be effectively used as a "stop action" case, allowing students to discuss what they would do when they first learn about the conflict (e.g., collect more information). The film also ends with the manager using an ineffectual strategy - - a mild form of the "providing impetus" style (see "Concluding The Exercise")--and students can evaluate why this strategy is commonly used but also commonly does not resolve the problem.

Parts II and III:

1. Participants should read The Mediation Guide prior to the session. The instructor should review the basics of mediation in a prior class or in the first 15-20 minutes of this class session. The "Steps in a Mediation Process" is a helpful way to summarize the process.

2. Participants should be divided into trios. Two of the three will play the roles of Harold Stokes and Brenda Bennett, disputants. The third will play the role of Sam Finder, the superior who will mediate. Roles can be assigned randomly, or those who want to play the role of "mediator" can be asked to volunteer. An observer may be assigned to each group if desired, and can use The Mediation Guide as an observation form.

3. Participants take approximately 15 minutes to read and prepare their role. This can also be done as an advance assignment.

Option: (10 minutes) Prior to actual role playing, all those playing Brenda Bennett can meet together, all those playing Harold Stokes can meet together, and all those playing Sam Finder can meet together. The purpose is to discuss and help participants "get into" their roles. Instructors should coach the disputants to play their roles sincerely, but be willing to make concessions and compromises as a result of the mediator's efforts. Instructors should spend their time with the Sam Finders, discussing tactics they will use to mediate the disputes. Answer questions and offer suggestions, but do not explicitly direct the participants on how to play their roles. Observers can be coached on how to observe mediation techniques.

1. The actual mediation in trios should take place in areas where groups can not overhear one another (i.e., spaced around a large room, in break rooms). Put the "mediators" in charge and define their time limits to return to the general session (approximately 20-30 minutes). Parties are not required to settle if they do not believe the resolution is advantageous to them.

2. Reconvene at the end of the time limit. Have various trios report on the role-play. Specifically focus on the following:

    a) Solutions to the problem arrived at by various trios. Comment on differences between groups, and praise groups for inventing new and unique ways to improve coordination, cooperation, and decision-making between Bennett and Stokes.

    b) Trios which did not come to resolution, and reasons why this happened. Look for what the mediator and/or the disputing parties did or did not do that led to impasse.

    c) Reports from the mediators (only) on specific tactics they used that were most and least unsuccessful. Elicit comments on the easiest and most difficult parts of mediation.

    d) Reports from the disputants (and observers) on productive and unproductive behaviors used by mediators.

    e) Discussions of the pros and cons of mediation as a technique for resolving disputes.

3. In general, the following results occur:

    a) Most pairs will settle. Several pairs will not, and it is useful for the discussion to focus on the reasons why.

    b) Disputants often feel more "comfortable" with the process than does the mediator; particularly if the mediator "naturally" uses an adversarial or inquisitive style, he/she will have a hard time not exerting influence over the actual outcome arrived at by the disputants.

    c) Many third-party role-players follow the mediation procedure well until the "generating solutions" stage, and then "they take over the problem" and exert a lot of control over the solution as well. Find out if this happened, and why (see previous point).

d) Ask participants whether they would be likely to continue using mediation in the back-home work environment. Many will be candid and say they would not because it still feels uncomfortable, they would violate others' expectations of them, and so forth.

Concluding the Exercise:

Part I

When managers consider and evaluate ways to intervene, they typically borrow models from the legal system or labor arbitration. Similarly, theorists themselves have borrowed the language and models of the legal system to describe what managers do. Thus, students often describe their actions as follows:

1. When discussing the case, students traditionally seek to achieve one (or more) of four primary objectives: efficiency, effectiveness, participant satisfaction, and fairness. These objectives can be applied to the *outcome* of the Joe-Charles conflict or to the *procedure* that the parties use to resolve their dispute (overhead: Conflict Management Concerns):

    a) *Efficiency.* To solve the problem with a minimum expenditure of resources--third party time, disputant time, capital outlay, and so forth. Solving the problem quickly would be an example of procedural efficiency; telling Charles he will have to live with Joe's plan is an example of an efficient outcome.

    b) *Effectiveness.* To solve the problem so that it is solved well and stays solved. Making sure that the third party listens to all parties who have a relevant perspective on the conflict is an example of procedural effectiveness (brainstorming) to invent the best possible solution and one that will "work" (i.e., one that will not bring the parties back in the next few weeks) are examples of outcome effectiveness.

    c) *Participant Satisfaction.* To solve the problem so that the parties are satisfied with the solution. Giving all sides an opportunity to "present their case" is an example of participant satisfaction for procedures; getting Joe and Charles to invent a solution they like and to which they are committed (even if impractical) would be examples of participant satisfaction for outcomes.

    d) *Fairness.* To solve the problem so that the parties believe the outcome is fair (by some standard of fairness-equality, equity, and so forth). Again, giving each party an opportunity to present their case is traditionally equated with procedural fairness. Giving Charles some opportunity to study the five-year plan and present his views (but not have them binding on Joe) might be seen by some of the parties as a reasonably fair outcome.

2. When intervening into conflict, third parties tend to use one of several styles. These styles have been described and classified by Sheppard (1983, 1984) according to the

degree of control that the third party is exerting over the outcome of the dispute and the process by which it is resolved (see Figures 2 and 3).

- a) *Judges* exert high degrees of control over the outcome of the conflict but not the process by which it is resolved. A judge typically acts like a judge in an American courtroom-he/she allows both sides to present whatever facts, evidence, or arguments each desires; and then the third party decides the outcome of the conflict and, if he/she has the power, enforces it on the disputants.

- b) *Inquisitors* exert high degrees of control over both the outcome and the process of conflict resolution. An inquisitor is more typical of a judge in a European courtroom, or a Magistrate in an American court. He/she directs the presentation of evidence by the disputants, may ask questions or act as a referee, call for evidence that was not willingly presented, and then decides the outcome of the conflict.

- c) *Mediators* exert high degrees of control over the process of conflict resolution but not the outcome. A mediator may initially separate the parties to interview each and determine their "side;" he/she may then bring the parties together or separate them and ferry proposals back and forth in order to help the disputants forge their own solution to the conflict.

- d) *Avoiders, Delegators,* and *"Impetus Providers"* exert low degrees of control over both the process and the outcome. Avoiders prefer to find ways to either ignore the conflict or minimize its importance. Delegators recognize that the conflict exists, but try to delegate it back to the disputing parties to get them to handle it or to give it to someone else to attempt resolution. Finally, the Providing Impetus style (often called "Kick in the Pants") delegates it back to the parties with a threat--either they resolve it themselves or the third party will resolve it for them, and "nobody will like the solution." Research by Sheppard (1983) and Lewicki and Sheppard (1985) indicates that managers in organizations tend to use the inquisitorial style most frequently, followed by the judge and providing impetus styles. Managers believe that they use the mediation style frequently, but in fact seldom give the disputing parties real control over the outcome. Managers are more likely to use strategies that exert control over the outcome when they are operating under time pressures, when they think disputants will not be likely to work together in the future, and when the settlement has broad Implications for the resolution of other disputes.

3. Third party styles and objectives. Based on research regarding the various third party styles and their impact, each third party style should be used to achieve one or more of the four objectives listed above. The relationship between the third party styles and the primary objectives they serve can be seen by overlaying the overheads, Types of Intervention Strategies and Strengths of Intervention Strategies on top of one another. While not all of these relationships have received direct empirical confirmation, strong arguments can be made that each style will yield these primary results, and that managers should strive for a "contingency" model of conflict management based on the primary objectives of their intervention.

Parts II and III

While Part I of this exercise focused on the variety of strategies managers use to resolve disputes, Part II has focused specifically on mediation. The reason for this emphasis is that mediation appears to have many advantages as a conflict-resolution strategy, but has been used less frequently than it might be compared to judicial and inquisitorial styles. The clear advantages of mediation, as described earlier, is that it helps disputing parties invent their own solutions to problems, thereby increasing the "ownership" of solutions, willingness to implement them and live by them, and hopefully showing them a process they can use in subsequent disputes.

Only one approach to mediation was presented in this unit. In fact, there are many different stylistic approaches to mediation. The approach presented here is one of the two most common, and can be described as the "orchestration" approach. In this approach, the mediator attempts to work with both parties in the same room at the same time. In contrast, a number of mediators prefer the "shuttle diplomacy" approach, whereby the third party carries proposals back and forth between the separated disputants and tries to forge a common agreement from the efforts. Kolb (1983) and Merry and Silbey (1982) have described differences in mediator style.

Mediation is enjoying increasing popularity as a mechanism for resolving disputes traditionally handled by the courts. In the past 8-10 years, mediation has become a popular and viable way of handling labor disputes, divorce, community conflicts, insurance claims, environmental and land disputes, and many small legal cases. Communities throughout the country are setting up mediation centers annexed to the court system to relive the significant backlog of trials awaiting courtroom dates. Mediation is preferred because it is frequently quicker than the courts, less costly in attorney and court fees, and, again, gives the disputing parties considerable control in shaping the actual settlement. In mediation, both parties can be winners; in adjudication, only one party wins, and sometimes, neither one wins (see Folberg, 1984 and Goldberg, Green and Sander, 1985 for reviews).

Mediation and its applications to management have also been receiving considerable research attention. Instructors may consult Bush and Folger (1994), Moore (1996) and Kolb (1994) for comprehensive treatments of the mediation process and selected research.

REFERENCES

Bush, R.A.B. and Folger, J. (1994). The promise of mediation. San Francisco, CA: Jossey Bass.

Folberg, J. and Taylor, A. (1984) *Mediation*. San Francisco: Jossey Bass.

Goldberg, S., Green, E. and Sander, F. (1985) *Dispute Resolution*. Boston: Little Brown.

Kolb, D.M. (1984) The Mediators. Cambridge, MA: MIT Press.

Kolb, D.M. (1994). *When talk works: Profiles of mediators*. San Francisco, CA: Jossey Bass.

Kressel, K. and Pruitt, D. G. (1985) "The Mediation of Social Conflict," *Journal of Social Issues*. 41(2).

Lewicki, R. J. and Sheppard, B. (1985) "Choosing How to Intervene: Factors Affecting the Use of Process and Outcome Control in Third Party Dispute Resolution," *Journal of Occupational Behavior* 6, pp. 49-64.

Merry, S. E. and Silbey, S. (1982) *Mediator Settlement Strategies: Authority and Manipulation in Alternative Dispute Resolution*. Paper presented at the American Anthropological Association meetings.

Moore, C.W. (1996). *The mediation process: Practical strategies for resolving conflict*. San Francisco, CA: Jossey Bass.

Sheppard, B. (1983) "Managers as Inquisitors: Some Lessons from the Law," In M. Bazerman and R. J. Lewicki (eds.) *Negotiation in Organizations*. Beverly Hills: Sage Publications.

Sheppard, B. (1984) "Third Party Conflict Intervention: A Procedural Frame-work," In B. Staw and L. L. Cummings (eds.) *Research in Organizational Behavior*. Greenwich, CT: JAI Publishing Co.

ROLE FOR BRENDA BENNETT
EXERCISE 15 THIRD PARTY CONFLICT RESOLUTION

You are Brenda Bennett, Director of Personnel for the Levver Corporation. You have just taken over the position of Director of Personnel, and have inherited a lot of ill-will and dead weight. Past personnel practices have been less than perfect. However, the people running the summer intern program this year are some of the best that you have.

Several weeks ago, the Engineering Department requested two summer interns. Jim Lexington, your subordinate and head of the intern program, informed Engineering that they would have to wait because the hiring would not begin for at least two weeks. Then, without further consultation, Engineering went and hired two students, themselves.

You are concerned for several reasons. First, the intern program comes out of your budget, and you will be damned if you will pay for two students not hired through your staff. Second, both students are white males - - sons of friends of Joe Barnes. You are concerned about the E.E.O. implications. Third, the intern program involves some general overall orientation and development work before students are assigned to projects, and these students will be out of phase. Fourth, from your view there seem to be better applicants. Finally, you feel it is necessary to begin establishing Personnel's "territorial rights," and this is as good a time as any. You have a good case.

With these thoughts in mind you called Stokes, and he put you off before you had a chance to explain your concerns. Thus, you called your boss, Samantha (Sam) Pinder to discuss the problem. You report primarily to the Vice President of Human Resources of Levver, who works at another location and only have an indirect ("dotted line") reporting relationship to Finder. Nevertheless, since Finder manages the office you work in, he/she has the responsibility to try to handle this problem.

You only had a chance to tell Pinder the basic problem on the telephone, but not any of the details. You know Pinder will expect some compromise from you, and you are willing to seek common ground- -provided most of all of your five concerns are somehow alleviated.

ROLE FOR HAROLD STOKES
EXERCISE 15: THIRD PARTY CONFLICT RESOLUTION

You are Harold Stokes, Vice President of Engineering for the Levver Corporation. Your electrical engineering group is far behind on a major power station project. Much of the work on this project involves relatively simple drafting; it requires minimal engineering competence if supervised properly. However, it must be started right away. You and your staff decided that a few summer interns would be perfect for the job. Joe Barnes, your manager of Electrical Engineering, tried to hire interns through the Personnel Intern program; however, he was told that hiring could not begin for at least another two weeks. Remembering your past skirmishes with the former Director of Personnel (Brenda Bennett's predecessor), you just told Barnes to go and hire two students (friends of Barnes' son in college) whom he knew, to get the job started.

You are aware that this action probably caused some trouble for the Personnel Department. As a matter of fact, you are sure of this because Bennett called Samantha (Sam) Finder, the Executive Vice President, to complain about your actions. Bennett is not necessarily like her predecessor and probably deserves a chance to prove herself. However, the two students are here now, and they appear to be working out well; when Bennett called in a real huff, you told her the students were here now, and "that's that!" Moreover, some of the interns that Personnel have sent in the past have been complete "duds." You feel that the placement officers in Personnel do not consult well enough with the host departments when making placement decisions.

Bennett's call to Finder has prompted Finder to get involved to try to resolve this conflict. Your reporting relationship at Levver is directly to the Senior Vice President for R & D, who works at another location. You don't report directly to Pinder and Bennett only reports to Finder indirectly; nevertheless, Pinder has the most direct responsibility for trying to resolve this conflict.

You know that Pinder is going to expect some compromise, and you and your department will accept anything reasonable - - provided the two students stay, acquires more control over intern hiring decisions.

ROTE FOR SAMANTHA ("SAM") PINDER.
EXERCISE 15: THIRD PARTY CONFLICT RESOLUTION

    You are Samantha (Sam) Pinder, Executive Vice-President Finance and head of the main office staff for Levver Corporation. Brenda Bennett (Director of Personnel) and Harold Stokes (Vice-President Engineering) are about to arrive in your office. Brenda phoned you this morning saying that she had to speak with you about Harold's violation of the procedure for hiring summer interns. Apparently, the Engineering Department (at Harold's request) has been hiring interns directly into the Department without going through Personnel. You asked if she had tried to discuss the problem with Stokes, and she said that she had.

    Neither Bennett nor Stokes works for you directly. Bennett reports to the Vice President for Human Resources (who works in another office); Bennett has an indirect ("dotted line") reporting relationship to you because she works in the main office. Stokes reports to the Senior VP for Research and Development in a different part of the organization. Nevertheless, you are the most logical one to try to solve this problem. Both Stokes and Bennett are tough, but reasonable, people. You feel that if you can bring the two of them together, the problem can probably be settled. You called Harold to set up this meeting.

CONFLICT MANAGEMENT CONCERNS

Procedural Attributes

1. Fairness
   Perceived fairness
   Degree of neutrality
   Degree of disputant control
   Protection of individual rights

2. Participant Satisfaction
   Degree of privacy
   Degree of involvement
   Degree of injury

3. Effectiveness
   Implementability
   Quantity/quality of Facts, ideas, arguments
   Degree to which dispute surfaces

4. Efficiency
   Cost of hassle
   Timeliness and time involved
   Disruptiveness

Outcome Attributes

1. Fairness
   Equity
   Consistency
   Need
   Consistency with norms
   Perceived fairness

2. Participant Satisfaction
   Commitment to solution
   Benefit to participants
   Level of animosity

3. Effectiveness
   Level of resolution
   Performance of solution
   Likelihood of similar future outcomes
   Impact on participants

4. Efficiency
   Resolves the problem at hand

CONFLICT INTERVENTION STYLES

Judge

Inquisitor

Mediator

Delegator

Avoider

Impetus Provider

STEPS IN A MEDIATION PROCESS

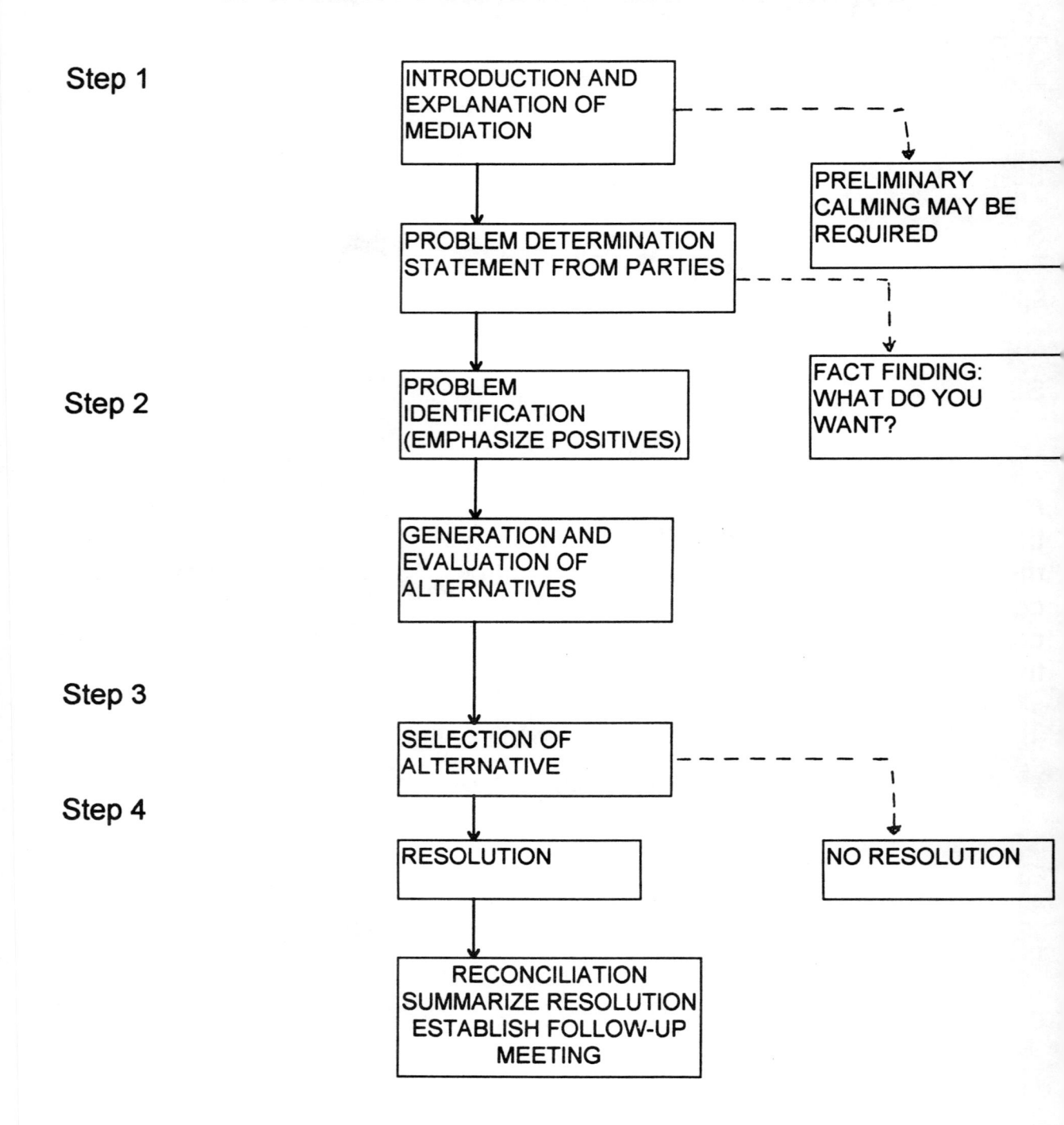

Step 1 — INTRODUCTION AND EXPLANATION OF MEDIATION → PRELIMINARY CALMING MAY BE REQUIRED

↓

PROBLEM DETERMINATION STATEMENT FROM PARTIES → FACT FINDING: WHAT DO YOU WANT?

↓

Step 2 — PROBLEM IDENTIFICATION (EMPHASIZE POSITIVES)

↓

GENERATION AND EVALUATION OF ALTERNATIVES

↓

Step 3 — SELECTION OF ALTERNATIVE → NO RESOLUTION

↓

Step 4 — RESOLUTION

↓

RECONCILIATION
SUMMARIZE RESOLUTION
ESTABLISH FOLLOW-UP MEETING

THE MEDIATION GUIDE

The Steps:

Step 1: Stabilize the Setting.

Step 2: Help the Parties Communicate.

Step 3: Help the Parties Negotiate.

Step 4: Clarify the Parties' Agreement.

Step 1: Stabilize the Setting

Parties often bring strong feelings of anger and frustration into mediation. These feelings can prevent them from talking productively about their dispute. You, as mediator, will try to gain their trust for you and for the mediation process. Stabilize the setting by being polite; show that you are in control and that you are neutral. This step helps the parties feel comfortable, so they can speak freely about their complaints, and safe, so they can air their feelings.

1. Greet the parties.

2. Indicate where each of them is to sit.

3. Identify yourself and each party, by name.

4. Offer water, paper and pencil, and patience.

5. State the purpose of mediation.

6. Confirm your neutrality.

7. Get their commitment to proceed.

8. Get their commitment that only one party at a time will speak

9. Get their commitment to speak directly to you.

10. Use calming techniques as needed.

Step 2: Help the Parties Communicate

Once the setting is stable, and the parties seem to trust you and the mediation process, you can begin to carefully build trust between them. Both must make statements about what has happened. Each will use these statements to air negative feelings. They may express anger, make accusations, and show frustration in other ways. But, with your help, this mutual ventilation lets them hear each other's side of the story, perhaps for the first time. It can help calm their emotions, and can build a basis for trust between them.

1. Explain the rationale for who speaks first.

2. Reassure them that both will speak without interruption, for as long as is needed.

3. Ask the first speaker to tell what has happened.

   a) Take notes.

   b) Respond actively; restate and echo what is said.

   c) Calm the parties as needed.

   d) Clarify, with open or closed questions, or with restatements.

   e) Focus the narration on the issues in the dispute.

   f) Summarize, eliminating all disparaging references.

   g) Check to see that you understand the story.

   h) Thank this party for speaking, the other for listening quietly.

4. Ask the second speaker to tell what has happened.

   a) Take notes.

   b) Respond actively, restate and echo what is said.

   c) Calm the parties as needed.

- d) Clarify, with open or closed questions, or with restatements.
- e) Focus the narration on the issues in the dispute.
- f) Summarize, eliminating all disparaging references.
- g) Check to see that you understand the story.
- h) Thank this party for speaking, the other for listening quietly.

5. Ask each party, in turn, to help clarify the major issues to be resolved.

6. Inquire into basic issues, probing to see if something, instead, may be at the root of the complaints.

7. Define the problem by restating and summarizing.

8. Conduct private meetings, if needed (explain what will happen during and after the private meetings).

9. Summarize areas of agreement and disagreement.

10. Help the parties set priorities on the issues and demands.

Step 3: Help the Parties Negotiate

Cooperation is needed for negotiations that lead to agreement. Cooperation requires a stable setting, to control disruptions, and exchanges of information, to develop mutual trust. With these conditions, the parties may be willing to cooperate, but still feel driven to compete. You can press for cooperative initiatives by patiently helping them to explore alternative solutions, and by directing attention to their progress.

1. Ask each party to list alternative possibilities for a settlement.

2. Restate and summarize each alternative.

3. Check with each party on the workability of each alternative.

4. Restate whether the alternative is workable.

5. In an impasse, suggest the general form of other alternatives.

6. Note the amount of progress already made, to show that success is likely.

7. If the impasse continues, suggest a break or a second mediation session.

8. Encourage them to select the alternative that appears to both to be workable.

9. Increase their understanding by rephrasing the alternative.

10. Help them plan a course of action to implement the alternative.

Step 4: Clarify Their Agreement

Mediation should change each party's attitude toward the other. When both have shown their commitment, through a joint declaration of agreement, each will support the agreement more strongly. For a settlement that lasts, each component of the attitudes toward each other -- their thinking, feeling, and acting -- will have changed. Not only will they now <u>act</u> differently toward each other, they are likely to <u>feel</u> differently, more positively, about each other, and <u>think</u> of their relationship in new ways.

1. Summarize the agreement terms.

2. Recheck with each party their understanding of the agreement.

3. Ask whether other issues need to be discussed.

4. Help them specify the terms of their agreement.

5. State each person's role in the agreement.

6. Recheck with each party **when** they are to do certain things, **where,** and **how**.

7. Explain the process of follow-up.

8. Establish a time for follow-up with each party.

9. Emphasize that the agreement is theirs, not yours.

10. Congratulate the parties on their reasonableness, and on the workability of their resolution.

TYPES OF INTERVENTION STRATEGIES

Third Party controls the decisions

	YES	NO
YES	INQUISTION	MEDIATION
NO	ARBITRATION	PROVIDING IMPETUS BARGAINING

Third Party controls the process

STRENGTHS OF INTERVENTION STRATEGIES

Third Party controls the decisions

	YES	NO
Third Party controls the process YES	EFFICIENCY EFFECTIVENESS	SATISFACTION FAIRNESS
NO	FAIRNESS EFFECTIVENESS	EFFICIENCY

EXERCISE 16
THE CONNECTICUT VALLEY SCHOOL

Objectives

The primary objective is to confront students with a realistic integrative bargaining problem. Participants must grapple with the following complexities.

1) Three parties. Unlike many negotiating exercises, this is not a simple dyadic face off. Success requires forging an agreement which simultaneously satisfies the most salient goals of all three parties. In this situation two parties may be tempted to coalesce and to slight the interests of the third party- particularly when the two parties have similar goals and the third party appears to be stubborn or uncooperative.

2) Sequential negotiations. The members of each group should agree on priorities and bargaining strategies before entering the negotiation. If a group is unable to forge an internal consensus, they may be ill prepared for the final bargaining session.

3) Ambiguous distribution of power. While the headmaster and the trustees have the authority to make budgeting decisions, the de facto power of the faculty may be considerable. The faculty's power is based on their understanding of the day-to-day operations of the school and the needs of the students. In addition, the morale of the faculty is critical to the mission of the school. Any outcome which leaves the faculty disgruntled should be unsatisfactory to the other parties.

4) Multiple success criteria. Again, there is no simple objective function which students can attempt to maximize. While promoting such qualitative objectives as "improving the quality of student life" and "promoting the school's liberal arts mission," each group must also deal with tangible financial constraints and the need to maintain the morale and commitment of the other players.

Given these complexities, participants should find that thorough preparation and a concerted effort to understand the viewpoints of other parties will pay off.

Group Size: There are two plans. The first runs the exercise as a single role play involving the whole class, while the second runs the exercise as a multiple role play. The instructor should assign each student to one of the three groups, depending on the plan:

Plan 1: Single Role Play

1) the Headmaster. The Headmaster can be assigned an assistant as well. (2 students)
2) the Trustees. (8-10 students)
3) the Faculty Budget Committee. (remaining students)

These numbers can be adjusted depending on the size of the class.

Plan 2: Multiple Groups Role Play

Running a single negotiation with large groups may invite social loafing. To encourage greater participation, a number of simultaneous bargaining sessions could be run with only 2 or 3 students assigned to a group in any one session. Students could then report their experience to the full class. This plan would reduce total time requirements but increase the portion of time needed for class discussion.

Time Required: 1.5 to 2.5 hours. Time requirements will depend on 1) the sophistication of the students and 2) how much preparation is done outside of class. If the "within group" preparation is done outside of class, only 1.5 hours of class time would be needed.

Special Materials: Copy and distribute role play information in this manual.

Special Physical Requirements: It is helpful to have rooms for each of the three parties to meet (to plan and caucus). At least two rooms are needed for the faculty and trustees to meet. If you run the multiple groups role play, each iteration needs a separate room to meet, and areas within the room for subgroups to plan and caucus.

Recommended Reading Assignments to Accompany this Exercise:

Roger Fisher and William Ury. *Getting to Yes: Negotiating Agreement Without Giving In*. New York: Penguin, 1981.

What to Expect:

A private secondary school must allocate a limited capital budget among seven competing projects. Three parties are involved in the discussions: the headmaster, the faculty budget committee and the board of trustees. While the three parties view the budgeting process differently and have slightly different priorities, their goals overlap and are fundamentally compatible. Conscientious, resourceful participants should be able to achieve a mutually satisfying, integrative outcome.

This is a realistic, integrative bargaining exercise in that participants are not given a simple unidimensional success criterion (i.e.- maximize profit, achieve outcome x). Instead, they must establish their own bargaining goals. Moreover, these goals are likely to be multi-dimensional, since the benefits promised by the projects cannot be collapsed to a single dimension.

This case has proven effective as a capstone exercise in undergraduate courses. It can be used at any point in an MBA course. It is interesting to use CVS early in an MBA course, before students have developed a facility for forging creative "win-win" solutions. Later in the course students can reflect back on integrative opportunities forgone.

Advance Preparation:

1. Read the exercise over so you understand how it works and what might happen. Decide whether you want to use the single group or multiple groups option.
2. Also decide whether you want to use the Faculty Budget Committee (A) or (B) option, and whether you want to introduce the *Memo from the Dean of Students* (see Teaching Options, below).
3. Photocopy the appropriate number of copies of the role briefing information from this book.
4. Decide whether you want students to prepare their roles outside of class, or during a class period.

Operating Procedure

1. The exercise requires two negotiating sessions. The first is a "within group" negotiation/discussion during which each group agrees on priorities, ranks the projects, discusses bargaining strategy and possibly selects spokespersons. Depending on the sophistication of the participants, this session may require 45-60 minutes- assuming that each participant prepares in advance. The second session, a between groups negotiation, will also require 45-60 minutes. At least 30 minutes should be reserved for discussion and debriefing.

2. Each student should read the case introduction (in the Reader) and be given a copy of his/her group's confidential role assignment. Unless you use one of the alternative options (see below), you should use
    a) - The Board of Trustees
    b) - John Loring, Headmaster
    c) - Faculty Budget Committee (A)

3. The assignment of roles may influence the dynamics of the subsequent negotiations. For this reason, the instructor may wish to assign students to specific roles. For example:
    a) - Chairperson of the Board of Trustees
    b) - Chairperson of the Faculty Budget Committee
    c) - Dean of Students (see "Teaching Options" below)
    d) This may set up a discussion of "personality effects" and the importance of separating positions from personalities.

4. Assign roles and hand out instructions in advance of the class. Ask students to study their roles and prepare for their group meeting.

5. Time options for running the exercise:
    a) Within Group Negotiation (45-60 minutes). Groups should be asked to prepare a ranking and rating (perhaps on a 5-point scale) of the projects, a list of the projects they would fund, and a brief statement of their evaluation criteria. This information should be submitted to the instructor at the conclusion of the group meetings. These a priori ratings can later be used to assess how well the groups achieved their original goals.

b) Between Group Negotiation (45-60 minutes). If class time permits, both negotiations can be conducted during the same class period. Due to the large number of participants, it may be useful to ask the Chairperson of the Trustees to moderate the discussion.

Teaching Options:

The instructor can fine-tune this exercise to the needs and sophistication of the class. Options include:

A) Distribute the *Memo from the Dean of Students*. This memo makes a compelling case for a new project, safety lighting on campus walkways. If it is distributed after the groups have begun their deliberations, it may encourage groups to critically reassess their ranking criteria. The memo can be hand delivered by a student playing the role of Nancy Clarke, Dean of Students.

B) Add a new project to the list of alternatives. (You can invent this issue as you wish).

C) Tighten the budget constraints. Either tightening the budget constraint or introducing a new project proposal can make the exercise more challenging for advanced students.

D) Assign several students to specific roles and coach them on how to play those roles. For example, a student playing the Chairperson of the Board of Trustees might be assigned responsibility for keeping the discussion on track and diffusing counterproductive hostility. Also, a student athlete could play the role of headmaster, since he might appreciate (better than the average student) the importance of athletics in the secondary school experience and be more sympathetic to the headmaster's agenda.

E) Give students an exhibit (Exhibit 1 or 2) which ranks projects by profitability index. While the more advanced students enjoy "running the numbers," others may get "bogged down" with the numbers and fail to adequately explore the critical qualitative issues. If the exhibit is provided, students can focus more on the issues (the Exhibit should be provided to both groups).

NOTE: Exhibit 2 is easier to process and tells a more complete story. Specifically, it provides two calculations not presented in Exhibit 1:

- NPV. Many students are "comfortable" with this measure and like to compare it with the profitability index. In the debriefing they often raise questions about NPV. (Both NPV and the profitability index are derived from the first two columns of the table.)

- Cumulative Investment. By explicitly listing the cumulative investment, Exhibit 2 emphasizes that the budget constraint will force some serious trade-offs. Students could easily do these calculations themselves.

However, Exhibit 1 more completely summarizes the assumptions stated in the case (project life, annual tangible benefits).

F) Ask the Faculty Budget Committee to develop their own criteria for ranking the projects. Two alternative role assignments are provided for the faculty. Role A provides ranking criteria. Role B requires that the faculty develop their own criteria. Role B makes the exercise more interesting and more challenging, especially for advanced students.

G) Measure Satisfaction (Optional). Immediately following the negotiation, the instructor could ask students to complete a brief questionnaire (several Likert-scaled questions) designed to measure satisfaction with the outcome, perceived fairness, and perceived success in achieving group goals. During the subsequent debriefing, these measures could be used as an indicator of success/failure in achieving an integrative solution.

Discussion and Debriefing:

(30 minutes). Questions:

1. Did the class agree on appropriate decision criteria before debating the merits of specific projects? Which party's decision criteria will best promote an integrative solution?

A "principled" approach (Fisher and Ury, 1981) to negotiation would favor discussing the appropriate decision criteria before debating the merits of specific projects. If the parties can agree on appropriate criteria, agreeing on a ranking of projects may be relatively easy. Moreover, groups who endorse the decision criteria are likely to be more accepting of necessary concessions.

Since the capital budget should achieve multiple goals, the multi-attribute decision criteria proposed by the faculty is most realistic. The faculty's approach also recognizes the need to make difficult trade-offs among objectives.

The Trustees' tentative decision rule is clearly too narrow and unidimensional- addressing only financial criteria. Usually the Trustees recognize that the faculty's "principled" approach can provide the foundation for a truly integrative solution, which will satisfy the most important goals of each group.

The Headmaster's confidential instructions suggest a "positional" approach (Fisher and Ury, 1981) to bargaining. However, students playing this role often reject the Headmaster's ill-defined political agenda in favor of a more principled approach.

2. What techniques were used to create a more integrative solution?

Students often mention the following:

EXPAND THE PIE. Implementing "cost saving" projects this year could free up funds to achieve other goals in the near future. Also, the pie can be expanded by identifying additional sources of funding (see #3 below).

IDENTIFY PROJECTS WHICH SATISFY MULTIPLE GOALS. For example, the Fine Arts Building improves the quality of student life and promotes the school's liberal arts mission, while also scoring high on financial criteria (see Exhibits).

IDENTIFY LOW COST/HIGH BENEFIT TRADE-OFFS. Some projects provide high benefits to one group at little cost to other groups. For example, renovating the women's locker room would support the faculty's top three priorities while costing a mere $20,000, less than any other project.

3. What is negotiable?

Some groups will focus narrowly on which projects to fund in the current year. Others will find creative solutions by expanding the *domain of the negotiation.* For example, all of the following could be negotiable.

THE BUDGET CONSTRAINT. The budget constraint could be relaxed. Untapped financing sources may be available. Perhaps a fund-raising campaign can center around the need to fund a specific project. Benefactors are sometimes more inclined to donate towards a tangible goal.

NEXT YEAR'S BUDGET ALLOCATION. Projects which are not funded this year could be promised priority next year. Could a project be partially funded this year and completed next year?

THE DECISION CRITERIA. See (1) above.

4. Which group possessed the greatest power? How did the distribution of power influence the outcome?

When students begin this exercise, they often assume that the Trustees will exert disproportionate influence on the decision process, since they are authorized to make the final choice of projects. However, as the negotiation unfolds the faculty's de facto power usually becomes apparent. The faculty draws power from at least three sources:

CRITICAL CONSTITUENCY. The faculty is so critical to the school's identity and mission that any outcome which does not satisfy the faculty should be unacceptable to the other groups. In addition, the faculty will exert influence by their sheer numbers.

PRINCIPLED NEGOTIATION. The faculty's decision criteria are so reasonable, that the Trustees and Headmaster usually accept them in part or in full.

EXPERTISE. The faculty's power is based in part on their detailed knowledge of the student needs and the day-to-day operation of the school.

5. How successful were the groups in achieving an integrative solution?

If the process was truly integrative, all groups should be reasonably satisfied with the outcome and the fairness of the process. If the instructor administered a "satisfaction" questionnaire at the conclusion of the negotiation, the results could be discussed here.

Often groups are quite satisfied even though they did not achieve their original goals. They may have revised their goals during the course of the negotiation.

6. How did personalities influence the bargaining process?

    Were groups able to separate personalities from issues? If so, how? If not, how might this problem have been better managed?

7. Did groups use a "net present value" calculation to determine the profitability of each project? Profitability measures do not capture many of the important benefits generated by these projects. Hence, if negotiators adopt a profitability index as the primary measure of project attractiveness, the legitimate needs of faculty and students will not be served. Since many of the projects provide huge intangible benefits, the profitability index is not the best decision criterion (obvious). The faculty should be prepared to make this case to the trustees. Bottom line: run the numbers, understand the numbers, but don't allow decisions to be driven by simplistic decision rules.

Exhibit 1
Connecticut Valley School
Ranking of Projects by Profitability Index

PROJECT	INITIAL INVESTMENT	ANNUAL TANGIBLE BENEFITS		EST LIFE (YRS)	PRESENT VALUE OF BENEFITS	PROFIT INDEX
Fine Arts Bldg.	$75,000	$150,000	1st yr		$150,000	2.00
Rink Roof	$30,000	$60,000	1st yr		$53,571	1.79
Buses	$135,000	$50,000		6	$205,570	1.52
Heating System	$400,000	$70,000		15	$476,761	1.19
Swimming Pool	$320,000	$50,000		15	$340,543	1.06
Women's Locker	$20,000	$20,000	1st yr		$20,000	1.00
Campus Lighting	$30,000	$30,000	1st yr		$30,000	1.00
Computer Lab	$60,000	$60,000	1st yr		$60,000	1.00

This exhibit uses the Trustees' profitability index to rank the projects. However, it considers all "tangible" benefits rather than just cash inflows and cost savings. For example, the Fine Arts Building would cost the school $75,000 in year 1. However, the school would receive a tangible benefit worth $150,000 in year 1 (i.e., the completed renovations are valued at $150,000). Therefore, the project's profitability index is 2.0 ($150,000/$75,000).

Exhibit 2
Connecticut Valley School
Ranking of Projects by Profitability Index

PROJECT	INITIAL INVESTMENT	PRESENT VALUE OF BENEFITS	NET PRESENT VALUE	PROFIT INDEX	CUMULATIVE INVESTMENT
Fine Arts Bldg.	$75,000	$150,000	$75,000	2.00	$75,000
Rink Roof	$30,000	$53,571	$23,571	1.79	$105,000
Buses	$135,000	$205,570	$70,570	1.52	$240,000
Heating System	$400,000	$476,761	$76,761	1.19	$640,000
Swimming Pool	$320,000	$340,543	$20,543	1.06	$960,000
Women's Locker	$20,000	$20,000	$0	1.00	$980,000
Campus Lighting	$30,000	$30,000	$0	1.00	$1,010,000
Computer Lab	$60,000	$60,000	$0	1.00	$1,070,000
			$266,445		

This exhibit uses the Trustees' profitability index to rank the projects. However, it considers all "tangible" benefits rather than just cash inflows and cost savings. For example, the Fine Arts Building would cost the school $75,000 in year 1. However, the school would receive a tangible benefit worth $150,000 in year 1 (i.e., the completed renovations are valued at $150,000). Therefore, the project's profitability index is 2.0 ($150,000/$75,000).

ROLE FOR THE BOARD OF TRUSTEES

EXERCISE 16: THE CONNETICUT VALLEY SCHOOL

The trustees feel that an optimal allocation of scarce capital funds can be achieved by applying the following decision rule:

1. Calculate a "profitability index" (or "benefit-cost ratio") for each project:

    PRESENT VALUE of   net cash inflows and cost savings
    　　　　　　　　　　　　　　initial investment

2. Reject any project with an index less than 1.

3. Select those projects with the highest profitability indexes - until all available capital funds have been applied.

According to one member of the Board of Trustees, this rule is particularly appropriate when funds are being rationed, since it promises the biggest "bang for the buck" -- that is, the highest ratio of present value to initial investment. (The school uses a 12 percent annual discount rate to evaluate all "cost saving" investment projects.) While they will consider using other decision rules, the trustees feel that this rule is "prudent." They view themselves as guardians of fiscal restraint. It is their job to hold spending within the budget and to veto questionable projects.

The trustees feel that it is important to include the faculty in the decision process. Some faculty members were vocal in their criticism of last year's spending priorities. They were upset that over half the budget was allocated to building or improving athletic facilities*** at the expense of other pressing needs. Accordingly, the trustees are determined to give the faculty a fair hearing.

The trustees plan to develop their own tentative ranking of projects before meeting with the headmaster and the faculty. Their objective is to forge agreement on a capital budget which will promote the long-run interests of the school.

*** Last year's projects included: 1) improving drainage on the soccer field, 2) building new stands for the football field, 3) constructing four new tennis courts, and 4) purchasing two new vans to transport men's interscholastic teams.

ROLE FOR JOHN LORING, HEADMASTER
EXERCISE 16: THE CONNETICUT VALLEY SCHOOL

Headmaster Loring had no difficulty identifying the most promising projects:

1. Swimming pool $320,000
2. Hockey rink roof $ 30,000
3. Buses $135,000

These projects are easily defended as financially prudent, and they are consistent with the school's commitment to a strong athletic program. Cost savings generated by projects 1 and 3 will take the pressure off the operating budget in future years and may free up funds for additional projects. Repairing the hockey rink roof is clearly essential and should draw no objections. In fact, Loring is considering asking for an additional $20,000 to fully enclose the hockey rink. As long as major construction is required on the roof, this additional improvement seems timely.

Last year some vocal faculty members criticized the headmaster for allocating too much of the capital budget to developing and improving athletic facilities. Last year's projects included: 1) improving drainage on the soccer field, 2) building new stands for the football field, 3) constructing four new tennis courts, and 4) purchasing two new vans to transport men's interscholastic teams. This year's recommendations are more "balanced." The headmaster expects to win faculty endorsement for his proposal, but recognizes that he must be prepared to defend his recommendations.

His objective is to secure funding for as much of his program as possible, while maintaining faculty support and morale.

ROLE FOR THE FACULTY BUDGET COMMITTEE (A)
EXERCISE 16: THE CONNETICUT VALLEY SCHOOL

After months of deliberation, the Faculty Budget Committee has agreed on an approach to ranking projects. They will rely on a qualitative assessment of the benefits promised by each project. The committee has agreed on the following priorities:

First priority: protecting the health and safety of the community
Second priority: maintaining current plant and property
Third priority: improving the quality of student life
Fourth priority: promoting the school's "liberal arts" mission
Fifth priority: reducing operating costs

The committee was very unhappy with last year's allocation of funds. They feel that spending decisions were driven more by the headmaster's political agenda than by the pressing needs of the faculty and students. The headmaster is a strong booster of athletic programs, and his capital spending priorities reflect this commitment. For example, last year's projects included: 1) improving drainage on the soccer field, 2) building new stands for the football field, 3) constructing four new tennis courts, and 4) purchasing two new vans to transport men's interscholastic teams. While all of these projects were worthwhile, the faculty feels the capital budget overemphasized athletics.

The Faculty Budget Committee must develop their own tentative ranking of projects before meeting with the headmaster and the trustees. They are determined to be heard.

ROLE FOR THE FACULTY BUDGET COMMITTEE (B)
EXERCISE 16: THE CONNETICUT VALLEY SCHOOL

Some of the proposed projects provide important "intangible" benefits, which cannot be easily quantified. Accordingly, the Faculty Budget Committee wants to develop qualitative criteria for evaluating and ranking the projects. The committee agrees that projects which promote the mission of the school and serve the interests of students should be highly valued. However, the faculty have not yet agreed on the specific criteria which they will use to rank projects.

The committee was very unhappy with last year's allocation of funds. They feel that spending decisions were driven more by the headmaster's political agenda than by the pressing needs of the faculty and students. The headmaster is a strong booster of athletic programs, and his capital spending priorities reflect this commitment. For example, last year's projects included: 1) improving drainage on the soccer field, 2) building new stands for the football field, 3) constructing four new tennis courts, and 4) purchasing two new vans to transport men's interscholastic teams. While all of these projects were worthwhile, the faculty feels the capital budget overemphasized athletics.

The Faculty Budget Committee must develop a set of guidelines which could be used to rank the investment projects. In addition, they must tentatively rank the projects before meeting with the headmaster and the trustees. They are determined to be heard.

The Connecticut Valley School

To: John Loring, Headmaster
      Board of Trustees
      Faculty Budget Committee

From: Nancy Clarke, Dean of Students

Re: Need for improved lighting on campus walkways

Last month a female student was assaulted while walking from the library to her dormitory late at night. The assailant has not been apprehended, but was probably from off campus.

We are fortunate that our campus is relatively safe. Only one other incident of this type has been reported in the past 9 months. However, we are determined to be proactive in maintaining campus safety.

Since the assault, I have talked extensively with both faculty and students about safety on campus. As a result of these discussions, the campus security office has been instructed to be more vigilant and students have been asked not to walk alone after dark.

Some faculty and students feel that the danger of assault is aggravated by a lack of lighting on walkways between the dorms, the library, and the student center. I agree. These paths are illuminated only by the light from nearby buildings, and it is usually necessary to carry a flashlight to see your way.

I have thoroughly researched possible remedies. The cost of installing lamp posts every 50 feet on these paths is $30,000. This lighting system would solve the problem without compromising the aesthetics of the campus. While lower cost options are possible, I feel that we should do this right.

EXERCISE 17
ALPHA-BETA

Objectives

This cross-cultural, interteam negotiation role play, a disguised version of the GE-Hitachi robotics negotiation of 1981, is designed to provide an introduction to the effects of different cultural styles and to the dynamics of interteam bargaining. It has been used for the first class of semester-long courses on international negotiation and for short workshops.

The role-play materials are rich enough for several uses, but this note describes two 2-hour formats: 1) Option A, one continuous round, and 2) Option B, one interrupted round (two phases). The continuous round involves a 15-20 minute negotiation period in which participants tend to focus on cultural factors and superficially deal with substantive issues, whereas the interrupted round provides 20-35 minutes for negotiations in which the parties can concentrate sequentially on cultural factors and on substantive details.

For both formats, a team should consist of 2 persons. When there are odd numbers of participants, assign the extra person to the Beta team.

Option A: One Continuous Round (Version A Materials)

Advance Preparation: None necessary.

Materials: *Important* --- use Version A materials for this option

For Alpha: Public Information (in Reader), Alpha Confidential Memo, and The Alphan Negotiating Style.

For Beta: Public Information (in Reader), Beta Confidential Memo, and The Betan Negotiating Style.

Number of Participants: 4 (2 per team)

Time Required:

- Preparation: - for individuals to read materials: 10-15 mins. For each team to plan for negotiations: 25 mins.
- Negotiations between teams: 15-20 mins.
- Debriefing: 20-30 mins.
- Total time: 1 hr. 30 mins. minimum (including setup and shuffling by participants)

Recommended Reading Assignments to Accompany This Exercise:

Readings: 11.1 (Phatak and Habib), 11.2 (Koh), 11.3 (Frank)
Text: Chapter 11

Additional Information:

For the team planning period, assign all of the Alphans (stereotypical Americans) to one room and all of the Betans (stereotypical Japanese) to another. The Betans, in particular, can benefit from actively practicing their negotiating styles and should be able to do so without the Alphans seeing those styles in advance.

The negotiations should be stopped while the teams are still using their assigned styles, that is, before they revert to their usual negotiating styles.

For the debriefing, have the Alphans sit on one side of the room, and the Betans on the other. As with any other negotiation exercise, the debriefing can address both outcomes and process, but the very beginning of the period, when the experience is still fresh, is the best time to get at affective dimensions. Each culture can be asked in turn to describe: 1) how they <u>feel</u> about the experience, how they felt during it [leaving cognitive and strategic factors aside for the time being]; and 2) the counterparts' negotiating style. Each set of observations can be recorded on a transparency split into two columns, one for each culture. (Slide 1 can be labelled "Feelings about this Negotiation" and split into a column for "Alphans'" and one for "Betans.'" Slide 2 can be labelled "Counterparts' Style" and split into a column for "Alphans' Style per Betans" and one for "Betans' Style per Alphans.") Work with one culture and column at a time, always covering the other column, eliciting and recording the observations quickly (as in a brainstorming session), and controlling interruptions from the other culture. Since these data will be on slides, you can always go back to them if you prefer to address outcomes before delving into aspects of process.

With regard to the cultural aspects of negotiation, this exercise dramatically makes or reinforces at least three major points:

1) How frustrating it is to deal with people whose styles differ greatly from one's own [refer to the first transparency]

2) How easy it is to be judgmental in one's observations about other cultures [refer to the second transparency "Counterparts' Style"]

3) How difficult it is to "do as the Romans do," even for a very brief period (Although the Betan style tends to differ the most from participants' usual styles, even the Alphan behavior can be challenging for some participants.)

Bonus lesson: Westerners who play a Beta role experience the "power of silence"

For features of the actual outcome, see "General Electric-Hitachi Robotics Negotiation." Note that the bargaining objectives stated in the confidential role-play materials are imaginary. The real objectives of the two companies are not known.

Option B: One Interrupted Round (Two Phases) - (Version B Materials)

Advance Preparation: None necessary.

Materials: Important --- use Version B materials for this option

    For Alpha: Public Information (in Reader), Alpha Confidential Memo, and The Alphan Negotiating Style

    For Beta: Public Information (in Reader), Beta Confidential Memo, and The Betan Negotiating Style

Number of Participants: 4 (2 per team)

Time Required:

Preparation: - for individuals to read materials: 20 mins. For each team to plan for negotiations: 25 mins.
Negotiations between teams:
    Phase 1: 7-9 mins.
    Debriefing 1: 10 mins.
    Phase 2: 20-35 mins.
    Debriefing: 20-30 mins.
Total time: 2 hrs. minimum (including setup and "shuffling" by participants)

Alternative Format:

    In advance of the session, distribute the confidential Alpha and Beta memos so that participants do not feel crunched for preparation time. Do not distribute the style sheets until the session itself, though, because they are unlikely to have as strong an impact on the participants. This format will reduce the 10 minutes spent on setup and the 45-minute, on-site preparation time.

Additional Information:

    During the team preparations, encourage students to circle the numbers in the tables that represent their given objectives (version B). They can be used as starting points for working through and understanding the tables. Also, emphasize the importance of using their prescribed styles. They should concentrate on both the style and the substance.

    Tell the participants before their preparation period that they will have 20 minutes total to negotiate. Then, once they are 7-9 minutes into their negotiations (when tension is visible), stop the action and do the "data dump" on transparencies described under Additional Information above. Set the transparencies aside, and direct the participants to return to their negotiations to try to reach an agreement in the next 20 minutes. They can let their Alpha and

Beta styles recede (not adhere to them rigidly) and should concentrate on reaching an agreement.

For the debriefing, outcomes can be plotted on a plane to facilitate comparisons between the participants' results and with various other possibilities, including pareto optimal packages. Cultural aspects of the negotiation process can be developed by going back to the transparencies and using them in the ways described under One Continuous Round.

GENERAL ELECTRIC-HITACHI ROBOTICS NEGOTIATIONS[1]

(1980-1981, 1982)

CHRONOLOGY

April, 1980
- GE asks Hitachi to license its technology and to provide OEM supply of its industrial robots;
- GE team staffed by future Automation System Group;
- Hitachi team headed by manager of Industrial Components and Equipment Group and includes manager of Narashino Works (makers of robots) and his technical engineers

April, 1981
- GE establishes new department, "Automation System Group" with Mirabal as head;
- GE introduces multi-arm, light assembly system called Pragma (manufactured with technology licensed from Italy's OEA SpA)

July, 1981
- Initial GE-Hitachi agreement reached

August 4, 1981
- Announcement of agreement

THE (1981) AGREEMENT

A. OEM supply of robots to GE by Hitachi

    1 Number of models: 3* general process; intelligent, seam-tracking, arc-welding (Mr. Aros); and spraying
    2 Quantity of units per year: 200? ["several hundred" over 2-3 yrs.]
    3 Territory: worldwide
    4 Label: GE
    5 Initial delivery date: Fall, 1981

*(as a result of a November, 1982 renegotiation, 4th and 5th models were added to the OEM supply agreement)

B Licensing of Hitachi robotics technology by GE

    1 Technology for advanced, programmable robots for use in arc-welding and in painting
    2 Proprietary know-how (patent): included
    3 Territory: worldwide
    4 Nonexclusive

---

[1] Copyright 1988, 1991, Stephen E. Weiss and Thomas N. Gladwin. Used with permission.

5   Royalties: [not announced, "top secret"]
6   Duration: 7 years, with option to renew

(GE did not agree to share its vision technology with Hitachi)

AFTERMATH

October, 1982
- CEO Jack Welch of GE sees market for factory automation products and services reaching $4 bn. in 1982, $30 bn. in 1990, which analysts consider optimistic because of lack of capital spending;
- GE wants 25% of market, but out of 75 company contacts, GE now has only 9 projects, 4 of them in GE's own plants
- GE has spent $1 billion to automate its own factories plus $500 mn. to acquire other concerns in factory automation; has 200 robots in its plants; est. 1000 by 1984

November, 1982
- OEM supply terms of original GE-Hitachi agreement renegotiated; two products added

November, 1983
- Westinghouse acquires Unimation Inc., which introduced the first industrial robot in the 1950's, for $107 mn.

March, 1984
- Robotics industry in US lost $83 mn. (49% of sales) in 1983, according to the International Trade Commission; actual domestic sales for 1983 were $137 million, although US Dept. of Commerce had predicted $270 mn.
- Sales of US-produced robots up 10% in 1983, but imports from Japan, W. Germany, Norway, and Sweden rose 92%
- 65% of working robots in world made and used in Japan

Sept 19, 1984
- GE and Ungermann-Bass form joint venture to develop network system to link factory automation equipment: GE contributes $6 mn.; for over 50% ownership, U-B contributes its technology and staff

March, 1986
- Since 1980, 100-200 new companies have entered machine vision business (camera-computer hookups); mergers and failures expected
- GE reportedly cuts back on its marketing efforts for machine vision systems; reportedly unsuccessful in efforts to sell complete automation packages (design through to shipping) adaptation of machines also reported to be problematic because makers do not understand environment or task, and companies not adequately training employees (GM has about 500 machine vision systems; wants 44,000)

June 6, 1986
- GE and Fanuc establish joint venture (GE-Fanuc Automation Corporation) in Charlottesville to sell machine-control equipment and systems; capitalized at $200 mn.

July, 1986
- GE has had losses of $120 mn. in automation market and still does not rank within top ten

August 9, 1986
- GE-Fanuc Robotics, US market leader, restructures and lays off 30% of its work force as GM cuts its capital spending

May, 1987
- Worldwide sales of automation equipment, including computer run machine tools, in 1986 estimated at $37.8 bn.; estimated 1987 sales for GMF Robotics are about $100 mn., representing a 35% drop off the 1986 total

June 6, 1987
- Westinghouse licenses to Prab Robots Inc. the right to make, sell and service its Unimate line of heavy-duty robots;
- Westinghouse closes a plant, lays off 350 robot sales for 1987 expected to be 30% below 1986 mark of $580 mn.; GMF Robotics, the industry leader, and Cincinnati Milacron, Inc, have sales of $186 mn. and $80 mn., respectively

IMPORTANT NOTE: BE SURE TO USE THE CORRECT VERSION OF THE MATERIALS FOR THE EXERCISE OPTION THAT YOU HAVE CHOSEN. USE THE VERSION (A) MATERIALS FOR OPTION A (ONE CONTINUOUS ROUND) AND THE VERSION (B) MATERIALS FOR OPTION B (ONE INTERRUPTED ROUND).

ROLE INFORMATION FOR ALPHA INC.

EXERCISE 17(VERSION A): ALPHA BETA

TO:
DATE: 1981
FROM: VP, Marketing

RE: Upcoming Negotiations with Beta Inc.

As you know, we initially approached, and have held preliminary discussions with, Beta Inc. on a possible robot manufacturing and marketing tie-up. Over the past five months, some very tentative understandings have been reached on the general nature of a collaborative arrangement, but the details still need to be worked out. Your negotiation team will soon go to Beta to discuss them. We would like you to wrap the deal up on this trip.

Our long-range strategic objective is to become a very profitable, innovative, global, full-service supplier of automation equipment and systems. We believe leadership in equipping the "factory of the future" will come by putting more pieces of the automation puzzle together than any other firm. Even in the robotics portion of this business, we believe that the key to success lies in having a broad range of models to offer industrial customers. We have also determined that we must get into the market now, not five years from now. We must accumulate experience and attempt to establish ourselves as the first and favored supplier to companies turning to automation to boost their quality and productivity.

Our top management has considered a variety of ways to achieve these goals. Our own robotics development program has begun to look too slow off the mark. Exciting things will pour out of the labs and into production in 3 to 4 years, but at the moment, the company cannot rely just on in-house capabilities. To establish an initial market presence, to learn the business and to bridge the transitional R & D gap, we must acquire and exploit now the leading edge robotics technology of other firms.

Licensing the best available technology, particularly from leading foreign firms, seems to make sense. After all, we have one of the largest industrial sales, distribution and service networks in Alpha and have more experience in selling factory automation packages than any other firm in the world. These qualifications have made us quite an attractive potential partner in the eyes of several foreign robot producers, including Beta Inc., whom we view as the leader in the field because of its broad line of high quality, proven and cost-competitive robots.

Our preliminary talks with Beta Inc. led to the following *tentative* agreements:

1) The tie-up over 7 years will proceed in two phases: a) in Phase 1 (Years 1-4), we will receive fully-assembled Beta Inc. robots for sale under our own brand name; b) in Phase 2 (Years 5-7), we will begin producing these robots ourselves in Alpha using Beta technology and key components;

2) The tie-up will focus on robots that Beta Inc. currently has on the market; and

3) The agreement will be nonexclusive, that is, Beta Inc. will be allowed to enter the Alphan market directly at any time and allowed to tie up with other Alphan firms.

The still undecided issues include (at least) these four:

1) **The number of different models involved** (we would like the number to be large, say 6 or 7, given our full line or "supermarket of automation" philosophy);
2) **The quantity of Beta Inc. units to be imported by Alpha during Phase 1** given market and other uncertainties, we would like to start with a small number (which includes all models), say 150 per year, and to increase the number as the market grows;
3) **The royalty rate to be paid to Beta during Phase 2** (we believe a rate of 3% on gross sales is reasonable); and
4) **Access to vision technology** (Beta Inc. has been hinting that it wants access to our proprietary research advances in artificial vision for robots, but since it may be the key to achieving significant innovation in robotics several years from now, we really do **not** want to share any of our advances).

I am confident that you will negotiate effectively, and I look forward to hearing back from you about the discussions.

THE ALPHA NEGOTIATING STYLE

Alphans generally see negotiation as a competitive process of offers and counteroffers in which one party's gains are losses for the other. Concerned about "getting the job done," Alphans concentrate on substantive types of issues such as price and quantity.

Negotiators from the Alpha culture typically use a "style" (set of behaviors) that is *individual, informal, impatient, direct, emotional,* and *aggressive*. It is vitally important that your team exhibit this style in today's negotiation with Beta Inc. Guidelines are provided below. Discuss each guideline with your teammate(s) and plan how each will be followed during the negotiating session. A little practice beforehand may be useful.

In the negotiations with Beta, you must behave:

1. **INDIVIDUALLY** -- Initiative is expected from each of you; you each have individual responsibilities and can make individual contributions. The words "I" and "you" should be prominent in your discussions at the bargaining table. Decisions by your side can be made either by voting (one person-one vote) or independently by the appointed group leader.

2. **INFORMALLY** -- Alphans don't attach much importance or significance to ceremony, protocol, tradition or formalized social rules. In fact, you consider a formal style to be pompous and arrogant. Alphans are easy-going, casual, relaxed, and friendly people; they like to kid and joke around. You greet people with vigorous handshakes and slaps on the back. With the Betans today, get on a first name basis as soon as possible.

3. **IMPATIENTLY** -- To be idle is wasteful and nonproductive in Alpha: "time is money." You want to get right down to business. Show annoyance when confronted with delay or opposition. But don't "cry over spilt milk." You are willing to make concessions throughout a negotiation. The idea is to settle one issue and move on to the next. What you want is an effective total package obtained in the most efficient manner possible.

4. **DIRECTLY** -- In the Alphan culture, it is a matter of honor to "get the cards on the table." No matter how much it hurts, the truth is "good for you," and it is a sign of strength and maturity to give and receive negative feedback. In today's meeting, "tell it like it is" and minimize ambiguity and uncertainty. Be completely open, explicit, and frank. Don't hesitate to "clear the air" if necessary.

5. **EMOTIONALLY** -- Alphans are quick to get angry or happy. They tend to be extroverts and show emotion easily, exuberantly and rapidly. Alphans also tend to be confident and optimistic. Enter the negotiation room today with confidence and talk assertively. (Remember that sincerity and warmth are also a big part of your style.)

6. **AGGRESSIVELY** -- Taking risks, being active, and using power intelligently are all virtues in the Alphan culture. You are full of enterprise and initiative. You are ready and willing to take issue, engage in direct action, and "wheel and deal." To persuade others, you are used to employing bluffs, threats and warnings.

ROLE INFORMATION FOR BETA INC.
EXERCISE 17(VERSION A): ALPHA BETA

TO:
DATE: 1981
FROM: VP, Marketing

RE: Upcoming Negotiations with Alpha Inc.

As you know, we were approached by, and held preliminary discussions with, Alpha Inc. on a possible robot manufacturing and marketing tie-up. Some very tentative understandings have been reached during the past five months regarding the general nature of a collaborative arrangement. You will be responsible for taking it from here to work out the details when the Alpha Inc. negotiating team comes here.

Our topmost need is to attain greater scale economies in production by significantly boosting overseas sales of robots. We especially want to develop a presence in the currently small but rapidly growing Alphan market. This implies, of course, the need for a high quality, industrial sales distribution and service network. The options of exporting directly to Alpha, establishing a joint venture there, or forming a wholly-owned subsidiary there are all suboptimal for a variety of reasons, including the difficulties in servicing robots from overseas, the somewhat inefficient current size of the Alphan market, and the pervasive cultural differences involved. So, like other Betan robot producers, we have decided that the Alphan market at this time can probably best be served via a licensing arrangement with a local Alphan company. We can offer that company proven, high quality robots, either in the form of fully assembled units or the technology and components needed to produce them.

Alpha Inc. looks like an ideal candidate to become our licensee--it has the desired technical competence, industrial marketing expertise, service network, quality control, distribution system, general management and business reputation. We are a bit concerned, however, that by helping Alpha Inc. we may create a competitive monster that comes back to haunt us in the future.

Our preliminary talks with Alpha Inc. led to the following *tentative* agreements:

1) The tie-up over 7 years will proceed in two phases: a) in Phase 1 (Years 1-4), Alpha Inc. will receive our robots, fully assembled, for sale under Alpha's own brand name; b) in Phase 2 (Years 5-7), Alpha will begin producing its own robots in Alpha using our technology and key components;

2) The tie-up will focus on robots that we are currently selling in the Betan market; and

3) The agreement will be nonexclusive, meaning that we can enter the Alphan market directly at any time and can tie up with other Alphan firms.

The still undecided issues include (at least) these four:

1) **The number of different models involved** (we would like the number to be small, say 4 at the most, given the advantages of long production runs);

2) **The quantity of our units to be imported by Alpha during Phase 1** (we would like the number (including all models) to be as relatively large, say 250 per year, given our desire for rapid growth and deep penetration);

3) **The royalty rate to be paid to us during Phase 2** (we believe a rate of 5% on gross sales is just and reasonable); and

4) **Access to vision technology** (we would like complete access to Alpha Inc.'s R&D advances in artificial vision (worth US$30 million) and the opportunity to sell vision-equipped robots in all viable markets).

I am confident that you will negotiate effectively, and I look forward to hearing back from you about the discussions.

THE BETAN NEGOTIATING STYLE

Betans see "negotiation" as an irrational, fluid and face-threatening process. They value harmonious (nonconflictual) personal relationships, so they tend to infer others' positions indirectly and adjust to the situation. Information is valued and expected to reveal "best solutions."

Negotiators from Beta culture typically use a "style" (set of behaviors) that is *collective, formal, patient, indirect, unemotional* and *passive*. It is vitally important that your team exhibit this style in today's negotiation with Alpha Inc. Guidelines are provided below. Discuss each guideline with your teammate(s) and plan how each will be followed during the negotiating session. A little practice beforehand may be useful.

In the negotiations with Alpha, you must behave:

1. **COLLECTIVELY** -- Loyalty to the group takes precedence over personal feelings. Use the word "we" today, not "I." Any decisions by your side must be reached via group consensus. If you cannot agree, then defer the decision. Remember the Betan proverb: "The nail that sticks up is hit."

2. **FORMALLY** -- Betans are "polite to a fault." You follow fixed customs, rules and ceremonies. When greeting Alphan negotiators today, bow several times (from the waist, with your arms at your sides and your back and neck straight--try it). Other formalities include use of last names (using first names is embarrassing for you), the exchange of calling cards, and sitting through the negotiation with erect posture.

3. **PATIENTLY** -- Patience and endurance are cardinal Betan virtues. Start the negotiation session with a discussion of something completely unrelated to the business deal. Later, stick with your demands as long as you can; you have faith in the righteousness of your goals and positions--they are just, proper and fair. Betans seldom make a first concession; make any concessions only at the very end of the bargaining session.

4. **INDIRECTLY** -- Ask many questions, while offering little information. Betans are tentative, vague and play hard to read. Don't look members of the Alpha team in the eye when you talk to them (you think that would be aggressive and individualistic); instead look down. Say "yes" when you mean "I hear you talking" or "I'm trying to understand." "No" is hardly ever used in Beta because answers in the complete negative lead to embarrassment and loss of face. Instead of "no," say "that would be very difficult."

5. **UNEMOTIONALLY** -- Do not show emotion easily or quickly. Betans go to great lengths to hide their inner feelings ("an able hawk hides his talons"). You limit facial expressions, emphasize reserve and modesty, and do not laugh easily with strangers. Nor do you openly disagree or lose your temper in a negotiation session: "a short temper means a lost spirit."

6. **PASSIVELY** -- Betans dislike crude or Machiavellian tactics such as bluffs, threats and escalating demands ("crude tactics cause great injuries"); bold uses of power; and excessively logical people. When pressed or challenged, try very hard not to get flustered, and instead of arguing back, try to change the subject or just remain quiet. You know how to pause, wait and experience long periods before proceeding with further talk.

ROLE INFORMATION FOR ALPHA INC.

EXERCISE 17(VERSION B): ALPHA BETA

TO:
DATE: 1981
FROM: VP, Marketing

RE: Upcoming Negotiations with Beta Inc.

As you know, we initially approached, and have held preliminary discussions with, Beta Inc. on a possible robot manufacturing and marketing tie-up. Over the past five months, some very tentative understandings have been reached on the general nature of a collaborative arrangement, but the details still need to be worked out. Your negotiation team will soon go to Beta to discuss them. We would like you to wrap the deal up on this trip.

Our long-range strategic objective is to become a very profitable, innovative, global, full-service supplier of automation equipment and systems. We believe leadership in equipping the "factory of the future" will come by putting more pieces of the automation puzzle together than any other firm. Even in the robotics portion of this business, we believe that the key to success lies in having a broad range of models to offer industrial customers. We have also determined that we must get into the market now, not five years from now. We must accumulate experience and attempt to establish ourselves as the first and favored supplier to companies turning to automation to boost their quality and productivity.

Our top management has considered a variety of ways to achieve these goals. Our own robotics development program has begun to look too slow off the mark. Exciting things will pour out of the labs and into production in 3 to 4 years, but at the moment, the company cannot rely just on in-house capabilities. To establish an initial market presence, to learn the business and to bridge the transitional R & D gap, we must acquire and exploit now the leading edge robotics technology of other firms.

Licensing the best available technology, particularly from leading foreign firms, seems to make sense. After all, we have one of the largest industrial sales, distribution and service networks in Alpha and have more experience in selling factory automation packages than any other firm in the world. These qualifications have made us quite an attractive potential partner in the eyes of several foreign robot producers, including Beta Inc., whom we view as the leader in the field because of its broad line of high quality, proven and cost-competitive robots.

Our preliminary talks with Beta Inc. led to the following *tentative* agreements:

1) The tie-up over 7 years will proceed in two phases: a) in Phase 1 (Years 1-4), we will receive fully-assembled Beta Inc. robots for sale under our own brand name; b) in Phase 2 (Years 5-7), we will begin producing these robots ourselves in Alpha using Beta technology and key components;
2) The tie-up will focus on robots that Beta Inc. currently has on the market; and

3) The agreement will be nonexclusive, that is, Beta Inc. will be allowed to enter the Alphan market directly at any time and allowed to tie up with other Alphan firms.

The still undecided issues include (at least) these five:

1) **The number of different models involved** (we would like the number to be large, say 6 or 7, given our full line or "supermarket of automation" philosophy);
2) **The quantity of Beta Inc. units to be imported by Alpha during Phase 1** (given market and other uncertainties, we would like to start with a small number (which includes all models), say 150 per year, and to increase the number as the market grows);
3) **The unit price to be paid to Beta** (we would like the lowest possible, assume one price for all models);
4) **The royalty rate to be paid to Beta during Phase 2** (we believe a rate of 3% on gross sales is reasonable); and
5) **Access to vision technology** (Beta Inc. has been hinting that it wants access to our proprietary research advances in artificial vision for robots, but since it may be the key to achieving significant innovation in robotics several years from now, we really do not want to share any of our advances).

Financial consequences of various possible arrangements appear in attached tables prepared by our staff.

I am confident that you will negotiate effectively, and I look forward to hearing back from you about the discussions.

ALPHA INC.

FINANCIAL PROJECTIONS FOR ALPHA-BETA ROBOT TIE-UP

PHASE 1 (YEARS 1-4): PROFIT FROM SALES OF ROBOTS SOURCED FROM BETA

Assumptions:

A. Units can generally be sold retail for $100,000. If they are purchased from Beta at $70,000, with ancillary costs of $10,000, Alpha can make a profit of $20,000 per unit.
B. To sell additional units past a certain level of demand, Alpha must discount the unit price, even to the point of taking a loss on these units.
C. Projected aggregate (4-year) profit is based on both the aggregate profit (unadjusted) in Table 1 and the adjustment derived from the unit price negotiated with Beta (see Table 2).

Table 1. AGGREGATE (4-YEAR) PROFIT (unadjusted) (US$ millions)

	\multicolumn{6}{c}{Total Number of Units Sold Over 4 Years}
# of Models	600	800	1000	1200	1400	1600
1	4.5	.6	-3.4	-7.4	-11.4	-15.4
2	12.0	13.3	13.2	9.2	5.2	1.2
3	12.0	16.0	17.9	17.9	16.8	12.8
4	12.0	16.0	20.0	20.5	20.5	19.3
5	12.0	16.0	20.0	21.2	21.2	21.1
6	12.0	16.0	20.0	21.9	21.9	21.9
7	12.0	16.0	20.0	22.6	22.6	22.6

Table 2. ADJUSTMENT TO AGGREGATE (4-YEAR) PROFIT (US$ millions)

	\multicolumn{6}{c}{Total Number of Units Sold Over 4 Years}
Beta's Unit Price	600	800	1000	1200	1400	1600
75,000	-3.0	-4.0	-5.0	-6.0	-7.0	-8.0
74,000	-2.4	-3.2	-4.0	-4.8	-5.6	-6.4
73,000	-1.8	-2.4	-3.0	-3.6	-4.2	-4.8
72,000	-1.2	-1.6	-2.0	-2.4	-2.8	-3.2
71,000	-0.6	-0.8	-1.0	-1.2	-1.4	-1.6
70,000	0	0	0	0	0	0
69,000	0.6	.8	1.0	1.2	1.4	1.6
68,000	1.2	1.6	2.0	2.4	2.8	3.2
67,000	1.8	2.4	3.0	3.6	4.2	4.8
66,000	2.4	3.2	4.0	4.8	5.6	6.4
65,000	3.0	4.0	5.0	6.0	7.0	8.0

(Note: This adjustment to profit is required regardless of the # of models sourced

PHASE 2 (YEARS 5-7): PROFIT FROM SALES OF ALPHA-MADE ROBOTS

Assumptions:

A. Royalty payments are based on suggested retail unit price of $100,000, regardless of any price discounting that Alpha does.
B. Our projected sales for this 3-year period: 2000 units.

Alpha's Aggregate (3-Year) Profit

Royalty Rate (Paid to Beta)	from Alpha-made Robot Sales (US$ millions)
3.0 %	34
3.5	33
4.0	32
4.5	31
5.0	30

VISION TECHNOLOGY

Assumptions:

A. Alpha Inc.'s total cost of developing vision technology: $30 million. Marketable in Year 8.
B. Beta Inc. can develop vision technology on its own for $30 million and also market it in Year 8, so the profit shares below will occur whether or not Alpha shares its technology.
C. Estimated capitalized net profits to be derived from vision technology over its entire useful life: $100 million in Alpha market, $100 million in rest of world.

Profit shares (in US$ millions) are expected to be as follows:

		Manufacturer		
Market	Alpha Inc.	Beta Inc.	Others	Total
Alpha	$50	$40	$10	$100
Rest of world	50	40	10	100
Total	$100	$80	$20	$200

Note: In considering vision technology for this negotiation (and to calculate $ consequences below), focus on 1 or 2 factors: 1) Alpha's savings in R&D cost (if Alpha and Beta agree to share in some % the $30 million total cost); and 2) net $ change in Alpha's profit shares (if, as part of a technology-sharing agreement, certain territories are restricted).

TOTAL VALUE OF THE TIE-UP

To calculate the projected total value to Alpha of a package proposed with Beta, add:

    _____Unadjusted profit from Table 1 (Years 1-4) associated with the proposal

+ _____Adjustment from Table 2 associated with the proposed unit price

+ _____Projected profit from sales in Years 5-7, given the proposed royalty rate

+ _____Consequences of arrangements concerning vision technology

= _____TOTAL VALUE

THE ALPHA NEGOTIATING STYLE

Alphans generally see negotiation as a competitive process of offers and counteroffers in which one party's gains are losses for the other. Concerned about "getting the job done," Alphans concentrate on substantive types of issues such as price and quantity.

Negotiators from the Alpha culture typically use a "style" (set of behaviors) that is *individual, informal, impatient, direct, emotional*, and *aggressive*. It is vitally important that your team exhibit this style in today's negotiation with Beta Inc. Guidelines are provided below. Discuss each guideline with your teammate(s) and plan how each will be followed during the negotiating session. A little practice beforehand may be useful.

In the negotiations with Beta, you must behave:

1. **INDIVIDUALLY** -- Initiative is expected from each of you; you each have individual responsibilities and can make individual contributions. The words "I" and "you" should be prominent in your discussions at the bargaining table. Decisions by your side can be made either by voting (one person-one vote) or independently by the appointed group leader.

2. **INFORMALLY** -- Alphans don't attach much importance or significance to ceremony, protocol, tradition or formalized social rules. In fact, you consider a formal style to be pompous and arrogant. Alphans are easy-going, casual, relaxed, and friendly people; they like to kid and joke around. You greet people with vigorous handshakes and slaps on the back. With the Betans today, get on a first name basis as soon as possible.

3. **IMPATIENTLY** -- To be idle is wasteful and nonproductive in Alpha: "time is money." You want to get right down to business. Show annoyance when confronted with delay or opposition. But don't "cry over spilt milk." You are willing to make concessions throughout a negotiation. The idea is to settle one issue and move on to the next. What you want is an effective total package obtained in the most efficient manner possible.

4. **DIRECTLY** -- In the Alphan culture, it is a matter of honor to "get the cards on the table." No matter how much it hurts, the truth is "good for you," and it is a sign of strength and maturity to give and receive negative feedback. In today's meeting, "tell it like it is" and minimize ambiguity and uncertainty. Be completely open, explicit, and frank. Don't hesitate to "clear the air" if necessary.

5. **EMOTIONALLY** -- Alphans are quick to get angry or happy. They tend to be extroverts and show emotion easily, exuberantly and rapidly. Alphans also tend to be confident and optimistic. Enter the negotiation room today with confidence and talk assertively. (Remember that sincerity and warmth are also a big part of your style.)

6. **AGGRESSIVELY** -- Taking risks, being active, and using power intelligently are all virtues in the Alphan culture. You are full of enterprise and initiative. You are ready and willing to take issue, engage in direct action, and "wheel and deal." To persuade others, you are used to employing bluffs, threats and warnings.

ROLE INFORMATION FOR BETA INC.

EXERCISE 17(VERSION B): ALPHA BETA

TO:
DATE: 1981
FROM: VP, Marketing

RE: Upcoming Negotiations with Alpha Inc.

As you know, we were approached by, and held preliminary discussions with, Alpha Inc. on a possible robot manufacturing and marketing tie-up. Some very tentative understandings have been reached during the past five months regarding the general nature of a collaborative arrangement. You will be responsible for taking it from here to work out the details when the Alpha Inc. negotiating team comes here.

Our topmost need is to attain greater scale economies in production by significantly boosting overseas sales of robots. We especially want to develop a presence in the currently small but rapidly growing Alphan market. This implies, of course, the need for a high quality, industrial sales distribution and service network. The options of exporting directly to Alpha, establishing a joint venture there, or forming a wholly-owned subsidiary there are all suboptimal for a variety of reasons, including the difficulties in servicing robots from overseas, the somewhat inefficient current size of the Alphan market, and the pervasive cultural differences involved. So, like other Betan robot producers, we have decided that the Alphan market at this time can probably best be served via a licensing arrangement with a local Alphan company. We can offer that company proven, high quality robots, either in the form of fully assembled units or the technology and components needed to produce them.

Alpha Inc. looks like an ideal candidate to become our licensee--it has the desired technical competence, industrial marketing expertise, service network, quality control, distribution system, general management and business reputation. We are a bit concerned, however, that by helping Alpha Inc. we may create a competitive monster that comes back to haunt us in the future.

Our preliminary talks with Alpha Inc. led to the following *tentative* agreements:

1) The tie-up over 7 years will proceed in two phases: a) in Phase 1 (Years 1-4), Alpha Inc. will receive our robots, fully assembled, for sale under Alpha's own brand name; b) in Phase 2 (Years 5-7), Alpha will begin producing its own robots in Alpha using our technology and key components;
2) The tie-up will focus on robots that we are currently selling in the Betan market; and
3) The agreement will be nonexclusive, meaning that we can enter the Alphan market directly at any time and can tie up with other Alphan firms.

The still undecided issues include (at least) these five:

1) **The number of different models involved** (we would like the number to be small, say 4 at the most, given the advantages of long production runs);
2) **The quantity of our units to be imported by Alpha during Phase 1** (we would like the number (including all models) to be as relatively large, say 250 per year, given our desire for rapid growth and deep penetration);
3) **The unit price to be paid to us** (we would like the highest possible (assume one price for all models));
4) **The royalty rate to be paid to us during Phase 2** (we believe a rate of 5% on gross sales is just and reasonable); and
5) **Access to vision technology** (we would like complete access to Alpha Inc.'s R&D advances in artificial vision (worth US$30 million) and the opportunity to sell vision-equipped robots in all viable markets).

Financial consequences of various possible arrangements appear in the attached tables prepared by our staff.

I am confident that you will negotiate effectively, and I look forward to hearing back from you about the discussions.

BETA INC.

FINANCIAL PROJECTIONS FOR ALPHA-BETA ROBOT TIE-UP

PHASE 1 (YEARS 1-4): AGGREGATE VALUE OF SUPPLYING ROBOTS TO ALPHA

Assumptions:
A. The first unit of any kind costs $65,000 to produce.
B. As production volume increases, unit cost drops.
C. The projected aggregate (4-year) value is based on both the cost savings in Table 1 and the profit in Table 2.

Table 1. AGGREGATE (4-YEAR) COST SAVINGS (US$ millions)

# of Models	600	800	1000	1200	1400	1600
1	4.8	8.4	13.8	19.4	26.0	33.6
2	2.6	4.4	6.8	9.6	13.0	16.8
3	1.8	3.1	4.9	6.6	8.9	11.5
4	1.4	2.4	3.6	5.1	6.8	8.8
5	1.2	2.0	3.0	4.2	5.6	7.2
6	1.1	1.8	2.6	3.6	4.8	6.2
7	1.0	1.6	2.3	3.2	4.2	5.4

(column header: Total Number of Units Sold Over 4 Years)

Table 2. AGGREGATE (4-YEAR) PROFIT FROM SALES TO ALPHA (US$ millions)

Beta's Unit Price	600	800	1000	1200	1400	1600
75,000	6.0	8.0	10.0	12.0	14.0	16.0
74,000	5.4	7.2	9.0	10.8	12.6	14.4
73,000	4.8	6.4	8.0	9.6	11.2	12.8
72,000	4.2	5.6	7.0	8.4	9.8	11.2
71,000	3.6	4.8	6.0	7.2	8.4	9.6
70,000	3.0	4.0	5.0	6.0	7.0	8.0
69,000	2.4	3.2	4.0	4.8	5.6	6.4
68,000	1.8	2.4	3.0	3.6	4.2	4.8
67,000	1.2	1.6	2.0	2.4	2.8	3.2
66,000	0.6	0.8	1.0	1.2	1.4	1.6
65,000	0	0	0	0	0	0

(column header: Total Number of Units Sold Over 4 Years)

(Note: These financial results occur regardless of the number of models provided to Alpha)

PHASE 2 (YEARS 5-7): ROYALTY REVENUE FOR TECHNOLOGY LICENSED TO ALPHA

Assumptions:

A. Royalty revenues are based on Alpha's projected $100,000 per unit retail selling price, regardless of any price discounting that Alpha may do.
B. Alpha expects to sell a total of 2,000 units between Years 5-7.

Royalty Rate / Expected Total (3-Year) Royalty Revenues

Royalty Rate (Paid by Alpha)	Expected Total (3-Year) Royalty Revenues (US$ million)
5.0 %	10
4.5	9
4.0	8
3.5	7
3.0	6

VISION TECHNOLOGY

Assumptions:

A. Alpha expects to bring robots equipped with artificial vision to market in Year 8.
B. Estimated cost of developing vision technology on our own: $30 million. Despite Alpha's head start, we believe we could also bring it to market in Year 8.
C. Estimated capitalized net profits to be derived from vision technology over its entire useful life: $200 million worldwide.

Profit shares (in US$ millions) are expected to be as follows:

Market	Alpha Inc.	Beta Inc.	Others	Total
Alpha	$25	$25	$10	$60
Rest of world	40	70	30	140
Total	$65	$95	$40	$200

Note: In considering vision technology for this negotiation (and to calculate $ consequences below), focus on 1 or 2 factors: 1) Beta's savings in R&D cost (if Alpha agrees to provide some % of the $30 million value); and 2) net $ change in Beta's profit shares (if, as part of a technology-sharing agreement, certain territories are restricted).

TOTAL VALUE OF THE TIE-UP

To calculate the projected total value to Beta of a package proposed with Alpha, add:

	_____	Savings from Table 1 (Years 1-4) associated with the proposal
+	_____	Profit in Table 2 associated with the proposed unit price
+	_____	Royalty revenues in Years 5-7
+	_____	Value of arrangements concerning vision technology
=	_____	TOTAL VALUE

THE BETAN NEGOTIATING STYLE

Betans see "negotiation" as an irrational, fluid and face-threatening process. They value harmonious (nonconflictual) personal relationships, so they tend to infer others' positions indirectly and adjust to the situation. Information is valued and expected to reveal "best solutions."

Negotiators from Beta culture typically use a "style" (set of behaviors) that is *collective, formal, patient, indirect, unemotional* and *passive*. It is vitally important that your team exhibit this style in today's negotiation with Alpha Inc. Guidelines are provided below. Discuss each guideline with your teammate(s) and plan how each will be followed during the negotiating session. A little practice beforehand may be useful.

In the negotiations with Alpha, you must behave:

1. **COLLECTIVELY** -- Loyalty to the group takes precedence over personal feelings. Use the word "we" today, not "I." Any decisions by your side must be reached via group consensus. If you cannot agree, then defer the decision. Remember the Betan proverb: "The nail that sticks up is hit."

2. **FORMALLY** -- Betans are "polite to a fault." You follow fixed customs, rules and ceremonies. When greeting Alphan negotiators today, bow several times (from the waist, with your arms at your sides and your back and neck straight--try it). Other formalities include use of last names (using first names is embarrassing for you), the exchange of calling cards, and sitting through the negotiation with erect posture.

3. **PATIENTLY** -- Patience and endurance are cardinal Betan virtues. Start the negotiation session with a discussion of something completely unrelated to the business deal. Later, stick with your demands as long as you can; you have faith in the righteousness of your goals and positions--they are just, proper and fair. Betans seldom make a first concession; make any concessions only at the very end of the bargaining session.

4. **INDIRECTLY** -- Ask many questions, while offering little information. Betans are tentative, vague and play hard to read. Don't look members of the Alpha team in the eye when you talk to them (you think that would be aggressive and individualistic); instead look down. Say "yes" when you mean "I hear you talking" or "I'm trying to understand." "No" is hardly ever used in Beta because answers in the complete negative lead to embarrassment and loss of face. Instead of "no," say "that would be very difficult."

5. **UNEMOTIONALLY** -- Do not show emotion easily or quickly. Betans go to great lengths to hide their inner feelings ("an able hawk hides his talons"). You limit facial expressions, emphasize reserve and modesty, and do not laugh easily with strangers. Nor do you openly disagree or lose your temper in a negotiation session: "a short temper means a lost spirit."

6. **PASSIVELY** -- Betans dislike crude or Machiavellian tactics such as bluffs, threats and escalating demands ("crude tactics cause great injuries"); bold uses of power; and excessively logical people. When pressed or challenged, try very hard not to get flustered, and instead of arguing back, try to change the subject or just remain quiet. You know how to pause, wait and experience long periods before proceeding with further talk.

EXERCISE 18
THE NEW HOUSE NEGOTIATION

Objectives

The purpose of this exercise is to provide a rich and complex negotiation situation which requires the following:

1. To extract relevant facts;
2. To decide on a strategy; and
3. To implement the strategy.

In addition, this simulation *requires the parties to work through an agent* (from the buyer's or seller's role), or to directly satisfy a constituent from the agent's role.

Group Size There are several possible variations:

1. Groups of four, assigned to buyer and seller roles, buyer's agent and seller's agent.
2. Groups of six, assigning a "husband/wife" team to buyer and seller role and single individuals to the two agents.
3. Assign extra parties as observers to groups.
4. The exercise may be done in a fishbowl format, so that only one set of buyers, sellers and agents negotiate while the rest of the class observes.

Time required Approximately 1 hour, as specified in the Operating Procedures Section.

Special Materials Copy and distribute role information from this manual.

Special Physical Requirements Breakout space for groups of 4-6 or a fishbowl setting in front of class.

Recommended Reading Assignments to Accompany This Exercise:

Readings: 3.1 (Aaronson), 3.2 (Craver), 3.3 (Dawson) 7.1 (Wokutch and Carson), 7.2 (Dees and Crampton), 9.1 (Colosi), 9.2 (Vanover)
Text: Chapters 3, 7, 9

What to Expect:

This negotiation produces traditional competitive dynamics, which are often enhanced when the parties have to "represent" the positions and interests of another party. Those who play the roles of "agents" will experience the dynamics of trying to represent what their respective "constituents" (buyers and sellers) want, while trying to get an agreement with the other agent. They then have to "sell" the agreement back to the constituent, and hence experience many of the dynamics of conflicting loyalties, compromise, etc. that is involved when one represents another in negotiation.

These dynamics can be enhanced if you have two buyers or two sellers and they disagree as to what they want. Hence the agent has to decide how to reconcile the different needs of the two buyers, how to represent both of their views at the table, and how to "sell" the agreement back to them.

These dynamics can also be enhanced if you use the fishbowl option. Negotiators now have to conduct themselves in front of an "audience" who will also provide evaluative feedback about how they are performing.

Advance Preparation

It is useful to have students read their role information in advance. It is not recommended that the Appraisal Form be given to students unless they request it.

Operating Procedures

1. Decide whether you want to do this as a multiple role-play or fishbowl setting. This will determine whether you want one set of role players, or assign roles to everyone in the class. Here are the approximate time allocations for each exercise:

Multiple Role Play Format:

Round 1:

10 minutes	Read information and familiarize self with role.
10 minutes	Buyer and seller's agents talk to their clients.
10 minutes	Agents talk to each other.

Rounds 2 and 3:

5 minutes	Buyer and seller's agents talk to their clients.
5-10 minutes	Agents talk to each other

Fishbowl Format:

Round 1:

10-15 minutes	Role players read information by themselves, rest of class (observers) are briefed.
10 minutes	Seller talks to agent in front of class.
10 minutes	Buyer talks to agent in front of class.
10 minutes	Agents talk to each other, buyers and sellers out of room.

Round 2 and 3:

5 minutes	Seller talks to agent in front of class.
5 minutes	Buyer talks to agent in front of class.
5 minutes	Agents talk to each other, buyers and sellers out of room.

2. Assign people to roles. This can be done randomly or by asking students whether they wish to be principals or agents (or observers).

   a) Buyers should also get the Buyer's Inspection Form.
   b) The "Appraisal" form can be given to the Buyers and Sellers automatically, or it can be withheld so that it is only distributed if someone asks for it! (Withholding it lets them define their own bargaining range based on their information only; giving appraisal gives them an "objective value" for the house that will tend to ground negotiations around that value.)

3. Tell parties they will negotiate in several "rounds" of discussion. Agents will first confer with principals. Then they will negotiate with each other. It is preferred that when agents negotiate, principals will be out of earshot (do this in the fishbowl variation). In the multiple role play variations, you can request this, you can allow principals to hear the negotiation but not speak, or you can let the agents control their principals as they wish.

4. Go through several rounds until agreement has been reached, the parties choose to break off negotiation, or you choose not to go further.

5. As an option, you can allow observers or class to participate between rounds, in terms of "offering advice," stop action format, etc.

Concluding the Exercise

There is a great deal that can be drawn out of this negotiation, depending on when it is used in the course. You may focus on any or all of the following points:

1. Basic negotiation strategy--distributive vs. integrative.
2. Use of distributive tactics, particularly those in which the agent plays off the principals against the opposing agent.
3. Degree to which information is disclosed truthfully vs. a great deal of bluffing and misrepresentation.
4. Effective and ineffective communication between principals and agents and between agents.
5. Understanding the dynamics of negotiation when principals are represented by agents-- how principals react, how agents react, etc.

DEBRIEFING--THE NEW HOUSE NEGOTIATION

- **WHAT NEGOTIATION STRATEGIES WERE PRIMARILY USED BY THE AGENTS WITH EACH OTHER? WERE THEY EFFECTIVE?**

- **HOW DID THE AGENTS NEGOTIATE WITH THEIR "CONSTITUENTS" (THE BUYERS AND SELLERS)?**

- **HOW MUCH TRUST WAS THERE BETWEEN THE AGENTS AND THEIR CONSTITUENTS?**

- **DID COMMUNICATIONS BREAK DOWN BETWEEN AGENTS AND CONSTITUENTS? WHAT CAUSED THIS BREAKDOWN?**

- **FOR THE "PRINCIPALS" (BUYERS OR SELLERS), WHAT WAS IT LIKE TO HAVE SOMEONE ELSE TRY TO NEGOTIATE FOR YOU? WAS THIS A SATISFACTORY OR UNSATISFACTORY EXPERIENCE?**

- **DID YOU KNOW THE APPRAISED VALUE OF THE HOUSE? HOW DID THIS AFFECT THE NEGOTIATION PROCESS?**

- **IF YOU DID THE "FISHBOWL" VARIATION, HOW DID THIS AFFECT NEGOTIATOR BEHAVIOR?**

- **DID YOU SEE EVIDENCE OF BLUFFING, MISREPRESENTATION OR OTHER "DISHONEST" BEHAVIOR? WHEN? HOW DID THIS AFFECT THE NEGOTIATIONS?**

SELLER'S SITUATION

EXERCISE 18: THE NEW HOUSE NEGOTIATION

Husband lost his job four weeks ago. He has accepted a new job in a distant city, starting in three weeks. His new salary will be $58,000 (this is a 10% increase in his pay). Wife is still employed at a job which pays $20,000 a year. She wants to quit in two weeks to pack and move to be with her husband. You would like to buy a new house in the new city, but don't believe you can make two house payments at once. Wife expects to be able to find a comparable new job within a week of beginning her search.

You have no children. You have $4,500 in savings, which you would like to add to your equity in the present house to use in making a down payment on another new home. You have two cars, one of which is paid for (a five-year-old Buick), and one of which you are making $400 monthly payments on (a one-year-old Honda Accord, loan balance, $14,000). Your only other debt is a $1,000 Master Card balance (credit limit $2,500). You paid $125,000 for this house three years ago. You anticipated a 4-5% rise in the market value of the house each year, but because of a local recession, you believe that the housing market has been flat for the past two years. Your house payments are $730 per month. There are 27 years remaining on the loan; the loan balance is $94,500. The next payment is due in seven days. You estimate your other living expenses for the next three weeks to be $800 (plus house payment and car payment) Husband's new employer will pay for all moving expenses (except those associated with selling the house), but you estimate the need to cover $1000 in out-of-pocket expenses before he is reimbursed in 30 days.

You like this house, and hate to leave it. You have put a lot of extra work into it since moving in, including building extra closet shelves and shelves in the garage, installing premium quality storm doors on front and back, installing a ceiling fan in the family room, adding accent lighting in the front and back yards, and adding a built-in microwave oven in the kitchen. You are also aware that the bath tub in the master bathroom has chronic problems with slow drainage, doors on the guest bedroom and hall closet are apparently poorly hung and do not close properly, the dishwasher has a broken latch which makes it extremely hard to open and close, and there are cracks in the plaster around the fireplace in the family room where the roof leaked last winter during an ice storm (the roof was never fixed as it apparently only leaks under the peculiar conditions of an ice storm). The roof, appliances, carpet, and paint are original. Carpet and interior paint show average wear, but should be able to go a couple of years longer before anything has to be done about them. The fan motor on the heating/air conditioner was replaced last year. Electric bills run about $200 per month in summer, and gas bills about $100 in the winter (72 degree thermostat).

You have signed a six-month contract with Agent (whose commission rate will be the standard 7%, to be paid by the Seller at closing). This means that you cannot sell the house through anyone but this agent (including selling it personally) for the next six months. House was listed for $140,000 at your request.

BUYER'S SITUATION

EXERCISE 18: THE NEW HOUSE NEGOTIATION

Husband and wife have been living in an apartment with their three-year-old son. You are looking for your first home. You want something with three bedrooms and two baths, and about 2,000 square feet. You very much desire a two-car garage with opener. Also important to you are a safe neighborhood, proximity to daycare (within 2 miles) and proximity to wife's work (within 5 miles). Husband, especially, is concerned that the house be energy efficient. Wife wants a shady back yard, and prefers nice landscaping.

Your joint income is about $48,000 per year. You have been living on a budget of approximately $3,000 per month, making $700 per month rent payments per month and $150 electric and gas payments, and saving $200 per month.

You were particularly interested in this house because the address in the multiple listings book puts it near the neighborhoods of several friends. This area of town is generally middle to upper middle class, which is important to you. This house is probably one of the least expensive in the area (which means it will probably appreciate in value), but it appears to be near the top of your price range, and will make your budget tight.

You have already looked at other houses. One of them in particular seems to come close to meeting your needs, having three bedrooms and two baths, but only a one-car garage (apparently half of the original garage was taken in to make a family room, which gives it a lot of living space). The yard is not well landscaped, but with a few hundred dollars and a lot of work, it could be made acceptable. However, this house is about 15 years old, and in a less-desirable neighborhood with some houses or lawns that are slightly run down (which will hurt its potential resale value). It *is* a viable alternative, however, being listed at $135,000. Given that the real estate market is very slow at the present time, it seems likely that this price is a bit too high.

You are interested in acquiring all the appliances in a house, if they are in good condition, as buying new refrigerator, washer and dryer could easily cost $1,500. You expect built-in range and dishwasher. You already have a counter-top model microwave oven.

Because this is your first house, you are very wary of any mechanical or structural problems in a house. You want to be sure you do not "get taken". In fact, you hope to strike a very good bargain so that you can make money on this house and move up in a few years.

You have only $8,000 in savings. You can qualify for a 5% down FHA loan, but would prefer to assume a loan to avoid paying the closing points, if you can come up with enough money to buy out seller's equity. You must give 30 days notice at your apartment complex before moving out, or will be charged an extra month's rent. You anticipate that your utility deposits will be transferable.

SELLER'S AGENT

EXERCISE 18: THE NEW HOUSE NEGOTIATION

You have had a bad year in this real estate market. You really need to get this deal put through so you can get your half of the 7% commission (which is paid by the seller), as you do not have a lot of hot deals working at the present time. On the other hand, you do not particularly like the buyer's agent, since she has beat you to the punch in several details over the past couple of years.

This house has been in multiple listings for two weeks now and has generated only three or four inquiries, no showings or offers--not unusual in the current market, but not a particularly good sign. You suspect that the price is too high. You saw a comparable house in this neighborhood stay on the market for six months before finally selling at $130,000 last month. You can get sellers an appraisal for $200 which will confirm the loan value of the house. You estimate closing costs for an assumption to be $1200 (seller's responsibility). For a new loan there would also be a 2 point (2% of loan amount) origination fee (buyer's responsibility).

The school system in this area is very progressive. Crime is low. Though traffic is a growing concern, it should not get much worse since the area has been mostly built up already.

You are aware that the potential buyers have just looked at the house, and you must get together with the sellers so you can prepare to meet with the buyer's agent.

BUYER'S AGENT

EXERCISE 18: THE NEW HOUSE NEGOTIATION

You have had a good year in this business, despite the downturn in real estate in the past couple of years. You always try to work hard for your buyers, but you know you won't make anything out of this if the house just sits there. You want these people to buy this house for some amount, and to collect your half of the 7% commission.

This house has been in multiple listings for two weeks now. You suspect that the price is too high. You saw a comparable house in this neighborhood stay on the market for six months before finally selling at $130,000 last month. Seller's closing costs would be about $1200 if their Note is assumed by buyer. If buyer has to get a new loan, they will be facing a 2 point (2% of loan value) origination fee.

Buyers have already looked at other houses. One of them in particular seems to come close to meeting their needs, having three bedrooms and two baths but only a one-car garage (apparently half of the original garage was taken in to make a family room, which gives it a lot of living space). The yard is not well-landscaped, but with a few hundred dollars and a lot of work, it could be made acceptable. However, this house is about 15 years old, and in a less desirable neighborhood with some houses or lawns that are slightly run down (which could affect the resale value, too). They seem to feel that it _is_ a viable alternative, however, being listed at $135,000. Given that the real estate market is very slow at the present time, it seems likely that the price is at least 5% too high, as sellers rarely realize the seriousness of the impact of the local recession on real estate values. The market will probably not pick up for awhile. Buyers seem willing to hold out for a while if they need to, but you would just as soon see them buy something soon so you can make some money! You have just taken them to see the house, and now you are ready to talk to them about an offer.

BUYER'S INSPECTION

EXERCISE 18: THE NEW HOUSE NEGOTIATION

Upon looking the house over, your first impression is that you like it very much and you **want** it. But you note several other specific impressions that should be weighed into your decision:

- All the trim on the outside needs to be painted--would run about $1,500 to have this professionally done (your guess).
- Carpet and interior walls are not terrible, but they are obviously original. You would really prefer to replace the carpet and have the walls repainted. Would run about $2,500 for carpet and $2,500 for professional paint job (your guess).
- A couple of doors do not hang correctly. Also there has been a ceiling leak near the fireplace. Has the foundation settled? Repair of the ceiling and roof would run about $500 (your guess).
- There is no shade on the back of the house at mid-day--this adds to the cooling load on the air conditioner.
- It is a **must** to have the draperies which cover the back windows (though when you close them to keep the sun out, you cannot **see** out).
- There are especially nice shelves in the closets.
- No evident problems with mechanical or electrical.
- Outside accent lights are a nice touch--but do they work?
- Yard looks OK, though pretty simple landscaping.
- Seller's appliances (refrigerator, washer, dryer) looked to be in good shape- -would meet your needs if you could get them in the deal.

You must now meet with your agent to discuss what offer you will make.

APPRAISAL

EXERCISE 18: THE NEW HOUSE NEGOTIATION

(Optional Information for Seller's Agent)

You had the house appraised by a reliable appraiser. It appraised for $135,000. You don't see any point in getting another appraisal because experience tells you that it won't differ by more than 1%.

EXERCISE 19
EUROTECHNOLOGIES, INC.

Objectives

To provide a negotiation opportunity to fully explore the dynamics of collaborative negotiation.

Group Size Any size. Each negotiating team should have 3-4 parties (paired teams of 6-8).

Time Required Minimum 60 minutes to read and have students prepare in teams, minimum 90-120 minutes to negotiate, 45-60 minutes to debrief. All but the debriefing can be done outside of class.

Special Materials Copy of role play briefing sheets (at the back of this note).

Special Physical Requirements Separate territories for groups to meet and to negotiate, out of earshot of other groups. If at all possible, each room should have a flipchart and markers. Flipchart output should be brought to the debriefing session. One of the instructional points here is that the use of a flipchart or blackboard often makes it easier to organize complex arguments and help the parties find integrative agreements.

Recommended Reading Assignments to Accompany This Exercise:

Readings: 4.2 (Anderson), 4.3 (Rubin), 8.2 (Sheppard), 11.2 (Koh), 11.3 (Frank)
Text: Chapter 4, 11

What to Expect

This is a negotiation scenario between the management of a firm and a group of key employees. Management finds it necessary to move the R&D laboratories to a different facility 40 miles away, and a key group of R&D scientists refuse to move. The negotiation is focused on finding creative ways for the parties to meet their interests.

Operating Procedures

Read this note over quickly.

Read the Eurotechnologies role play scenario, particularly the Background Information.

Remember that students may use "out of class time" to:
    Read role-play materials
    Meet with their teammates to prepare strategy
    Actually conduct the role play

Create the context for why students are doing the role play--e.g. as an exercise in negotiation, collaborative negotiation, etc. You may assign theory, readings, etc. in advance if you wish. We advise that you specifically instruct students to attempt to model a win-win (integrative) bargaining process in their role play. It will defeat the purpose of this scenario if you permit students to prepare for the role play as a traditional competitive, distributive negotiation.

Give students sufficient time to read the information and study it. Also give time to prepare in teams (e.g. discuss strategy, pick negotiators to play each of the key characters). However, we do not recommend long preparation periods--e.g. no more than 45 minutes. Our experience is that the longer the preparation time, the more rigid groups become in their negotiating positions, and the harder it is to "loosen them up" into more win-win negotiation modes.

Check the financial page of your local newspaper for the current value of the Deutschmark against your local currency. Being able to do the translation may help students interpret the value of their concessions in local currency. At this writing (late 1997), the DM was worth about $.55 U.S.

Assign students to negotiation "territories". Territories should have a blackboard, flipchart or other visual aid to enable them to create work document and output as they work. Tell students they have approximately 2-3 hours (optimally) to negotiate the problem. (Parties cannot negotiate this case in less than 90 minutes, and may take up to 3-4 hours if they become bogged down in competitive dynamics).

Encourage participants to use the flip charts and blackboards to define a problem, and to work out "solutions" to a problem. To the degree possible, observe selected groups to determine what kind of progress they are making. Be ready to make input on this after the groups have ended their negotiation.

Concluding the Exercise

Have groups return to the main classroom. First, ask for groups that did not settle. Determine how far they got, how and why negotiations broke down, and what factors appeared to contribute to their failure to agree.

Ask those groups which settled to present their solution. They should also comment on:
How satisfied is each side with the solution they achieved?
What were easiest and most difficult parts of the negotiation in achieving the solution?
If they had it to do over again, what would they do?
Integrate theoretical material on integrative bargaining, collaboration, etc. and apply to the specific strategy and tactics used by groups to the conceptual models employed.

BIBLIOGRAPHY

Fisher, R., Ury, W. & Patton, B. (1991). *Getting to Yes*. Second Edition. Boston: Houghton Mifflin.

Gray, B. (1988). *Collaboration*. San Francisco: Jossey Bass.

Lax, D. and Sebenius, J. (1986). *The Manager as Negotiator*. New York: Free Press.(see esp. the sections on creating value).

Pruitt, D.C. (1983). "Achieving Integrative Agreements." In M.A. Bazerman and R.J. Lewicki (Eds.), *Negotiating in Organizations*. Beverly Hills: Sage Publications.

Scheidel, Thomas & Crowell, Laura. (1979). *Discussing and Deciding: A Desk Book for Group Leaders and Members*. New York: MacMillan.

Weiss, S. (1994) "Negotiating with Romans". Part I. *Sloan Management Review*, Winter, Vol. 35, # 2, 51-61.

Weiss, S. (1994). "Negotiating with Romans". Part II. *Sloan Management Review*, Spring, Vol. 35, # 3, 85-99.

ROLE POSITION FOR THE R&D SCIENTIST COMMITTEE
(O'HARA, LOEW, BERKOWITZ, SHARFSTEIN, JONES, AND BLACK)

EXERCISE 19: EUROTECHNOLOGIES, INC.

You are to negotiate a solution to the problem with the Management Team if possible. Assign roles to your group members which correlate with the characters listed above. If you have more characters than group members, decide which characters to delete. You may choose to use your own names and simply represent the interests of R and D without adopting individual character identities.

As stated in the background information, there are six of you who signed the letter as the Research and Development Employment Committee

- J. O'Hara, age 52, 1 year seniority; has personal and social ties to Munich that s/he does not want to break, and which will be strained by a long commute.
- H. Loew, age 49, 24 years seniority; is the most likely to succeed the current Vice President for Research and Development.
- L. Berkowitz, age 42, 15 years seniority; has children in high school and worried about moving them at this point.
- A. Sharfstein, age 47, 22 years seniority; has children in high school and worried about moving his children at this point.
- F. Jones, age 36, 5 years seniority;
- T. Black, age 32, 4 years seniority; spouse is employed as a Radiologist at Munich General Hospital near downtown, and does not want to change locations if at all possible.

You are interested in saving the company. Your mass defection from the firm would surely end its existence. However, it is clear the Management does not understand how the move to Wasserburg they are considering would affect your morale and reduce your effectiveness in providing high quality research and development for the firm. In going to the upcoming meeting, your Committee has agreed to the following discussion points:

- Remember that you have offered to take *up to* a 20% pay cut per person to stay in Munich. Any negotiations should take that offer into consideration. Estimated dollar value of this "give back" is DM 366,750 for the group.

- The last thing on your mind is to put the company in a disadvantageous position with its competitors. You believe that you are doing the best thing possible by strongly requesting an alternative to the relocation, so you don't lose the critical professional stimulation which is so vital to your work.

- Moving from downtown Munich would put you at a significant disadvantage in gaining new ideas, information, and interaction with your peers, particularly those outside of the company. Not only "business lunches," but informal contact with peers at Munich University and other similar institutions has done more for your group's growth and development than all of the journals and technical seminars you could pursue. This proximity to fellow professionals and to the ideas generated by such interaction is essential to your individual personal growth and to the long-run excellence of the company.

- If moving to Wasserburg is the only option, it would require either a very difficult commute for some of you--particularly during a period when you might be spending morning, noon, night and weekends to meet some deadline or solve some problems. In certain cases, houses would have to be sold and families moved. A few of you have children in high school, and do not want to move the children at this time. Others are concerned about the quality of schools in the more rural Wasserburg area.

After agreeing to these points, you decided as a group to try to negotiate for some alternative other than moving to Wasserburg. You believe that the money slated for improving the Wasserburg facility would be better spent on an alternative solution, and you wish to explore a creative approach to solving the problem.

If you are unsuccessful discovering another solution to the problem, you believe that some members of the R&D staff would agree to the move if the following accommodations from the company were a part of the package. If you can find an alternative to moving, these concessions may be irrelevant. Key items on the list include the following:

- Annual funding for a research seminar series to attract scientists to Wasserburg, to enhance the stimulating nature of the climate. It is estimated that a well-funded seminar would cost approximately DM 16,300 annually.

- Personal days for each employee to visit other scientists in Europe and elsewhere. An allotment of up to 10 "personal enrichment days" has been suggested, plus DM 4075 per employee per year for travel costs on these days.

- Improved food service facilities at Wasserburg, including a separate cafeteria for scientists and executives, completed as quickly as possible.

- Laboratory facilities as good or better than what currently exist in Munich, with all current equipment moved to Wasserburg, completed as quickly as possible. A group of you is drawing up a list of new equipment needs.

- Assistance in helping those of you who are willing to move to Wasserburg by providing free real estate services, new mortgage cost, and "matching" the low-rate mortgages currently held by several members.

- Assistance in helping those of you who do not intend to move their residence and instead will drive to Wasserburg by improving the road and subsidizing personal automobile expenses.

Evaluate your interests and discuss them with other members of your scientist team. Be prepared to represent your point of view with the management team you are about to meet. You cannot afford to lose the intellectual contact with Munich colleagues which is so vital to your personal satisfaction and organizational effectiveness. Any solution which saves the company, reduces overhead significantly, and which keeps key employees an board is acceptable if your group can agree to it.

ROLE POSITION FOR THE MANAGEMENT TEAM
(PRESIDENT P. JENSEN, VP FOR RESEARCH AND DEVELOPMENT, VP FOR HUMAN RESOURCES, AND OTHERS)

EXERCISE 19: EUROTECHNOLOGIES, INC.

You are to prepare to negotiate a solution to the problem with the Research and Development committee if possible. Assign roles to the members in your group inventing appropriate roles in addition to those specified above. Alternatively, you may choose to use your own names in this simulation and simply represent management's interests without adopting these specific character identities.

As the management group for Eurotechnologies, Inc., you are interested in saving the company and you recognize that the loss of the majority of your Research and Development staff would be a crippling blow to the firm. Your fundamental interest is in Eurotechnologies' survival.

Several things are on your mind as you attempt to discover a solution to the relocation problem:

1. You are currently on very "shaky" ground with GYRO, your parent company, because of the reduced competitiveness of Eurotechnologies, Inc. The loss of top R&D personnel and continued high operating costs would make the situation even worse.

2. Regardless of your company's technical leadership, your customers will not award any more contracts to Eurotechnologies, Inc. if overhead costs are not reduced. You see the relocation of the facility to Wasserburg as the obvious way to accomplish this cost reduction. That relocation would create considerable difficulty and you would prefer to minimize those problems. If there are viable alternatives, you have not discovered them, but you are willing to keep searching.

3. You have tried to be as fair as possible in managing the possible relocations for those affected. You believe that getting the R&D personnel to move is one very important element of the plan. So far, you have not sensed organized resistance from any other employee group; some may be waiting, however, to see how this group's resistance is handled. Even if no other group assumes a similarly rigid position, you must be conscious of the issue of fairness to other employees, as making additional concessions to this group could exacerbate the morale problems which already exist and enhance the perception that Munich employees always receive favorable treatment.

4. You know that you will have *extreme* difficulties in replacing the R&D personnel. If they all decide to leave the firm, the largest single problem will be in maintaining progress in R&D while new people are being hired and trained.

5. Some members of the Research and Development group, particularly O'Hara and Loew, may not really be willing to leave the company. O'Hara is getting on in years, and you have heard that s/he has just bought a new home; Loew is a close personal friend of the company President and is strongly connected in Munich social circles. One of you (the Vice President for Research and Development) has announced plans for early retirement a

year from now, and people have been openly talking about Loew as a replacement. You know that s/he is keenly interested in the job. Finally, do not hesitate to appeal to the professional responsibility and loyalty of all of these scientists--particularly the older ones. This is a time when the whole company will have to pull together to solve the financial crisis.

6. You are concerned about the subcontracting (consulting on behalf of the company) that has been done by this group in their Research and Development work. On the one hand, it does bring in revenues, it does have a good ROI, and it has been much more convenient than using the Wasserburg facilities. On the other hand, it has fostered morale problems for the Wasserburg group. Constant duplication of equipment and materials, as well as morale problems, will be reduced if the group moves to Wasserburg.

7. You are all aware of the personal strains that a move will create. Your own families are personally attached to Munich as well, and some of you will be required to move your homes in order to minimize the "impossible" daily commute.

8. You are aware of the advantages that Munich offers in terms of the abundant scientific, academic and technical resources in its environment. You must deal with the employees' claims that a move to Wasserburg would destroy Eurotechnologies, Inc. research and development advantage by diminishing the "intellectual stimulation" that the environment provides for these people.

Dealing with the Committee's Position

In spite of the above concerns, you would be willing to listen to any proposal which reduces overhead costs by a figure close to the DM 13 million target. It is clear that significant savings can be achieved with the Wasserburg move and you are willing to make some concessions in order to change the R&D department's mind about relocation. Your primary interest in this negotiation is to find a way to save the company through drastic cost reduction while maintaining technical quality.

One major concern is to find a way to save the company money without losing key personnel. If moving everyone to Wasserburg becomes the only viable plan, you are prepared to consider some of the concessions which appear below. *Cost savings are a primary factor, so don't concede to do more than is absolutely necessary.* Also, explore alternatives for "packaging" concessions and tradeoffs wherever possible. However, if you can find a viable alternative to relocating everyone to Wasserburg which satisfies your primary interests, these modifications in the Wasserburg site will be irrelevant to this negotiation.

Cafeteria, Food Service, etc.:
The cafeteria, banquet facilities and other facilities for the professional staff at Wasserburg are scheduled for renovation in 6 months at a cost of DM 326,000. In a pinch, facilities could be renovated in as little as 4 months, but 20-30% additional cost expenditure would be required.

Renovation of laboratory facilities:
You intend to completely renovate the Wasserburg R&D labs over the next 8 months, at an estimated cost of DM 407,500. Reduction of any duplicate equipment and machinery will only occur with the consent of the scientists. All revenue from the sale of existing apparatus will go to improving the new

laboratory. Renovation of the lab could be speeded up to 4 1/2 months, but would increase costs by as much as 50%.

For those moving to Wasserburg:
You agree to provide real estate assistance, information about schools, and limited financial assistance (e.g. paying points for new loans and offering second mortgages at 2% below market rates). In a pinch, you might also agree to payment of real estate agent's fees for sale of one's own primary residence. Covering agent's fees would cost DM 9780 for each employee who chooses to move. You are already negotiating with the regional highway authority to improve the road; they have promised a response soon. You would be willing to help organize a car pool for drivers from the same location. Under pressure, you might be able to provide a company van and driver for a van pool.

Scholarly interaction:
A research seminar series to attract visiting scholars to Wasserburg would cost approximately DM 8,000 annually. You might also offer increased flexibility in work hours and a program of "personal days" for the scientists to meet with colleagues in Munich or other locations. Under significant pressure, you might be willing to double the seminar fund and provide approximately DM 2500 for the scientists to travel to professional meetings.

Cash incentives for employees to move:
Only as a last resort, you might be willing to offer a flat cash outlay of DM 2500 per employee for "relocation expenses," paid to the employee directly, with no strings attached.

Evaluate your interests and discuss them with other members of your management team. Be prepared to represent your point of view with the committee you are about to meet. You must close the Munich facilities *in their current highly expensive form;* that is an inevitable fact. If some other form of a Munich facility is needed and cost effective, you may consider such a proposal. Any solution which saves the company, reduces overhead significantly, and keeps the majority of key employees on board is acceptable if your group can agree to it.

EXERCISE 20
THE PAKISTANI PRUNES

Objectives

1. To introduce students to the challenges of integrative bargaining.

2. To demonstrate the effects of low trust on information disclosure.

3. To demonstrate the need to diagnose whether goals are incompatible or whether information is not being adequately shared, before acting cooperatively or competitively.

Group Size Any size group, either paired (to negotiate the exercise) or trios (with an observer).

Time Required 15 minutes to prepare, about 15 minutes to negotiate, 15 minutes to debrief.

Special Materials Copies of the two role briefing sheets following these instructions.

Special Physical Requirements None

Recommended Reading Assignments to Accompany This Exercise:

(It is recommended that these be done AFTER doing the negotiation):
Reader: 1.3 (Savage, Blair and Sorenson), 4.1 (Barbara Gray), 4.2 (Anderson), 5.3 (Tramel and Reynolds)
Text: Chapters 4, 5

What To Expect

The major benefits are that this exercise contains a lot of important learning points about cooperation and competition in a very short time period. Participants find the Pakistani Prunes situation intriguing, and discussion is lively.

Experienced instructors will recognize this activity as a variation on the popular "Ugli Orange" exercise. All dynamics are similar.

Advance Preparation

Prepare copies of the two role briefing forms as handouts.

Operating Procedure, Hints, And Cautions

The *key element* in this case is that Sanchez and Wilson need *different parts of the* prune. Sanchez needs the *mash* and Wilson needs the *pits.* If each person discloses enough information" to let them realize that their goals are not incompatible, they are likely to develop more trust and arrive at a satisfactory solution. If they withhold too much information and mistrust each other, they go on thinking that they each need the entire prune (an incompatible goal), engage in competitive behavior, and neither has their needs met.

To run this exercise, you can simply divide the class in half and then pair them up in a somewhat random manner, or you can systematically use observers (in which case, the class should be divided into trios). You should coach the observers while those playing Drs. Wilson and Sanchez are preparing their role information. Privately instruct the observers to look for the following:

- How much disclosure is there on each side about (a) how many prunes they want, and (b) what they want to use the prunes for?

- Do the parties appear to trust each other (the role play materials clearly encourage mistrust and suspicion)?

- How creative or complex is their "solution" (if they arrive at one)? Even pairs which learn that they need different parts of the prune still distrust one another sufficiently such that they have to work out very complex agreements for transporting and sharing the prunes with each other!

Instruct the pairs that if they reach some agreement to keep it to themselves and not let other groups overhear it! Often, when they discover that they need different parts of the prune, their enthusiasm leads them to be overheard by other pairs.

Stop the exercise after about 10 minutes. Usually at this point about half of the groups have reached a solution. In the discussion, focus first on those groups which have NOT solved the problem (try to keep the groups which have solved the problem under control --they will be very enthusiastic about sharing their settlement publicly!)

You will find that all groups will reach agreement fairly quickly (10-15 minutes) if you let them. Some people realize they need different parts of the prunes even faster than that. However, you will still see evidence of low trust behavior--extremely elaborate "holding companies" which will receive the prunes and use tight security procedures to ensure that each company gets its part of the prunes. On the other hand, high trust groups may simply agree to offer the market price for ordinary prunes and have the prunes shipped first to Dr. Sanchez' company, where the pits will be removed. In other words, the game is not over if people discover they need different parts of the prune.

When the groups have finished negotiating (or when you have stopped them), post the information from each group on a chart that looks like this:

<u>Solution?</u>   <u>Full Disclosure?</u>   <u>Trust?</u>   <u>Work together again?</u>   <u>Creativity?</u>

There is often an inverse relationship between trust and the creativity (or complexity) of the solution. The solution is often very creative when trust is low. Check to see if this phenomenon occurs in your groups.

Alternatives And Variations

1. In large groups (more than 40), you may not have the time for each group to individually report back to the total class. One option is for only some of the groups to report. Ask for volunteers to describe what happened in their groups, and solicit feedback from as many groups for which you have time. (If the group feedback takes too long, the rest of the class will get bored.)

2. Another option for large classes is to take a poll of the class with a show of hands for each issue. First ask a few observers to describe what happened in their group and use these descriptions as examples of high or low trust behavior and high or low disclosure. You might get at this by asking, "Did anyone see behavior indicating high trust in his group?" (hands will go up). "Can someone describe that high trust behavior?" Then ask for examples of low trust, then of high and low disclosure.

3. Next, fill out the following table by asking for a show of hands for the various cells. Start by asking how many groups had high or low disclosure. Then ask how many of the high disclosure groups had high trust, then how many would want to work together again or not, then how many had complex or simple solutions. Then ask how many of the low-disclosure groups experienced each of the other conditions. After all the numbers are posted, ask what conclusions people can draw from the table. Usually with high disclosure you will find high trust, high satisfaction, and low complexity.

Disclosure?	Trust?	Work Together Again?	Solution Complexity
High =	High =	Yes =	High =
	Low =	No =	Low =
Low =	High =	Yes =	High =
	Low =	No =	Low =

Concluding The Exercise

A number of conflict models can be used to explain the different patterns of results achieved by pairs and groups. For example, the basic dynamics of distributive vs. integrative bargaining can be used to describe the different approaches to the negotiation (see the Savage, Blair and Sorenson article). Second, one might specifically examine the degree to which the parties share their underlying *interests*, as opposed to their *positions* (see the text discussion of interest-based negotiations). Finally, different approaches to this problem can be related to the five different types of conflict management proposed by Killman and Thomas (Thomas, 1976): collaborative, competitive, compromising, avoiding, and accommodating. Collaborative solutions would be ones in which the parties agreed to buy the entire year's production of the prunes and split the pits to one party and the pulp to the other. Compromising solutions would be ones in which they each agreed to take half the prunes. Competitive-accommodating solutions would be ones in which one party got 2/3 of the supply and the other got 1/3, while competitive-competitive solutions would be no agreement on how to divide the prunes at all.

Specific concluding points regarding the discussion questions are as follows:

1. What is the relationship between trust and the disclosure of information?

There is a mutual interaction between open disclosure of information and trust. Each can stimulate the other, just as a lack of openness can stimulate mistrust. Thus, in many situations, as in this exercise, it is possible to observe trust cycles in which the trust level steadily increases or decreases.

2. In a bargaining situation such as this, before competing or collaborating with the other person, what should you do first?

It is important to identify whether goals are compatible **before** deciding whether competition or cooperation is appropriate. We often tend to assume competition exists when it may not be appropriate.

3. How does mistrust affect the creativity or complexity of bargained agreements?

Where trust is low, negotiated agreements tend to be very complex, with elaborate controls, checks, and balances to ensure good faith and compliance. Under conditions of mistrust, much creative energy is wasted by dreaming up ingenious strategies to take advantage of the other person or to avoid being taken advantage of.

Source Materials

Fisher, R., Ury, W. and Patton, B. *Getting to Yes*. Second Edition. Boston: Houghton Mifflin, 1991.

Rubin, J. Z., Pruitt, D. and Kim, S. H. *Social Conflict: Escalation Stalemate and Settlement*. Second Edition. New York: Random House.

Thomas, K. Conflict and Negotiation Processes in Organizations. In M. Dunnette and L. M. Hough, *Handbook of Industrial and Organizational Psychology,* Second Edition. Volume 3. Palo Alto, CA: Consulting Psychologist's Press, 1992.

DEBRIEFING: THE PAKISTANI PRUNES

How much disclosure was there on each side about

    (a) how many prunes each side wanted?

    (b) what they want to use the prunes for?

Do the parties appear to trust each other?
    Why or why not?

How creative or complex were the "solutions"?

Did the parties negotiate about positions or interests?

What does this exercise say about the ease or difficulty of reaching integrative agreements?

ROLE FOR THE UNITED NATIONS REPRESENTATIVE, DR. SANCHEZ
EXERCISE 20: THE PAKISTANI PRUNES

You are Dr. Rubio Sanchez, a research scientist employed by the United Nations Standing Committee on World Hunger. Your organization's sole purpose is to develop methods to increase production of the world's food supply, particularly in third world countries. The more successful your organization is, the more likely it will be that you can reduce the millions of deaths that occur worldwide from malnutrition and starvation.

Your committee has discovered a substance that, when added to the soil, dramatically reduces the amount of moisture needed in the soil to grow a variety of staple crops (high protein grains). Preliminary studies around the world indicate that the use of this substance in drought areas would effectively allow currently fallow and drought-parched land in that area to grow crops. This new substance also has the promise, long term, to slow the process of the land turning into desert ("desertification") and might eventually increase the ability of desert areas to produce crops with a lot less water.

This new substance can only be found in the Pakistani Prune, which grows on trees in certain parts of Pakistan. The trees are in a deserted and remote part of the country, making them highly inaccessible for easy harvesting. All efforts to transplant the trees to regions of the world where production would be easier and cheaper have failed; there seems to be some combination of the trees themselves and the quality of the agricultural and weather conditions that only allow the trees to thrive in this area. Moreover, efforts to expand the production in this area have been unsuccessful, since the climate and soil conditions appear to change just enough in neighboring regions to yield healthy trees but no fruit!

Pakistani prune trees bear fruit only once every two years (a ripe prune is about the size, color and texture of a plum). The process for obtaining the soil additive from the prunes requires picking them, washing them, and then extracting and pulverizing the pits of the prunes into a fine powder. It has been estimated that the powder from the pits of an entire harvest would be sufficient to produce enough soil additive to reclaim land that would support a population of 20,000 people. Your scientists claim that they are at least 5 years away from solving the problem of how to create the conditions to grow fruit-bearing trees in other parts of the world, and at least 10 years away from being able to create a synthetic powder in the laboratory. Moreover, the trees must have a dormant year in between the years they produce fruit. All efforts at "genetic engineering" with the trees to produce a crop annually have failed.

The biannual harvest has just been completed. The output from the entire harvest of Pakistani Prunes is being controlled by the Ministry of Agriculture which will sell the batch to the highest bidder. Knowing the importance of the powder and the potential lives that might be saved by using it in the right way, you are eager to make this purchase. You have been authorized by the United Nations Committee to spend up to $ 2 million to obtain the prunes.

You have just learned that a competitor, Dr. Kim Wilson, working for an American company, also has plans to make a bid on the prunes. You have no information about Wilson or what he wants, but you know that you must get the prunes to continue working on this important problem! In an effort to save time, and obtain the prunes as quickly as possible, you have decided to contact Dr. Wilson and influence him not to purchase the prunes. You called him at his hotel and he agreed to meet with you in a cafe near your hotel in Karachi. You have no idea what you will encounter, but you have heard that Dr. Wilson is quite ruthless and very clearly wants the prunes for his company. You know that Dr. Wilson's company is one of the biggest biotech firms in the U.S.--you heard that Wall Street sent the stock soaring about two years ago. As a result, Kim Wilson probably has a lot of money to throw around.

ROLE FOR DR. KIM WILSON OF TECHNOGEN
EXERCISE 20: THE PAKISTANI PRUNES

You are Dr. Kim Wilson of TechnoGen of San Jose, California. Your firm is a world leader in the development of genetic engineering processes, biomedical technology and the creation of "new" products for the agricultural and health sciences. Your firm has a multi-million dollar annual budget for the development and testing of new products.

TechnoGen has spent millions of dollars on the research and development of a new drug that will actually reduce blood cholesterol levels. This new substance was discovered accidentally in the process of working on an industry product to develop a good tasting, low fat medical nutritional supplement. If you are successful in developing this product, people could take the product and significantly reduce their blood cholesterol levels AND cholesterol buildup in their bodies simply by diet alone, and without any change in their current exercise program. This product could be taken as part of a dietary program, or added to nutritional supplements and sold over the counter. You suspect that the market for this product would be huge.

This new substance can only be found in the Pakistani Prune, which grows on trees in certain parts of Pakistan. The trees are in a deserted and remote part of the country, making them highly inaccessible for easy harvesting. All efforts to transplant the trees to regions of the world where production would be easier and cheaper have failed--there seems to be some combination of the trees themselves and the quality of the agricultural and weather conditions that only allow the trees to thrive in this area. Moreover, efforts to expand the production in this area have been unsuccessful, since the climate and soil conditions appear to change just enough in neighboring regions to yield healthy trees but they bear no fruit!

Pakistani prune trees bear fruit only once every two years (a ripe prune is about the size, color and texture of a plum). The process for obtaining the key compound from the prunes requires picking them, washing them and then extracting the pulp ("meat") from the prunes. This pulp "mash" is then biochemically treated and subject to several genetic engineering processes. It has been estimated that the mash extract of an entire harvest would be sufficient to produce enough compound to treat more than 20,000 high-cholesterol-risk people. Your scientists claim that they are at least 5 years away from solving the problem of how to create the conditions to grow fruit-bearing trees in other parts of the world, and at least 10 years away from being able to create a synthetic mash in the laboratory. Moreover, the trees must have a dormant year in between the years they produce fruit, and all efforts at "genetic engineering" with the trees to produce an annual crop of prunes have failed.

The biannual harvest has just been completed. The output from the entire harvest of Pakistani Prunes is being controlled by the Ministry of Agriculture which will sell the batch to the highest bidder. Knowing the importance of the mash and the potential lives that might be saved by reducing heart attack risk in high cholesterol patients, you are eager to make this purchase for your company. You have been authorized by TechnoGen to spend up to $5 million to obtain the prunes.

You have just learned that a potential competitor, Dr. Rubio Sanchez, working for some United Nations agency, also has plans to make a bid on the prunes. You don't know any more about the competitor or why he wants the prunes, but you know that you must get the prunes to continue working on this important problem (which promises fabulous profits for your company)! You were just about to call Dr. Sanchez and request a meeting when you received Sanchez's call, requesting a meeting. The two of you have agreed to meet in a cafe near your hotel in Karachi. You have no idea what you will encounter, but you have heard that Sanchez is quite ruthless and very clearly wants the prunes for his organization. As a world government organization, they probably have a lot of money to throw around if they want to!

EXERCISE 21
PLANNING FOR NEGOTIATIONS

Objectives

The purpose of this exercise is to give students a practice experience with a negotiation planning process. There is frequent criticism that negotiators--particularly American ones--do not engage in adequate preparation prior to actually meeting the other "at the table." The purpose of this exercise is to create a practice session for rehearsing that preparation process.

This exercise is pretty straightforward, but also has the advantage of letting students apply the planning process to a real negotiation in their own lives, and of allowing them to see the universal applicability of planning to all negotiations. It also lets them see the frequently common structure and conduct of negotiations across a wide variety of settings.

Group Size This exercise works best in groups of four or five for classes of 25 to 35. If the class total exceeds 35 or so, the break-out groups can be increased in size accordingly, such that no more than six (6) teams have to "report out" at the end of the class period.

Time Required Students may be asked to think of a "focus" negotiation prior to class; otherwise, all activities are conducted according to one of three options:

Option 1: One class period; all steps (1-5) will take approximately two hours, or more depending on how much extra time the instructor uses for debriefing the exercise.
Option 2: Two class periods of approximately one hour each; Steps 1 and 2 are conducted in the first class, followed by Steps 4 and 5 in the following class. If this option is used, in lieu of Step 3, students should be instructed to put their presentation on a transparency sheet and to provide a hard copy of that sheet for duplication and dissemination to the class.
Option 3: One class period of approximately one hour, during which Steps 4 and 5 are conducted. If this option is chosen, Steps 1 and 2 can be assigned as an out-of-class activity, and transparencies and hard copies should be required for class, as specified in Option 2.

Special Materials Copy and distribute materials from this manual.

Special Physical Requirements If Option 1 or Option 2 is used, the ideal facilities will provide a breakout room for each work group. Alternatively, groups can be allowed to "spread out" to do their discussions, returning to the classroom at the end of Step Two. If Option 1 is used, sufficient board space is required to allow each group (maximum 6 groups) to post the product of its deliberations in legible outline form.

Recommended Reading Assignments to Accompany this Exercise:

Reader: Articles 1.1 (Greenhalgh) and/or 3.2 (Craver); 2.1 (Kuhn), 2.2 (Scott), or 2.3 (Tannen); 5.2 (Neale & Bazerman), 6.3 (Keys & Case), 8.3 (Kaplan), and/or 10.3 (Greenhalgh & Gilkey). Text: Chapter 2.

Advance Preparation

None, unless Option 3 is used.

Concluding the Exercise

For Step 4, each group's presentation (either board or transparency/handout) should consist of a list of information and intentions ordered in accordance with the list of key elements set forth in Step 2 of the student copy of the Exercise (i.e., understanding of the problem, understanding of the relationship and context, intended strategies, tactics, and tones. etc.)

Once Step 4 has been finished, the instructor concludes the exercise by conducting Step 5, the debrief and summation. Typically, the range of negotiations presented will be both wide and entertaining. At a minimum, Step 5 should include:

1. A chance for the class participants to see both the parallels across negotiation types and the differences that do occur among certain types of negotiations (e.g., salary negotiations, performance appraisals, wedding arrangements, tenant/landlord problems, etc.).

2. A review of the strategies planned by each group for their particular negotiation, including a chance for questions and comments from the class with a mind to helping the actual negotiator improve his or her plan.

3. Discussion of the importance of negotiation planning and of the advantage it gives planners over parties who do not make an investment in the planning process.

EXERCISE 22
SANIBEL ISLAND

Objectives:

1. To explore the nature of negotiation processes between a land developer and an environmental group over a proposed real estate development project.

2. To explore factors that might lead the parties toward pursuing either a distributive or an integrative strategy.

Group Size No restrictions. Can be run as a 1:1 negotiation. Possible to run as a group-on-group.

Time Required 60-90 minutes (30 preparation, 30 negotiation, 30 debrief)

Special Materials Copy and distribute the role information from this manual.

Special Physical Requirements None

Recommended Reading to Accompany this Exercise:

Scott (2.2), Tannen (2.3), Anderson (4.2), Rubin (4.3)

What to Expect:

This is a relative low-intensity negotiation, unless the parties have strong views about environmental development. There are three major issues in a real estate development project in a proposed resort community on Sanibel Island, Florida. (The scenario is based on real information). Parties play the role of either a developer who wants to construct a resort property on a "wetland" on the Sanibel Island coast, or a representative of an environmental group who wants to limit and constrain that development. Several alternative options are specified for each issue; each alternative has points attached, thus making the exercise scorable. While the scorability of the exercise permits easy logrolling by the negotiators, we have often seen parties who want to truly explore an integrative agreement approach this problem quite creatively, and develop "bridging" settlements outside the bounds of these specified options.

While we state that the conflict is generally of "low intensity", conflict level can be enhanced to the degree that you assign students who have strong pro-environmental values to the environmental role, and those who have strong pro-development values to the developer role. We find that this tends to produce a more competitive standoff between the parties and increase the tension level.

Advance Preparation:

Students may read the common Sanibel Island Information (in the student manual) and their individual role briefing information before class.

Operating Procedures:

1) Decide whether you want students to prepare in class or prior to class. Assign the common briefing information and individual role information as homework.

2) You may assign students to roles randomly, or ask students whether they see themselves as *pro-environmental* or *pro development* and assign roles accordingly. If you SWITCH roles (e.g. assign developers to the environmental role and vice versa), we predict that you will enhance the likelihood of easy agreement.

3) If you decide to make this a group-on-group exercise, give students extra time to prepare their small group strategies.

4) If students are preparing in class, give them approximately 25-30 minutes to read and get ready. If students are already prepared, negotiations can begin on cue. Give the students approximately 30-40 minutes to negotiate.

5) You may tell students that their solutions must stay within the boundaries of the specified options for each of the three issues. If they do so, they will generally develop logrolling solutions to the overall negotiating problem. In contrast, you may say nothing, or you may indicate that if they wish, they can go outside the boundaries of the options if they can find a more creative way to resolve the issues. This final instruction is often a *cue* for negotiators to pursue more creative/integrative options. Unique and interesting configurations often emerge here as negotiators explore options such as building over the marsh, putting in parking decks rather than parking lots to reduce surface runoff, etc.

6) If you assign negotiators with strong pro-environmental or strong pro-development values to their respective roles, the likelihood of deadlock and more distributive agreements increases. There is an ethic in the environmental movement that advocates *no net loss* of wetlands, and some environmentalists interpret this as a mandate to not negotiate away **any** part of a wetland. In short, compromise is equivalent to failure. This orientation can be a scenario for stand-off against a committed developer, but it can also be the motivation to truly search for a configuration on the site that might meet the needs of both sides.

7) The payoff structures for both parties and point combinations is presented in the attached overhead.

8)   Debrief the class in pairs by asking them to report out:

- the nature of their settlements
- the point values for each side
- *creative* solutions that go beyond the point values (ask pairs to share their agreements and the configuration of the development on the site)
- instances of deadlocks, breakdowns, or inability to agree

Concluding the Exercise:

Tie the settlements to basic principles of distributive and integrative bargaining:

- pairs where one party did significantly better than the other
- pairs where both parties did poorly
- pairs where both parties achieved the maximum number of points
- pairs which developed unique and creative options.

SANIBEL ISLAND ROLE PLAY
ISSUES AND PREFERENCE FUNCTIONS

Issue	Developer	Environmentalist
No Net Loss of Wetland	0	+ 30,000
Pool Access	+30,000	0
Building Height:		
3 Stories	0	+ 15,000
4 Stories	+5000	+ 10,000
Add. Floors	+5000	− 5,000
Paved Surfaces:		
Buffer Zone	0	+ 5,000
Retention Pond	0	+ 10,000
Both	0	+ 20,000
No Buffer Zone	+5000	0
No Ret. Pond	+10,000	0

CONFIDENTIAL INFORMATION FOR ENVIRONMENTALIST
EXERCISE 22: SANIBEL ISLAND

You are asked to participate in this negotiation as an environmentalist. Study this information carefully and empathize with the character you have been assigned.

Who you are

You are the leader of a local environmental protection group, *Citizens for Sanibel*. You are interested in protecting the natural resources of Sanibel Island against further land development, and you hope to persuade others of this goal. You are especially concerned that rising tourist demands and subsequent development is damaging the area. Your group is made up of other concerned citizens, and they have nominated you to represent their interests in the discussion session about the proposed hotel development.

Your specific perspective on these issues is described below. Each issue has a corresponding *Green-Point* value (green--as in *environment*). These points translate into funds which are likely to be donated to your cause if you are successful. **Your task is to negotiate an agreement that maximizes your total number of Green Points for the entire agreement.**

Issue 1: DEVELOPMENT PLAN

The developer has a resort that includes a hotel near the beach, a swimming pool, and a parking lot (see map). The developer proposes to use some of the wetland as a nature preserve. The plan includes building elevated boardwalks to permit tourists to view the wetland. The idea of attracting more tourists concerns you; however, the idea of boardwalks meets with your approval since it will not significantly affect the wetland.

Also included in the overall development plan is a patio area allowing access from the hotel to the pool through the wetland. In addition, an access road will be built from the existing road to the parking lot. The destruction of the wetland concerns you. Your perspective on this issue is as follows:

- The developer should not destroy any part of the wetland.
- If you negotiate "no net loss" of wetlands, you can earn **30,000** Green Points.
- If there is any net-loss of wetland, you will earn **0** Green Points.

Issue 2: BUILDING HEIGHT

The citizens of Sanibel Island have historically put a limit on the height of new buildings to three (3) stories. Aesthetically speaking, the concern is that the natural beauty of Sanibel Island could be harmed by allowing tall, multi-storied hotels and condominiums to be erected. The purpose of the building height restriction is to facilitate an unobstructed view of the island from all vantage points. Your perspective on the building height issue is as follows:

- You would like to see the current building height maintained at three (3) stories.
- If the building height limit remains at three stories, you can earn **15,000** Green Points.
- For each additional level agreed to, you will decrease your Green Points by **5,000**. (e.g.. 4 stories = **10,000** Green Points; 5 stories = **5,000**; 6 stories = **0**)

Issue 3: PAVED SURFACES

In the course of development, roads and parking lots must be constructed to allow access to the hotel. Unfortunately, asphalt and concrete create impermeable surfaces on otherwise permeable sand surfaces on Sanibel Island. These paved surfaces increase water runoff and erosion, and may lead to pollution buildup in freshwater wetlands. Generally speaking, you wish to limit additional paved surfaces. Therefore, your perspective on this issue is as follows:

Paved surfaces should be severely restricted. When paved roads and lots are necessary, developers should be required to minimize erosion and pollution effects. Developers should build water retention ponds to gather excess runoff from paved surfaces. Additionally, developers should be required to build a buffer zone (a large area of plants between paved surfaces and wetlands) whenever paved surfaces come near wetlands.

- If neither the buffer zone nor the retention pond is built, you earn **0** Green Points.
- If the buffer zone is built, you earn **5,000** Green Points.
- If the retention pond is built, you earn **10,000** Green Points.
- If **both** are built, then you earn **20,000** Green Points.

CONFIDENTIAL INFORMATION FOR DEVELOPER

EXERCISE 22: SANIBEL ISLAND

You are asked to participate in this process as a land developer. Study this information carefully and try to assume the orientation of the party you have been assigned.

Who you are

You are a hotel owner and developer from Sanibel Island. Rising tourism has led to an increase in your business in recent years, and you hope to continue to make profits. You have many developments on Sanibel Island, and you hope to continue your past success. However, obtaining a permit to build is often a problem, especially due to the time delays involved in the permitting process. You are responsible to your financial backers, and it is up to you to guarantee a good return on their investment.

You have borrowed a great deal of money from a bank in order to build this hotel. Therefore, most of your revenues from the hotel will go toward repaying this loan. However, you do forecast a profit of $25,000 the first year, but you expect this profit margin to increase significantly in subsequent years.

Your viewpoint on development

While you do see the logic in protecting natural resources, you believe that development is necessary to meet the demands of the tourist industry, Sanibel's chief source of income.

It is in your best interests to come to an agreement with the environmentalists, since further delay costs you money and resources. You have agreed to participate in this discussion to assess the issues surrounding the proposed hotel development. Your position on these issues is described on the following pages.

Each issue has a corresponding *Green Point* value (green--as in *money*). These points translate into funds which you are likely to save on the construction of the project. **Your task is to negotiate an agreement that maximizes your total number of Green Points for the entire agreement.**

Issue 1: DEVELOPMENT PLAN

You have proposed a hotel development on a piece of property that you've recently purchased (see Exhibit 2 in text). This includes a hotel near the beach, a swimming pool, and a parking lot. Also included in the plan is a patio area allowing access from the hotel to the pool. Building the patio entails construction through a portion of the wetland on your property. This proposal has become a cause for concern among the environmentalists, since it will destroy some of the wetland. However, access to the pool is necessary for the success of this resort. In fact, you estimate that with proper pool access, you can attract more tourists and increase your profits significantly.

In addition, an access road will be built from the existing road to the parking lot. The remainder of the wetland will be designated as a nature preserve. You envision raised boardwalks to allow tourists to enjoy the wetland without intruding upon the wetland itself. Your perspective on this issue is as follows:

- You see your development plan on the map as being reasonable.
- If there is pool access, then you will earn **30,000** Green Points.
- If there is no pool access, then you will earn **0** Green Points.

Issue 2: BUILDING HEIGHT

The citizens of Sanibel Island have historically put a limit of three (3) stories on the height of new buildings. The purpose of the building height restriction is to facilitate an unobstructed view of the island from all vantage points.

In your opinion, Sanibel Island's tradition of limiting building height to three stories is extreme. You estimate that by adhering to the current building height restriction, you are losing the opportunity to increase the value of the development. For example, if you could increase the building height from three stories to four stories, you could add more rooms to your hotel and increase your profits.

Other beach front communities allow higher developments. In fact, Casey Key (a neighboring city to the north) allows six (6) story developments. You would like to see the same building height standard at Sanibel Island. Your perspective on the building height issue is as follows:

- Building height on Sanibel Island should be increased to six (6) stories.
- You will earn **5,000** Green Points for each floor over three (3) you build. (e.g.. 3 stories = **0** Green Points; 4 stories = **5,000**; 5 stories = **10,000**; etc)
- Additionally, if you can build 6 stories or more, you will earn a **5,000** point bonus. (e.g.. 6 stories = **15,000** + **5,000** point bonus--for a total of **20,000** Green Points)

Issue 3: PAVED SURFACES

In the course of your development, roads and parking lots must be constructed to allow access to the hotel. Unfortunately, asphalt and concrete create impermeable surfaces on otherwise permeable sand surfaces on Sanibel Island. Environmentalists want you to pay for environmental safeguards for your access road and parking lot. Specifically, they are asking you to build a retention pond (to catch water runoff) and a buffer zone (a large area of plants between paved surfaces and wetlands). You believe that environmentalists are exaggerating the detrimental effects of paved surfaces, but you have *already included the costs* of building a retention pond and a buffer zone in your development plans and forecasts. Your perspective on this issue is as follows:

- The city government should pay for any additional environmental safeguards it finds necessary with regards to paved surfaces. You should not be required to build a retention pond or a buffer zone.
- By **not** building a retention pond, you could earn **10,000** Green Points.
- By **not** building a buffer zone, you could earn **5,000** Green Points.

EXERCISE 23
THE PLAYGROUND NEGOTIATION

Objectives

This case presents a true-to-life public administration issue. It is framed around a decision whether to fund a neighborhood playground with limited special project funds. It is one of several projects which will be presented to the Ithaca Special Projects Task Force (ISPTF) during the course of the year; the members of the ISPTF cannot know whether these other projects will be more, less, or as deserving of funding as the neighborhood playground.

This case is purposely structured loosely. By keeping the roles and guidelines fluid, students will think through the possible goals and objectives and be creative in their negotiation process. There are few situations where all elements of a negotiation are crystal clear and solutions can be chosen from a menu. Our emphasis is to encourage the examination of negotiation process rather than to focus on the outcome.

While the ISPTF negotiators share the superordinate goal of "bettering Ithaca" by making the best decision possible and they realize they have constituents in common, they also have conflicting interests. The Parks Department Representative has the goal of maintaining jobs in the Parks Department. The Community Volunteer Representative, on the other hand, wants as much support, financial or otherwise, for the Community Volunteer Association as possible. As both are elected officials, they must maintain happy constituencies. Moreover, their constituencies may overlap; a Parks Department employee by day may be a community volunteer at night.

The case is based loosely on news articles relating the experiences of Leathers and Associates, an internationally-recognized, Ithaca-based firm that specializes in coordinating and developing community-planned and community-built playgrounds. Over 1300 Leathers and Associates playgrounds can be found in practically every state and in several foreign countries. For example, the panda pen at the U.S. National Zoo is an easily-identified Leathers' project (Tousignant, 1995; Wilding, 1995). Leathers and his colleagues occasionally find their projects stalled by political considerations, including partial community opposition, lack of funding, or vandalism (e.g., Tousignant, 1995; Nagler, 1995). Such stories helped form the basis of this case.

The case is suitable for use in teaching negotiations emphasizing interpersonal and/or intergroup relations. Undergraduate students or graduate-level students enrolled in general negotiations courses should find this case absorbing and challenging. The case can be used in conjunction with the topics of "multi-interest negotiation," "low conflict negotiation," and "individual differences in negotiation." It is equally appropriate to use it in teaching intergroup dynamics using the vehicle of negotiation.

Specific Learning Objectives

The objectives of learning for this course are as follows:

1. The playground negotiation involves a "low conflict" negotiation in which the interests of the parties are characterized by a shared superordinate goal as well as by divergent personal and public interests. In analyzing the case, students should be encouraged to understand the public policy issues, including the diversity of the community, the potential conflict of disparate interests among constituent groups, the relative neglect of the community in funding decisions by the ISPTF in the past, and the effect of political concerns on a negotiator's perceptions of an issue. Students should realize that there is no one "right way" to resolve issues such as these.

2. The case illustrates how incipient interpersonal and intergroup conflict can be moderated by broader shared goals. The *conflict* between the negotiators personal goals is only one element of a larger community-wide decision making structure in which participants must operate effectively. As a result, *neither hard bargaining nor compromise will be completely satisfactory* in this case. It is therefore useful in discussing the types of concepts Lax and Sebenius (1986) or Gray (1989) address.

3. A variety of factors, including which interests the negotiator represents and each negotiator's sensitivity to community issues, will affect the negotiator's interpretations of the material provided. To successfully navigate this negotiation, students must develop their ability to stretch their "frames" of reference in this case, to articulate and incorporate the views of *all interested parties,* including, but not limited to, the views of the "other side." This case offers an opportunity to manage the negotiation on two levels:

    Interpersonal level: Interpersonal factors such as sensitivity, openness, and trust toward the other party can be highlighted. In addition, this is an excellent opportunity to discuss the implications of the choice of distributive vs. integrative bargaining strategies (Walton & McKersie, 1965), conflict-handling styles (competing, collaborating, avoiding, accommodating, or compromising), and the four steps of principled negotiation (Fisher & Ury, 1981):

    1. Separate the people from the problem;
    2. Focus on interests, not positions;
    3. Invent options for mutual gain; and
    4. Insist on objective criteria.

    Intergroup level: In addition to the above concepts, issues involving intergroup dynamics including in-group favoritism and out-group bias, stereotyping, and power differentials can be raised. In negotiations characterized by group identification, loyalty and commitment to the group can cause negotiators to overvalue their own group's position, priorities, and goals, and undervalue the points of view of outgroups. This can lead to a "we-they" orientation, even in a low-conflict situation (see Thomas, 1991). The use of strategies for minimizing conflict based on group identification are elaborated later in this note.

4. Diversity in the community is a leading concern in public as well as private administration. This case allows examination of a variety of diversity concerns: ageism, racism, and classism (see Cox, 1993 for an excellent treatment of this topic). In some classes, differences between how the different genders negotiate may also become an important discussion issue. Gender differences that were found in a study using this case (Halpern & McLean Parks, 1996) are discussed in a later section of this paper.

Group Size The group size depends on the version you choose to run. You can do the following:

1. This case could be conducted as a fishbowl exercise, with two students assigned opposing roles negotiating in front of the class. (Option 1) This version works best in classes no larger than about 30 students to permit maximum participation in the discussion. Remaining students could be assigned roles as representatives of the different constituencies represented in the case. The proceedings might be conducted as a public mock session of the ISPTF, with representatives of the various constituencies interjecting questions or comments during the meeting. Role descriptions for this version are provided at the end of this section of the manual.

2. The case could be used as a role-playing activity in dyads, with one student assigned to the role of the Parks Department Representative to the task force and a second student to the role of Community Volunteer Representative. (Option 2) Each dyad would negotiate a solution, and then the entire class would convene to discuss the various solutions.

3. Another possibility would be to create teams of Parks Department Representatives and Community Volunteer Representatives. Teams would have to negotiate among themselves about how best to present their case prior to negotiating with the other side. This approach would introduce elements of intraparty bargaining and representation to the case.

Teaching hint: When the case is conducted as a fishbowl or public hearing exercise, each group's interests are likely to be well articulated. However, in a role play or team approach with only two roles, each representative should be prompted to focus on the interests of different constituencies. For example, the Parks Department Representative may stress the low socioeconomic status of the community in order to argue for the importance of new jobs in advocating the construction and maintenance of a new playground. The Community Volunteer Representative, on the other hand, may focus on the diversity of the community and the need to pull people together in order to prevent further decline in a vulnerable area.

Time Required 90-120 minutes

Special Materials Copy and distribute the role information from this manual.

Special Physical Requirements If done in pairs, none. If done as a "large group," space for small groups to plan and caucus, and space for a formal meeting area in the front of the classroom.

Recommended Reading Assignment to Accompany This Exercise:

Readings: 2.3 (Tannen), 4.1 (Gray), 4.2 (Anderson), 5.2 (Tannen)
Text: Chapters 2, 4, 5

Advance Preparation:

It is preferred to have the students read the information in the student manual in advance of class. Role descriptions are short and can be read in class, unless you wish to have the groups prepare out of class and before the negotiation begins.

Operating Procedure:

Once you decide on which option to use, simply follow the general procedures. Options 1 and 2 are likely to lead to a relatively low conflict encounter in which the parties may arrive at some unique and creative solutions. Option 3, in which various community groups play audience members, yields a more typical and challenging opportunity for negotiators to respond to, and "manage," various constituencies. We believe this particular option is more challenging and offers something unique and different not found in more traditional two-party negotiations. You may orchestrate this Option as you wish, permitting the audience to participate throughout the discussion, or only after the two negotiators have had a chance to openly discuss playground options for a while.

Concluding the Exercise

The process your students go through to reach their particular outcomes is more important than which outcome they choose. It is important to emphasize the social and political goals of the negotiators and their constituents, and to discourage students from concentrating on the actual costs or playground elements. The exact cost and the specific elements included in the design of the playground are *not* issues. In fact, there is no "right answer" for this case. For example, when the case was run in a university in the Northeast, the dominant outcome was to have a wooden structure with sand--in keeping with the style of the city surrounding that university. In a midwestern university, on the other hand, the overwhelming choice was the metal and vinyl structure which the Northeastern students found anathema.

By keeping the focus on process, you can help students recognize that negotiation involves issues of justice and fairness that go beyond outcomes. In one class where this case was run, many of the students spent most of their time determining who had more *clout* and how they could make unpopular choices palatable to their constituencies. In one exchange, for example, one negotiator was concerned that parents seemed to find sand "unclean." The partner proposed a public education campaign to deal with that concern.

A strength of this case is that the relative lack of specific costs and other data encourages "thinking outside the box," creativity, and innovative approaches such as collaborative problem solving. Instructors should emphasize that students need to focus on the *interests* of the parties, rather than on the *positions*.

Goals of Parties. Each party to this case--the Parks Department Representative and the Community Volunteer Representative-has conflicting as well as shared goals. The Parks Department Representative and the Community Volunteer Representative must decide how much of the ISPTF money for this year should be allotted to the development of a community playground and which designs should be used.

The Parks Department Representative has a partial goal of attempting to funnel as much funding to the Parks Department as possible. This representative's objective is to maintain jobs. If the department does not make full use of its employees, positions may be eliminated. The ISPTF funds are a potential windfall, because the Parks Department claims it does not have enough money to build a new playground in an area where one already exists, despite many demands for an expanded playground. The Parks Department representative, an elected official, also seeks to maintain a happy constituency.

On the other hand, the Community Volunteer Representative has a partial goal that as much of the ISPTF money goes to projects that involve volunteerism as possible. The support of volunteers in the community provides benefits in terms of saving money during times of economic stress, as well as in terms of building cohesiveness and pride in the neighborhood--a well-known antidote to neighborhood decline. Moreover, there is a spillover effect of community involvement in local activities onto increased citizen participation in other civic activities, such as school board elections and neighborhood crime watches. The Community Volunteer Representative, an elected official, also seeks to maintain a happy constituency.

Both representatives share the common goal of bettering the community for everyone by making the best decision on how to use the ISPTF funds. Moreover, because Ithaca is a small town, people who are employed by the Parks Department may also be members of the Community Volunteer Association in their free time. Therefore, they both seek to avoid alienating each other's constituencies.

There is no single best way to negotiate this case. A strictly competitive approach is likely to alienate the other representative and his or her constituency--which may overlap with the competitive representative's own. A strictly compromising approach may lead to a non-optimal solution for the playground as well as for future projects. For example, splitting the ISPTF funds evenly between the playground and unknown upcoming projects, one possible compromise, may shortchange the playground and leave too much money for less ambitious projects. Each pair of negotiators must find their own solution, depending on how they present their constituency's interests and on their own approach to negotiating.

Low-Conflict Nature of the Case. This case constitutes a weak situation that does not cue particular behaviors (see, e.g., Mischel, 1977). Strong contexts may swamp some differences by cueing particular behaviors, such as adversarial acts, or profit maximizing decisions.

Solidarity between the negotiators is likely to develop in a low-conflict case, encouraging the use of more egalitarian distributive principles as opposed to the economic, task-oriented, or impersonal distribution rules that would be found in the classic high-conflict case (cf. Deutsch, 1973). The weak situation of a low-conflict case is more likely than the stronger situations of traditional negotiation research to reveal individual differences, such as those between male and female negotiating styles. As a result, individuals may have different interpretations of stimulus materials and estimations of the balance between cooperative and competitive behavior.

Low-conflict does not necessarily imply friendly, quiet, or polite proceedings: many community board meetings are raucous and even vituperative, as, for example, when senior and single taxpayers debate the merits of pay increases for music teachers in neighborhood schools with these teachers and parents of children in the orchestra (Halpern & McLean Parks, 1996).

No rewards favor one response over another in this low-conflict case; there is no right answer. Consequently, field-dependent individuals are able to choose behaviors other than those suggested by the situation. Individuals can be either competitive or cooperative, an opportunity which is not customarily available in the vast majority of negotiation studies.

Environmental Factors. The proposed playground would be built as part of a currently existing recreation area with softball fields, an outdoor basketball court, and a small playground. It is located in a neighborhood with a very diverse population, including welfare families living in a public housing facility (Landmark Square), low- to moderate-income homeowners, and senior citizens living in a senior citizen's housing facility. The existing playground seems inadequate for the community's needs because young children have been playing in the streets.

The decisions that the ISPTF representatives reach must reflect the socioeconomic and physical realities of the situation. There is no optimal solution, as happens in many public policy situations.

Political Factors. Both representatives to the ISPTF were elected. While the case does not indicate that this is an election year, representatives must always be aware that their actions may affect them at election time. Moreover, the representatives must be aware that the distinction between "community volunteer" and "Parks Department employee" is not that clear-cut; it is reasonable to assume in a town of this size that Parks Department employees may *also,* in their free time, be members of the Community Volunteer Association.

Both representatives should be aware, based on the past years' budget allocations, that funding has not been directed to this or any other lower-income area of Ithaca. It is reasonable to be concerned that there may have been some discrimination in the past against the diverse population in this area. Therefore, the ISPTF representatives should be concerned that they reach an agreement that will allow this area to benefit from ISPTF moneys.

Demographic Factors. The various needs and interests considered by the diverse constituencies in the case can be understood through an analysis of the elements that comprise the social system influencing the negotiation. This analysis requires listing each constituency to the negotiation, identifying its specific interests, and considering the interaction among these various groups. There may be regional differences in the interests and nature of the interactions discussed, based on the particular political climate surrounding your university. For example, discussions in classes at a northeastern university almost always draw in the apparent socioeconomic discrimination the ISPTF has shown in the past. However, a group of students from the Midwest did not discuss discrimination, but focused more on ways to expand the allocations for all citizens.

For the Parks Department employees, concerns over jobs and funding for the department predominate. For community volunteer advocates, community participation in the construction of the playground is critical. Groups like this consider projects such as the playground as a means for creating strong and vital neighborhoods to combat an alienated citizenry.

Politics of city government play a role. Political issues involved include the following: what it means when one group or the other gets its choice of play-ground; who is ultimately benefited by the playground; who will have control over the playground once it is built; and who has been benefited by the ISPTF in the past. As can be seen from the map, the projects that ISPTF has funded in previous years are all located in "better" neighborhoods, with a mostly white constituency. Votes and financial backing are also important considerations, as the negotiators are elected officials.

The Titus Flats Community is comprised of three main constituents: property owners, residents of the senior citizens' home, and renters at Landmark Square. Each group (and most probably, several subgroups) is likely to have different reactions to the proposed playground. They have different concerns and see different advantages or problems. The property owners want to limit their liability for injuries that may occur if children play in front of their homes. They would most likely want to see the children playing in a safe playground. On the other hand, if the playground proves to be a magnet for older teenagers and drug dealers, the property owners want no part of it. They also pay the most taxes of the neighborhood groups and may expect to have greater influence on decisions as a result.

Senior citizens, for the most part, prefer a quieter neighborhood than a large playground would permit. The current set-up is small enough, and the ball games seasonal, so that the area doesn't seem constantly noisy, even in summer or on weekends. Some of the senior citizens' home residents, however, have their own grandchildren visiting, and wouldn't mind a small, safe playground, perhaps with benches off to the side where they could visit with their friends while watching the little ones. Like the property owners, the senior citizens fear the magnetic attraction of a playground to drug dealers after dark.

Landmark Square residents are low-income renters. Many of them are welfare recipients. A high proportion are African-American. Most of the renters do not share the property owners concerns about liability, nor the senior citizens' home residents' concerns about noise, since most residents are families and are accustomed to children's noise. The renters want to have a safe playground for their children, but prefer to have some assurances about security against rougher teenagers or drug dealers. They also want to have recreational facilities for their teenagers, such as good basketball courts and playing fields. They do not wish to be seen as a source of trouble, an unfortunately frequent consequence of stereotypes about their status as welfare recipients and low-income renters. At the same time, they feel they have as much right as anyone else in the neighborhood to have their interests and needs considered.

Intergroup Conflict. Representatives should be aware that the different issues and needs of these demographic groups can create conflict between the groups, even though there is little conflict between the representatives themselves. The following framework for analysis of the intergroup conflict has been adapted from Cox (1993, pp. 137-158). Intergroup conflict generally springs from one or more of five sources. Students should examine each of the five sources in order to properly diagnose the nature of the friction between groups and then develop a strategy for defusing it.

Sources of conflict. The sources of conflict are as follows:

Competing goals. There are many possible competing goals in this case: maintaining jobs for Parks Department employees, providing a safe place for children to play, developing citizen involvement, preserving a quiet retreat for elderly neighbors, and retaining a recreational facility for the youth living in Landmark Square. Some of these goals favor building the playground, some argue against it.

Competition for resources. Resources are tight, and different groups have different priorities for their use. ISPTF funds are limited, and the entire community is eligible to compete for a share. The Parks Department is also concerned about creating ongoing jobs by using the ISPTF funds as seed money.

Space is another scarce resource that must be budgeted wisely. A new and expanded playground will take up space formerly used for another purpose. For example, a ball field, a basketball court, or quiet sitting areas used by the elderly may have to be eliminated to make room for the playground.

Demographic or cultural differences. Misperceptions and misunderstandings concerning the motives and actions of others can result from conflicting priorities and interests. A decision to eliminate a basketball court to make room for the play-ground may be seen as racist, for example, if African-American teenagers are more likely to use the basketball court while white children are more likely to use a playground.

Likewise, enlarging the playground by decreasing the available sitting area may be seen as an example of how the needs of the elderly are ignored. As the negotiation proceeds, students should be urged to take the perspective of the different groups and see the issues through their eyes.

Power discrepancies. Each group has something to gain and something to lose in terms of influence. The Parks Department wants to maintain control over city playgrounds, the Community Volunteer Association wants to empower the community (an outcome which may be seen as threatening by the city government), the youth of Landmark Square may want to protect what they see as their "turf," *and* the senior citizens' home residents have similarly come to view the park as an extension of their own grounds. Finally, property owners will expect to be influential by virtue of the taxes they pay.

Identity affirmation. In situations such as these, each group can be expected to show concern about threats to its status and autonomy. Each group will make an effort to validate the interests of the group and affirm its importance. Students should be on guard for signs that a group's identity has been threatened.

Strategies for Managing Intergroup Conflict. When this case is used as a fishbowl exercise or a public hearing simulation, the ISPTF representatives will need strategies for managing the conflict that may emerge among the different groups present. To the extent that any group's goals, resources, influence, or identity is threatened, conflict will erupt. It is important that students recognize these threats to a negotiated solution to the case and minimize or eliminate them.

Focusing on shared goals, rather than on the subordinate goals of their groups, can minimize the effects of conflicting goals and competition for resources. By emphasizing the similarities in the groups' interests, the ISPTF representatives may be able to reframe divisive issues as the search for a "win-win" solution. For example, creative positioning of the playground might make it possible for the area to comfortably support multiple uses but cost no more than the ISPTF representatives are willing to budget for the playground.

Clear communication, emphasizing active listening, is key to the process of perspective-taking which allows each party to understand the interests, needs, and concerns of the others, and to reduce misperceptions. Open meetings involving all interested parties, as well as committees involving representatives of all groups will also reduce conflict based on cultural differences.

Power struggles will be minimized if an effort is made to guarantee all parties a voice in the decision-making process. It may also be helpful if the ISPTF representatives redefine the issues so that the primary task is seen as not just building a playground, but creating a park where the multiple needs of the neighborhood can be accommodated. These tactics should also serve to protect the integrity of each party from threats to group identity.

Questions for Discussion:

1. *What is the overall goal of the ISPTF?* This committee makes recommendations to the City Council for the use of special project funds for the betterment of the Ithaca community.

2. *How would you describe the relationship between the Parks Department Representative and the Community Volunteer Representative?* The answer to this question may depend on the attitudes towards the negotiation and towards their role as champion of their constituencies that the representatives brought to the table. Under most circumstances, the relationship will be cooperative as the representatives focus on the shared goal of the betterment of Ithaca. There should be little conflict between the two representatives if they use problem-solving techniques as they approach the negotiation. However, in situations where either the negotiators' egos become involved or if they choose to be radical adversarial champions of their constituencies, the relationship may turn hostile. This should be avoided.

3. *Identify all persons or groups likely to have a stake in the outcome of the negotiation. What are their interests likely to be? Which interests are shared?*

    - **Parks Department Representative**: promote betterment of Ithaca; maintain job opportunities for Parks Department employees; maintain favor in the eyes of the electorate.
    - **Community Volunteer Representative**: promote betterment of Ithaca; maintain and increase community involvement; maintain favor in the eyes of the electorate.
    - **Parks Department employees**: advocate jobs and funding for the Parks Department.
    - **Community involvement advocates**: support projects such as the playground as a means for creating strong and vital neighborhoods to combat an alienated citizenry.
    - **Property owners**: limit liability for injuries that may occur if children play in front of their homes; have children playing in a safe playground; avoid drug dealers; get representation for their greater tax dollars.
    - **Senior citizens' home residents**: maintain a quiet, safe neighborhood without drug dealers; maintain benches for their own use; perhaps provide a small, safe playground.
    - **Landmark Square residents**: provide a safe playground for their children that won't attract drug dealers; provide recreational facilities for teenagers, such as good basketball courts and playing fields; fight stereotypes as "troublemakers."
    - **Shared interests include the following:** for the politicians, a "better Ithaca," however the constituents define it. They are also "on the same side" in terms of both being members of the ISPTF. For the residents, shared interests include a safe, drug-free playground which takes the needs of others into account (e.g., not too noisy, and doesn't eliminate other recreation

opportunities). The residents also share an interest in having their voices heard and fairly interpreted.

4. *What decisions do the representatives face?* Their main decision is to fund or not to fund the playground, and to determine a funding level They must keep in mind that within the year, they will have to consider other projects that may be more, less, or equally deserving of funding. Once this decision is made, they then need to decide on a type of playground structure (the different options reflect different interests of their constituencies) and on a ground cover.

5. *What are the social issues with which the representatives should be concerned in making the decision to fund or not to fund the playground?* The representatives must be aware of the social tensions between the different groups in Titus Flats. They therefore need to take into account the elderly people's desire for quiet; the property owners' desire for voice and freedom from liability; the Landmark Square residents' concerns about stereotyping and preferential treatment of the property owners; everyone's desire for a drug-free neighborhood; as well as parents' concerns about the type of playground structure and ground cover that will be used. Issues of racism, ageism, and classism are likely to influence people's response to the representatives' decision if those representatives do not handle the decision thoughtfully.

6. *What are the economic issues with which the representatives should be concerned in making the decision to fund or not fund the playground?* ISPTF funds are fixed, and do not roll over from one year to the next. Moreover, the funds are a one-time grant, so the ISPTF cannot make any recommendations that require sustained financing.

7. *What are the political issues with which the representatives should be concerned in making the decision to fund or not to fund the playground?* The representatives are elected officials and must be concerned about not alienating their constituencies. However, the constituencies tend to overlap. Ithaca is small, so people who are Parks Department employees may at the same time be community volunteers. Moreover, the representatives must maintain the credibility and viability of the ISPTF planning board. Voters could potentially eliminate it if they were dissatisfied with its operation The representatives must take into consideration the fact that Titus Flats has not received ISPTF funds in the past. Previous funding has gone to wealthier areas than Titus Flats, or to projects that mostly benefit wealthier Ithacans.

8. *What differences can you find between this low-conflict situation and a high conflict negotiation?* In this low-conflict negotiation, the representatives share a common goal and common concerns about being re-elected--perhaps by the same people, since they have overlapping constituencies. The financial situation of funding the playground is not "zero-sum" as it may be in a high-conflict negotiation; one representative's gain does not necessarily mean a loss for the other representative. There is potential for conflict in this case: representatives can choose to be confrontational, at enormous political risk to themselves. If the case is handled as a public hearing, there is also potential for

conflict among members of the various constituencies. However, unlike high-conflict negotiations, these forms of conflict will not always surface.

Additional Information for the Instructor

This case, while not based on an actual incident, is nonetheless true-to-life. There are several community-based project architects. One of these, Robert Leathers, an Ithaca native, is known internationally for his designs and direction of construction for neighborhood playgrounds built mostly with community labor. Several playgrounds in Ithaca are Leathers' work. The kinds of discussion referred to in the case are very similar to actual discussions on city planning boards as Leathers' designs are considered (cf. Nagler, 1995; Tousignant, 1995; Wilding, 1995).

Students who are accustomed to payoff matrix-style negotiations may find this exercise awkward at first--there is a lot here that is unknown, and the best students will quickly realize that there is no one right answer. It is important to warn students in advance that this exercise is different from those they have done in the past, and that, as in "real life," they need to do the best they can with their wits and dealing with the uncertainties of unknown projects, and inexact pricing of playground elements. Real-world negotiations don't always come equipped with payoff tables; nor are costs of elements of the substance of the negotiation (in this case the parts of the playground) always the most important focus of the discussion.

It is also important that students not be allowed to "solve" the problem by "expanding the pie" by levying fees and taxes, or counting on enormous donations. Such solutions would be fiscally irresponsible, since the ISPTF has the power to make recommendations about the playground only, not about other civil fiscal matters. When this case was run in an experimental setting, gender differences in the negotiation process and outcome emerged (Halpern & McLean Parks, 1996). Females allocated less of the budget than males to the playground. Content coding of audio transcripts created by single-sex dyads revealed very different negotiation processes and styles underlying these different outcomes. Males and females emphasized different aspects of the case and saw different implications in the same materials. For example, males discussed their positions on the subject more than females, while females sought more interpersonal information than males. Males also tended to bring up monetary issues earlier during the negotiation than did females. Males in one class discussed the liability of different parties if children who used the parking lot as a playground got hit by a car as a result: nowhere does the case mention the possibility of legal problems.

Males and females' styles differed: for example, males used humor, while females did not. The males' jokes tended to be strategic. As an example, one of the male participants did not want to spend a lot of money on sand for ground cover. His negotiation partner had suggested a much higher dollar allocation for sand. The first negotiator responded: "Yeah, we need to get some sand, but we're not trying to build Malibu Beach here, man." With this joke, he made the other negotiator's request for more sand look ridiculous. Consequently, they ordered less sand.

In another example, a negotiator wanted to limit the expenses associated with the number of playground structures being considered. His issue was whether to allocate money for a climbing tower with a turret. "A turret? You want to pay to build a turret? Ivanhoe needs a turret. Rapunzel needs a turret. These kids do not need a turret." Consequently, they did not build a turret (Halpern & McLean Parks, 1996).

Females were more concerned about the reactions of other constituent groups than males were. For example, the case materials indicated that some parents had concerns a sand ground cover might attract cats who would use the sand as a litter box. Males tended to dismiss these concerns: Male Participant: "Well, I don't agree that there are any sanitary concerns with sand, so let's not worry about it."

Females, on the other hand, demonstrated a greater tolerance of, compassion for, and responsiveness to, others. Even when females disagreed with the parents' concerns, they still acknowledged that using sand might create a problem simply because the parents had doubts about it. Female Participant A: "Well, I don't agree, but if the mothers aren't comfortable, the children won't use it..." Female Participant B: "Maybe we could start an educational campaign?" Other demographic differences in the negotiation process could be an interesting area to pursue with the negotiators.

As a postscript, the area in Ithaca known as Titus Flats now has an expanded playground constructed of colorful plastic, and designed without turrets. It has a rubberized ground cover. One ballfield was eliminated, and two new basketball courts moved to the area directly adjacent to the four-lane road. It was not a Robert Leathers project.

References

Cox, T. H. Jr. (1993). *Cultural Diversity in Organizations: Theory, Research, and Practice*. San Francisco: Berrett Koehler.

Deutsch, M. (1973). *The Resolution of Conflict*. New Haven, CT: Yale University Press.

Fisher, R., & Ury, W. (1981). *Getting to Yes: Negotiating Agreement Without Giving In*. Boston: Houghton Mifflin.

Gray, B. (1989). *Collaborating: Finding Common Ground for Multi-party Problems*. San Francisco, CA: Jossey Bass.

Halpern, J. J., & McLean Parks, J. (1996). Vive La Difference: Differences Between Males and Females in Process and Outcomes in a Low-conflict Negotiation. *International Journal of Conflict Management*, 7, 45-70.

Lax, D. A., & Sebenius, J. K. (1986). *The Manager as Negotiator: Bargaining for Cooperation and Competitive Gain*. New York: Free Press.

Mischel, W. (1977). The interaction of Person and Situation. In D. Magnusson & N. S. Endler (Eds.), *Personality at the Crossroads: Current Issues in Interactional Psychology* (pp. 333-352). Hillsdale, NJ: Erlbaum.

Nagler, E. (1995, January 1). The view from Westbrook: What's Gone Wrong With the Campaign for a New Playscape? *New York Times*, Connecticut Weekly Desk, 13 CN, p.2.

Thomas, K. W. (1991) Conflict and Negotiation Processes in Organizations. In M. D. Dunnette & L. M. Hough (Eds.), *Handbook of Industrial and Organizational Psychology* 2nd ed. Vol. 3, pp. 651-717). Palo Alto, CA: Consulting Psychologists Press.

Tousignant, M. (1995, March 19). Splintered Over New Playgrounds, Some Parents Object as Fairfax Replaces Old Wooden Structures. *Washington Post*, Sunday Final Edition, Metro, p. B 01.

Walton, R. E., & McKersie, R. B. (1965). *A Behavioral Theory of Labor Negotiations: An Analysis of a Social Interaction System*. New York: McGraw-Hill.

Wilding, K. (1995, June 11). It Takes a Whole Town to Build Paradise Park. *Pittsburgh Post Gazette,* East Week Edition, Metro, p. EW 4.

THE PLAYGROUND NEGOTIATION
CONCLUDING POINTS

1. Goals of the parties:
   - Common elements
   - Divergent elements

2. Impact of goals on negotiating strategy

3. "Low-conflict" nature of problem

4. Environmental issues

5. "Political" nature of elected representatives

6. Diverse demographics of neighborhood

7. Sources of group-on-group conflict:
   - Competing goals
   - Competition for resources
   - Demographic/cultural differences
   - Power discrepancies
   - Identity of different groups

Discussion Questions:

1. What is the overall goal of the ISPTF?

2. What is the relationship between the Parks Department Representative and the Community Volunteer Representative?

3. What groups have a stake in the outcome? What are the interests of each of these groups?

4. What decisions must the representatives make?

5. What are the "social tensions" between groups in the funding decision?

6. What are the economic issues facing the representatives in making the decision?

7. What are the political issues facing the representatives in making the decision?

8. What are the differences between a low-conflict situation and a high-conflict situation?

ROLE OF THE PARKS DEPARTMENT REP(S) OPTION 1
EXERCISE 23: THE PLAYGROUND NEGOTIATION

In this negotiation, you represent the Ithaca Parks Department. You were elected to the City Council on a platform that called for job protection for city employees. Recently, the mayor appointed you to the Ithaca Special Projects Task Force (ISPTF). This task force makes recommendations to the full Council for funding special projects which will benefit the Ithaca community. The Council then provides one-time funding for these special projects which are not included in the budgets for any other department. The ISPTF does not guarantee ongoing support for the projects it funds; thus, most projects are those that can be completed within one fiscal year.

You and your task force partner(s) are to consider a proposal for an expanded playground at Titus Flats (see accompanying maps). This playground will require ISPTF funds, some Parks Department sponsorship (including human resources), and volunteer effort. You must determine what kind of configuration and materials will be used for the playground, who will construct the playground, and who will provide maintenance.

As a former employee of the city, you are acutely aware of the dynamics of funding decisions. You know that if a department does not make full use of its employees, positions can be eliminated. Thus, you have strong preferences for projects that insure that as much work as possible is done by Parks Department employees rather than outside contractors or other parties, initially and in the future. However, your experience has made you realistic about not always getting what you want. You have no way of knowing how the playground proposal stacks up against other funding proposals not yet considered by the ISPTF. These other proposals may involve the Parks Department to a greater degree than this project does, or may not involve Parks Department employees in any way. In any case, as an elected official, the support of your constituents means a lot to you.

This exercise has three parts. In the first part, you will review the materials and formulate your position. The second part is a public hearing before the ISPTF. At this hearing, citizens can ask questions and express their views. In the third part, you and the other member(s) of the ISPTF will negotiate a resolution to the issue and a budget, should you decide to fund the project. Under the state open meetings law, this session must take place in front of the citizen audience.

ROLE OF THE COMMUNITY VOLUNTEER REP(S) OPTION 1
EXERCISE 23: THE PLAYGROUND NEGOTIATION

In this negotiation, you represent the Ithaca Volunteer Association. You were elected to the City Council on a platform that called for increased citizen participation in community development. Recently, the mayor appointed you to the ISPTF because of your extensive work with grassroots community improvement efforts involving volunteers from all segments of the Ithaca community. This task force makes recommendations to the full Council for funding special projects which will benefit the Ithaca community. The Council then provides one-time funding for these special projects which are not included in the budgets for any other department. The ISPTF does not guarantee ongoing support for the projects it funds; thus, most projects are those that can be completed within one fiscal year.

You and your task force partner(s) are to consider a proposal for an expanded playground at Titus Flats (see accompanying maps). This playground will require ISPTF funds, some Parks Department sponsorship (including human resources), and volunteer effort. You must determine what kind of configuration and materials will be used for the playground, who will construct the playground, and who will provide maintenance.

From your experience, you find the benefits of citizen involvement to be substantial, not only in terms of saving money during times of economic stress, but also in terms of building cohesiveness and pride in Ithaca neighborhoods. You therefore want as much support, whether financial or otherwise, for the Community Volunteer Association as possible. One beneficial side effect of community involvement in the past has been increased citizen participation in other civic activities, including school board elections and neighborhood crime watches. Projects that involve community "ownership" of the project and require ongoing volunteer effort seem to be particularly helpful in this regard. Although you feel that citizen participation is the wave of the future (especially in the light of severe federal and state budge cuts), your experience has made you realistic about not always getting what you want. In any case, as an elected official, the support of your constituents means a lot to you.

You have no way of knowing what other projects will be proposed to the task force. These proposals may open up opportunities for greater citizen participation, involve a larger cross-section of the community, or have greater visibility than this project. Or they may not involve community volunteers in any way.

This exercise has three parts. In the first part, you will review the materials and formulate your position. The second part is a public hearing before the ISPTF. At this hearing, citizens can ask questions and express their views. In the third part, you and the other member(s) of the ISPTF will negotiate a resolution to the issues and a budget, should you decide to fund the project. Under the state open meetings law, this session must take place in front of the citizen audience.

ROLE OF LOCAL PROPERTY OWNER(S) OPTION 1
EXERCISE 23: THE PLAYGROUND NEGOTIATION

In this exercise, you represent the local property owners who live in the Titus Flats neighborhood. You were elected to this position in an ad hoc meeting of concerned neighbors. You will be attending a public hearing by the ISPTF. This task force makes recommendations to the City Council for funding special projects which will benefit the Ithaca community. The Council then provides one-time funding for these special projects which are not included in the budgets for any other department. The ISPTF does not guarantee ongoing support for the projects it funds; thus, most projects are those that can be completed within one fiscal year.

The task force members are to consider a proposal for an expanded playground at Titus Flats (see accompanying maps). This playground will require ISPTF funds, some Parks Department sponsorship (including human resources), and volunteer effort. The task force will determine what kind of configuration and materials will be used for the playground, who will construct the playground, and who will provide maintenance.

Property owners are concerned with several issues regarding the playground. First, they are concerned that children presently play in the streets and sidewalks in front of their homes. There is some concern about damage to vehicles parked on the street and lawns from this practice. In addition, although there have been no automobile accidents involving serious injury to children, many property owners worry that it is just a matter of time. Finally, property owners are concerned about their liability for injuries that may occur to children playing in front of their homes.

While a safe playground would address these issues, property owners are concerned that a larger playground could become a magnet for teenage gangs and drug dealers. Some parents already avoid taking their children to the Park because of the ever-present basketball games. They feel their children are intimidated by the boisterous teens and young adults on and around the court. Some property owners fear that the costs could outweigh the benefits, and they want to be sure the Task Force addresses security issues. While you know the Park serves the entire community, you also know that property owners pay the most taxes and expect to have the greatest influence on this decision.

This exercise has three parts. In the first part, you will review the materials and formulate your position. The second part is a public hearing before the ISPTF. At this hearing, you can ask questions and express your views. In the third part, member(s) of the ISPTF will negotiate a resolution to the issues and a budget, should they decide to fund the project. Under the state open meetings law, this session must take place in front of the citizen audience. You do not negotiate, but you can indicate your pleasure or displeasure with statements made through your facial expressions.

ROLE OF THE SENIOR CITIZEN(S) AT TITUS TOWERS OPTION 1
EXERCISE 23: THE PLAYGROUND NEGOTIATION

In this exercise, you represent the senior citizens who live at Titus Towers adjacent to the Titus Flats Neighborhood Park. You were asked to represent the residents at a regularly scheduled meeting of the residents. You will be attending a public hearing by the Ithaca Special Projects Task Force (ISPTF). This task force makes recommendations to the City Council for funding special projects which will benefit the Ithaca community. The Council then provides one-time funding for these special projects which are not included in the budget for any other department. The ISPTF does not guarantee ongoing support for the projects it funds; thus, most projects are those that can be completed within one fiscal year.

The task force members are to consider a proposal for an expanded playground at Titus Flats (see accompanying maps). This playground will require ISPTF funds, some Parks Department sponsorship (including human resources), and volunteer effort. The task force will determine what kind of configuration and materials will be used for the playground, who will construct the playground, and who will provide maintenance.

The main concern of the residents is the preservation of a quiet and safe neighborhood around the Towers. Residents like to sit in the Park on warm days, and some walk to nearby Tops Supermarket and a drugstore. Although a wooded area provides a visual and sound screen between the Towers and the Park, many residents still complain about the softball games and especially the basketball games, which they characterize as raucous and profane. In addition, the court seems to serve as a hangout for groups of teens who congregate in the sitting area next to the courts. On the other hand, a number of residents like to take visiting grandchildren to the playground, which is viewed as manageable because it is small. There is some fear that a larger playground would be more crowded with children running and throwing things and could easily cause injury to a senior citizen through carelessness. While you know the Park serves the entire community, you also know that residents of the Towers view the Park as an extension of their own grounds and feel that as the nearest neighbors to the playground, they should have the greatest influence on this decision.

This exercise has three parts. In the first part, you will review the materials and formulate your position. The second part is a public hearing before the ISPTF. At this hearing, you can ask questions and express your views. In the third part, member(s) of the ISPTF will negotiate a resolution to the issues and a budget, should they decide to fund the project. Under the state open meetings law, this session must take place in front of the citizen audience. You do not negotiate, but you can indicate your pleasure or displeasure with statements made through your facial expressions.

ROLE OF RESIDENT(S) AT LANDMARK SQUARE OPTION 1
EXERCISE 23: THE PLAYGROUND NEGOTIATION

In this exercise, you represent the residents of Landmark Square, a public housing project in the Titus Flats neighborhood. You hold this position as an elected officer with the Landmark Square Tenants' association. You will be attending a public hearing by the Ithaca Special Projects Task Force (ISPTF). This task force makes recommendations to the City Council for funding special projects which will benefit the Ithaca community. The Council then provides one-time funding for these special projects which are not included in the budgets for any other department. The ISPTF does not guarantee ongoing support for the projects it funds; thus, most projects are those that can be completed within one fiscal year.

The task force members are to consider a proposal for an expanded playground at Titus Flats (see accompanying maps). This playground will require ISPTF funds, some Parks Department sponsorship (including human resources), and volunteer effort. The Task Force will determine what kind of configuration and materials will be used for the playground, who will construct the playground, and who will provide maintenance.

Landmark Square residents are low-income renters; many of them are welfare recipients, and a high proportion are African-American. Parents at Landmark Square depend on the playground at Titus Flats Neighborhood Park because there are no facilities in the project. Their older teens use the basketball court heavily, and parents feel this keeps them from hanging out on the streets. In fact, the court is constantly busy, and teens are frequently seen waiting for it to open up. Some members of the tenants' association are talking about organizing summer leagues for basketball and baseball to help keep their children out of trouble. As a result, residents would like to see improvements in not only the playground, but also more basketball courts and improved ballfields.

Like others in the community, residents of Landmark Square do not want to see the area turn into a hangout for gangs and drug dealers. They are worried that the city will provide inadequate security because the city does not pay adequate attention to their needs and concerns. While they do not wish to be seen as "troublemakers," they feel that they have just as much right as anyone else in the neighborhood to have their interests and needs considered.

This exercise has three parts. In the first part, you will review the materials and formulate your position. The second part is a public hearing before the ISPTF. At this hearing, you can ask questions and express your views. In the third part, member(s) of the ISPTF will negotiate a resolution to the issues and a budget, should they decide to fund the project. Under the state open meetings law, this session must take place in front of the citizen audience. You do not negotiate, but you can indicate your pleasure or displeasure with statements made through your facial expressions.

ROLE: PARKS DEPARTMENT REP(S) OPTION 2
EXERCISE 23: THE PLAYGROUND NEGOTIATION

You and your task force partner(s) are to consider a proposal for an expanded playground at Titus Flats (see accompanying maps). This playground will require ISPTF funds, some Parks Department sponsorship (including human resources), and volunteer effort. You must determine what kind of configuration and materials will be used for the playground, who will construct the playground, and who will provide maintenance.

In this negotiation, you represent the Parks Department. You were elected as a City Council representative and later appointed to the Ithaca Special Projects Task Force (ISPTF). As a former employee of the city, you are acutely aware of the dynamics of funding decisions and are particularly committed to the Parks Department. You know that if a department does not make full use of its employees, positions can be eliminated. During times of economic stress (like now), this is a particularly serious concern, and you keep a close eye on projects which will use existing personnel most efficiently. However, while your previous experience leads you to prefer to see current employees used in projects, your more recent experiences on the City Council have made you realistic about not always getting what you want. Furthermore, as an elected official, the support of your constituents means a lot to you.

Your task force partner, like you, is an elected official. However, your partner was appointed to the task force partly because of his or her extensive work with grassroots community organizations. You are aware that the agenda your constituents have for you, and your partner's agenda, may overlap; this is not necessarily a win-lose situation.

ROLE: COMMUNITY VOLUNTEER REP(S) OPTION 2
EXERCISE 23: THE PLAYGROUND NEGOTIATION

You and your task force partner(s) are to consider a proposal for an expanded playground at Titus Flats (see accompanying maps). This playground will require ISPTF funds, some Parks Department sponsorship (including human resources), and volunteer effort. You must determine what kind of configuration and materials will be used for the playground, who will construct the playground, and who will provide maintenance.

In this negotiation, you represent the Community Volunteer Association. The CVA is a non-governmental, non-profit coalition of several voluntary community action groups such as neighborhood organizations, Jaycees, historic preservation groups, etc. You were elected as a City Council representative and later appointed to the Ithaca Special Projects Task Force (ISPTF) due to your extensive work with grassroots community improvement efforts involving volunteers from all segments of the community. From your experience, you find the benefits of citizen involvement to be substantial, not only in terms of saving money during times of economic stress, but also in terms of building cohesiveness and pride in Ithaca neighborhoods. One beneficial side effect of community involvement in the past has been increased citizen participation in other civic activities, including school board elections and neighborhood crime watches. Although you feel that increased citizen participation is the wave of the future (because of government budget cuts), your experience on the City Council has made you realistic about not always getting what you want. Furthermore, as an elected official, the support of your constituents means a lot to you.

Your task force partner, like you, is an elected official. However, your partner was appointed to the task force partly because of his or her extensive knowledge of and experience with funding decisions in local organizations such as the Parks Department. You are aware that the agenda your constituents have for you, and your partner's agenda, may overlap; this is not necessarily a win-lose situation.

EXERCISE 24
COLLECTING NOS

Objectives:

1. To provide an opportunity for students to practice making requests and to understand how they make requests, and whether their particular strategies are effective or ineffective.

2. To allow students to examine their "theories" of what it takes to get people to take action.

Time Required   The exercise is designed to be given as homework. The only class time required is for exploring what happened with student efforts to make requests. This can take as little as 20 minutes, or as much as 60 minutes, depending on how the instructor is using the exercise and what areas (see below) are chosen for exploration.

Special Materials   None

Special Physical Requirements   None

Readings Related to this Exercise:

Kuhn (2.1), Scott (2.2), Craver (3.2), Dawson (3.3)

What to Expect:

This exercise engages students in formulating and making requests that are intended to produce "No" as the response. One reason people often give for not making requests of other people is that they do not want to experience the rejection of being told "No." This exercise is specifically designed to have getting a "No" a success! Students are successful when they are told "No!" Thus, the exercise may help students be more assertive, learn how to ask for things more directly, or discover the real "limits" to a reasonable or unreasonable request.

There are three things that reliably happen with this exercise:

1) People generally say "Yes" to requests. We have found that it takes approximately 6 requests to get one "No." And, to even get that one "No," students generally have to make their requests more and more unreasonable. That is, they have to ask for much more of something than they think is "reasonable", or to ask for it with a deadline much shorter than they expect. Students are generally amazed at what people will say "Yes" to in the way of a request, and are often surprised how outrageous they need to be to get a genuine, clear-cut, unambiguous "No."

2)   When people do decline requests, they do not generally come right out and say "No." They may say, "I'll think about it", or "I'll get back to you," or "Maybe," etc. Discovering this is part of the exercise, and exploring why people do not come right out and say "No" is worthy of exploration. In probing for the reasons why people just don't say "No," students will uncover many underlying beliefs which shape the way we communicate in organizations.

Parts B and C of the exercise raise other issues worthy of exploration. Part C allows people to explore how persistent they are in getting a request accepted and their relationship to making repeated requests. In this area, it is worth noting that some people relate to a "No" as a permanent, irrevocable response, rather than as what was said at the time. There are lots of reasons why people may say "no." But what are the reasons for not asking a second or even third time? This allows students to explore not only their own commitments, but also the beliefs and assumptions that stop them from making requests.

Part C provides students with the opportunity to actually learn what they would have to do to get a "Yes." People have reasons for saying "No," and most of these reasons can be successfully addressed if the student is willing to find out what would address them. So, when the student is told "No," there is an opportunity to find out what actions can be taken to make it a "Yes." Then the student can decide if they will take the action. Again, it allows the student to explore their commitment in getting a yes and what they are willing to do to get the "yes."

Advance Preparation:

A solid understanding of requests and their structure is needed before students are given this assignment (see following "Brief Guide to Requests," which may be copied and distributed). Students should be directed to formulate and make requests using the canonical structure provided in the "Brief Guide to Requests." It is recommended that students be given an opportunity to formulate and make requests in class so that they have some practical experience before doing the homework. Instructors would also do well to read the recommended reference material.

Operating Procedure:

There is no special operating procedure other than a willingness to let the discussion explore different issues as they come up.

What Happens?

In general what happens is that students have a hard time getting 10 "Nos." Students generally expect people will say "no," and when they don't, they are surprised. Incidentally, this exercise has been used with all types of managers at all different levels in organizations, and the results are very reliable. The only thing that varies is the actual responses people get.

The other thing that happens is that when people say "No," they generally give a reason or an excuse for not accepting the request immediately. It is worth looking with students to see what types of excuses are made e.g., "too busy," "no time," "other commitments," etc. and then to talk about the social acceptability of the excuses given. There are cultural and organizational excuses that make it O.K. to say "No," and we never really challenge the excuse, we just accept it. It is worth exploring why some excuses are acceptable and others are not. The reference on "Accounts" is particularly useful here.

Concluding the Exercise

Students generally find this exercise informative and empowering. What they find empowering is that they can make requests and generally get what they want. This is a real revelation to students and it gives them considerable power in getting things done. At the same time, however, they can find it confronting because making requests can appear "pushy" or "intrusive" to some. So students are left with deciding for themselves how far they are willing to go in making requests. A good way to conclude this exercise, therefore, is simply to acknowledge this while pointing out to them that they have demonstrated that they can get many of the things they want, and some things they never expected they could get, through well formulated requests. It is up to them how and when they will use this newfound power.

Recommended References:

Goss, T. (1996). *The Last Word on Power*. New York: Currency Doubleday. pages 170-186.

Scott, M. & Layman, S. (1968). Accounts. *American Sociological Review*, Vol. 33, pp. 45-62

Wheeler, Michael. (1997). Getting to No. *Negotiation Journal*. Vol. 13, No. 3.

"BRIEF GUIDE TO REQUESTS"

Requests are speech acts which call another person into action. Although there are many forms of requests (see Goss, 1996), the canonical form is:

- I request that you [intended result] by [deadline].

Requests, therefore, ask someone else to produce a specific result by a specific deadline. A specific result is something that is unequivocal and not subject to interpretation. This means that someone other than the parties to a request could tell if the request has been satisfied. The following are examples of equivocal and unequivocal results:

Equivocal: increase sales

(It is equivocal because we do not know how much of an increase is wanted)

Unequivocal: 25% increase in sales

Equivocal: give me support at the sales meeting (it's equivocal because we do not know what is meant by support or how one would know if it was given)

Unequivocal: speak on behalf of and vote for my new pricing policy at the sales meeting

What makes requests hard is that the person making the request must be very clear about what they want and communicate it as a specific result.

The other part to a request is the "by when" the result is wanted. Again, the deadline is to be unequivocal so that the person fulfilling the request can be certain that the deadline has been met. The following are examples of equivocal and unequivocal deadlines:

Equivocal: ASAP (it's equivocal because we do not know when this is needed)

Unequivocal: by 3 PM this afternoon

Equivocal: next month (its equivocal because we do not know when next month)

Unequivocal: by the 15th of next month

So, not only does someone need to know what they want, they have to know when they want it. This requires some work on behalf of the person making the request to be clear about the deadline.

When requests are well formulated, both people know what is being asked for and can easily determine if the request has been satisfied.

EXERCISE 25
500 ENGLISH SENTENCES

NOTE: This material is also available as a case (Case 7, 500 English Sentences). Instructors are advised to use either the roleplay or the case, but not both because they overlap considerably. Choosing whether to use the roleplay or case materials depends on your goals for the class and the level of sophistication and cross-cultural experience of the students. For homogeneous classes with little previous cross-cultural experience, one option is to use the case to teach the cross-cultural nuances of American-Japanese negotiations and to follow this with Exercise 26 (Sick Leave), a roleplay with many similar lessons to 500 English Sentences.

Objectives

The two participants in this roleplay frame the negotiation in very different ways. For Scott (the American Assistant English teacher) it is an issue of right-wrong. There are several errors in the manuscript *500 English Sentences*, he is a native speaker of English and he has a university degree in English literature so he knows that he is right. For Mr. Honda (the Japanese Head of English) it is an issue of honor, reputation, and face. He has worked in the same school board for more than 20 years and he wants to avoid embarrassing his superiors in the Board of Education, who initially authored the first edition of the book several years before. The differences in framing reflect nicely the cross-cultural differences in the way that Americans and Japanese negotiate.

1. To negotiate in a cross cultural situation where pride and face are very important.

2. To practice understanding the interests that underlie the other party's positions, especially when the negotiation is framed quite differently by the two parties.

3. To learn a different meaning to the term win/lose bargaining.

Group Size Students work in pairs. Any number may participate, limited only by the size of the space available.

Time Required 60-90 minutes

Special Materials Copy and distribute role information from this manual.

Special Physical Requirements None.

Recommended Reading Assignments to Accompany This Exercise

Reader: 11.1 (Phatak & Habib), 11.2 (Koh), 11.3 (Frank)
Text: Chapter 11

What to Expect

The role play pits the participants' egos and goals against each other in a situation where there appears to be no compromise (Scott either signs the endorsement or he doesn't; he can't "half-sign"). The addition of two different cultural styles complicates the resolution of the problem. Some groups will try to compromise (include half of the revisions to the text); this is a very Western way of handling the situation because more than a couple of changes will cause the original authors to lose face. Participants who are more competitive will have trouble reaching an agreement and understanding the perspective of the other party.

Advance Preparation

Students and the instructor should be familiar with cultural and business differences between Japan and North America. Dated, yet still appropriate, is Howard Van Zandt's *How to Negotiate in Japan,* from the Harvard Business Review of Nov/Dec 1970, more current is *Smart Bargaining* by John Graham and Yoshihiro Sano, *The Influence of Japanese Culture on Business Relationships and Negotiations* by Naoko Oikawa and John Tanner Jr., *International Dimensions of Organizational Behavior*, chapter on Negotiating with Foreigners by Nancy J. Adler, and *Cultural Approaches to Negotiations: Understanding the Japanese* by Brian Hawrysh and Judith Zaichkowsky.

In addition, the instructor (but not the students) should read Case 7 (500 English Sentences) because, while written from Scott's point of view, it contains a good description of the broader content of the situation surrounding the publication of the book.

Operating Procedure

Care needs to be taken when assigning students to the roles in this exercise. If there are students who are from, or who have lived in, Japan then they should be assigned the role of Mr. Honda. It is also possible to conduct this negotiation as a fishbowl, where the person most familiar with the Japanese negotiation style would play Mr. Honda. Some participants may have trouble playing the Japanese role, so it may be a good idea to split the class in half during the preparation for the negotiation and to discuss with the students who are playing the Japanese role the nuances of the approach. Participants should read the information in the text along with handouts dealing with differences in negotiation styles between Japanese and North Americans (see below). On the surface, this is a very straightforward situation: will Scott sign the endorsement or not? The cultural differences, however, make it essential to Mr. Honda that Scott signs and equally essential to Scott that he doesn't.

Concluding the Exercise

Debriefing of the exercise should begin with a discussion of the outcome of the negotiation. Proceed by using the following questions:

1. How many people playing the role of Scott decided to endorse the book? For those that decided to sign the endorsement, why did you? For those deciding not to sign, why didn't you?

2. Speaking to those playing the role of Scott only, what was this negotiation about? (Use the blackboard to record all of the responses). Next, repeat the process for those playing the role of Mr. Honda.

3. Next, discuss the process of the negotiation. How did people approach the negotiation? How was it similar and different to other negotiations in the class? Was it easier or more challenging than other exercises? Why?

4. What were the most important intangibles in the negotiation? Was saving face more important to Scott or Mr. Honda? Why?

The discussion should conclude with a good summary about Japanese and North American negotiation styles and culture. When negotiating in Japan it is often important to give in for the sake of peace and harmony, or relationships may be harmed beyond repair. Deciding *how* to negotiate cross-culturally remains a challenge for every negotiator that negotiates across a border. One of the best pieces discussing this was written by Stephen Weiss ("Negotiating with 'Romans': A Range of Culturally-Responsive Strategies," *Sloan Management Review*, 35, No. 1, pp. 51-61; No. 2, pp. 1-16) and a summary of this work makes a nice conclusion to the class.

Final Note

Although this exercise has been modified somewhat it is based on an actual situation that occurred in Japan (names and location have been changed). "Scott" is currently completing a Master's degree in East Asian Studies at a Northeastern American University and is looking forward to returning to Japan. He continues to study Japanese and to perfect his karate. Mr. "Honda" continues as a loyal employee of his school. After thinking carefully about the situation during the week of the negotiation, "Scott" decided to endorse the book.

CULTURAL NEGOTIATION STYLES[1]

Japanese

- Status relationships are very important (e.g., older, larger, more prestigious have more power)

- Buyers have more status than sellers, but buyers look out for seller's interests

- Focus is long-term and on the relationship (not the contract)

- Maintaining harmony is more important than the deal

- Decision making is by consensus

- Important concessions and negotiating is done before the formal meeting, which is used as a place to approve what has already been discussed

- Do not say "no"

- Discuss items holistically

- A contract represents the beginning of the negotiation and furthering of the relationship

---

[1] Based on the book *Smart Bargaining: Doing Business with the Japanese* by John Graham and Yoshihiro Sano. New York: Harper Collins, 1989.

CULTURAL NEGOTIATION STYLES[1]

American

- Status relationships are not very important; status is based on what you can do, not who you are

- Buyers and sellers have equal status; negotiators look out for their own interests

- Focus is short term and on the contract (not the relationship)

- The deal is more important than maintaining harmony

- Decision making is individualistic

- Important concessions and negotiating is done at the formal meeting

- Do not accept "no" for an answer (there is always a way...)

- Discuss items sequentially

- A contract represents the end of the negotiation and is enforceable

CONFIDENTIAL ROLE INFORMATION FOR SCOTT
EXERCISE 25: 500 ENGLISH SENTENCES

You have been working for Nishi High School in Japan as a member of their English teaching staff for the past 6 months. Previous to this position, you taught a year at the Naka High School but changed schools because you thought Nishi High provided more of a challenge. You are one of two foreign teachers on the Nishi staff although you have been working in Japan longer than the other teacher. You have a degree in English literature and this is your first job after graduating from university in the United States.

This is the first time that you have ever been to Japan. Previous to your living there, you had never studied Japanese nor knew anything about the Japanese culture. You applied for and accepted a teaching job in Japan because you heard that the pay was higher than starting positions back home in the United States, in spite of the higher cost of living. You are trying your best to adapt to the Japanese way of life. You are currently attending Japanese classes and have read everything you can get your hands on about the Japanese culture so that you don't make any major faux pas on the job.

You feel that your relationship with the teaching staff at Nishi has been very cordial for the short time that you have been there. Japanese people are extremely group oriented and it usually takes time to break into the inner circle, as your experiences at Naka High confirm. The teachers at Nishi seem to appreciate the extra hours you put into work and your efforts to speak Japanese. Your relationship is also helped by the fact that you are on good terms with Mr. Honda, the head of English at Nishi. You have known Mr. Honda for over a year since he also taught at Naka High School and transferred to Nishi high about the same time as you. At Naka High School, you had assisted Mr. Honda with several projects and teaching seminars, which you felt were very successful. Another reason that you feel explains your acceptance by the teachers is that 3 months ago, Nishi High School hosted a prefecture wide English Teaching conference at which you gave a demonstration teaching class. The demonstration was a huge success and resulted in Nishi receiving an outstanding commendation from the prefectural Board of Education and from each of the other schools in attendance. To show his gratitude and his faith in your abilities, Mr. Honda has put you in charge of the Advanced English program. This is a special cram class for the senior students who are studying for their university entrance examination. This exam is extremely tough and important as only those students with the highest scores have any hope of being accepted to the top universities. To be trusted with this class shows that the teachers and Mr. Honda think highly of you as a teacher.

One afternoon about two weeks ago, you were working at your desk in the staff room when you were approached by a group of smiling Japanese English teachers headed by Mr. Honda. The teachers put a copy of *500 English Sentences* on your desk. You feared that they were going to ask you to make more use of this textbook in your classes since you are the only teacher in the department who does not use the book. You know that the book was written several years ago by senior English teachers of Nishi high school who since have been promoted to higher positions at the Board of Education and that the book has gone on to be used by virtually every English department in the prefecture, but you also know that the text is full of glaring grammatical inconsistencies, misspelling and archaic forms of English. You would never use such an inferior textbook in your classes. What you find most appalling about the book is that it is endorsed by an American English teacher who you think must be the worst if not the stupidest teacher alive for promoting such an abysmal text.

To your relief, the entourage of teachers are there to ask for your input to correct and update the *500 English Sentences* for a revised edition planned to be published soon. Mr. Honda tells you that Nishi High School has the great honor of being assigned the task of editing the text and submitting it to the publisher in time for the deadline. You agree to do the work and ask Mr. Honda when he would like you to finish the revisions. He tells you that the corrected manuscript must be on the publisher's desk in 10 days. You find this an unreasonably short amount of time for such a big project. You don't believe that you will have enough time to do the work and ask why the publisher has given the school such a quick deadline. Mr. Honda tells you that he has known about the project for at least six months. You ask Mr. Honda why he did not come to you sooner, but your question is greeted with coughs and silence. You decide that it is probably better that you don't know the reason since you will probably not be happy with the answer, and tell Mr. Honda that you will go ahead with the project.

You take the project home with you and work on it for 4 days non-stop. You return the manuscript all covered with red marks, sample replacement sentences and complete explanations as to why the changes you made were necessary. To your surprise, instead of thanking you for your efforts, Mr. Honda looks very uncomfortable, smiles nervously and takes the manuscript from you.

Two days later, while sitting at your desk, the same group of English teachers approach you, thank you for all your hard work, and then while coughing and humming and hawing, tell you that your corrections cannot be used. You cannot believe what they are telling you. You demand to know why and they tell you that it would be too much trouble for the publisher to make so many changes at such a late date. You stare at the group of teachers incredulously and tell them that maybe they should have thought of this six months ago. As the teachers retreat, you wonder which is more important to them, the publisher or students?

The next day, Mr. Honda comes over to your desk. In his hand is the uncorrected manuscript that he is going to send in to the publisher along with an endorsement paper that he has prepared and wants you to sign. You cannot believe this. Not only are they going to send in the text without any of your corrections, but they want you to endorse it. You realize that you have no power to force Mr. Honda to send the manuscript with your corrections into the publisher, but you can control whether you sign the endorsement or not. You have read the last endorsement in the previous edition and you have openly made fun of the foreign teacher who signed his name to such a flawed textbook. There is no way that you want your name associated with such a substandard text and you feel that your integrity and reputation as an educator would be compromised if you sign.

CONFIDENTIAL ROLE INFORMATION FOR MR. HONDA
EXERCISE 25: 500 ENGLISH SENTENCES

Six months ago, you were transferred from Naka High School to Nishi High, where you took over the position of head of English. You are originally from Osaka and have been teaching English for more than 22 years. Your department hires several foreign teachers specifically to teach the advanced classes and help the senior students prepare for the English portion of the rigorous university entrance examinations. One of the current foreign teachers on your staff, Scott from the United States, has been working at your school for the past six months. You believe that you have a good relationship with Scott since you have known and worked with him at your previous high school.

You are very proud of Scott and think that he is coming along fine as your protégé. You see yourself as a mentor, not only to Scott, but to all of the junior English teachers in your department. Like any good Japanese manager, you see it as your role to protect and guide your subordinates, not only on the job, but also in life. You advise them on everything from good lesson planning and teaching methods, to appropriate marrying times. In your opinion, good employees are those who listen to their mentors and act on their advice and not act independently, since they are too inexperienced to know any better. Scott's conduct and teaching ability are making you as his supervisor very proud. Scott also conducted a very impressive teaching demonstration at your school during a teachers' conference which brought high commendations to your school from the Board of Education and the other schools in attendance.

Your English department uses, among others, a textbook called *500 English Sentences* which was written several years ago by senior members of your English staff who have since moved on to higher positions at the Board of Education. The book went on to become a standard and has been adopted by nearly every high school in the prefecture. Your school is very proud of this achievement and you feel deeply honored to be working at Nishi, the school which produced such distinguished authors.

The publisher of the book has decided to revise *500 English Sentences* since it has been several years since the text was first published. Nishi High School has been chosen to do this task, which you consider to be another great honor, because they feel that you continue to have an excellent English department. You use the text in your classes and feel that the book is flawless. You imagine that only a few minor changes will be needed, at most a morning of your time, so you put the manuscript into your "To Do" basket on your desk.

One day, while going through some papers on your desk, you come across the manuscript and realize that you had almost forgotten about it. You check the date when the manuscript is due back at the publisher and discover that it is only 10 days away. You decide to ask Scott to look over the manuscript for you since he is a native English speaker and has studied English literature at a university in the United States. You feel that he should be able to look through the book in a couple of hours since there are not many changes that need to be made.

Scott does not appear too happy when you ask him to do this favor for the school. Instead of listening and accepting responsibility like a good *kohai* (subordinate), he tells you that the publisher is being unreasonable by insisting that a whole manuscript be edited within 10 days. You think Scott's accusation is out of line but you explain that the publisher is not at fault and that you have known about the project for the past six months. You decide that this is further proof that foreigners are simply argumentative and are not always eager to help out. To your satisfaction, Scott agrees to look over the manuscript.

You don't see anything from Scott by the end of the day but aren't too concerned since you told him when the deadline was. After a couple of days, you begin to worry and wonder why Scott hasn't returned the manuscript. You hope that he has not forgotten about the project. On the fifth day, Scott comes to you with the manuscript so covered with red ink that it looks like he has rewritten the entire work. You thank him for his efforts and take the papers.

You cannot believe that Scott found so many errors. You look over his work and discover, much to your embarrassment that, indeed, most of his changes are justified. You know that the publisher wants to update the book so the changes that can be attributed to the evolving usage of the language pose no problem. However, most of the changes are simply corrections of errors on the part of the original authors. You realize that if you make all of these changes, it will result in a great loss of face for the authors who are currently high level members of the board of education. You have no intention of making these senior men look bad nor do you want to risk other people thinking that your school's teachers are impudent.

Two days later you return to Scott and tell him that perhaps you will not be able to use all of his corrections. Scott appears very agitated and upset and demands to know why. You explain that perhaps it will be a problem for the publisher if he has to change so much at such a late date. You don't anticipate any argument from Scott on this issue since you believe he is a team player and will understand.

The next day, you go over to Scott's desk and ask him to sign an endorsement which will go in the inside cover of the "revised" *500 English Sentences*. The first edition is also endorsed by a Native English Speaker and the Board of Education has asked you get have Scott sign it because they feel that his signature will add legitimacy to the book.

To your complete surprise, Scott flatly refuses to sign the endorsement. If he doesn't sign there will be a great loss of face for your school. The original authors of the text will be insulted and will probably lose face since people will speculate as to why Scott didn't endorse the book. You will probably be passed up on the promotions in the spring, if not demoted. You hope that you can convince Scott to endorse the text.

EXERCISE 26
SICK LEAVE

NOTE: This material is also available as a case (Case 8, Sick Leave). Instructors are advised to use either the roleplay or the case, but not both because they overlap considerably. Choosing whether to use the roleplay or case materials depends on your goals for the class and the level of sophistication and cross-cultural experience of the students. For homogeneous classes with little previous cross-cultural experience, one option is to use the case to teach the cross-cultural nuances of American-Japanese negotiations and to follow this with Exercise 25 (500 English Sentences), a roleplay with many similar lessons to Sick Leave.

Objectives

The root of this negotiation is a deep cross-cultural misunderstanding that has transformed into a much larger incident involving important intangible factors such as saving face and maintaining principles. Specific objectives of the role play include:

1. To negotiate in a cross-cultural setting where the two parties have framed the conflict very differently.

2. To practice negotiating a conflict where the two parties have large personal stakes.

3. To negotiate a conflict where the intangible factors are much larger than the tangible factors being discussed.

Group Size Students work in pairs. Any number may participate, limited only by the size of the space available.

Time Required 60-90 minutes

Special Materials Copy and distribute the role information from this manual.

Special Physical Requirements None.

Recommended Reading Assignments to Accompany This Exercise

Reader: 11.1 (Phatak & Habib), 11.2 (Koh), 11.3 (Frank)
Text: Chapter 11

What to Expect

If both parties play their roles seriously, this can be a very frustrating, conflictual negotiation. The negotiation tends to start, and for some will finish, very competitively. Both sides want to "win" and there doesn't seem to be a halfway point for compromise.

Kelly frames this negotiation as one of her rights to have the sick leave, which is written into her contract. Mr. Higashi frames this negotiation much broader and wants Kelly to "fit in" at work and to be treated the same as Japanese workers. While the issue in this roleplay is quite straightforward, it is very representative of the types of conflict that occur in cross-cultural negotiations between Americans (rights based, contract as enforceable) and Japanese (relationship based, contract as beginning).

Advance Preparation

Students and the instructor should be familiar with cultural and business differences between Japan and North America. Dated, yet still appropriate, is Howard Van Zandt's *How to Negotiate in Japan*, from the Harvard Business Review of Nov/Dec 1970, more current is *Smart Bargaining* by John Graham and Yoshihiro Sano, *The Influence of Japanese Culture on Business Relationships and Negotiations* by Naoko Oikawa and John Tanner Jr., *International Dimensions of Organizational Behavior*, chapter on Negotiating with Foreigners by Nancy J. Adler, and *Cultural Approaches to Negotiations: Understanding the Japanese* by Brian Hawrysh and Judith Zaichkowsky.

In addition, the instructor (but not the students) should read Case 8 (Sick Leave) because, while written from Kelly's point of view, it contains a good description of the broader content of the situation surrounding the sick leave discussion.

Operating Procedure

Care needs to be taken when assigning students to the roles in this exercise. If there are students who are from, or who have lived in, Japan then they should be assigned the role of Mr. Higashi. It is also possible to conduct this negotiation as a fishbowl, where the person most familiar with the Japanese negotiation style would play Mr. Higashi. Some participants may have trouble playing the Japanese role, so it may be a good idea to split the class in half during the preparation for the negotiation and to discuss with the students who are playing the Japanese role the nuances of the approach. Participants should read the information in the text along with handouts dealing with differences in negotiation styles between Japanese and North Americans (see below). On the surface, this is a very straightforward situation: will Kelly get her contractually guaranteed sick leave benefits or not? The cultural differences, however, make this a high stakes negotiation for both parties, in which the importance of the intangible factors far outweighs that of the tangible factors.

Concluding the Exercise

Debriefing of the exercise should begin with a discussion of the outcome of the negotiation. Proceed by using the following questions:

1. What were the outcomes of the negotiation? How many people playing the role of Kelly negotiated an agreement to use their sick leave? How many did not use any of their sick leave? Were there any other outcomes?

2. What was this dispute about for Kelly? For Mr. Higashi? In these types of conflicts is a compromise possible?

3. Next, discuss the process of the negotiation. How did people approach the negotiation? How was it similar and different to other negotiations in the class? Was it easier or more challenging than other exercises? Why?

4. What were the most important intangibles in the negotiation? Was saving face more important to Kelly or Mr. Higashi? Why?

The discussion should conclude with a good summary about Japanese and North American negotiation styles and culture. When negotiating in Japan it is often important to give in for the sake of peace and harmony, or relationships may be harmed beyond repair. Deciding *how* to negotiate cross-culturally remains a challenge for every negotiator that negotiates across a border. One of the best pieces discussing this was written by Stephen Weiss ("Negotiating with 'Romans': A Range of Culturally-Responsive Strategies," *Sloan Management Review*, 35, No. 1, pp. 51-61; No. 2, pp. 1-16) and a summary of this work makes a nice conclusion to the class.

Final Note

Although this exercise has been modified somewhat it is based on an actual situation that occurred in Japan (names and location have been changed). In the actual incident, "Kelly" received her sick leave but the relationship was seriously harmed and work became more and more uncomfortable. Kelly decided not to renew her contract, and left Japan at the end of the school year.

CULTURAL NEGOTIATION STYLES[1]

Japanese

- Status relationships are very important (e.g., older, larger, more prestigious have more power)

- Buyers have more status than sellers, but buyers look out for seller's interests

- Focus is long-term and on the relationship (not the contract)

- Maintaining harmony is more important than the deal

- Decision making is by consensus

- Important concessions and negotiating is done before the formal meeting, which is used as a place to approve what has already been discussed

- Do not say "no"

- Discuss items holistically

- A contract represents the beginning of the negotiation and furthering of the relationship

---

[1] Based on the book *Smart Bargaining: Doing Business with the Japanese* by John Graham and Yoshihiro Sano. New York: Harper Collins, 1989.

CULTURAL NEGOTIATION STYLES[1]

American

- Status relationships are not very important; status is based on what you can do, not who you are

- Buyers and sellers have equal status; negotiators look out for their own interests

- Focus is short term and on the contract (not the relationship)

- The deal is more important than maintaining harmony

- Decision making is individualistic

- Important concessions and negotiating is done at the formal meeting

- Do not accept "no" for an answer (there is always a way...)

- Discuss items sequentially

- A contract represents the end of the negotiation and is enforceable

CONFIDENTIAL ROLE INFORMATION FOR KELLY
EXERCISE 26: SICK LEAVE

You have been working for the Soto Board of Education in Japan for the past six months. You are the only foreigner working in the office and were hired to assist with the English language program in the city's public schools.

You recently graduated with a degree in management from the University of Alberta in Edmonton, Canada. Although not a prerequisite for this position, you have studied and speak some Japanese. You decided to spend some time in Japan in order improve your Japanese and to make yourself more marketable when you return to Canada to start your career. This is your first time in Japan and aside from the inevitable culture shock, you have had relatively no problem adjusting to your new surroundings. You attribute your ease of adjusting to the Japanese culture to the organization back in Canada which hired you. They were very thorough in briefing you about life in Japan and provided you with what you considered to be excellent pre-departure training.

One aspect that you find hard to adjust to is the commitment which the Japanese have for their work. The day begins at 8:30 a.m. and officially ends at 5:00 p.m., but no one ever leaves the office before 7 or 8:00 p.m. The Japanese employees also work on Saturdays, which you find absurd since it infringes on what you consider to be personal and family time and you know that their salaries do not reflect the extra time put in on the weekends. You have a standard North American contract that you were given before leaving Canada which stipulates your hours, number of vacation days, how many days sick leave you're entitled to, etc. You work from Monday to Friday, 8:30 to 5:00 p.m., but stay later if you have legitimate work to do (which is practically never). No one has ever asked you to stay after 5 p.m. and you have never been requested to come in on the weekend. You know that you receive what could be considered preferential treatment but the conditions of your employment were carefully outlined in your contract, and the people in your office seem to be following them to the letter which suits you fine.

The only person in your office who speaks English is your supervisor, Mr. Higashi, and since your Japanese is not very good, you rely on him for all important office communications. Mr. Higashi is what you consider to be a traditional middle aged Japanese man. He works late every night and often goes out with the other men in the office to discuss business at the local sake establishments. He seems to have very conservative values and frowns upon innovation or change. His wife stays home to run the household and raise their two children, and Mr. Higashi doesn't think that women should be in the work force after marriage.

Mr. Higashi is constantly bugging you to immerse yourself in Japanese culture and lifestyle. When you started practicing Kendo, a Japanese style of fencing, he was very pleased and you hoped he would drop the issue once and for all. You don't mind trying or adopting some of the Japanese ways, but you don't like feeling pressured to convert. After all, you have been hired only on a one year contract basis, which is renewable to a maximum of three, so you know that you are not going to be staying in Japan forever.

Last Monday you woke up with a severe fever and sore throat. You called in sick and were told by Mr. Higashi to rest until you were better, but to bring in a doctor's note when you came back to work. After hanging up the phone, you thought that it was a bit ridiculous to get out of bed and go see a doctor about a simple flu, but you went to the clinic and got a note for your office. Two days later you returned to the office and brought with you the note from the physician. Mr. Higashi seemed concerned about your health and asked if you were feeling any better. You handed him the note telling him it was from your doctor. He took it without so much as a thank you and threw it onto a pile of papers on his desk.

Around mid-morning, the office accountant comes to your desk with forms for you to sign. In spite of your limited Japanese, you are able to understand that these forms had to do with your absence and that you are signing for two days of your paid vacation time. You assume that she has made a mistake and try to explain to her that you were not on vacation, but were sick and that your contract allows you to take sick leave. The accountant appears to not understand, and motions for you to sign the papers.

You go over to Mr. Higashi's desk and tell him about the misunderstanding. To your surprise he tells you that there is no misunderstanding and that this is standard procedure in Japan. He tells you that since you work for a Japanese company, you may as well start behaving like a Japanese employee. He tells you that Japanese employees normally do not take their allotted paid vacation time each year because of their dedication to their work. He also says that when Japanese employees are sick, it is not uncommon for them to deduct the time off from their paid vacation and not use their sick leave out of respect for their employers. Mr. Higashi says that this is what you should do. You are so dumbfounded that you go back to your desk without speaking.

Back at your desk you cannot believe what just happened. You know that your contract allows more than twenty days of sick leave and this is the first time that you have been sick. Your contract says nothing about having to bring in a doctor's note, but you think that it should help to strengthen your case since it proves that you really were ill. You realize that your supervisor wants you to "blend in" to the Japanese way of doing things, but this is a fine time for him to start and besides, you have already planned a big vacation in the spring. If you lose two days now, you won't be able to go on your trip.

The accountant has already come back twice to have you sign the paper and you have sent her away both times. You have approached your supervisor again on the subject and he is still adamant on the fact that this is the Japanese way of doing things and that it is time for you to "Do as the Romans do". You try to reason with him but he refuses to talk to you.

There is no way that you are going to sign the paper for paid vacation. Your contract says that you are entitled to sick leave and you have a doctor's certificate to prove that you were. You know that you aren't being unreasonable, you just want what is rightfully yours. It is more than the spring vacation at stake, it is the principle of the matter.

CONFIDENTIAL ROLE INFORMATION FOR MR. HIGASHI
EXERCISE 26: SICK LEAVE

You were born and have lived all your life in Soto, Japan. You taught high school English in and around Soto for more than twenty years. Two years ago you received a promotion and now work at the Board of Education as an advisor to all English teachers in the city. This was a career making promotion, one that most teachers will never experience and if everything goes well, you could end up as the principal of one of the high schools. About 8 years ago, the government started hiring English speaking foreigners to assist teachers in the schools and work as advisors at the Board of Education. The Soto Board of Education has had a foreigner working in it for the past 6 years. Since the foreign English assistants are hired on a one year contract basis, renewable to a maximum of three, your office has already seen several of these people come and go.

The government agency responsible for hiring the English advisors does not require any knowledge of Japanese as a prerequisite. Since you are the only person in the office who speaks fluent English, you find that you spend a lot of your time as interpreter and writer for the foreign English advisors since they are not able to do many of the day to day tasks on their own. For example, you have to go and help these people open a bank account, show them how to use the automated teller machines, show them how to read a gas bill, etc., tasks which you don't believe should be necessary for you to do.

Most of these foreigners have been good workers, but the past six years have not been trouble free. The men in your office have worked hard for many long years to reach such high positions within the Board of Education, and many of them are insulted to be working at the same level with people who are so inexperienced and so much younger. You also know that despite the obvious age difference and lack of experience, these temporary foreign advisors earn almost as much as you each month. (Although they don't get the twice a year bonus.) Another problem is that the foreign English advisors are not very committed workers. They are hired on a one year contract basis, renewable only up to three years. Many of them regard their time in Japan as a stepping stone to somewhere else and do not take their jobs seriously enough. Since they are in your office for such a short period of time, they don't really try to become part of the group. They do not work as long as the other Japanese workers in the office and it seems like they are always away on vacation. The foreign advisors' contract allows them up to four weeks of paid vacation on top of the Japanese national holidays and compared to Japanese employees who rarely make use of their paid leave, these foreigners use every available day. You know that if you took such long and frequent holidays, you would not be respected by the other members of your office and would never have made it to the position that you are in now. It makes you and some of the other Japanese employees upset to see that they get special treatment. You feel that if they are going to work in Japan for the Japanese government, they should at least behave and be treated like the Japanese.

You have a few problems with the current foreign advisor in your office. Kelly seems nice, but is not very hard working and has made no attempt to fit in to the Japanese way of doing things. You have never seen Kelly work after five o'clock, while everyone else in the office stays until at least 7:00 p.m., and Kelly has told you repeatedly that Canadians do not work on weekends. Kelly drinks coffee instead of Japanese tea during the breaks and often comes in late in the morning, constantly disrupting the morning meetings which you find utterly disrespectful. When you've mentioned it, Kelly just smiles and says that it won't happen again. Kelly has also been away on several vacations in the short six months that she has been working for you. Some of the employees think Kelly is not dedicated to the job, while some of the office members are envious because they think Kelly must be making more money than they do since they could never afford to travel so much in such a short time.

You have talked to Kelly about fitting into Japanese society and work culture, but felt like your advice was being ignored. Kelly seems more interested in doing things the Canadian way even though you have pointed out that some of these actions might be considered rude in Japan.

Last Monday Kelly phoned in sick just before the 8:30 morning meeting. You thanked Kelly for phoning and asked for a doctor's note when she got back to the office. Since Kelly has never missed a day of work so far, you believed the story, but you had heard that foreigners sometimes pretend to be sick on Monday in order to take long weekends, and so you asked for the doctor's note just to be sure. Two days later, Kelly returned to the office with a note from a doctor. You took the note over to the accountant so she could prepare the necessary documentation.

A few hours later, Kelly is at your desk looking upset. She says that there has been a mistake because the papers that she was given to sign were for paid leave, not for sick leave. Kelly starts getting angry, raises her voice and tells you that she has a contract and that you should honor it. You try to calm Kelly down, and explain that Japanese employees have similar contracts which outline sick leave and paid vacation. You tell Kelly that Japanese employees are not in the habit of using their vacation pay since they are so dedicated to their work. You also mention that typical Japanese employees use their vacation time when they are sick, and not their sick leave to show their dedication to their employers and also to show that they are not trying to take time off work at the company's expense. Since Kelly is working for a Japanese company, you feel that she should "Do as the Roman's do".

Kelly sits down and refuses to sign the papers. She comes back to your desk a few hours later and starts yelling and waving the contract at you saying that you must give her sick leave since it is written in the contract. You look at Kelly and think that this is typical North American behavior. When they don't get what they want they raise their voices and complain. You are also very insulted that Kelly has waved the contract in your face. In Japan, contracts are not as important as the relationships behind them, and Kelly is not making this relationship very easy. You think Kelly is being very impertinent and prefer to say nothing rather than lose your temper.

You are already under pressure from your superiors to "handle the foreigner" without making a scene and from your co-workers who think that she has more perks and is more favored than the rest of the office. You are also worried that if you do give in to the young foreigner, it will undermine your authority and will make you lose face in the office. Also, you are up for another promotion this spring, and you know that your superiors are watching how you handle the situation.

EXERCISE 27
TOWN OF TAMARACK

NOTE: There are two versions of the Town of Tamarack material and they are quite different. Exercise 27 is a scorable exercise that has the potential to be either distributive or integrative. Exercise 7 (Twin Lakes Mining) allows a free discussion of the challenges that the Town and Company face and explores the dynamics of trying to negotiate integratively under conditions of very different levels of power. We suggest that you choose which material suits your needs in the course and that you *use only Exercise 27 **or** 7 and not both* because while they are similar they are different enough to cause confusion among the students.

Objectives

The Town of Tamarack role play is a multi-issue negotiation scenario that has the potential to be either distributive or integrative. Some groups will become highly competitive, particularly if they try to assign total responsibility for the pollution and cleanup problems to the other party (the Company to the Town, and vice versa). However, other groups are more likely to assume joint responsibility for the problems, and hence engage in mutual problem solving toward a constructive resolution. In addition, there is the opportunity for integrative negotiating across issues because the issues are worth different point values to each party.

Learning objectives for this simulation include:

1. Strategy planning and preparation for a negotiation with distributive or integrative potential.

2. Identifying integrative potential in what is apparently a distributive situation.

3. Practice creating and using persuasive arguments when both parties have equivalent power.

Group Size   There is no limit on group size for this negotiation. Students work in dyads.

Time Required   30 minutes of preparation, and 30-45 minutes of negotiation time.

Special Materials   Copy and distribute role information from this manual.

Physical Requirements   Space for dyads to meet comfortably, out of earshot of other dyads.

Recommended Reading Assignments to Accompany This Exercise:

Readings: 2.1 (Kuhn), 2.2 (Scott), 2.3 (Tannen), 4.1 (Gray), 4.2 (Anderson), 4.3 (Rubin) 5.1 (Neale and Bazerman), 5.2 (Tannen)
Text: Chapters 2, 4, 5

Operating Procedure

Follow the general procedure described for comparable exercises (e.g., Exercise 3). This is a very straightforward exercise. Some students will fail to find the integrative solutions possible, especially if they are overly competitive, or if this is their first exercise with integrative potential.

Concluding the Exercise

There are many levels of discussion for this exercise. Generally it is best to discuss the content of the different outcomes first, followed by a discussion of the negotiation process, and concluding with a more general discussion of integrative negotiating.

1. Content of Outcomes

Ask the students to post their results on the blackboard. Begin the discussion by asking different groups to describe the process they used to go about this negotiation. Focus on several different types of groups:
- Groups that had very low point totals for both sides. These groups are likely to have used a more distributive, competitive approach to these negotiations.
- Groups in which one party did very well and the other did poorly. In these groups one negotiator is likely to have acted competitively or deceptively towards the other.
- Groups in which both parties did well. In these groups, an integrative process was likely to have been initiated by one or both sides.

For each group, discuss their:
   a) Strategy and tactics planned prior to negotiation.
   b) Strategy and tactics actually used as negotiation progressed.
   c) Target points and resistance points developed by each group, and their impact on settlement.
   d) Actual settlements arrived at by the groups

2. Process of Negotiating

   a) How did the negotiation begin? What happened next?
   b) Was this negotiation integrative or distributive? Why?
   c) Did one side have more power in the negotiation? Why?

3. General Discussion

   a) What were the important ethical dimensions in this negotiation? How did they influence the strategy and tactics of the Town Council and the Company?
   b) What strategy and tactics were used by the dyads that reached the most integrative solutions? How can these be applied to other negotiation situations?
   c) What did groups reaching suboptimal outcomes do? What could they have done differently?

TOWN OF TAMARACK (PUBLIC BACKGROUND INFORMATION)

INTRODUCTION

In this role-play, you will negotiate a conflict between a mining company and the government of a small town regarding an environmental cleanup and other issues. You are a member of a negotiating team consisting of members of the Town Council of Tamarack, a small town in which the Twin Lakes Mining Company operates. Your team will negotiate against a team comprised of top managers from the Twin Lakes Mining Company.

BACKGROUND INFORMATION

The largest regional office of the Twin Lakes Mining Company is located in Tamarack, Minnesota, in the northern part of the state. It was established there in 1941. The town of Tamarack has a population of approximately 12,000. Although there is a growing revenue that accrues to the town as a result of heavy summer tourism (summer homes, fishing, etc.) and several "cottage industries," Tamarack is basically a one-industry town. Two thousand five hundred people, 60 percent of whom live within town limits, work for the Twin Lakes Mining Company; 33 percent of the town's real estate tax base consists of Twin Lakes property and operations. Both in terms of direct tax revenue and indirect contribution to the economic stability of the local population, Tamarack is strongly dependent on the continued success of the Twin Lakes Company.

The primary activity of the Twin Lakes Mining Company consists of mining iron ore from open-pit mines. Open-pit mining consists of stripping the top soil from the ore deposit with the use of a power shovel. Train rails are then laid, and most of the ore is loaded into railroad cars for transportation to a central collecting point for rail or water shipment. As mining operations progress, rails are relaid or roads constructed to haul ore by truck. The ore is transported to a plant located on the outskirts of Tamarack, where it is crushed, washed, concentrated, blended, and agglomerated into larger lumps or pellets. After the ore proceeds through this process of cleaning and agglomerating, it is shipped by railroad car to steel mills throughout the Midwest. Rejected materials are returned to parts of the mine where the mining process has been completed. Mines that are no longer in use are called "consumed" mines.

Twin Lakes' plant is located approximately five miles outside of Tamarack. As a result of the expansion of the residential areas of the town, summer home development and various Twin Lakes operations, the plant has become an environmental problem for local citizens. The primary problem is that the mining operations pollute the air with dust. For years, the Tamarack Town Council has been pressing the company to clean up the most problematic operations. Although several discussions between the town and the company have occurred, Twin Lakes has done little to remedy the major concerns. Now, as a result of more stringent environmental laws and regulations, Twin Lakes has come under pressure from both the state of Minnesota and the federal government for environmental cleanup. Both the State and the Federal Environmental Protection Agency have informed Twin Lakes that they are in major violation of air pollution quality standards, and that immediate action must be taken. Because Twin Lakes is now mining reasonably low-grade ore and because foreign competition in the steel market has significantly eroded the demand for ore, the high cost of environmental compliance might force the company to shut down its Tamarack operations. Many local citizens, as individuals and through the local chapter of the United Mineworkers Union, are putting significant pressure on the Town Council to help the Twin Lakes Company in its environmental cleanup operations.

The imposition of the environmental controls on Twin Lakes, and the resulting pressure from all segments of the community, has led to renewed discussions between company and town officials about the future of Twin Lakes in the Tamarack area. As a result of these discussions, the following major issues, including environmental issues and others, have emerged:

Air Quality - Paving Dirt Roads. The entire process of mining, transporting, and crushing ore generates large amounts of dust. This has significantly increased the levels of particulates in the air. During the dry summer months, the operation of many large trucks along dirt roads intensifies the problem considerably.

Twin Lakes believes that it can control a great deal of the dust generated immediately around the plant, and is planning to incur this expense without help from Tamarack. The most significant debate with the town has been over a series of roads around the outskirts of town. They need to be paved to reduce the dust in the air to acceptable levels. Many of the roads are town-owned, and some have been specially constructed by the company for the transportation of ore and material. Almost all of the roads, including those constructed by the company, are used frequently by tourists. All of the roads have to be paved for Twin Lakes to comply with the environmental regulations and stay in business.

Air Quality - Road Maintenance. The roads in question currently require a minimal amount of maintenance. They will require a much higher degree of maintenance if they are paved, however, especially because the harsh winters tend to break up paved roads. To keep the roads in an acceptable condition, the town and company will have to agree on who will maintain them.

Site of Next Mine. Twin Lakes has been testing several locations in the Tamarack area to determine the extent of iron ore deposits. Several of the locations have enough ore to be profitable, and Twin Lakes would like to open a new mine. Although the actual mining may not begin immediately, the decision concerning the location of a new site has to be made now to allow time for both the company to plan for a new mine and the town to plan its expansion around any new mining site.

Restoration of Consumed Mines. The consumed mines that are no longer used by the company are outside of the town limits. Some of these mines lie alongside main roads leading into the town from the most popular resort areas on local lakes. The town considers the consumed mines unsightly and is afraid that tourists may be repelled by the mines. The company has restored the land to the extent required by law, but the town would like to see further restoration.

Tax Rate on Company Land. The land for the mine currently in operation is outside of town limits. However, the plant lies within township boundaries, and Twin Lakes pays a substantial amount of money in taxes. The company has always felt that the Tamarack taxation rate is excessive.

Both the company and the town believe that if some resolution could be obtained on these major issues, the remaining problems could be easily resolved, and Twin Lakes would agree to keep its operations in the Tamarack area in business. Toward this end, a formal negotiation has been arranged between the Town of Tamarack and the Twin Lakes Mining Company.

ROLE INFORMATION FOR TOWN OF TAMARACK
EXERCISE 27: TOWN OF TAMARACK

Your negotiation team, consisting of members of the Tamarack Town Council, has the authority to enter into any agreement that it deems to be in the best interest of the town of Tamarack. The problems that were described in the "Background Information" have existed for a long time. Town officials have met periodically with officials of the Twin Lakes Mining Company to discuss these problems. While some small cleanup measures have been taken by the company, the meetings have always ended with the major issues unresolved. The Twin Lakes representatives have always maintained that they did not have the economic resources to spend that much money on cleanup activities. Now the federal and state agencies have mandated a cleanup. While you are pleased that the company people are under pressure to make some changes, you would rather not see the company close its operations. This outcome would have a negative economic impact on the town of Tamarack.

Of course, you would prefer to pay for as little of the cleanup projects as possible, while still having Twin Lakes stay in business. You hope to continue to develop tourism in your town, and that industry is in a growth phase that requires a considerable amount of money. By getting Twin Lakes to finance as much of the cleanup as it possibly can, you can channel your resources into the tourism industry and the town can develop with the support of both the mining and tourist industries. If Twin Lakes does go out of business in the Tamarack area, tourism will take over as the primary industry, and will receive most of the resources Tamarack has at its disposal. Several options for each of the issues have been discussed in the last few meetings between the town of Tamarack and the Twin Lakes Mining Company. Both parties have agreed on which options for each issue are the most feasible. A detailed explanation of each issue and the available options is provided in this confidential memorandum. In addition, a point system has been devised so that all of the issues can be rated on a common metric, to assist you in negotiating. The point system allows you to combine several interests - minimizing expenses and maximizing current and future revenues, while incorporating opportunity costs and legal considerations - into a single "currency." Each option has been assigned a point value to indicate the quality of that option to you. Within each issue, an option with a high point value is a better outcome for you than options with lower point values. Across the five issues, more important issues are assigned a higher maximum level of points than less important issues. The more total points you gain, the better the outcome is for you. Your task is to try to earn as many points as possible in this negotiation.

1. *Site of Next Mine.* There are five locations that the Twin Lakes Mining Company is considering for a new mine site in the Tamarack area. You would certainly like to see the revenues that would accrue to the town as a result of a new mine site. Any of the sites would generate about the same revenue for the town. However, the location of the new mine could have a dramatic effect on future revenue from tourism. Open-pit iron ore mines and tourist resorts are not compatible when they are in close proximity. Some of the potential mining locations have great potential for drawing tourists, and you plan to see that resorts are built in at least some of these areas. Ideally, you would like to see the new mine located at the Eagle Falls Site, because this location has virtually no value to you as a potential tourist area. This is the best option for you. The remaining four potential mine sites are all relatively valuable to you as future resort locations. They would not make good mining sites from your perspective.

According to your projections, there should be enough resort development over the next few years to make use of all four of these sites. Locating a new mine at any one of these four sites could cut substantially into future revenue from tourism. They include the Devil's Pass Site, the Clearwater Lake Site, the Buffalo Bridge Site, and the Allen Road Site. The Allen Road Site is an especially attractive prospect for new resorts. Allowing a mine at the Allen Road Site could seriously curtail the growth of Tamarack's tourist industry. Twin Lakes wants to open a mine at one of these sites if they are going to continue operating in the Tamarack area. The point values for these mining sites are:

- Eagle Falls Site   150
- Devil's Pass Site   60
- Clearwater Lake Site   45
- Buffalo Bridge Site   30
- Allen Road Site   0

2. *Restoration of Consumed Mines.* Twin Lakes has met its legal obligation by filling the consumed mines and putting enough rejected ore or rock in place to decrease the likelihood of erosion. However, the laws the company has followed were obviously designed to minimally restore the health of land typically located in remote places, not in the middle of a tourist area. You justifiably think the consumed mines, which are alongside busy tourist roads, are an eyesore that place Tamarack at an obvious disadvantage compared to neighboring tourist towns. You would like to see Twin Lakes, as an upstanding member of the community, obey the spirit as well as the letter of the law, and restore the old mines in an aesthetically agreeable manner. It is not your responsibility to restore land that was naturally beautiful before Twin Lakes started mining it. There are two further levels of restoration above the current level ("legal restoration") that are typically discussed. Partial restoration refers to planting enough vegetation to further reduce the risk of erosion and to make the land blend in more naturally with the rest of the surrounding country. In the mining industry, this is sometimes referred to as "descarring" the land. Full restoration, as the name implies, refers to planting enough vegetation to bring the land back to very near its pre-mining state. There are several consumed mines in question, some of which run along main roads, while others are further back in the country. Restoring the mines near the main roads is of primary importance right now. The other mines, however, also need to be restored because resort developers are always looking for new areas to develop, and a remote location could turn into a new resort area if it is attractive to a developer. The options for restoration by the company and the associated point values are given below:

- Company fully restores all consumed mines   120
- Company fully restores mines near tourist roads
  / restores other mines partially   90
- Company partially restores all mines   60
- Company partially restores mines near tourist roads 30
- No further restoration by company of consumed mines 0

3. *Air Quality - Road Maintenance.* Unlike several of the other issues, which are one-time expenses, this issue involves a continuing expense. The paved roads will require a far greater amount and a different kind of maintenance than the current dirt roads require. Although there are many tourist vehicles on the roads, especially during the summer, the mining trucks tear up the roads much more than the cars driven by tourists. Most road damage occurs in the winter

because the weather conditions make the roads more vulnerable to wear and tear. In the winter, there are far fewer tourists than in the summer, but the mining trucks continue to damage the roads throughout the winter. The options for maintaining the roads are similar to those for paving the roads. These options, and their point values, follow:

- Company maintains all roads   90
- Company maintains all roads it currently uses / Town maintains others   69
- Company maintains roads it has constructed / Town maintains others   48
- Company maintains roads on company-owned land / Town maintains others 24
- Town maintains all roads   0

4. *Air Quality - Paving Dirt Roads.* This issue involves reducing road dust by paving the dirt roads around the outskirts of the town. Many of the roads in question are owned by the town, and all of the roads are used by people from the town and by tourists. They are in relatively good shape even though they are not paved, and are certainly adequate in their present condition for all the needs of the town. The mining company has been instrumental in constructing many roads throughout the region. It is true that several of these are now used more by tourists than by the company's trucks. The company's trucks currently use most of the dirt roads around the town. These mining trucks stir up large amounts of dust because of their size and weight. It is undeniable that paving the roads will be a nice improvement for the town, both as a practical and an aesthetic matter. However, it would be an unnecessary improvement, except for the fact that the mining trucks stir up so much dust. The importance you place on this issue stems directly and singularly from your desire to keep the Twin Lakes Mining Company in business. All of these roads have to be paved for the Twin Lakes Company to stay in business. The options for paving the roads that have been discussed prior to this negotiation, and the point values for each option, are:

- Company paves all roads   60
- Company paves all roads it currently uses / Town paves others   42
- Company paves roads it has constructed / Town paves others   27
- Company paves roads on company-owned land / Town paves other roads   15
- Town paves all roads   0

5. *Tax Rate on Company Land.* Naturally, you need to generate tax revenues to fund the various projects on which the town is working. In your view, the current tax rate for the company is in line with the rest of the area, and you have proposed the same 4% tax rate increase for the mining company that will apply to everyone else. The company has argued that they should pay a lower rate than the residents of the town, and have proposed a tax rate reduction of 4%. The local taxes paid by the company comprise a substantial portion of the town's tax revenues, and any reduction in this amount would be sorely missed. You think the tourist industry is about to take off, and its expansion will require substantial funding. Of course, you have channeled funds toward the mining company in the past, and will probably do so in the future, if they stay in the area. The options on the table and their point values are:

- Increase tax 4%   30
- Increase tax 2%   24
- Maintain current tax   18
- Reduce tax 2%   9
- Reduce tax 4%   0

The town of Tamarack wants the Twin Lakes Mining Company to maintain their operations in the Tamarack area, and you certainly would like to get the environment cleaned up. However, there are limits to the amount you are willing to do to keep the company here. You have high hopes for the growth of the tourist industry, and money spent on keeping the mining company in the area obviously cannot be used to expand the tourism industry. There are high opportunity costs associated with money spent on the projects being discussed in the negotiation today. You want to reach the highest quality outcome possible. Your objective for this negotiation is to try to earn as many points as you can.

Because there are opportunity costs associated with the money that may be allocated by your town in this negotiation, and because the company has been reluctant to fully address these issues in the past, you have decided that you need to reach an agreement that yields at least 198 points, or you will break off negotiations and invest further in the tourist industry. An outcome of less than 198 points would indicate a poor overall investment, and the town could achieve higher returns from other investments. Of course, this number represents a minimum for you, and you certainly hope to surpass this number. You have to gain 198 points or more from the final agreement or you will not settle with the company. The final settlement must include an agreement on one option for each of the five issues. If this does not occur, the Twin Lakes Mining Company will shut down its Tamarack operations, and the tourist industry will replace it as the largest industry in the area.

TOWN OF TAMARACK - CONFIDENTIAL PAYOFF SCHEDULE

Issues: **Points:**

Site of next mine:
Eagle Falls Site	150
Devil's Pass Site	60
Clearwater Lake Site	45
Buffalo Bridge Site	30
Allen Road Site	0

Restoration of consumed mines:
Company fully restores all consumed mines	120
Company fully restores mines near tourist roads / restores other mines partially	90
Company partially restores all mines	60
Company partially restores mines near tourist roads	30
No further restoration by company of consumed mines	0

Air quality - Road maintenance:
Company maintains all roads	90
Company maintains all roads it currently uses / Town maintains others	69
Company maintains roads it has constructed / Town maintains others	48
Company maintains roads on company-owned land/Town maintains others	24
Town maintains all roads	0

Air quality - Paving dirt roads:
Company paves all roads	60
Company paves all roads it currently uses / Town paves others	42
Company paves roads it has constructed / Town paves others	27
Company paves roads on company-owned land/ Town paves other roads	15
Town paves all roads	0

Tax rate on company land:
Increase tax 4%	30
Increase tax 2%	24
Maintain current tax	18
Reduce tax 2%	9
Reduce tax 4%	0

DO NOT LET THE OTHER PARTY SEE THIS SHEET AT ANY TIME!

ROLE INFORMATION FOR TWIN LAKES MINING COMPANY

EXERCISE 27: TOWN OF TAMARACK

Your negotiation team, consisting of members of the top management group of the Twin Lakes Mining Company, has the authority to enter into any agreement that it deems to be in the best interest of the company. Twin Lakes has several mines in northern Minnesota and Canada; the Tamarack operation is second in both "productivity" and contribution to corporate profit. Your negotiating team includes the top person from the Tamarack operation, along with others from corporate headquarters in Duluth, Minnesota.

Most of the problems that were described in the "Background Information" have existed for a long time. Officials of the company have met with town officials several times to discuss these problems. Although you agree with community concerns, you frankly think that the town has overstated the problems in order to get you to pay for public improvements. Hence you have agreed to remedy several of the most obvious concerns in the past, but have not had to incur major costs up to this point. Now that the state and federal agencies have mandated a cleanup, things have changed considerably. Some major improvements will have to be made in order to keep the Tamarack operations running.

You are committed to keep the Tamarack mine and plant open if possible, but not at all costs. You do not want to spend large sums of money to keep this operation running. Some of the newer mining operations in other areas have revealed rich deposits, but will require large investments to gain access. If the costs of continuing the Tamarack operations are too high, you could close this mine and plant and invest in other operations. You want the town to help with the improvements, especially because they will benefit the town as well as the company. In addition, everyone involved knows that keeping the Tamarack area operations running is very important for the Tamarack economy. Naturally, you would like to settle as cheaply as possible.

Several options for each of the issues have been discussed in the last few meetings between the town of Tamarack and the Twin Lakes Mining Company. Both parties have agreed on which options for each issue are the most feasible. A detailed explanation of each issue, including the available options, is provided in this confidential memorandum. In addition, a point system has been devised so that all of the issues can be rated on a common metric, to assist you in negotiating. The point system allows you to combine several interests - minimizing expenses and maximizing current and future revenues, while incorporating opportunity costs and legal considerations - into a single "currency." Each option has been assigned a point value to indicate the quality of that option to you. Within each issue, an option with a high point value is a better outcome for you than options with lower point values. Across the five issues, more important issues are assigned a higher maximum level of points than less important issues. The more total points you gain, the better the outcome is for you. Your task is to try to earn as many points as possible in this negotiation.

1. *Site of Next Mine.* There are five locations that would be profitable for you to mine, but they vary widely in their relative attractiveness. They are all projected to bring back a positive return on investment. The Allen Road Site contains the largest iron ore deposit of the five, and has by far the highest profit potential. The ore located at this site is concentrated as well as

abundant, making it a very attractive site. Your company does not come across mining sites with this kind of profit potential very often. Mining the ore from this site could make the Tamarack area the most productive and profitable region in the company. The Buffalo Bridge Site, the Clearwater Lake Site, and the Devil's Pass Site, in order of desirability, are three other sites that you are interested in. These do not have ore deposits as large as the Allen Road Site, and are in more remote locations. Based on the testing conducted on these sights, they do not compare favorably with the Allen Road Site, but they would be profitable. The Eagle Falls Site has the lowest potential of the five sites under consideration, but it would still bring a positive return on investment. Starting up a new mine would have the added advantage of bringing production at the Tamarack plant to near full capacity, achieving further economies of scale. The company only has enough resources at its disposal to invest in one of these mines. Because the town of Tamarack either owns some of the land at potential sites, or owns land that provides access to a potential site, an agreement must be reached with the town concerning which site will be mined. The point values for these mining sites are:

- Allen Road Site   100
- Buffalo Bridge Site   40
- Clearwater Lake Site   30
- Devil's Pass Site   20
- Eagle Falls Site   0

2. Air Quality - Road Maintenance. Unlike several of the other issues, which are one-time expenses, this issue involves a continuing expense. The paved roads will require a far greater amount and a different kind of maintenance than the current dirt roads do. Although the mining trucks do tend to tear up the roads, you do not think it should be an ongoing cost of business to maintain roads that are used primarily by tourists, based on the number of vehicles on the road. The options are similar to those for paving the roads, although this issue is more important to you because it is an ongoing expense. If your company is going to operate in this area for an extended number of years, it is important to establish a precedent that the town takes care of the roads. The options, and their point values, follow:

Town maintains all roads	80
Company maintains roads on company-owned land/Town maintains other roads	60
Company maintains roads it has constructed / Town maintains others	40
Company maintains all roads it currently uses / Town maintains others	20
Company maintains all roads	0

3. Air Quality - Paving Dirt Roads. You have already agreed to make significant investments to reduce dust around the plant. The major problem with the town concerns reducing road dust by paving the dirt roads around the outskirts of the town. An increasing number of tourists are using the dirt roads that need to be paved, many of which are owned by the town. Your company has been instrumental in constructing many roads throughout the region. Several of these are now used more by tourists than by the company's trucks. Your trucks currently use most of the dirt roads around the town. There are some dirt roads, however, that you have used in the past but no longer need to use. The mining trucks obviously stir up a lot of dust because of their size, but smaller tourist vehicles vastly outnumber the mining trucks, and account for what you feel is a substantial portion of the dust. Although getting the roads paved is now a necessity for your company because of the air pollution, it will also be a nice improvement for the town, both as a practical and an aesthetic matter. All of these roads have to be paved for your company to stay in business in the Tamarack region. The options for paving the roads that have been discussed prior to this negotiation, and the point values for each option, are:

- Town paves all roads   60
- Company paves roads on company-owned land/Town paves other roads   46
- Company paves roads it has constructed/Town paves others   32
- Company paves all roads it currently uses/Town paves others   16
- Company paves all roads   0

4. Tax Rate on Company Land. You have been arguing with the town constantly about the tax rate for company-owned land, and feel that their rates are ridiculous. You believe the basic problem is that the rate on the company land is very similar to rates on private residential land, when in fact you argue that it should be considerably less. The town wants to increase your tax rate, as the taxes you pay represent a major portion of their revenue base. You know that the town wants to expand its tourism industry, and you suspect that they will use your tax dollars to fund this growth. This scenario is clearly unacceptable. You would ideally like to see the town reduce your tax rate by 4%, putting it in line with rates on company property in similar towns. The options on the table and their point values are:

- Reduce tax 4%   40
- Reduce tax 2%   28
- Maintain current tax   18
- Increase tax 2%   10
- Increase tax 4%   0

5. Restoration of Consumed Mines. Your company has met its legal obligation by filling the consumed mines and putting enough rejected ore or rock in place to decrease the likelihood of erosion. There are two further levels of restoration above the current level ("legal restoration") that are typically discussed. Partial restoration refers to planting enough vegetation to further reduce the risk of erosion and to make the land blend in more naturally with the rest of the surrounding country. In the mining industry, this is sometimes referred to as "descarring" the land. Full restoration, as the name implies, refers to planting enough vegetation to bring the land back to very near its pre-mining state. There are several consumed mines in question, some of which run along main roads, while others are further back in the country. You realize that the consumed mines are not as attractive as the surrounding area, and that this may have some indirect effect on tourism. You are trying to run a profitable business, however, and feel that meeting the requirements of the law should be sufficient. Although the town may realize increased revenues because of the prettier landscape, the only benefit accruing to the company from further restoration would be heightened goodwill in the eyes of the town, making it at best an uncertain investment. The options for restoration by the company and the associated point values are given below:

- No further restoration by company of consumed mines   20
- Company partially restores mines near tourist roads   16
- Company partially restores all mines   12
- Company fully restores mines near tourist roads / restores other mines partially   6
- Company fully restores all consumed mines   0

Your company wants to maintain its operations in the Tamarack area. However, you do not want to incur high costs in meeting the environmental cleanup demands required for continued operation. You have mining operations in other locations that are competing with the Tamarack site for company resources. There are high opportunity costs associated with money spent on the Tamarack operations. You want to reach the highest quality outcome possible. Your objective for this negotiation is to try to earn as many points as you can.

Because there are opportunity costs associated with the money that may be allocated by your company in this negotiation, and because the town has been reluctant to help the company in the past, you have decided that you need to reach an agreement that yields at least 132 points, or you will break off negotiations and invest in other operations. An outcome of less than 132 points would indicate a poor overall investment, and the company could achieve higher returns from other investments. Of course, this number represents a minimum for you, and you certainly hope to surpass this number. You have to gain 132 points or more from the final agreement or you will not settle with the town. The final settlement must include an agreement on one option for each of the six issues. If this does not occur, your company will shut down its Tamarack operations.

TWIN LAKES MINING COMPANY CONFIDENTIAL PAYOFF SCHEDULE

Issues: Points:

Site of next mine:
    Allen Road Site   100
    Buffalo Bridge Site   40
    Clearwater Lake Site   30
    Devil's Pass Site   20
    Eagle Falls Site   0

Air quality - Road maintenance:
    Town maintains all roads   80
    Company maintains roads on company-owned land / Town maintains others   60
    Company maintains roads it has constructed / Town maintains others   40
    Company maintains all roads it currently uses / Town maintains others   20
    Company maintains all roads   0

Air quality - Paving dirt roads:
    Town paves all roads   60
    Company paves roads on company-owned land / Town paves other roads   46
    Company paves roads it has constructed / Town paves others   32
    Company paves all roads it currently uses / Town paves others   16
    Company paves all roads   0

Tax rate on company land:
    Reduce tax 4%   40
    Reduce tax 2%   28
    Maintain current tax   18
    Increase tax 2%   10
    Increase tax 4%   0

Restoration of consumed mines:
    No further restoration by company of consumed mines   20
    Company partially restores mines near tourist roads   16
    Company partially restores all mines   12
    Company fully restores mines near tourist roads/
    restores other mines partially   6
    Company fully restores all consumed mines   0

DO NOT LET THE OTHER PARTY SEE THIS SHEET AT ANY TIME!

CASE
CAPITAL MORTGAGE INSURANCE CORPORATION

Learning Objectives

This is a six-part case that provides a "positive example" of a well-conducted (but competitive) negotiation, effectively allowing the instructor to emphasize key aspects of preparation for negotiation, and the "give and take" of the negotiation process. The case is a business acquisition, set in the context of the real-estate market. Although a great deal of financial information is given, the case can be taught to audiences with only a small amount of sophistication in reading and understanding financial transactions. The following key points can be made in the case discussion:

1. The importance of thorough preparation and "doing homework" to get ready for a negotiation and the dimensions on which homework must be done;

2. The process by which negotiators determine their opening bids, resistance points and bargaining range;

3. Procedures for evaluating a negotiating opponent;

4. The use of negotiation strategy and tactics - in this case, a commitment or "playing hard to get" strategy.

In addition, because the case is divided into six parts, (Cases B-F are in the Appendix of the student manual), the format provides an involving "stop action" feature to the discussions of negotiations, allowing students to commit themselves to strategic options and then evaluate what really happened.

Update to Instructors for the Third Edition:

This case was originally written in 1979, and still contains financial information from the first writing. The editors of this volume have been unable to secure permission to revise and update the financial information. However, we believe the teaching points in the case continue to justify its use with the original financial information.

Case Summary

Frank Randall and Jim Dolan are senior executives with Capital Mortgage Insurance Corporation, a firm that provides mortgage guaranty insurance to banks, savings and loans and mortgage bankers. They are interested in acquiring another business, Corporate Transfer Services, in order to expand and diversify the mortgage insurance business. In the (A) case, Randall and Dolan prepare for the negotiations, and lay out their strategy. In the subsequent cases (B-F), they play out this strategy in order to obtain the acquisition at their desired price.

Recommended Reading Assignment to Accompany This Case:

Reader: 2.1 (Kuhn), 2.2. (Scott), 3.1 (Aaronson), 3.2 (Craver), 3.3 (Dawson)
Text: Chapter 2, 3.

Assignment Questions (A Case):

1. Be ready to discuss preparation and the negotiating strategy that Randall and Dolan use in the (A) case.

2. What do you think CTS is expecting to get for the company?

Case Analysis

Capital Mortgage Insurance Corporation is a firm that provides mortgage guaranty insurance to banks, savings and loans, mortgage bankers and others who lend money for home mortgages. The purpose of mortgage insurance is to protect these lenders against payment default by borrowers. Lending institutions normally lend up to only 70-80% of the appraised value of a property; when mortgage insurance is available, however, an institution can lend up to 95% of the value, since the insurance protects the lender more completely. Mortgage insurance was typically sold to borrowers through contacts made with the financial institutions, and connections made through real-estate brokers who could identify new clients that might be interested in this form of protection.

The company was founded in 1972. By 1979, it had lost sizeable market share, and was "bailed out" by another organization that bought and sold homes for employee relocation companies so that people could dispose of their homes quickly when they moved. As Randall and Dolan evaluated the marketplace, they discovered Corporate Transfer Services - a third party equity company created by several real estate brokers. Because of the nature of the company, and ties that it had to a large network of brokers, Randall and Dolan decided that this would be the company they would negotiate to acquire.

The remainder of the (A) case describes the key facts about CTS, and the preparation done by Randall and Dolan for their negotiation. Major aspects of this preparation in the case include:

1. An understanding of the potential for growth and development of CTS and its marketplace.
2. The current assets, liabilities and financial health of the company.
3. A profile of the four "key actors" in the CTS organization, and the roles they are likely to play in the negotiation.
4. Evaluation of the negotiation package, and determination of an opening offer and "bottom line" for negotiation.
5. Procedures for obtaining the approval of the proposed acquisition by the Board of Capital Equipment Company.

The (A) case walks through these points in some detail, and provides a complete picture of how this group prepares for their negotiation. The case ends with some discussion between Randall and Dolan as to what CTS is probably expecting as a price and offer package, and how their initial offer is likely to be received.

The (B) case discusses how Randall and Dolan finalize their plans for negotiation. They decide to make one modification in their strategy--proposing to retain one of the four owners as consultant-- and prepare for the first meeting with CTS. The opening statements of both sides are described. The parties make their opening bids and demands, and discover that they are approximately $4.6 million apart.

In the (C) case, Randall and Dolan describe how they arrived at their opening offer, and ask CTS to describe how they arrived at their opening demand. These questions reveal that CTS' opening demand was poorly developed and supported, and within a few minutes, CTS drops its demand from $5 million to $2 million.

In the (D) case, Randall and Dolan extend the negotiation to other issues: the value of the connection to the real estate network provided by CTS, and are challenged by the key CTS negotiator (Burr) to work something out. Randall and Dolan decide to leave instead, telling the other side to consider CMI's first offer, which is still on the table.

In the (E) case, Randall and Dolan go out for dinner to evaluate the progress of negotiations. They do not return a phone message from Burr, and are awakened the next morning by Burr, who has dropped CTS' demand from $2 million to $1 million. Randall and Dolan are still noncommittal.

Finally, in the (F) case, Randall and Dolan affirm the correctness of their negotiation strategy. They return home and "play the waiting game," putting time pressure on CTS to drop their demands. Finally, several days later, CTS calls back and requests $750,000; Randall offers $600,000--the limit he had set in his negotiation planning several weeks earlier--and CTS accepts.

Teaching Strategy

Students should read the (A) case for homework and class preparation. As stated earlier, the case contains a great deal of financial information. Students who can handle this information because of prior experience and preparation should be allowed to "wallow through it," even though they are likely to come out with the same conclusions as Randall and Dolan. Students who do not have the background to manage this financial information should be told to accept Randall and Dolan's calculations at "face value"--that the company is worth about $420,000 in book value (assets), and that anything over that is payment to CTS for "goodwill." Randall and Dolan have decided that this good will is worth no less than $400,000 additional and no more than $600,000 additional. Burr, in contrast, has at least mentioned that it is worth about $5 million (over book value).

(30 minutes) Discuss the (A) case in class. This discussion should emphasize the following:

1. An understanding of the nature of the business that these people are in, and what they want to acquire (short lecture may be helpful).
2. "History" of each side's growth and development as a business.
3. What each side "brings" to the negotiation as major chips to negotiate with-i.e., what does CMI have going for it in the negotiation, and what does CTS have going for it in the negotiation?

4. "Personalities" and expected styles of key negotiators (particularly the four CTS negotiators).
5. The manner in which opening bids were developed, and (assuming their financial assessment was correct) whether CMI have left themselves enough room to make concessions (e.g. if CTS starts with a very high offer, is $200,000 enough "room" for CMI to negotiate in?)

Discussion questions:

- How good has CMI's preparation been?
- Is there anything that they have left out?
- How do you think CTS will react to this offer?

(15 minutes) Students read the (B) case in the Appendix. Note that Burr was hired as a consultant (usually one of the suggestions). Discussion can then focus on the opening minutes of the meeting between the two groups.

Discussion questions:

- How did CTS respond to the opening offer? As expected? Why?
- What should CMI do next? (Push for those who want to make a concession, vs. those who want to "hang tough" and get the other side to defend its position. Get each side to defend its approach, and encourage debate among students in the class.)

(10 minutes) Students should read the (C) case. Test out how good the "plans" were against what Randall and Dolan did. Through the effective use of questions, they discovered that CTS' opening negotiating position was weak and indefensible. CTS has made major concessions in a short period of time.

Discussion Questions:

- What had happened? What is the significance of these events?
- What should Randall and Dolan do now?

(10 minutes) Students should read the (D) case. Test out the students' action plans against what actually occurs (Randall and Dolan push for a few more points, then adjourn negotiations).

Discussion Questions:

- What will CTS do next? (Poll for those who think they will stay with $2 million, or change to a lower demand.)
- What should CMI do next? (Poll for those who think that CMI should stay with its demands, vs. those who think it is time for them to make a concession.)

(10 minutes) Students should read the (E) case. Students will be amused at CMI's "tough" negotiating position. Ask them whether they think this is appropriate or not. The answer should depend on whether this a long-term or short-term negotiation for CMI--i.e., will they need to work with CTS people in the future and is their "reputation" really important here?

Discussion Questions:

- How do you feel about the negotiating strategy being used by CMI? Do you think it will work or backfire?
- What should CMI do next?

   (5 minutes) Students should read the (F) case. At this point, students can summarize what they feel were the most important aspects of CMI's negotiating strategy.

Summary Discussion (15 minutes)

The instructor should pick up on the following major summary points:

1. The importance of effective preparation and "doing homework"--knowing about one's own needs, the opponent and his needs, the history and background of the business, and the nature of the issues (marketplace) that you are negotiating.

2. The setting of key negotiating points:
   a) A resistance point (maximum they will pay)
   b) An opening bid (where to start)
   c) An expected or desired settlement

3. Understanding the bargaining range (difference between the two opening bids, and the likelihood that, through the negotiation process parties move to the middle of this range). In this case, that precedent was violated because of CMI's negotiating strategy of "hanging tough." If they had moved to the middle of the range, they would have settled a a point around $3 million.

4. Assessment of opponent's enthusiasm to settle, and willingness to make quick concessions, as an indicator that a) the opponent does not have much faith in his own opening offer, and b) the opponent is likely to concede quickly and rapidly.

5. The strategy used by CMI- -A "hold tight" or commitment strategy.

6. The "10 act play of negotiation"- -that bargainers begin far apart, and move toward some central point through a rather predictable series of concessions.

7. Assessment of the negotiating styles of key parties, particularly those for CTS--e.g., Burr Winder and Lehman.

CAPITAL MORTGAGE COMPANY CASE
SUMMARY POINTS

ROLE OF HOMEWORK AND PREPARATION

- UNDERSTAND OWN NEEDS

- ANTICIPATE OTHER'S NEEDS, OTHER'S NEED TO SETTLE

- HISTORY, TRACK RECORD OF OPPONENT

- IMPORTANCE OF THE LARGER MARKET ANALYSIS

ROLE OF PRESENCE/ABSENCE OF OPTIONS

SETTING KEY POINTS:

- TARGET

- OPENING BID

- WALKAWAY, RESISTANCE POINT

POWER OF THE "BARGAINING RANGE"

IMPORTANCE OF "THE NEGOTIATION DANCE"

KEY ROLE OF STRATEGY:

- MODEST OPENING
- STINGY CONCESSIONS
- "FIRST MOVE" DYNAMICS

CASE 2
PACIFIC OIL COMPANY

Learning Objectives

Pacific Oil Company is a case about a negotiation failure. Set in the context of a renegotiation of a purchase agreement for liquefied chemical, Pacific Oil Company highlights the consequences of ineffective planning and negotiating strategy. The failure of the key negotiators to define clear objectives and a bottom line, failure to define a strategy, and failure to understand the importance of time deadlines all contribute to a weak and ineffectual strategy. The case ends on an action note--whether Pacific's chief negotiator should yield one more concession--and students are asked to determine whether there is anything that can be done to "salvage" the contract negotiation for Pacific.

Specific learning objectives include:

1. Reinforcing the importance of planning, goal setting, and preparation for negotiation;
2. Reinforcing the importance of developing a strategy, and the liabilities of being on the defensive, responsive to the opponent's strategy;
3. Demonstrating the important role played by time and deadlines in negotiation;
4. Showing how negotiators are liable to "entrapment" in negotiations, and demonstrating ways to understand and prevent these dynamics.

Case Summary

Pacific Oil Company, like many major oil companies, produces fuel and diesel oil, gasoline, and a variety of industrial chemicals. One of it's major industrial chemical lines is Vinyl Chloride Monomer--VCM--primarily used for the manufacture of polyvinyl chloride plastics. Pacific Oil had a number of VCM customers in its European market, one of whom was Reliant Corporation, which manufactured plastic pipe and pipe fittings for residential and industrial plumbing. Pacific had negotiated a sales agreement with Reliant that had been renewed. During the term of the contract and because of changing market conditions, Pacific decided to try to get the contract extended beyond its current expiration date.

The case describes the actions of two negotiators for Pacific--Fontaine and Gaudin--and their efforts to get Reliant's cooperation in a contract extension. Reliant's negotiators primarily use the tactics of delay, limited authority, "nibbling" and tough negotiating to undermine Pacific and minimize their effectiveness. As the case ends, Fontaine is being pressed to give "one last concession" to assure the Reliant deal, while a staff advisor is trying to talk him out of it.

Recommended Reading Assignment to Accompany This Case:

Reader: 2.1 (Kuhn), 2.2. (Scott), 3.1 (Aaronson), 3.2 (Craver), 3.3 (Dawson)
After the case: 12.1 (Rubin), 5.1 (Neale and Bazerman)
Text: Chapter 2, 3.

Discussion Questions:

1. Identify the strengths and weaknesses of Fontaine's and Gaudin's negotiating strategy in their deliberations with Reliant Chemical Company.

2. Identify the strengths and weaknesses of Hauptman's and Zinnser's negotiating strategy.

3. What action should Fontaine take at the end of the case?

Case Analysis:

In 1968, Pacific Oil Company had established a four-year agreement with Reliant Chemical to sell VCM. In October 1972, this agreement was successfully renegotiated to extend to December, 1977. However, by December of 1974, Pacific was deeply concerned about the status of the contract, for the following reasons:

1. The market for VCM had been in a significant "shortage" situation for years. However, a number of new chemical plants were being built, and between the added capacity to produce VCM and a drop in demand, it was clear that the market would be oversupplied in a few years.

2. The market was dominated by a few large customers that bought **huge** amounts of VCM. It was therefore important to keep contracts with these customers, because if a company lost one, it would be almost impossible to make up the business with new customers.

3. Corporate headquarters of Pacific Oil was talking about setting up a new company division to produce its own line of PVC products. If Pacific entered the PVC market, it would buy its own VCM chemical stock and not have to be as dependent on external sales.

As a result, Fontaine and Gaudin decided to try to get an extension of their contract with Reliant past the 1977 expiration date, while at the same time trying to determine whether Pacific was going to get into the PVC business on its own. The case describes the deliberations between Fontaine and Gaudin and Reliant's two major negotiators, Zinnser and Hauptmann. Fontaine and Gaudin approach the negotiation process, ineffectively, in the following ways.

1. Failure to Plan for Negotiations

    Fontaine and Gaudin did no systematic planning, other than to be motivated to "get Reliant to resign." As a result of the vagueness of this objective, the two are so eager for a contract extension that they make a number of needless concessions in an effort to assure some kind of deal. No goals were defined for the new contract, and no "bottom line" was ever set to determine what would be a minimally acceptable agreement.

2. Failure to Understand the Role of Deadlines

    Fontaine and Gaudin were aware of several things when they reopened negotiations with Reliant in early 1975:

    - The current contract had three years to run;

    - Reliant had no reason to want to extend the contract at this time;

    - Reliant probably knew that the market was going soft (hence it would be in Reliant's best interest to wait until the contract almost ran out, and then approach a number of suppliers to get the best possible deal).

    Yet Fontaine and Gaudin did not create any incentives for Reliant to want to resign before the expiration. As a result, they left themselves wide open to delaying and "nibbling" tactics by Reliant- - tactics Hauptmann and Zinnser used. Reliant strung the negotiations out. They only discussed one issue at a time, while making Fontaine believe that this was "the last issue to be settled" before signing. Finally, Hauptmann and Zinnser introduced "dummy issues" to stall the negotiations. One example of this was the pipeline metering problem--a question that would not normally be dealt with in negotiations but through independent inspection and monitoring.

3. Differences in Negotiating Style

    Fontaine and Gaudin are often described as naive, clumsy and careless as negotiators. Their styles may also be contrasted against the calculating, tactical, precise "German" style evidenced by Hauptmann and Zinnser. (While executives and some students will be aware of cultural differences and their impact on negotiating style, be careful about generalizations and "stereotypes" that you, the instructor, use in class.)

4. Failure to Define a Strategy

    By failing to set objectives, set deadlines, and understand how to achieve their objectives in the time period, Fontaine and Gaudin did not define a clear strategy. They had no "plan" for knowing how to proceed. Moreover, by not having a strategy, they were forced to play by the strategy defined by Hauptmann and Zinnser--one of delay and "nibbling." When opponents use delay and "nibbling" tactics, negotiators must be able to:

- Define a deadline for the negotiations. If the deadline is not identical with the other's deadline, then negotiators must invent ways to attract the opponent toward a quick resolution.
- Define a bottom line, or a minimally acceptable deal. Negotiators must know what is the least satisfactory contract they will sign.
- Aggressively seek out options (other new customers or even closing the plant).
- Protect themselves from "nibbling" by not allowing any new issues to be opened up unless the opponent is also willing to discuss issues previously settled. Contracts must be viewed as an acceptable package; if the opponent wants to discuss a new issue after everything is settled, the entire contract should be put on the table for renegotiation.

5. Failure to Manage and Deal with One's Own Constituency

Fontaine and Gaudin have several major problems with their own organization that affect their negotiations:

a. The lines of responsibility for senior management regarding this problem are muddy and unclear. It isn't clear whether Meredith or Saunders should be monitoring this negotiation, but one or the other clearly should have intervened to "stem the damage" and stop the constant concessions being made. Kelsey (a staff person) finally takes the most active role in trying to persuade Fontaine not to give any more away. The matrix organization of Pacific makes this problem even more serious.

b. Pacific undermines its own negotiators and their use of a key bargaining point by deciding midway through negotiations not to go into the PVC market themselves. In addition, they publish it in the newspaper, thereby announcing to the world that Pacific will not be a major consumer of VCM. This weakens Fontaine and Gaudin's ability to tell Reliant that *"You* better sign up now before we decide not to sell it to you."

6. Entrapment

By virtue of the strategy they use (or, more precisely, don't use), Fontaine and Gaudin unwittingly make themselves susceptible to entrapment. Entrapment has typically been described in terms of waiting lines, or stock market investments, or "bad loan psychology" in banks. The instructor can learn more about entrapment by referring to the article by Jeffrey Rubin (12.1), and by referring to the other references listed at the end of this section. A set of "lecture notes" on entrapment is also included in these case notes.

Teaching Strategy

For students who have no knowledge of contracts and contract negotiations in the petrochemical industry, they should first read "Petrochemical Supply Contracts: A Technical Note." Then read the case, and prepare the discussion questions.

(20-40 minutes) Review the major events in the case. The following discussion questions and strategies may be used:

- a) What was Pacific Oil's problem in late 1974?
- b) How effectively did Fontaine and Gaudin approach the negotiation?
- c) How effectively did Hauptmann and Zinnser approach the negotiation?
- d) What were the events that transpired, beginning in January of 1975? (It is extremely helpful to draw a "time line" on the blackboard and summarize the events so that students can see the progress to the current state).
- e) How did Fontaine and Gaudin "get themselves into this situation"?

(20 minutes) It is common for students to be very critical of Fontaine and Gaudin by this point. One teaching strategy that adds a lot of life to the discussion is for the instructor to role play Fontaine at this point. Create a name tent for Fontaine, sit at the front of the room at a desk or table, and begin as follows:

"My name is Jean Fontaine. I have been sitting in the back of the room, at the invitation of Professor _____, listening to your comments. However, I don't think that 'what to do' in this negotiation is quite as simple and clear cut as you try to make it!"

At this point, the instructor can specifically respond to some of the students earlier comments, or simply invite suggestions and criticism about how Fontaine has handled the negotiation. In addition, Fontaine should push the students to specifically address how he should deal with Kelsey's advice at the end of the case. In playing this role, Fontaine should try to convey the following:

- You always thought that you were just about to sign the deal, and that this was the last concession.

- You felt that your objective was to get a deal, almost at any price, and that was the objective you pursued.

- You did not get a lot of help with this problem from Saunders and Meredith, and, in fact, the company put you in an even bigger mess when they announced that the company was not going to go into the PVC business.

- The company people back in the United States always have a lot of helpful advice, but really don't understand what it is like over here "on the front lines."

- What would they have you do now--abort the entire negotiations over one small concession in the contract language? You've worked so hard and so long to get to this point! Beside, what are you going to do with all that VCM in an oversupplied market?

Continue the role play until students see the binds that Fontaine feels and experiences. Then, step out of role and summarize the discussion.

Read the "B" case to students (reprinted following these notes). This will confirm that the scenario did not end well, but ended predictably given the previous events.

(20 minutes) Stand back from the role play and try to get the students to identify with Fontaine's feelings of being "trapped" by the circumstances. Talk about other analogous situations where people feel "trapped" and what they do about it.

As an option, you may choose to do the Dollar Auction exercise at this point, to demonstrate entrapment dynamics. (See Lewicki, Bowen, Hall & Hall, 1988 for complete information).

Proceed to the lecturette on Entrapment if time allows.

(10 minutes) Summarize the key negotiation failures depicted in the case:

a) Failure to adequately define objectives.
b) Failure to define a bottom line, or minimally acceptable deal.
c) Failure to cultivate alternatives to resigning a new agreement with Reliant.
d) Failure to set a deadline, and incentives for the other party to meet that deadline.
e) Failure to define a clear negotiating strategy, and as a result, to be manipulated by the other's strategy.
f) Failure to manage one's constituency--bosses and information sources-- so that they give the negotiator the advice and support he needs.
g) Failure to recognize the "nibbling" strategy used by Hauptmann and Zinnser--and to combat it by only being willing to negotiate a package deal, rather than one concession at a time.
h) Failure to recognize that entrapment was occurring, and that only by setting limits and defining resistance points (and sticking to them) would they be able to "hold the line."

References:

Bazerman, M. & Neale, M. (1992), *Negotiating Rationally*. New York: Free Press.

Brockner, J., Shaw, M. C., & Rubin, J. Z. (1979). "Factors Affecting Withdrawal from an Escalating Conflict: Quitting Before It's Too Late. *Journal of Experimental Social Psychology* 15, 492-503.

Staw, B. M. (1981). "The Escalation of Commitment to a Course of Action." *Academy of Management Review.* 6, 577-587.

Teger, A. I. (1979). *Too Much Invested to Quit: The Psychology of the escalation of conflict.* New York: Pergammon Press.

KEY NEGOTIATION FAILURES DEPICTED IN THE CASE:

- Failure to adequately define objectives.

- Failure to define a bottom line, or minimally acceptable deal.

- Failure to cultivate alternatives to resigning a new agreement with Reliant.

- Failure to set a deadline, and incentives for the other party to meet that deadline.

- Failure to define a clear negotiating strategy, hence to be manipulated by the other's strategy.

- Failure to manage one's constituency--bosses and information sources- -so that they give the negotiator the advice and support he needs.

- Failure to recognize the "nibbling" strategy used by Reliant, and to combat it.

- Failure to recognize that entrapment was occurring, and to limit it by setting limits and defining resistance points.

LECTURETTE ON ENTRAPMENT

WHAT IS ENTRAPMENT?

- Commitment of resources to a course of action

- Action does not produce return, may produce loss

- Decision is made to commit further resources in order to "turn the situation around"

- Process may repeat and escalate several times as additional resources are invested

EXAMPLES:

- "Bad loan" psychology
- "Waiting line" psychology
- Stock market psychology--"Buy more while the price is down"
- Military escalation

- Application to negotiation-failure to set specific objectives and deadlines *in advance*; leads to failure to "bracket" the limits of commitment (time or resources), and hence be prone to commit more at each failure.

WHAT CONTRIBUTES TO ENTRAPPING SITUATIONS?

- Emotional commitment to an objective or possible solution

- Wishful thinking

- Bigger the investment, more severe the possible loss, more prone to try to "turn it around"

- Diffused responsibility

- HOW actor is being evaluated by others:

    - Get a deal (any deal)
    - Establish a good deal
    - Behave in a certain way

HOW CAN ENTRAPMENT BE PREVENTED?

- Get several perspectives-avoid tunnel vision

- Avoid inaction--DO something

    - Don't "wish or hope"
    - Don't let time work it out
    - Set a limit for commitment, be willing to cut your losses

- Redefine the situation

    - Not the same old problem but a new problem to be dealt with (often helps to change decision criteria)

- Diversify responsibility and authority

    - Define/redefine accountability
    - Play "devil's advocate"

- Watch out for the organizational pressure to "settle at all costs"

    - Beware of the "Don't come home empty-handed" message

CASE STUDY

PACIFIC OIL COMPANY (B)

Kelsey called Meredith the next day. They both agreed that a resale clause would be a dangerous commitment and an even more dangerous precedent for Pacific Oil. They made an appointment for a conference call to Saunders for the following morning. When they talked to him, they learned that Saunders had approved the concession, that Fontaine had already talked to Hauptmann and told him it was O.K. to include it in the revised agreement.

CASE 3
A POWER PLAY FOR HOWARD

Learning Objectives

1. To understand how the broader social context can have a large influence on negotiations.

2. To examine how agents exert influence on the negotiations process.

3. To learn a different meaning to the term "win/lose bargaining."

Case Summary

This case describes a series of negotiations for the contract of professional basketball player Juwan Howard that occurred during the summer of 1996. The case describes several tangible and intangible factors in the negotiation, outlines how the league as an interested third party played a critical role in determining the outcome of the negotiation, and describes how Howard and his agents negotiated contracts with two different teams during the summer.

Recommended Reading Assignments to Accompany This Case

Reader: 8.1 (Rubin and Sander), 9.1 (Colosi), 12.1 (Rubin), 12.3 (Keiser)
Text: Chapter 8, 12

Teaching Strategy

The case describes a high stakes situation where the participants' egos and goals conflict and several tangible and intangible factors play important roles in the negotiation.

Proceed by using the following questions to discuss the case:

1. Was the Washington Bullets General Manager Wes Unseld correct when he stated that this negotiation "was simply about bucks"? Why or why not?

2. What were the important tangible and intangible factors in the case?

3. What role did Howard's agents, David Falk and Curtis Polk, play in the negotiation? Where they a positive or negative force in the negotiation? When should agents be

used in a negotiation and when do they simply "get in the way"? (see Rubin and Sander's article)

4. Was the league action of violating the initial contract between the Miami Heat and Juwan Howard predictable or not? What could Miami have done differently, if anything?

5. What are the lessons from this negotiation for other NBA teams? What general lessons are there for all negotiators in this case?

6. How is negotiating with a star player similar to and different from negotiating with a "customer you can't afford to lose"? (see Keiser's article)

CASE 4
CREATING THE GM-TOYOTA JOINT VENTURE: A CASE IN COMPLEX NEGOTIATION[1]

Learning Objectives

This is a one-part case describing a complex business negotiation, with strong industrial and international overtones. It serves **primarily** as a discussion piece, conveying the detail and intricacy of large-scale negotiations that encompass many parties, with varying agendas, conducted simultaneously at multiple levels. The case describes the initial contacts and subsequent negotiations between two major manufacturers in a sensitive political and economic environment. Communication, critical to the process, occurs within and across cultural boundaries; negotiators must manage differences not only of language, but of managerial and operational philosophy. Key points to be developed in class discussions vary, depending on how the case is used (see "Teaching Strategies" below).

Case Summary

Leaders of two major auto manufacturers, General Motors (U.S.) and Toyota (Japan), perceive a number of advantages in forming a business alliance producing motor vehicles in and for the U.S. domestic market. Each corporation enters the negotiation with its own particular agenda, with differing needs and interests between them. In addition, a variety of other parties become involved in the negotiation as advisors to the main negotiators, or as external (but highly interested) parties.

Case Analysis

On April 11, 1984, the U.S. Federal Trade Commission (FTC) approved of plans for GM and Toyota to form a joint venture to manufacture automobiles in the U.S. That venture, New United Motor Manufacturing, Inc. (NUMMI), was the culmination of negotiations between GM and Toyota that began formally on December 21, 1981 with high-level talks between senior managers of the two firms. Subsequent negotiations leading to the 1984 agreement, described by some participants as "long," "hard," and "frustrating," took place at multiple levels, with a bewildering array of parties, interests and agendas, in an atmosphere charged with questions of domestic and international trade, politics, competition, management oversight and employee job security.

Factors motivating the major players in the negotiations were many and varied. Both GM and Toyota were concerned about their own corporate performance in light of volatile market conditions. In the U.S., an increasing attraction for Japanese manufacturers, the setting was marked by two things. First, the "oil shocks" of the 1970's created official and

---

[1] This teaching note was prepared by Professor Stephen Weiss, Faculty of Administrative Studies, York University. It is used with permission.

consumer interest in more fuel efficient autos, a strength of the Japanese product. Japanese response to this interest created, in turn, concern among U.S. manufacturers and government officials on matters such as market share, import limitations, and "domestic content" legislation seeking to secure for the U.S. economy the benefits of a robust domestic auto manufacturing sector. In partial response, Japanese interests self-imposed a system of voluntary export restraints, while various Japanese auto manufacturers investigated a variety of options involving the manufacture of "Japanese" autos in U.S. facilities, primarily using American labor. Both GM and Toyota had interests which, while differing substantially from the other's, might be served by an innovative agreement such as a joint manufacturing venture. Any potential GM-Toyota agreement, though, was only one of a range of strategic options for each company.

Given the U.S. domestic location of any such GM-Toyota joint venture, two other actors had primary "first-order" interests in the negotiations--U.S. labor and the U.S. government. Negotiations involving these additional parties might be considered "ancillary" to those between GM and Toyota, but were critical nonetheless given the political and environmental aspects of the negotiation setting. U.S. labor, represented by the United Auto Workers (UAW), had clear interests involving the maintenance of its traditional bargaining relationship with GM, in participation in novel "cutting edge" activities in ventures differing from the traditional model, and in the rights and precedents relevant to the reemployment of UAW workers laid off by GM but still available to work in the proposed joint venture facility. The U.S. government participated in two main ways, directly through the offices of the Federal Trade Commission (FTC), and indirectly through legislation passed by the U.S. Congress. The FTC's primary concern was the negotiating firms' compliance with existing anti-trust law; an additional issue regarded the FTC's request for company information from the firms, which Toyota in particular was reticent to provide. Congress' "participation" was through the passage of controversial "domestic content" legislation, in response to pressure from a variety of U.S. interests regarding the protection of American jobs and manufacturing capabilities.

The negotiation process is viewed as a two-phase process, preceded by a preparation stage. "Preparation" covers the period prior to March 1, 1982, and includes each side's general experiences, environmental awareness, and specific (negotiation-related) activities. For instance, while Toyota's failed negotiations with Ford affects its approach to GM, "preparation" here involved a focus on GM as a negotiation prospect in light of such related events and market conditions. "Phase One," from March 1, 1982 until February 17, 1983, culminates in a GM-Toyota "Memorandum of Understanding" (MOU) stipulating a broad outline subject to further negotiation. "Phase Two," from February 17, 1983 to February 21, 1984, encompasses the preparation of a more detailed document, resulting in the initiation of the joint venture, per se.

Yet another alternative for analyzing complex cases such as GM-Toyota is the "Relationship-Behaviors-Conditions" (or "RBC") model developed by Professor Weiss, the case author. This approach is described in greater detail by him in his article "Analysis of Complex Negotiation in International Business: The RBC Perspective" (*Organizational Science, 4*, 269-300). Several overhead masters representing this analytical approach follow this case note; instructors should feel free to contact Professor Weiss directly for a copy of the full article (Professor Stephen E. Weiss, Faculty of Administrative Studies, York University, 4700 Keele St., North York, Ontario, Canada, M3J IP3).

The case goes on to examine the "ancillary" negotiations involving the UAW and the FTC, closing by proposing and briefly discussing the strategic implications of the entire process. More specifically, these involve:

1. Preparation for and monitoring of the negotiations;
2. The nature and role of top management participation;
3. The role of intermediaries and external experts;
4. "Fractionalization" of complex negotiations; and
5. Periodic reference to the "big picture."

The "phased" structure of this presentation lends itself to an analytical approach to the study of this negotiation in two ways. First, it provides a "framework/detail" model for complex negotiations, with the development of a broad formula or framework for agreement in Phase One, which then guides discussion toward a detailed agreement during Phase Two. Second, an analytical approach allows observers a chance to investigate the richness and complexity of such negotiations through sensitivity to factors such as multiple-level actors (i.e., organizations, groups, and individuals) with varying relationships, constituencies, perspectives, and levels of involvement. Also valuable is the chance to study the effect of "ancillary" (but critical) negotiations on the main negotiation itself.

Teaching Strategies and Assignments

Case as-Stand-Alone. The case can be used as a self-contained exercise. Given its length and complexity, it should be assigned for individual reading before class. Another option is that it be read, then discussed in groups before or during class (allow 60 minutes, if the discussion occurs during class). Whichever option is used, the assignment questions should be some variation of:

1. Given the environmental and communication problems set forth, why/how did GM and Toyota reach satisfactory agreement in this case?

2. If you were describing this case to those unfamiliar with negotiations, what structure or framework would you use to make it understandable to them?

While the groups discuss the case, in class or out, the post-group, in-class discussion can take the analytical approach mentioned at the end of the case analysis above. Starting with the assignment question, the instructor can guide subsequent discussion of alternate scenarios. For instance, how the negotiation might have differed if both firms had been U.S. corporations, how they might have differed if Toyota's failed negotiations with Ford had not occurred, or what the effect might have been of the absence of "domestic content" legislation by the U.S. Congress. Another approach to this option might be to assign such alternate scenarios to separate groups, asking them to develop and present their findings independently to the whole class so as to highlight the likely effects of differing actors, settings, or processes.

Alternatively, students can be asked specific questions, such as who "won" or "lost," what specifically was "won" or "lost," or what behaviors, tactics of strategies seemed more or less effective, given the outcomes (one example of this last sort might be the UAW's willingness to enter into non-traditional agreements, as it exhibited in this case).

A third option is to have students do a "power" analysis, identifying sources of power for the various negotiating parties and assessing how (and how well) such power was applied to the negotiation process.

Depending on time available, class discussion can take 60 to 90 minutes (not including in-class, pre-discussion group time, if that option is used).

Case as Debriefing Packet. Professor Weiss has also prepared a role-play version of this case which is designed to occupy up to twelve participants in an extended (6-8 hour) negotiation. Instructors may wish to contact Professor Weiss directly for access to these materials. As constructed, the role play version begins at the beginning of "Phase Two" (i.e., just after the signing of the GM/Toyota MOU) and focuses an the ancillary negotiations and the "detailing of the Phase One framework." It is assumed that most (if not all) of the roleplayed negotiation will be conducted outside of class, with settlement results and subsequent debriefing confined to 60 to 90 minutes of class time.

The case as presented here can then be used as a debriefing packet, to be read prior to class but after the role play is concluded. It can also be read after reports of negotiation outcomes are made, but before a subsequent class which can then be devoted to a "postmortem" analysis of the role play. This second option will take up two classes, of approximately 60 to 90 minutes each.

Case as Counter-Point. Finally, the case can be used as a linked assignment, connected to use of the "Alpha-Beta" role play (Exercise 17, in the *Readings, Exercises and Cases* book), which presents a Japanese/American negotiation in the electronics industry. We suggest that "Alpha-Beta" be set up and conducted first, as suggested elsewhere in this Manual, followed by the use of this case as presented here, as described above under "Case as Stand-Alone." Time for the discussion of this case (normally 60 to 90 minutes) can be shortened as appropriate to allow time for developing comparisons and contrasts between the two settings, and the two exercises.

CASE UPDATE

(WRITTEN BY PROFESSOR STEVE WEISS)

June, 1983 Usery goes to Toyota in Japan with UAW demand for assurance that it can represent joint venture workers

June 6, 1983 National Tooling and Machining Association asks FTC to block joint venture on grounds that it will damage tooling industry; GM is industry's largest customer, but it is building in-house capacity via $200 million capital investment program and may import from Japan for joint venture needs

June 10, 1983 UAW threatens to "go to war" if joint venture does not hire its members (WSJ)

June 13, 1983 Request for bids for building Fremont stamping plant sent out; Toyota to bring in all welding systems and other assembly equipment from Japan; Kawasaki Heavy Industries and Yasakawa Electric Co. are likely suppliers

June 20, 1983 Last day of 120-day period set up in Feb. 17 memorandum; earlier direct appeal by Usery to Roger Smith secured an approval conditional upon Toyota's continuing interest; Toyota agrees to extension

July 9, 1983 Japanese government may drop export restraints for 1984-85 period (beginning April 1) (Economist)

July 4, 1983 Via Usery, Toyota sends to UAW a proposal with its original demands concerning production standards, compulsory overtime, job classification, seniority, etc. UAW later rejects them

July 18, 1983 $1-2 million contract awarded to Shoketsu Kinzoku Kogyo for supply of pneumatic equipment to joint venture

July, 1983 Usery and Ephlin negotiate for three days in Washington; meetings end in deadlock over rehiring issue; Usery sets aside attempt to arrive at contract, proposing a binding letter of intent as an alternative goal; he returns to Tokyo as second deadline approaches, asks for another extension

July 27, 1983 GM reports that its earnings for 2nd quarter increased 86% to $1.04 billion; best showing in four years

Aug 25, 1983 FTC commissioners' opinions are rumored to be split with Clanton the sole commissioner undecided (International Herald Tribune); Toyota announces earnings of $829 million for year ending June 1; first annual report for new Toyota Motor Corp.

Sept 2, 1983 UAW Local #1364 sues GM and UAW International for depriving its members of voice; wants its charter back (International revoked it) and nullification of any labor agreement made without a vote by local members

Sept 9, 1983 Federal Judge Spencer Williams refuses to issue an injunction in UAW local's favor

Sept 16, 1983 For first time in history, GM invites a UAW Vice-President (Donald Ephlin) to address stockholders; also $7 million retraining program announced for 9,300 laidoff workers in Flint

Sept 21, 1983 Ford Motor Company announces that it may join Chrysler in antitrust suit against the joint venture

Sept 23, 1983 UAW officials reach agreement in principle ("Letter of Intent") with joint venture without vote by laid-off workers; represents first time UAW will organize a Japanese-run auto plant in the U.S.

Sept 25, 1983 Commissioner David Clanton's term expires; Toyota has reportedly not provided documents to FTC because of "translation problems;" some suggest that Toyota has waited until Commissioner Clanton, who opposes joint venture, is replaced by appointee Terry Calvani

Oct 6, 1983 GM announces plains to import 200,000 subcompacts from Isuzu Motors Ltd. and 100,000 minicars from Suzuki Motor Co.

Oct 19, 1983 Toyota given "one last chance" by FTC to provide cost and profit information; reports circulate that Toyota only entered joint venture to avoid domestic content legislation in U.S. that no longer looks imminent; Roger Smith says he is "anxious"

Fall 1983 Toyota's negotiations with the Government of Taiwan for an auto joint venture fall through

Nov 1, 1993 after a month of bargaining with USTR, Brock and other U.S. officials, Japanese officials announce a fourth year of voluntary auto export restraints (April 1, 1994 - March 31, 1985) at 1.85 million cars (a 10% increase); GM opposed continuation of restraints because of desire to increase imports from Isuzu and Suzuki

Nov 16, 1983 Terry Calvani, Vanderbilt University professor appointed by President Reagan, begins term as FTC Commissioner; Toyota agrees to provide FTC with documents concerning cost and profit information so it can make a ruling

Nov 28, 1983 Toyota made deal with FTC; usually after provision of such data, deal may be consummated after 20 days; Toyota gave FTC as much time as it wants in exchange for FTC's restricting access to the data

Dec 19, 1983 FTC staff has proposed that GM and Toyota sign an agreement to avoid antitrust violations; proposal is said to be delaying an FTC ruling; could take 6-12 more months

Dec 21, 1983 GM will sign a FTC consent accord with Toyota that bars anticompetitive practices such as price-fixing, expanding output, and lengthening duration of venture

Dec 22, 1983 GM and Toyota sign consent accord and FTC gives provisional approval to permit venture; order subject to 60 day period for public comment

Dec 27, 1983 News article reports that according to documents submitted by Toyota to FTC, company wants to take over the joint venture at its termination

Jan 1984 GM reports record profit for 1983 of $3.7 billion

Jan 10, 1984 Chrysler asks FTC to investigate joint venture and to delay 60-day waiting period before consent agreement takes effect; asks FTC to release contents of original pact between GM and Toyota

Jan 16, 1984 Chrysler files suit, asking U. S. District Court to find GM and Toyota in violation of the Clayton and Sherman Acts and asks for compensation for unfair competition resulting from the joint venture

Jan 30, 1984 Rep. J. Florio rejects unusual FTC request that he delay a Commerce subcommittee hearing on the FTC's tentative approval of the joint venture

Feb 2, 1984 Consumer Federation of America announces its support for Chrysler's antitrust suit against GM and Toyota

Feb 9, 1984 FTC votes 3-2 against releasing non-public GM and Toyota documents to Chrysler; Iacocca testifies before House subcommittee reviewing GM-Toyota agreement that if every American auto maker adopted GM's "Japan strategy," the U.S. would lose 300,000 jobs

Mar 1984 GM and Toyota send 5,000 letters to former Fremont workers to solicit job applications

Apr 11, 1984 FTC grants final approval to joint venture in a 3-2 vote; Pertschuk and Bailey voted against it

Final Agreements

UAW - GM/Toyota "Letter of Intent" (announced September 23, 1983)

- UAW recognized as bargaining agent at plant once hiring begins
- GM and Toyota to hire 2,500 of the 4,000 workers laid off in 1982
- GM and Toyota need not preserve seniority of laid off workers
- Workers' wages to be pegged to "going rates" in the U.S. auto industry
- UAW agrees to be flexible on work rules and job classifications
- A detailed labor agreement will be negotiated starting in April; to be concluded by June, 1985

Other provisions, source uncertain (Letter of Intent? later contract?)

- Four job classifications: 1 for all production workers (80% of workers at plant); 3 for skilled trades (20 is common in U.S.; some GM assembly plants have over 100)
- Workers will have employment for life of joint venture (12 years); jobs will not be lost because of automation
- No grievance protection
- Workers will wear uniforms; morning exercise is optional

FTC Decision and Order (April 11, 1984)
Joint venture approved subject to following conditions:
- No other joint venture may be formed between GM and Toyota
- Venture will not last longer than 12 years after the start of production or Dec. 31 1997, whichever comes first
- GM and Toyota will not exchange non-public information about prices of new cars or parts, or about costs, sales and production forecasts of GM or Toyota products not necessary for the joint venture; no marketing plans for any products are to be disclosed
- GM and Toyota will not exchange information about model changes, sales and production forecasts not related to the joint venture; nor cost information about GM or Toyota parts supplied to the joint venture
- GM and Toyota shall each keep files of all communications and logs of all meetings between them

GM-Toyota Detailed Agreements

- Reinvestment of profits or pay out in dividends is up to Board of Directors
- Venture to be named New United Motor Manufacturing, Inc.
- GM to sell the NUMMI car as Chevrolet Nova
- Product liability [terms unknown]
- Suppliers to be used [see names listed in above chronology] ultimately, total of about 70

Other provisions probably reached in Feb. 17th memorandum:

- NUMMI to be managed by 30 staffers from Toyota, incl. President (and CEO), Chief Operating Officer, and Vice-President of Manufacturing
- 2.5% royalty to Toyota on each car produced (Ind Mgt - Canada - 4/83)
- NUMMI car to be sold to GM on cost-plus basis
- 2500 workers

THE RBC MODEL FOR COMPLEX NEGOTIATIONS
(STEVE WEISS, *ORGANIZATIONAL SCIENCE*)

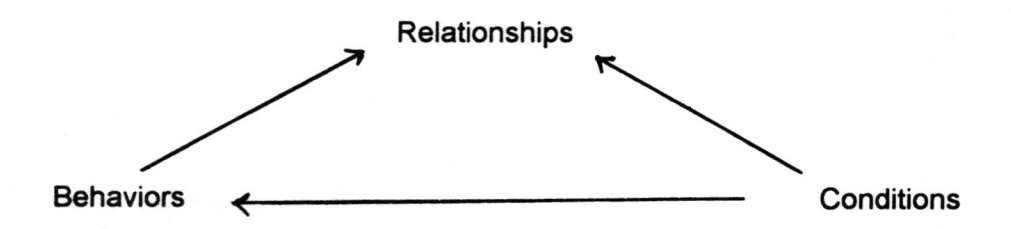

```
              Relationships
              ↗         ↖
       Behaviors ←———————— Conditions
```

RELATIONSHIPS BETWEEN PRIMARY PARTIES
Interorganizational
Intergroup
Interpersonal

BEHAVIOR OF PRIMARY PARTIES
    Organizations
    Groups (Teams)
    Individuals

CONDITIONS
Circumstances
Capabilities
Cultures
Environments

CASE 5
COLLECTIVE BARGAINING AT MAGIC CARPET AIRLINES: A UNION PERSPECTIVE

CASE OVERVIEW

This case describes the bargaining process from the perspective of the League of Flight Attendants (LFA) union negotiators, as they sought their second contract against Magic Carpet Airlines (MCA). It describes the steps the negotiating team members followed as they identified their bargaining objectives and pursued them through collective bargaining. Because of the confidential nature of the bargaining process, all names, dates, conversations, financial data, and figures used in this case are disguised. However, the survey data are real.

Part (A) of the case covers the union's preparation for bargaining, forming initial positions and the early negotiation sessions. These sessions illustrate "contending" tactics, distributive ("win-lose") bargaining, and "power plays" on the part of management. It also raises issues pertaining to the dynamics within the ranks of management's own team ("Intra-organizational bargaining," Walton and McKersie, 1965).

Part (B) covers the middle phase of negotiation. Serious ethical questions are raised about management's approach to bargaining. Even so, integrative ("win-win") bargaining also occurs. This phase also illustrates some distributive bargaining and intra-organizational bargaining within the union team at a time when their chief negotiator cannot attend the sessions.

Part (C) covers the latter phase of negotiation. It illustrates one mediator's approach to helping the parties resolve their dispute and his gamble designed to shock the parties into serious negotiations as a strike deadline loomed.

At the end of the teaching note, what actually happened at the end of negotiations is revealed along with a table describing the final settlement.

SUGGESTED COURSES AND APPROACHES

This case is appropriate for either an undergraduate or graduate negotiation course, labor-management relations course, or a mediation course. It can be given in parts [note that Part (B) and Part (C) cannot be used independently of Part (A)]; alternatively, the entire case may be given as one assignment. It makes an excellent integrative case (end-of-the semester) for collective bargaining courses. It is suitable for class discussion or for a paper assignment (e.g. as a part of a take-home examination).

TEACHING OBJECTIVES

The teaching objectives for this case include the following:

1. To describe the collective bargaining process;

2. To portray preparation for bargaining from the union negotiators' perspective (the case outlines the union's preparation for bargaining, telling how the union identified its goals and what its strategies were for achieving these goals);

3. To help the student determine the strategies that MCA managers used (the tactics are shown, but not told, to the reader);

4. To illustrate various models of influence and persuasion techniques (techniques such as rational argument, inaction, integrative bargaining (e.g., swapping,) or "logrolling" issues) are illustrated (Lewicki, Litterer, Minton, & Saunders, 1993);

5. To illustrate how various mediation tactics, such as posing "what if..." questions are used (see Wall, 1981, Ross, 1988, or Carnevale, 1986 for discussions of mediation);

6. To help students learn about ethical issues in negotiation; and

7. To help students become more sensitive to gender concerns in the workplace by noting the way that managers treated the female flight attendant negotiators.

QUESTIONS

The following questions might be helpful for class discussion:

Part (A)

1. What did the union do to prepare for negotiations? What additional sources of information might it have used?

The union surveyed the members and used wage comparison data gathered from sources such as *Monthly Labor Reports* for industry comparisons. Additionally, the League of Flight Attendants (LFA) negotiators examined the pilots and mechanics unions' pay, benefits, and working conditions. The previous contract as well as arbitration rulings were also consulted. The union could have sought information from the following: The Department of Labor, various Bureau of Business and Economic Research offices in the domiciles (for geographic wage comparisons and local cost of living data), the pilots'and mechanics' contracts, and recent legislation bearing upon their jobs.

2. What were the union's primary objectives?

The union's primary objectives were:
- Implementation of a "duty rig" provision, whereby flight attendants are paid a percentage of their "duty time" (whether flying or not), rather than a straight for those hours when the aircraft was moving;
- Some sort of job security provision to protect the workers in the event of a layoff or merger;
- An increase in the level of pay;

- Improved benefits, such as more time off and an improved sick leave program; and
- Improved working conditions.

As an example of improved working conditions, attendants who swapped routes with each other currently had to give management five days advance notice. They wanted this practice eliminated or changed.

3.   What were the union's strategies? Were they reasonable?

The union strategies were as follows:

Keeping union members informed via newsletters. The student might criticize this tactic because negotiators tend to be unwilling to make serious concessions when they are aware of -- and are accountable to -- their constituents.

Involvement by all members of the negotiating team. This is good for insuring all members contribute ideas and accept tentative agreements. It may also be useful for ensuring team member commitment to the agreement -- necessary for securing contract ratification from the rank-and-file members. Involvement has a disadvantage also. It necessitates more caucusing, taking longer to conclude an agreement.

Allowing only one spokesperson. This is generally a good idea for avoiding sending "mixed signals" to the opponent.

Submitting an initial offer that was close to the union's resistance point (anticipated final offer). Further, this was close to the industry average for many clauses. Students could argue that this strategy was not wise because the union did not leave itself sufficient room to make concessions.

4.   What were the company's goals?

One goal seemed to be to get the LFA to give up hope for a new contract. If that were impossible, then the goal appeared to be to pay as little to the union as possible. For example, the company readily agreed to items that were unchanged, or to items that cost the company little, financially.

5.   What were the company's strategies?

During negotiations, MCA's team appeared to use stalling tactics that also communicated its lack of concern over whether the union struck or not.

The company sent confusing signals. For example, Mr. Windham, MCA's CEO, began negotiations by making a speech about how MCA did not want to take anything away from the flight attendants. After this speech, he left, whereupon the company negotiators proceeded to present the union with demands for wage and benefit concessions. Mr. Orleans, the industrial relations director, delivered a speech about the company's poor financial health and how the company could be bankrupt at any time. However, in the history of Magic Carpet Air, there had never been a year ending when the company showed a loss on its financial statement.

The company would not release all of the LFA committee members from work to participate in negotiations each session. This tactic was ineffective.

The company would not give LFA an adequate number of days for negotiations. The company would schedule three or four days each month. The managers were often "too busy" to meet with LFA. LFA began accepting any days that the company allotted to them for bargaining.

Management gave the impression that the union simply was not important. The company would schedule negotiations and after only a few minutes would want to caucus. The managers would "caucus" for the remainder of the day, leaving the union negotiators to wait in vain for their return. All the managers were doing was going back to their offices and conducting their daily business. It was unclear whether some of their sexist remarks were reflective of actual prejudice or were part of their apparent strategy of attempting to intimidate the union.

6. How did the deregulation of the airline industry in the late 1970s influence labor relations at Magic Carpet Air?

The deregulation created a climate where airline managers were quite concerned with containing labor costs. It also made mergers and acquisitions acceptable for managers, but created job insecurity for the workers, which led to these flight attendants unionizing. A handout on deregulation's effects on labor relations in the airline industry follows.

Part (B)

1. What tactics did management use that they had not attempted to use previously?

Management and LFA reached tentative agreements on various sections of a new contract. Mr. Orleans would have his assistant type those sections. However, upon review, LFA negotiators often discovered that those sections contained the same concessionary proposals that the company had proposed the first week of negotiations. Section after section would have to be retyped to reflect the actual compromises.

Management negotiator Mr. Sanders also used a "back-channel" type of informal negotiations by approaching the union during lunch. He offered an integrative "package" settlement (sometimes called "logrolling") which satisfied each side's interests. The union accepted the general terms of the package, but then used the more contending tactics of distributive bargaining ("nibbling") to try to get a slightly more favorable package. This process, where integrative bargaining is followed by distributive bargaining, is analogous in some ways to the process described by Lax and Sebenius (1986) where they discuss negotiators "creating value" and "claiming value."

2. What role did ethics play in this case?

Many of MCA managers' actions could be viewed as unethical. Mr. Orleans had new contract sections "mistyped" by his secretary, including MCA's original proposals instead of the negotiated clauses. The managers attempted to "buy off" the union by offering perks for union officers, rather than benefits for members. Also, managers pretended to caucus but actually went back to their jobs. Some bluffing and distortion of information also occurred. Many students will argue that these things are to be expected and that ethics are not important in negotiations. However, such unethical behavior may harm the long-term MCA-LFA relationship.

3. Why did Mr. Orleans only have contract sections "mistyped" when his boss, Mr. Irving, was not attending the meetings? How, if at all, is this related to Mr. Orleans' demotion?

Answers will vary. One possibility is that Mr. Orleans simply made honest mistakes. Another is that he wanted to "look good" to his new boss by securing union concessions. A third possibility is that he wanted to put the union on notice that MCA would stop at nothing to achieve its goals and that the LFA should not interfere with management's plans. A fourth possibility recognizes the presence of "organizational politics." Mr. Orleans may have hoped that no one would catch the mistakes until later. In this way he may have wanted to embarrass his boss, Mr. Irving, in the eyes of the CEO, Tom Windam. This may have been part of a long-term strategy for Mr. Orleans to win his old job back.

Part (C)

1. What strategies did the mediator use?

The mediator used several strategies, such as pressuring the parties to agree, posing "what if..." questions, devising creative (integrative) solutions, creating package settlements ("logrolling"), and inaction. He made statements to show to the negotiators that he was an expert. He presented proposals as his own ideas rather than as concessions from the other side so that the ideas would be considered on their merit, rather than viewed as opportunities for exploiting an opponent's weaknesses. These techniques are commonly used by mediators, although not universally used. And he quit, which is not widely used by mediators.

2. Why did the mediator quit?

His leaving was unusual. Apparently, he left because this dramatic (and some would say, unethical) form of inaction communicated three things to the negotiators:

1. They could resolve the dispute themselves;
2. He didn't care how they resolved the issues; and
3. He thought the negotiators were spending their energies trying to make their opponents look bad in front of the mediator, rather than trying to solve the problems they faced.

By "putting them on the spot," he forced them to accept responsibility for their own contract.

3. What was the "me-too" clause? Did the LFA use it wisely?

The "me-too" clause specified that the LFA would get the same terms as another union's contract. By seeking a "me-too" clause for job security, LFA hoped to leave this section of the contract for the pilots to negotiate; it was probably a wise strategy, given that the pilots had a more powerful union.

4. What should the union do next? Justify your decision.

    Answers will vary. Some students will encourage a strike as the only way to get management to bargain seriously. Some may urge that the union file a complaint with the federal government, charging that the firm is bargaining in bad faith (a charge that could be difficult to prove). Some will request another mediator. Some will urge the negotiations to resume without the mediator, noting that progress had been made on some issues and perhaps the mediator's leaving (and the approaching deadline) would be the catalyst needed to get management to make serious concessions. Some will request that Mr. Irving be present at future negotiations, because he seemed more congenial than Mr. Orleans.

Additional questions that might be given with this case, particularly if it is given as an out-of-class assignment:

1. Analyze the bargaining situation in light of at least five situational factors (see Druckman, 1971, 1994 for general reviews of these factors), recognizing that the situation is dynamic. Be sure to consider *the power relationship* as one of your factors.

2. Pruitt and Carnevale (1993) discuss matching and mismatching of concessions in both size and rate. To what extent did you see the type of matching/mismatching processes found throughout the "negotiation cycle" as described by Pruitt & Carnevale? Give examples to support your position.

3. In his 1985 book *You Can Get Anything You Want (But You Have To Do More Than Ask).* Roger Dawson describes several types of contending tactics (often called "gambits"). Find at least three examples of different contending tactics and identify each for what it is. Was each tactic used effectively and/or appropriately?

4. Find examples of at least two different techniques of integrative problem solving bargaining techniques. Tell why each example illustrates a different technique of integrative bargaining. Were there any examples of creativity?

REFERENCES

----(1982). "Title 45 United States Code," In U.S. Documents, *The Railway Labor Act*, Washington DC: U.S. Government Printing Office.

Adams, J.S. (1976). "The Structure and Dynamics of Behavior in Organizational Boundary Roles," In M.D. Dunnette (Ed.) *Handbook of Industrial and Organizational Psychology,* Chicago, IL: Rand McNally College Publishing Company, pp. 1175-1200.

Carnevale, P.J.D. (1986). "Strategic Choice in Mediation," *Negotiation Journal.* 2, 41-56.

Dawson, R. (1985). *You Can Get Anything You Want (But You Have To Do More Than Ask).* Phoenix, AZ: Regency.

Druckman, D. (1971). The Influence of the Situation In Interparty Conflict. *Journal of Conflict Resolution, 15*, 523-554.

Druckman, D. (1994). Determinants of Compromising Behavior in Negotiation: A Meta-analysis. *Journal of Conflict Resolution, 38*, 507-556.

Kochan, T.A. & Jick, T. (June, 1978). "The Public Sector Mediation Process: A Theory and Empirical Examination." *Journal of Conflict Resolution, 22*, 209-240.

Lax, D. A., & Sebenius, J. K. (1986). *The Manager as Negotiator: Bargaining for Cooperation and Competitive Gain*. New York: Free Press.

Lewicki, R. J., Litterer, J. A., Minton, J. W., & Saunders, D. M. (1993). *Negotiation, Second Edition*. Homewood, IL: Irwin.

McKelvey, J. T. (Ed., 1988). *Cleared for Takeoff*, Ithaca, NY: ILR Press.

Mills, D.Q. & McCormick, J. (1985). *Industrial Relations in Transition*, New York, NY: John Wiley & Sons.

Pruitt, D., & Carnevale, P. J. D. (1993). *Negotiation in Social Conflict*. Monterey, CA: Brooks/Cole.

Ross, W. H., Jr. (1988). "Situational Factors and Alternative Dispute Resolution." *The Journal of Applied Behavioral Science, 24*, 251-260.

Rubin, J.Z. & Brown B.R. (1975). *The Social Psychology of Bargaining and Negotiation*, New York, NY: Academic Press.

Wall, J. A., Jr. (1981). "Mediation: An Analysis, Review, and Proposed Research." *Journal of Conflict Resolution, 25*, 157-180.

Walton, R. E., & McKersie, R. B. (1965). *A Behavioral Theory of Labor Negotiations*. New York: McGraw-Hill.

MAGIC CARPET AIRLINES: CLIMATE OF THE AIRLINE INDUSTRY

Prior to the Deregulation Act of 1978, the airline industry was federally regulated in regards to the routes airlines flew and the fares they charged. Typically, when carriers negotiated labor contracts they gave a specific percentage increase in wages and then petitioned the government for a similar percentage increase in their fares. With full deregulation, airlines were free to fly any routes, pay any wages, and to charge any fares they wished.

Deregulation resulted in the formation of many new airlines. These new carriers were usually non-union and had substantially lower labor costs; thus, they charged lower fares. Competition for passengers forced the older carriers to lower their fares and to reduce service to smaller cities with unprofitable routes.

To cope with deregulation, companies made other changes. Airlines realigned their route systems. They developed "hub and spoke" systems whereby passengers were funneled into a hub city by a small regional carrier utilizing small aircraft (as represented by a spoke on a wheel). Travelers connecting at a hub city from a small airline then transferred to the major. To encourage these transfers, major airlines began contracting with smaller regional airlines to provide this spoke system for their hub cities. This arrangement gave new opportunities to regional carriers. However, to obtain such arrangements, regional airlines had to also cut costs. Typically, regional carrier pilots earn less than one-half of what national carrier pilots earn. Flight attendants also earned significantly less at regional carriers.

Many airlines sought to trim their labor costs. Deregulation led to confrontational bargaining with labor unions. This was exacerbated by the recession of the early 1990s. It became normal for companies to ask for wage concessions.

Owners also formed holding companies that controlled the airline itself. Holding companies could divert assets, revenues, and profits from the airline to the holding company. This could paint a false picture of the airline's true profitability, enabling the carriers to skirt issues in collective bargaining agreements.

Airline deregulation shifted the stress of uncertainty of a carrier's future to the bargaining table. Management had tested labor's power and found they could conquer it, such as Frank Lorenzo did by putting Continental Airlines in bankruptcy and nullifying their labor contracts in 1983. He then cut workers' wages in half. This had a profound effect on the industry. Soon two-tier wage provisions appeared, whereby a reduced wage rate was paid for the same job category for newly-hired employees.

Although profitability returned to the airline industry during the mid-1990s, labor faced new challenges. Historically, unions at major carriers had provisions stating that only their members could work on jet service (at national carrier wage levels). Now major carriers were encouraging regional airlines to switch from propeller planes to small jets, and then demanding that their pilot and flight attendant unions agree to this change. The unions feared that this could ultimately lead to layoffs due to major carriers subcontracting some of their routes to regional, low-wage airlines flying jets. Labor no longer worked in a protected environment. Deregulation made union leaders rethink their goals.

MAGIC CARPET AIRLINES: WHAT ACTUALLY HAPPENED:

An evening caucus revealed that the "bottom line" of members of the negotiating team was that they would accept a small wage increase for new hires, but still needed at least $1.00 per hour raise (to $21.20) for flight attendants with five-years experience. They further agreed not to make any large concessions to management until Saturday evening (August 30th).

Saturday morning, the two sides agreed on a compromise for job security--the mediator's proposal that management had rejected one week earlier. The two sides also agreed on the length of the contract: three years. Both sides also lowered their wage demands. By Saturday evening, the union was demanding $15.10 for new hires and $24.55 for those with five years experience and management was offering $14.05 and $21.05 for these two groups respectively.

After a 9:30 break, management came in with a new offer.

ORLEANS: Your wage proposals are too much. We can't give new workers $15.10 an hour! If you come down to $14.25 per hour for starting workers and $21.75 per hour for experienced workers, we will agree to a one hour's pay per three hours work' duty rig.

The union caucused. Knowing that wages were a high priority for the union members, the caucus was lengthy and the discussion grew lively.

ROGERS: I think we should hold out for more money. They can afford to do better than that. Besides, a $14.25 starting wage is only bringing us up to the regional airline industry average.

HARDY: Maybe, but I think the industry average is good enough; I'm ready to settle.

BOAZ: I'm in no mood to strike over this, either. Let's take their offer.

LEE: OK, we'll accept it, but I'll try to `nibble' just a little more before settling. Agreed?

When they returned to the bargaining table, Dixie sat directly across from Mr. Orleans and looked straight at him.

LEE: Mr. Orleans, we are willing to consider your duty rig offer. However, you know the industry standard is `one hour's pay for two hours work'--not three hours work. If you are going to pay us such a low rate, then we need a higher base wage, such as $14.75 an hour for new attendants and $23.00 for those with five years.

ORLEANS: (pause while calculating costs) Too expensive. (another pause while calculating) How about an increase to $14.35 per hour for new workers and fifteen cents more per hour for experienced workers. So the rate will be $21.90 per hour for those with five years experience.

LEE: How about $14.50 per hour for new workers and $22.00 for those with five years experience?

ORLEANS: (without any hesitation) Agreed!

ROGERS: Look at the clock---11:35. We just met the deadline.

LEE: We can bargain for more in the remaining twenty-five minutes, if you'd like!

ORLEANS: Thanks, but no thanks! Everyone laughed.

As the two sides hammered out some specific wording of the contract provisions, Peggy summarized the major aspects of the agreement for the final Negotiations Update Newsletter (see Table TN-1).

IRVING: How about a late supper? MCA's treat, and I promise---we won't `talk shop'!

LEE: Agreed! After all, we want to keep y'all in a good mood for when we have to do this all over again in three years!

TABLE TN-1

CHANGES IN THE MAGIC CARPET AIR---
LEAGUE OF FLIGHT ATTENDANTS CONTRACT

CONTRACT PROVISION	1994-1997 CONTRACT	UNION PROPOSAL	FINAL SETTLEMENT
COMPENSATION			
Base Wage	$13.00	$15.45	$14.50
Wage after five years	$20.20	$25.55	$22.00
Duty rig pay	none	1 hr. pay per 2 hr. duty (50%)	1 hr. pay per 3 hr. duty (33%)
Daily guarantee	3.25 hours	4.5 hours	3.5 hours
Holiday pay	none	8 holidays at "double time" rate	none. Two paid (regular rate) personal holidays.
JOB SECURITY			
Successorship	none	contract will still be binding	"me-too" clause with pilots and and mechanics unions, so attendants will be treated no less favorably than those employees in the event of a merger or buyout.
Protection of	none seniority rights in the event of a merger	arbitrator combines MCA seniority list with that of other airline.	
WORKING CONDITIONS			
Trip trading lead time	5 days	24 hours	24 hours prior
Shoe allowance	none	$100/year	$25/year
Winter Coat	none	Total cost	$60/three years
Uniform maintenance	$16/month	$20/month	$18/month

CASE 6
VANESSA ABRAMS

Learning Objectives:

To explore various ways that gender issues surface in negotiation. This includes looking at gender in a number of different ways:

- As an issue of identity--that one's masculinity or femininity are more or less central to certain people and under certain conditions.
- As an interactional issue--that certain circumstances call forth gendered expectations and stereotypes.
- As an issue of power--that power relationships in organizations and society limit what is possible.

Summary:

Vanessa Abrams, a successful consultant in the health care business, is engaged in contentious negotiations with her boss, Jerry, over the signing of a non-compete agreement. Although routine, she has never had to sign one and sees this move on Jerry's part as an effort to undermine her power and authority. The situation escalates when she hires an attorney. Although she gets an agreement, it changes their relationship. In the B case, she has to negotiate with Jerry again about her role in the business and her career options.

Recommended Reading Assignment to Accompany This Case:

Greenhalgh and Gilkey (10.3), Fisher and Davis (10.2)

Case Preparation Study Questions:

1. At the conclusion of the non-compete negotiations, Vanessa Abrams said, "I ended up giving in." Do you agree?
2. How did she get herself in this position? What other choices did she have? Why didn't she pursue them?
3. Have you had similar experiences? What were they and how did you handle them?
4. As Vanessa prepares to negotiate further with Jerry about a range of personal and business issues, based on your analysis of her previous experience, what advice would you give her?
5. What gender issues do you see in this case? How relevant are they to our understanding of what occurred?

Discussion of the A Case:

(Note: If you are unfamiliar with the current research and theory on gendered approaches to negotiation, see the references at the end of this note).

1. Do people identify with Vanessa? Have you signed non-compete agreements? Have they been an issue? Why are they here?

2. Look at the problem from the perspectives of the different key actors:

    - How does Vanessa interpret what is happening to her?
    - How does she see Jerry's actions?
    - How does she think Jerry interprets her actions?

    - How does Jerry see what's happening?
    - How does he see their relationship?
    - How does he interpret her actions?
    - How does he think Vanessa interprets his actions?

    Neither sees the other's actions as legitimate. Each believes the other is at fault, and feels he/she is being betrayed by the other. Both feel vulnerable and there is no trust.

3. How did Vanessa and Jerry get into this situation?

    To effectively analyze this, the student needs to look at their past relationship. Note how they negotiated in the past--i.e. very much in a gendered way. Vanessa took on a feminine role, Jerry took on a masculine role. The current negotiations have these past negotiations as a background to their current interaction. However, this time Vanessa changes tactics, and the different tactics she takes stand out in stark contrast to the past. His brinksmanship, and also pulling her off the committee, are also departures from his past behavior. Each is defying the other's expectations and hence decreasing predictability and trust.

    Second, the student needs to assess why this became such a big issue for her. Why does she see herself as so vulnerable? Why does she feel that she will lose her influence if she signs? Focusing on her own vulnerability blocks her seeing other sources of influence that she may have in the organization, i.e., she is the rainmaker and can use this as a source of power from which to negotiate.

4. Why does he get so upset when she consults a lawyer? Are his feelings influenced by gender? If Vanessa were a Van (i.e. male), how might the situation be different?

5. How does Vanessa perceive her gender? Does she think gender is a factor here? Do you think Jerry thinks it is a factor? (People will notice that Vanessa's physical appearance is described and overlook that Jerry is described too).

6. What other choices do they have? How could they break out of this impasse? Were there other ways she could have approached this negotiation? Other ways for Jerry to approach it?

7. At the end of the A case, she gets most of what she wants. Is it a good outcome? What will be the consequences for their relationship?

8. At the end of the case, it is apparent that she will negotiate with Jerry again in the near future. What advice would you give her?

Have students read B case. Then work through the discussion questions:

- Ask if she took their advice. Most people say, "generally not."
- There are a number of themes to pick up in the B case:
  - It is not clear what she wants, so it is difficult to have a way to get it.
  - If she decides to stay, she needs to know where her colleagues are and what they are thinking. She doesn't know this yet.
  - She misses opportunities to negotiate:
    ◊ Over payment.
    ◊ There are other possibilities
  - When Jerry asks what her plans are, she thinks he wants her to leave. What are 5 good reasons he may have had to ask this question, other than that he wants her to leave?
- Vanessa gets help. How does she use it? Instead of helping her think through what is happening, she tends to take on the style and persona of the person she is talking to.

What actually happened:

She consulted finally with her brother (a lawyer), who told her she needed to give Jerry an ultimatum--to state her demands. She and Jerry reached agreement that she would work part-time, with the prorated based salary and bonus. They signed a contract to that effect. During this time, Vanessa felt more empowered, and challenged Jerry directly on his decisions. Even though her group made their goals, five months later Jerry fired Vanessa. Her parachute went into effect.

Case Summary:

A. Gender comes up in this case in a number of ways.

1. Vanessa and Jerry as a man and woman. Do they react in "typically gendered" ways? Who gets emotional? Who takes risks?

2. Jerry and Vanessa's relationship. They expect each other to enact the gendered roles that characterized their relationship—she is supposed to accede to him or be manipulated by him.

3. Power and influence. Despite her success, she is in a subordinate relationship. How much of a possibility is negotiation in these circumstances? In the end she was fired. Her feelings of vulnerability turn out not to be misplaced. Gender-based dynamics also has us look at the social structures within which negotiations occur.

4. Gender and values. In this case, their "relationship" is reduced to a commodity that is bargained over. In negotiating a relationship, the general advice is that emotions and feelings are to be managed and controlled.

B. Other Negotiation Issues raised in the Case

1. Context is important in understanding your negotiating options. How you are positioned to negotiate shapes the possibilities.

2. Role is important. When you negotiate for yourself (and not on behalf of others), self esteem and worth issues become more salient.

3. How you feel--vulnerable or in control -- influences how you see choices and possibilities. Support can help expand understandings of what is happening and possible choices; but you need to assess advice.

4. Negotiations have histories. Past negotiating relationships set the context for the current negotiation and shape peoples' interpretations of behavior.

5. More issues than you think are negotiable but you need to be positioned (situationally and psychologically) to open them up for discussion.

6. Gender can impact negotiation at various levels --style, roles, structures, meanings, power, values.

Suggested Background Readings on Gender for the Instructor:

Gray, Barbara (1993) The Gender-Based Foundations of Negotiations Theory. In Lewicki, Roy, Blair Sheppard and Robert Bies, Eds. *Research on Negotiation in Organizations.* Vol. 4. Greenwich, CT: JAI Press, pp. 3-36.

Kolb, Deborah M. and Coolidge, Gloria. (1991) Her Place At The Table. In J. W. Breslin and J.Z. Rubin, *Negotiation Theory And Practice.* Cambridge, MA: Program on Negotiation at Harvard Law School, pp. 261-277.

Kolb, Deborah M. and Putnam, Linda L. (1997) Through the Looking Glass: Negotiation Theory Refracted Through the Lens of Gender. In Sandra Gleason (Ed.) *Workplace Dispute Resolution: Directions for the Twenty-First Century.* East Lansing: Michigan State University Press, pp. 231-259.

CASE 7
500 ENGLISH SENTENCES

NOTE: This material is also available as a roleplay (Exercise 25, 500 English Sentences). Instructors are advised to use either the roleplay or the case, but not both because they overlap considerably. Choosing whether to use the roleplay or case materials depends on your goals for the class and the level of sophistication and cross-cultural experience of the students. For homogeneous classes with little previous cross-cultural experience, one option is to use the case to teach the cross-cultural nuances of American-Japanese negotiations and to follow this with Exercise 26 (Sick Leave), a roleplay from a different context that has many similar lessons to 500 English Sentences.

Learning Objectives

This case is written from the perspective of Scott, an American Assistant English teacher working in Japan. Scott initially frames this situation as an issue of right-wrong. There are several errors in the manuscript *500 English Sentences;* he is a native speaker of English and he has a university degree in English literature so he knows that he is right. For Mr. Honda (the Japanese Head of English) it is an issue of honor, reputation, and face. He has worked in the same school board for more than 20 years and he wants to avoid embarrassing his superiors in the Board of Education, who initially authored the first edition of the book several years before. The differences in framing reflect nicely the cross-cultural differences in the way that Americans and Japanese negotiate. More specific objectives of the case include:

1. To understand a cross-cultural situation where pride and face are very important.
2. To examine how cultural differences influence the way a negotiation is framed.
3. To learn a different meaning to the term "win/lose bargaining."

Case Synopsis

This case describes a cross-cultural situation where an American (Scott) teaching English in a Japanese highschool is asked to endorse a book (500 English Sentences) that is seriously flawed. The case describes the dilemma facing Scott, the structural background of how several layers of the Japanese government work together to bring approximately 5,000 English teachers to Japan every year, and Scott's experience his first year in Japan. The case concludes with Scott's dilemma about whether or not to endorse the manuscript.

Recommended Reading Assignments to Accompany This Case

Reader: 11.1 (Phatak & Habib), 11.2 (Koh), 11.3 (Frank)
Text: Chapter 11

Background Preparation

None is required. The instructor (and optionally the students) should be familiar with cultural and business differences between Japan and North America. Dated, yet still appropriate, is Howard Van Zandt's *How to Negotiate in Japan,* from the Harvard Business Review of Nov/Dec 1970, more current is *Smart Bargaining* by John Graham and Yoshihiro Sano, *The Influence of Japanese Culture on Business Relationships and Negotiations* by Naoko Oikawa and John Tanner Jr., *International Dimensions of Organizational Behavior,* chapter on Negotiating with Foreigners by Nancy J. Adler, and *Cultural Approaches to Negotiations: Understanding the Japanese* by Brian Hawrysh and Judith Zaichkowsky.

Teaching Strategy

The case describes a situation where the participants' egos and goals conflict in a situation where there appears to be no compromise (Scott either signs the endorsement or he doesn't; he can't "half-sign"). The addition of two different cultural styles complicates the resolution of the problem. Some people may suggest a compromise (include half of the revisions to the text); this is a very Western way of handling the situation because more than a couple of changes will cause the original authors to lose face.

On the surface, this is a very straightforward situation: will Scott sign an endorsement or not? The cultural differences, however, make it essential to Mr. Honda that Scott signs and equally essential to Scott that he doesn't.

Proceed by using the following questions to discuss the case:

1. How many people think that Scott should endorse the book? For those who think he should sign the endorsement, why? For who think he shouldn't, why not? What are the long and short-term consequences of signing (not signing) the endorsement?

2. For Scott, what is this situation about? For Mr. Honda, what is this situation about?

3. What are the tangible factors in this situation? What are the intangible factors? Is saving face more important to Scott or Mr. Honda? Why? Which are more important, the tangible or intangible factors? Is this true for both Scott and Mr. Honda?

The discussion should conclude with a good summary about Japanese and North American negotiation styles and culture. When negotiating in Japan it is often important to give in for the sake of peace and harmony, or relationships may be harmed beyond repair. Deciding *how* to negotiate cross-culturally remains a challenge for every negotiator that negotiates across a border. One of the best pieces discussing this was written by Stephen Weiss ("Negotiating With 'Romans': A Range of Culturally-Responsive Strategies," *Sloan Management Review*, *35*, No. 1, pp. 51-61; No. 2, pp. 1-16) and a summary of this work makes a nice conclusion to the class.

Final Note

Although this exercise has been modified somewhat it is based on an actual situation that occurred in Japan (names and location have been changed). "Scott" is currently completing a Master's degree in East Asian Studies at a Northeastern American University and is looking forward to returning to Japan. He continues to study Japanese and to perfect his karate. Mr. "Honda" continues as a loyal employee of his school. After thinking carefully about the situation during the week of the negotiation, "Scott" decided to endorse the book.

CASE 8
SICK LEAVE

NOTE: This material is also available as a roleplay (Exercise 26, Sick Leave). Instructors are advised to use either the roleplay or the case, but not both because they overlap considerably. Choosing whether to use the roleplay or case materials depends on your goals for the class and the level of sophistication and cross-cultural experience of the students. For homogeneous classes with little previous cross-cultural experience, one option is to use the case to teach the cross-cultural nuances of American-Japanese negotiations and to follow this with Exercise 25 (500 English Sentences), a roleplay with many similar lessons to Sick Leave.

Learning Objectives

This case is written from the perspective of Kelly, a 22 year old Canadian Assistant English teacher working in Japan. The root of the conflict in this case is a deep cross-cultural misunderstanding that has transformed into a much larger incident involving important intangible factors such as saving face and maintaining principles. Specific learning objectives include:

1. To understand how two parties have framed a conflict very differently in a cross-cultural setting.

2. To explore the differences between positions and interests in a cross-cultural negotiation.

3. To understand a conflict where the intangible factors are much more important than the tangible factors.

Case Synopsis

On the surface, this case is very straightforward. Kelly, a 22 year old Canadian working as an Assistant English teacher in Japan, is sick with the flu, misses 2 days of work, and wants to claim these as legitimate sick days as described in her contract. Her supervisor, Mr. Higashi, insists that she take these days as part of her paid vacation days because that is the Japanese way. The sick leave conflict is symptomatic, however, of a much deeper conflict that Kelly and the other Assistant English teachers have with Mr. Higashi and the other Japanese English teachers. Dynamics underlying this conflict include face saving, adapting to a different culture, the meaning of contracts in different cultures, and the influence of reference groups on behavior.

Recommended Reading Assignments to Accompany This Case

Reader: 11.1 (Phatak & Habib), 11.2 (Koh), 11.3 (Frank)
Text: Chapter 11

Background Preparation

Students and the instructor should be familiar with cultural and business differences between Japan and North America. Dated, yet still appropriate, is Howard Van Zandt's *How to Negotiate in Japan*, from the Harvard Business Review of Nov/Dec 1970, more current is *Smart Bargaining* by John Graham and Yoshihiro Sano, *The Influence of Japanese Culture on Business Relationships and Negotiations* by Naoko Oikawa and John Tanner Jr., *International Dimensions of Organizational Behavior*, chapter on Negotiating with Foreigners by Nancy J. Adler, and *Cultural Approaches to Negotiations: Understanding the Japanese* by Brian Hawrysh and Judith Zaichkowsky.

Teaching Strategy

Kelly frames this negotiation as a right to have the sick leave, which is written into her contract. Mr. Higashi frames this negotiation much broader and wants Kelly to "fit in" at work and to be treated the same as Japanese workers. This situation is very representative of the types of conflict that occur in cross-cultural negotiations between Americans (rights based, contract as enforceable) and Japanese (relationship based, contract as beginning).

On the surface, this is a very straightforward situation: will Kelly get her contractually guaranteed sick leave benefits or not? The cultural differences, however, make this a high stakes negotiation for both parties, in which the importance of the intangible factors far outweighs that of the tangible factors.

Proceed by using the following questions to discuss the case:

1. What should Kelly do? Should she call CLAIR, or discuss this further with Mr. Higashi?

2. What is this dispute about for Kelly? For Mr. Higashi? In these types of conflicts is a compromise possible?

3. What are the tangible factors in this situation? What are the intangible factors in the negotiation? Is saving face more important to Kelly or Mr. Higashi? Why? Which are more important, the tangible or intangible factors? Is this true for both Kelly and Mr. Higashi?

The discussion should conclude with a good summary about Japanese and North American negotiation styles and culture. When negotiating in Japan it is often important to give in for the sake of peace and harmony, or relationships may be harmed beyond repair. Deciding *how* to negotiate cross-culturally remains a challenge for every negotiator that negotiates across a border. One of the best pieces discussing this was written by Stephen Weiss ("Negotiating With 'Romans': A Range of Culturally-Responsive Strategies," *Sloan Management Review*, 35, No. 1, pp. 51-61; No. 2, pp. 1-16) and a summary of this work makes a nice conclusion to the class.

Final Note

Although this exercise has been modified somewhat it is based on an actual situation that occurred in Japan (names and location have been changed). In the actual incident, "Kelly" received her sick leave but the relationship was seriously harmed and work became more and more uncomfortable. Kelly decided not to renew her contract, and left Japan at the end of the school year.

QUESTIONNAIRE 1
PERSONAL BARGAINING INVENTORY

Objectives

1. To help identify beliefs and values that are central to the negotiation process;

2. To help students understand how their views are similar to (different from) other people in the class;

3. To encourage students to identify and examine these differences in beliefs and values through classroom learning exercises.

Group Size Any size group can be used with Option 1. Option 2 becomes somewhat unwieldy with groups larger than 50.

Time Required 75-90 minutes for the exercise. Students should complete the questionnaire outside of class. If completed in class, add 20-30 minutes to do the questionnaire.

Special Materials For Option 2, enough 3x5 file cards (or scraps of paper about this size) to give six to each person, and rolls of masking tape. Name tags also desirable if students do not know one another.

Physical Requirements None for Option 1. For Option 2, the exercise will require a large open area to freely move around, e. g. an open hallway, lounge area or the front of a classroom.

Recommended Reading Assignments to Accompany This Exercise:

Readings: 10.1 (Rackham), 10.2 (Davis), 10.3 (Greenhalgh and Gilkey)
Text: Chapters 1, 10.

Advance Preparation

For Option 1, none. For Option 2, read over the procedure carefully before the activity begins.

What to Expect

The purpose of the two variations of this exercise is to help students understand their own personal philosophy of negotiation - - how they see themselves and how they view the negotiation process. The exercise can be used at three different time points in a course:

1. At the beginning, as an icebreaker to help students get acquainted and talking about negotiation, as well as to help them begin to identify their individual negotiation styles;

2. In the middle, when students are ready to explore individual personal styles in more detail;

3. At the end, as a way to help students clarify personal beliefs and self-perceptions that may have surfaced during the course.

Operating Procedure

Option 1

This option is easier to administer, and a bit more tame. It is designed to help students identify their own beliefs about themselves as negotiators, and about how to negotiate effectively.

The operating procedure is described in the *Readings, Exercises and Cases* book. Make sure to encourage students not to argue with one another about what is right or proper, or to put one another down for beliefs or attitudes about negotiation that are "dumb" or "wrong." State clearly that **there are no "right" answers**; there is no one right way to negotiate. A short session on active listening may be useful here to help people listen clearly; students must be supportive of one another's views, even if those views are dramatically different from their own.

Groups should be encouraged to make brief reports at the end of their group meetings. The instructor should try to identify different styles or philosophies as they are reported by groups, and to develop a list (on the blackboard, flip chart, etc.) of several different styles and types as groups identify them.

Option 2

This option is a bit more chaotic to orchestrate, but is more energizing and fun for students. It is particularly useful as an icebreaker in the first class. The overall objective is to have students identify key descriptors of themselves, and then to "negotiate" those key descriptors with others as they form larger groups. As these groups form, the groups will take on distinctly different "identities" in negotiation philosophy and style.

1. (10 minutes) Students should write their six statements on cards clearly and legibly, one on each card. Encourage them to write the statement large (so it can be easily seen), to condense the text of the statement to 2-3 key phrases, and to indicate whether the statement is characteristic or uncharacteristic.

2. Once the statements are written on cards, announce to the class as follows:

"Now that you've identified several statements that you believe to be very descriptive of you, I'd like to give you the opportunity to share these with others, and to see how others have described themselves. We have experimented with a variety of ways to do this, and the most effective method also turns out to be a bit awkward and embarrassing in the beginning. But once you get started, you'll see that the procedure works very well."

3. Using six blank cards as a demonstration, hang the cards on a long strip of masking tape so that all six are lined up with the tape across the back of the cards. Then stick the tape to your chest so that the statements hang from you and are clearly visible to others. Distribute rolls of tape around the classroom and ask all students to do the same. Also ask them to make name tags for themselves (out of extra cards and tape) if they don't know one another.

4. State the following:

"Now that your statements are clearly visible, I'd like you to get acquainted with the other people in this room and what they believe in. The easiest way to do this is to move around so that you can read other people's statements."

Students at this point should move to the open area of the classroom, hallway, etc. where free movement is possible. For the interim, students should simply move around to read others statements. At the beginning, there is much laughter and awkwardness--natural for this rather absurd activity--but it soon abates into interested examination of other people's statements.

5. (10 minutes) Once all students are up and have moved around for several minutes, announce that their next task is to find another person whose statements are reasonably **compatible** with their own. By compatible we *do not mean identical*; instead, we mean that you can be "reasonably comfortable" with most of the statements that the other individual displays. Once they have found that person, they are to pair-off, and remove themselves from the promenade area of the floor.

Note: Those who pair up easily leave the floor quickly, and those who take longer may find that their choices for compatible partners are diminished. This is natural and necessary. Individuals must get into pairs, and you must push them by setting firm time limits for pairing up. If there are an odd number of individuals, form a trio.

6. (5-10 minutes) Now announce that the objective is for the pair to take the 12 statements that they have between them (18 if they are a trio) and arrive at six statements to represent the group. No duplicate statements are allowed. They can select these six by any decision-making method they choose. When they are finished, they are to hang the six agreed upon statements on a piece of tape (new tape may be necessary); the remaining statements are to be discarded.

7. (10 minutes) The objective of the pair (or trio) is now to re-enter the promenade area and to find another group whose statements are compatible. Encourage them to move around and read the statements of several groups before making their choice.

8. (10 minutes) Once again, they are to take the statements of both groups and to reduce them to a single list of six statements that best represent all of the group members. Again, any decision method can be used. The new statements should be hung on a piece of tape.

9. (5 minutes) Groups re-enter the promenade and have a choice: a) if possible, to find another group whose statements are compatible; or b) to choose to remain as a group of

four. If an eight-person group is chosen, the statements must again be narrowed down to six statements to represent the group as a whole.

10. (10 minutes; optional) Once groups of eight have been formed, (or some have chosen to stay as a group of four), each group must take the six statements and rank order them in terms of their relative importance to the group. Any method of decision making may be used.

11. (30 minutes) Each group should appoint a recorder who will list the six ordered statements on a flipchart, or part of the blackboard. Names of group members should also be identified. Each recorder then makes a presentation to the entire class about 1) how the group members see themselves, and 2) how they arrived at the six statements that represent them. Other groups may ask questions, and are asked to describe their impressions of the presenting group.

12. If the instructor has the resources to do so, it is useful to save the sheets from the flipchart, or to have them typed and the output distributed to the entire class. This information is useful later to examine individual progress through the course, and for people to re-examine later how they saw themselves.

Concluding the Exercise

Instructors will note that as the groups form, class members will self-select themselves into groups that can be characterized along a dimension from highly trusting and cooperative to highly tactical and competitive. Second, the group processes within these groups (making decisions about the statements) will reflect the group's style--cooperative groups will work rather quickly and quietly, competitive groups will be boisterous and take more time as individuals hold out to win their view on which cards to hold or drop. Finally, individuals who are more (less) effective in advocating their viewpoint will find that their group's final statements are more (less) synonymous with their original self-descriptive statements. Individuals may be asked to reflect on the group decision making process as one piece of data about their negotiating style. Instructors should bring these points out in discussion if the observations do not spontaneously occur.

Instructors should note how the different groups reflect different approaches and styles of negotiation. It is **very important that the instructor not judge** whether one style or another is "better" or "worse" or "more effective" or "less effective." Encourage the students to be similarly open-minded. The instructor should stress that individuals are (or will be) given lots of opportunities to test the validity of these individual characterizations, and to determine the positive and negative elements of any style that they identify. Many of the other simulations and questionnaires used in the course can be evaluated by returning to the value statements surfaced in this exercise.

QUESTIONNAIRE 2
THE SINS SCALE

Objectives

To help students explore their views toward the use of marginally ethical and unethical tactics in negotiation, and to compare these views with others in the class and with national norms.

Group Size   No restrictions.

Time Required   60-90 minutes.

Special Materials   None

Special Physical Requirements   None

Recommended Reading Assignments to Accompany This Exercise:

Readings: 7.1 (Carson), 7.2 (Dees and Crampton), 7.3 (Friedman and Shapiro).
Text: Chapter 7.

What to Expect:

The questionnaire in this section measures an individual's perceptions of a collection of tactics which are often judged to be marginally ethical in a negotiation. These tactics are often described as "lying" or "cheating." The issue of what is ethically appropriate or inappropriate often provokes strong reactions among students, and stimulates engaging discussion.

Advance Preparation

It may be useful for the instructor to be aware of the basic processes of ethical reasoning and ethical decision making. If you are not familiar with these approaches, we suggest a basic text such as Boatright, 1993; Donaldson & Werhane, 1996.

Operating Procedure

1. The questionnaire may be assigned as an out-of-class assignment, or done in class. At least 15 minutes should be allowed for completing the questionnaire in class.

2. Instructors may wish to begin the discussion of this material by recalling any "ethics debates" that have occurred as a result of earlier role plays, cases, etc. in the class.

For example, ask students whether there were instances of lying, spying, cheating, subterfuge, etc. that occurred in earlier negotiations such as the Disarmament Game, Pemberton's Dilemma, Coalition Bargaining, etc.

A CAUTIONARY NOTE TO INSTRUCTORS:

Care must be taken that neither the instructor nor students in the class are permitted to become normative in the discussion of what is ethically appropriate. Nothing can kill a good discussion of this topic faster than permitting students to be prescriptive of what are the "right" answers to the questions, or the "right" ethical position to assume regarding negotiating strategy and tactics. THERE ARE NO RIGHT ANSWERS TO THESE QUESTIONS. Instead, the instructor must take care to help students recognize their own ethical views and the consequences of these views for the way they behave and judge others. Thus, for example, individuals with strong absolutist views are likely to be very prescriptive about what is "right" and "wrong," both for their own conduct and the conduct of others; similarly, individuals with strong relativistic views will want to know a lot more about the situation before making their judgments (and probably will have a harder time with the second questionnaire because very little situational information is presented).

3. Students should be asked to complete the questionnaire on their own. They may then:

   a) Hand the instrument to the instructor, who may compile class averages and then hand the questionnaires back. To assure candid answers to the questions, we encourage you to explicitly instruct students to put a CODE NUMBER on the questionnaire, not their name.

   b) Discuss their answers to the questionnaires in small groups. Students are encouraged to share their ratings on each of the tactics, share their perceptions of the tactics which are most/least appropriate, and determine the factors which lead them to rate those tactics as more/less appropriate.

   c) Compare their ratings with the ratings in Table 1 (you may reproduce and distribute or post as an overhead transparency). The SINS was compiled to explore perceptions of deceptive tactics that are often used in negotiation. The questionnaire is the result of a stream of research on those tactics which negotiators judge as ethical or unethical (Lewicki and Spencer, 1990, 1991; Lewicki & Stark, 1995; Lewicki & Robinson, 1996; Robinson, Lewicki & Donahue, 1996). Students at two major universities, over a period of several years, have been asked to determine which tactics are ethically appropriate or inappropriate. Table 1 presents the mean ratings of appropriateness and likelihood for 320 respondents from The Ohio State University (Lewicki & Robinson, 1996). These ratings are representative of several student groups who have completed the questionnaire.

4. Photocopy the SCORING KEY at the end of this exercise. This key aggregates the items into five clusters:
   a) Traditional Competitive Bargaining
   b) Attacking Opponent's Network
   c) False Promises
   d) Misrepresentation
   e) Inappropriate Information Gathering

These five clusters emerged from factor analyses of student data from Harvard and Ohio State University MBAs over a two year period. A brief description of each factor is as follows:

The first factor was named *Traditional Competitive Bargaining*. The three items in this factor were examples of common techniques employed during traditional distributive bargaining situations: 6 (making a very high/low opening offer), 7 (stalling) and 14 (extreme opening offer).

The second factor is labeled *Attacking Opponent's Network*, also contains three items: 3 (attempting to get your opponent fired), 9 (threatening to make your opponent look weak or foolish) and 12 (talking directly to the people your opponent reports to).

The third factor, *False Promises*, also contained three items: 1 (promise good things will happen to your opponent), 8 (offer to reciprocate your opponent's concessions when you really never intend to follow through) and 15 (guarantee your constituency will comply with a settlement when you know they probably will not).

The fourth factor is named *Misrepresentation*, and includes four items: 2, 4, 10 and 11. The commonality in these items is that the negotiator is explicitly lying about some form of information, either to one's opponent or one's constituency.

The final factor, named *Inappropriate Information Gathering* included items 5, 13 and 16. These items involve gaining information about your opponent's negotiating position by employing various tactics generally viewed as unacceptable in traditional bargaining situations.

Students may wish to aggregate their scores into the five categories and then compare them in their small groups.

5. Instructors may also wish to make an overhead of Table 2 and share this data with the class. This information reflects data collected from Harvard Business School students in the required Negotiations class, broken down by mean scores on the five factors and aggregated by Gender, Ethnicity, Nationality and Undergraduate Major and correlated with age, years of prior work experience, amount of prior negotiating experience, and self-rated evaluations as a generally Cooperative or Competitive negotiator.

Concluding the Discussion

Ask students to report out from their small group discussions and the comparisons. After students report out from these groups, the instructor should try to summarize the major dimensions identified by the groups. The essence of the cautionary note stated above should be repeated. Instructors may attempt to steer the discussion toward situational elements which may temper or moderate these ethical judgments: their relationship with the other party, expectations of future interactions with the other, commitment to the specific goal or objective of the negotiation, etc. Students should also be encouraged to identify other areas where their ethical judgment will affect their behavior in competitive situations--sports, politics, and business in general--and to continue to test their own ethical judgments against those of their friends and associates.

References

Boatright, John (1993) *Ethics and the Conduct of Business*. Englewood Cliffs: Prentice Hall.

Carr, A. (1968, January-February). "Is Business Bluffing Ethical?" *Harvard Business Review*. 143-153.

Donaldson, T. and Werhane, P. (1996). *Ethical Issues in Business*. Englewood Cliffs, NJ: Prentice Hall. See esp. pp. 129-177 on "Truth Telling."

Lewicki, R.J. and Spencer, G. "Lies and Dirty Tricks." Paper presented at the International Association of Conflict Management, Annual Meetings, Vancouver, Canada, June, 1990.

Lewicki, R.J. and Spencer, G. "Ethical Relativism and Negotiating Tactics: Factors Affecting Their Perceived Ethicality." Paper presented at the Academy of Management meetings, Miami, Florida, August 1991.

Lewicki, R.J. and Stark, N. "What's Ethically Appropriate in Negotiations: An Empirical Examination of Bargaining Tactics." *Social Justice Research*, 1995.

Lewicki, R. J. and Robinson, R. "A Factor Analytic Study of Negotiator Ethics" *Journal of Business Ethics*, 1997, in press.

Newton, L. and Schmidt, D. (1996) *Wake Up Calls*. Belmont, CA: Wadsworth.

Rion, Michael. (1990) *The Responsible Manager: Practical Strategies for Ethical Decision Making*. New York: Harper & Row, 1990.

Robinson, R. J., Lewicki, R. J., & Donahue, E. M. (1997). A Five Factor Model of Unethical Bargaining Tactics: The SINS Scale. *Australian Industrial and Organizational Psychology Best Paper Proceedings*, 131-137. Melbourne.

FIVE CLUSTERS OF MARGINALLY ETHICAL TACTICS

1. **Traditional Competitive Bargaining**

2. **Attacking Opponent's Network**

3. **False Promises**

4. **Misrepresentation**

5. **Inappropriate Information Gathering**

SINS SCALE-SCORING KEY

(BASED ON ROBINSON, LEWICKI AND DONAHUE, 1997)

Traditional Competitive Bargaining

Item 6	_____ (5.90)
Item 7	_____ (5.70)
Item 14	_____ (4.90)
Total	_____ 16.50

Attacking Opponent's Network

Item 3	_____ (1.68)
Item 9	_____ (1.88)
Item 12	_____ (2.16)
Total	_____ 5.72

False Promises

Item 1	_____ (2.07)
Item 8	_____ (2.19)
Item 15	_____ (1.91)
Total	_____ 6.17

Misrepresentation

Item 2	_____ (2.80)
Item 4	_____ (2.88)
Item 10	_____ (3.53)
Item 11	_____ (2.90)
Total	_____ 12.11

Inappropriate Information Gathering

Item 5	_____ (2.44)
Item 13	_____ (2.57)
Item 16	_____ (2.06)
Total	_____ 7.07

Table 1
Appropriateness and Likelihood Ratings of Tactics

Tactic Number and Description	Mean Approp.	S.D.	Mean Likelihood	S.D.
6. Gain information about an opponent's negotiating position and strategy by "asking around" in a network of your own friends, associates, and contacts.	6.10	1.47	6.04	1.59
5. Make an opening demand that is far greater than what one really hopes to settle for.	5.84	1.48	5.62	1.65
4. Hide your real bottom line from your opponent.	5.75	1.58	5.07	1.52
13. Convey a false impression that you are in absolutely no hurry to come to a negotiation agreement, thereby trying to put more time pressure on your opponent to concede quickly.	5.37	1.79	5.22	1.86
3. Lead the other negotiator to believe that they can only get what they want by negotiating with you, when in fact they could go elsewhere and get what they want cheaper or faster.	4.28	1.70	4.31	1.78
10. Make an opening offer or demand so high (or low) that it seriously undermines your opponent's confidence in his/her own ability to negotiate a satisfactory settlement.	4.18	2.03	3.73	2.01
16. Intentionally misrepresent the nature of negotiations to the press or your constituency in order to protect delicate discussions that have occurred.	3.41	2.01	3.43	2.05
12. Talk directly to the people who your opponent reports to, or is accountable to, and try to encourage them to defect to your side.	3.18	1.92	2.93	1.77
7. Gain information about an opponent's negotiating position by paying friends, associates, and contacts to get this info for you.	3.07	1.90	2.77	1.83

18.	Intentionally misrepresent factual information to your opponent when you know that he/she has already done this to you.	2.94	2.00	3.35	2.12
9.	Gain information about an opponent's negotiating position by cultivating his/her friendship through expensive gifts, entertaining, or "personal favors."	2.83	1.71	2.80	1.79
17.	Intentionally misrepresent the progress of negotiations to the press or your constituency in order to make your own position or point of view look better.	2.61	1.69	2.82	1.79
14.	Threaten to make your opponent look weak or foolish in front of a boss or others to whom he/she is accountable.	2.35	1.59	2.33	1.54
11.	Talk directly to the people who your opponent reports to, or is accountable to, and tell them things that will undermine their confidence in your opponent as negotiator.	2.20	1.53	2.13	1.50
2.	Promise that good things will happen to your opponent if he/she gives you what you want, even if you know that you can't (or won't) deliver those good things when the other's cooperation is obtained.	2.20	1.43	2.39	1.45
1.	Threaten to harm your opponent if he/she doesn't give you what you want, even if you know you will never follow through to carry out that threat.	2.10	1.87	2.15	1.83
8.	Gain information about an opponent's negotiating position by trying to recruit or hire one of your opponent's key subordinates (on the condition that the key subordinate bring confidential information with him/her).	2.02	1.41	1.98	1.42
15.	Intentionally misrepresent factual information to your opponent in order to support your negotiating arguments or position.	1.99	1.43	2.44	1.55

Table 2: Comparison of Various Groups on the 5 Factor Scales

Group	N	Factor 1 Trad. Compet. Bargaining	Factor 2 Attacking Opponent's Network	Factor 3 False Promises	Factor 4 Misrepresentation	Factor 5 Inapprop. Information Gathering	All Factors (16-items)
	762						
Means:							
GENDER[1]							
Females	225	5.45	2.82	1.76	1.62	1.93	2.73
Males	557	5.52	3.11*	2.18**	2.02**	2.53**	3.07**
ETHNICITY[2]							
Asian	45	5.59	3.04	2.11	1.99	2.57	3.06
Black	36	5.35	2.80	1.94	1.81	2.13	2.80
Hispanic	25	5.69	3.16	2.08	1.73	2.39	3.02
White	408	5.55	2.99	1.87	1.89	2.23	2.91
NATIONALITY[3]							
Asia: Pacific	58	5.19	2.95^a	2.59^B	1.97	2.91^D	3.11
Asia: Other	34	5.61	2.99	2.50^B	2.04	2.44^e	3.11
Latin America	44	5.61	3.27	2.37^B	2.03	2.42^e	3.15
USA & Canada	492	5.55	2.96^a	1.87^b	1.83^c	2.21^d	2.89^f
Western Europe	63	5.37	3.42^A	2.27^B	2.23^C	2.80^{DE}	3.23^F
UNDERGRAD. MAJOR							
Arts.	108	5.35^a	2.81^b	1.72^c	1.90	2.07^e	2.77^g
Business / Econ.	316	5.53^a	3.02	2.05^{Cd}	1.88	2.33^f	2.97^h
Engineer / Science	175	5.48^a	3.16^B	2.21^C	2.00	2.58^E	3.09^G
Math / Physics	36	5.91^A	3.31	2.37^{CD}	2.07	2.75^{EF}	3.29^{GH}
Soc. Sciences	75	5.56	3.05	2.06^C	1.86	2.29^f	2.97^h
Correlations:							
Age	762	-.125**	-.102**	-.009	-.111**	.003	-.105**
Yrs. work exper.	762	-.118**	-.100**	-.032	-.138**	-.034	-.125**
Prior. negot. exper	762	-.109**	.006	.125**	.038	.046	.025
Cooperativeness	762	-.132**	-.137**	-.141**	-.056	-.078*	-.167**
Competitiveness	762	.028	.052	.056	.092*	.074*	.087*
Course Z-Scores	762	.049	.075*	.012	.066	.045	.073*

* - $p < .05$
** - $p < .01$

[1] - Means for all subjects. Using only subjects from the USA produced the same result pattern.
[2] - USA subjects only. Only groups with large enough Ns were reported and analyzed (e.g. 2 subjects reporting themselves as Native American were excluded from this analysis).
[3] - Means with uppercase superscripts (e.g. ^{A}) are significantly larger than means with corresponding lowercase superscripts (e.g. ^{a}).

QUESTIONNAIRE 3
THE INFLUENCE TACTICS INVENTORY

Objectives

To explore the tactics that people use to influence people (e.g., their superiors, co-workers, and subordinates) at work. To explore why some forms of influence are more powerful than others.

Group Size Any size.

Time Required 30-60 minutes

Special Materials Provide each student with a copy of the enclosed scoring sheet.

Special Physical Requirements None.

Recommended Reading Assignments to Accompany This Exercise:

Readings: 10.1 (Rackham), 10.2 (Davis), 10.3 (Greenhalgh and Gilkey) 6.2 (Cohen and Bradford), 6.3 (Keys and Case)
Text: Chapters 10, 6.

What to Expect

This questionnaire is designed to probe the choice of tactics that people use when they want to influence someone. It was initially developed by David Kipnis, Stuart Schmidt, and Ian Wilkinson. Class discussion of the different influence tactics and how they vary across influence targets provides a richer understanding of how influence tactics work.

Advance Preparation (instructor)

Familiarity with the eight classes of influence tactics (assertiveness, ingratiation, rationality, sanctions, exchange, upward appeal, blocking, coalitions) is important. Instructors should study the items on the scale included in the exercise to ensure that they understand the concept clearly; further information may be gained by consulting Kipnis et al.'s original work.

Operating Procedure: Hints and Cautions

1. Have the students complete the questionnaire before class. Allow 20 minutes of class time if students are to complete it in class.

2. Distribute the scoring key. Have students sum their responses for the 8 categories of influence tactics for each of the three target groups rated.

3. Have students record their score on the blackboard separately for the 8 groups of influence tactics for the three target groups (a large 3 X 8 matrix can be drawn on one or several boards with the 8 influence tactics written across the top and the 3 targets written down the board).

4. Ask students to describe any patterns that they perceive across the scores. Determine what are the most and least likely form of influence tactics for each of the target groups, and discuss why this occurs.

5. Discuss how the different types of influence tactics relate to negotiation, and how they may be important for understanding why negotiations between superiors, co-workers and subordinates differ.

Concluding the Exercise

Ask students to volunteer to relate what they have learned from this exercise and how it will influence their future negotiations.

Reference

Kipnis, D., Schmidt, S.M., & Wilkinson, I. (1980). Intraorganizational Influence Tactics: Explorations in Getting One's Way. *Journal of Applied Psychology, 65*, 440-452.

INFLUENCE TACTICS INVENTORY
SCORING KEY

	Superior	Subordinate	Co-Worker
Assertiveness			
1	___	___	___
9	___	___	___
17	___	___	___
Total	___	___	___
Ingratiation			
2	___	___	___
10	___	___	___
18	___	___	___
Total	___	___	___
Rationality			
3	___	___	___
11	___	___	___
19	___	___	___
Total	___	___	___
Sanctions			
4	___	___	___
12	___	___	___
20	___	___	___
Total	___	___	___
Exchange			
5	___	___	___
13	___	___	___
21	___	___	___
Total	___	___	___
Upward Appeal			
6	___	___	___
14	___	___	___
22	___	___	___
Total	___	___	___
Blocking			
7	___	___	___
15	___	___	___
23	___	___	___
Total	___	___	___
Coalitions			
8	___	___	___
16	___	___	___
24	___	___	___
Total	___	___	___

TYPES OF INFLUENCE TACTICS

Assertiveness	Demanding, ordering, setting deadlines
Ingratiation	Making others feel important, acting humble, acting very friendly.
Rationality	Give information, explain, present detail, construct logical arguments
Sanctions	Use promises of positive consequences or threats of negative consequences.
Exchange of Benefits	Offer exchanges, transactions, tit-for-tat, chits
Upward Appeal	Appeal to higher level of authority, responsibility to use their "good offices"
Blocking	Hinder the other from achieving their goals
Coalitions	Obtain support of others and make a "group appeal," strength in numbers

QUESTIONNAIRE 4
THE TRUST SCALE

Objectives:

This questionnaire is designed to diagnose the current state of trust between the respondent and the person being rated.

Group Size   No restrictions

Time Required   10 minutes to complete; 30-60 minutes to debrief.

Special Materials   You may wish to make copies of the questionnaire in the student volume, in order to be able to have students rate several people or groups, or use this questionnaire in conjunction with different exercises and activities.

Special Physical Requirements   None

Recommended Reading Assignments to Accompany this Exercise:

Readings: 10.1 (Rackham), 10.2 (Davis), 12.3 (Keiser)
Text: Chapters 4, 12.

What to Expect:

This is a short questionnaire which has been developed to measure several different types of trust. It is based on a research program conducted by one of the authors, Roy Lewicki (see references below). It can be used to measure:

- The level of trust toward one individual at one point in time;
- The changing level of trust toward a single individual over time;
- Trust levels toward different individuals in different negotiation and working relationship contexts.

Advance Preparation:

It may be useful to read one or more of the research articles mentioned below. The Kramer and Tyler book is also an excellent resource on recent trust research.

Operating Procedures:

1. Assign the questionnaire prior to a negotiation, or after a negotiation. Students can complete the questionnaire in 5 minutes or less.

2. Have students "score" the questionnaire according to the key in the Appendix. The first six items measure the level of Calculus-Based trust; items 7-9 measure the level of Knowledge-Based trust; and items 10-15 measure the level of Identification-Based trust. (See the description of these categories in the student manual and in the research articles listed below.)

3. Students may wish to meet with the person whom they rated and share their scores. The purpose of this activity should be to comment on the specific behaviors that the other has shown which lead to these ratings.

4. Some students may be interested in attempting to "repair" or improve trust between them and the other. One suggested model for repairing trust is presented in the Lewicki and Bunker (1996) paper. However, our informal research shows that trust is a very difficult thing to repair. Students who DO successfully repair trust and improve their relationship with each other should be encouraged to share their strategy for improving their trust of each other.

Concluding the Exercise:

For students who wish to improve the trust level in negotiation, the following prescriptive steps may be effective (from Lewicki and Stevenson, 1997). It is presumed that these steps are initiated AT THE BEGINNING OF A RELATIONSHIP with the other. If a relationship has already been established, then the parties may either benefit from that prior relationship (if positive) or need to "repair" the past relationship (if negative).

1. **Does the party expect a short term, focused negotiation transaction with the other party, or a long term relationship with the other party?** One of the factors that drives the claiming value vs. creating value strategy is the party's expectations about the expected importance of the relationship (e.g. Savage, Blair and Sorenson, 1989.) These authors suggest that parties negotiate differently when they expect the negotiation process to be transactional--i.e. a one-time exchange of goods or services--vs. relational--i.e. embedded in a relationship in which the parties anticipate future dealings. When negotiation occurs in the context of a relationship, the parties should be mindful that their negotiating activities should either sustain the existing trust or serve to enhance it, but NOT reduce it. Therefore, negotiation in the context of an existing relationship should not employ competitive or unethical tactics which may be likely to reduce or destroy trust.

2. **If the parties anticipate a short term, transactional negotiation, then trust development actions are necessary only to assure that the parties can effectively complete the transaction.** We propose three things that need to be addressed:

First, they **need only address the elements of calculus-based trust**, since these elements are the ones which are most critical to completing a transactional deal. To build calculus-based trust, the party needs to:

- Create and meet expectations--to behave consistently and predictably
- Convince the other that the benefits of trusting outweigh the liabilities--to openly discuss these benefits and liabilities and make a persuasive case to the other in support of the benefits;
- Make and keep short-term promises--to commit to doing certain things and deliver on those things, even if they may be small procedural elements such as keeping to agreed-upon meeting times and locations, delivering what was committed to, etc.
- Establish credibility--to do what they say they will do, which may be addressed in the context of meeting expectations and keeping promises,
- Establish a reputation for trustworthiness--which may be created by the way one presents oneself, introducing references to attest to one's reputation, etc.

Second, the may wish to **propose safeguards which anticipate the opponents' possible distrust of the actor, and assure the other protection against possible consequences of trust abuse.** These safeguards may include insurance and liability protection processes, penalty clauses, fines, compensating the victim if distrustful actions occur, neutral forums in which grievances may be heard and ruled upon, etc. In addition, if the actor pre-emptively proposes such actions to the other, the other's trust may increase simply because the actor has anticipated the other's possible distrust and has expressed a willingness to help the other protect against possible distrustful actions.

Finally, the negotiator who wishes to create trust in the other should **seek evidence of the other's trustworthy behavior.** Again, this evidence should be based upon those actions which are primarily calculus-based, including the following:

- Does the other create and meet expectations? Does the other behave consistently and predictably?
- Is there evidence to determine whether the benefits of trusting outweigh the liabilities of not trusting? Is it possible to openly discuss with the other these benefits and liabilities and make a persuasive case to the other in support of the benefits?
- Does the other make and keep promises? Does the other commit to doing certain things and deliver on those things, even if they may be small procedural elements such as keeping to agreed-upon meeting times and locations, delivering what was committed to, etc.?
- Is the other credible? To what extent do they do what they say they will do, which may be addressed in the context of meeting expectations and keeping promises, and
- Does the other have a reputation for trustworthiness, which may be created by the way one the other presents (him)self, introduces references to attest to (his) reputation, etc.? Background and reputation checking on the other may be a highly valuable and informative process in establishing sound calculus-based trust.

3. In contrast, **if the parties anticipate that the upcoming transaction is the opening sequence in a long term relationship**, then trust development actions must follow a different pattern, as follows:

   a) The parties must **successfully pursue the development of calculus-based trust**, as described in the previous section.

b) As calculus based trust is solidified, the parties should also begin to **initiate activities which established knowledge-based trust**. These actions should include:

Frequent interactions. These interactions may occur simply as a function of repeated transactions, but may also occur as the parties initiate interactions which are not focused around an explicit transaction such as a purchase, sale, contract, etc. For example, salespeople often call on customers regularly simply to "check in," talk about business conditions or problems, or even simply socialize. The purpose of these activities is to establish frequent interaction and easy communication.

Establish familiarity. Interactions should be designed to help the other get to know the actor, and vice versa. Visiting the other's business location or manufacturing site, understanding the other's business challenges and problems, or establishing personal familiarity with the other's likes, preferences, wishes, aspirations, etc. are consistent with this familiarization process. The broader and richer the familiarity with the other, the more likely each will be to understand the other.

Be accurate in one's prediction of the other's actions and reactions. This tactic is an extension of establishing familiarity and frequent interaction. It is also an extension of the components of expectations, promise keeping and credibility discussed under calculus-based trust. The difference here is that greater information about the other allows each party to more accurately predict how the other will act and react, and **to use that predictive information in a manner which enhances the relationship--i.e. looks out for the other's specific interests and concerns.**

a) Finally, when the parties wish to develop a strong relationship with the other, they should engage in actions which strengthen identification-based trust. These actions should include:

Establish or affirm similar interests. To the degree that one sees one's own interests as compatible with the other's, one should highlight and affirm those similar interests.

Establish or affirm similar goals and objectives. To the degree that one sees one's own goals and objectives as compatible with the other's, one should highlight and affirm those similar goals.

Establish or affirm similar actions. To the degree that one sees one's own actions as compatible with the other's, one should highlight and affirm those similar actions. This may include proposing action strategies or implementation plans consistent with what the other would do or want to do, collaboratively designing joint actions for the future, or suggesting ways that the parties can work together on things that are now being pursued separately or in parallel.

Summary:

Trust is a complex process. It has been defined very differently by different authors, and viewed differently by various social science disciplines. The ideas represented here represent our current level of progress. We hope that those of you who teach negotiation and write about it can embellish upon and develop these ideas in the future.

References:

Kramer, R. and Tyler, T. (1996) *Trust In Organizations*. Thousand Oaks, CA: Sage Publications.

Lewicki, R.J. and Bunker, B. B. (1995) Trust in Relationships: A Model of Trust Development and Decline. In Bunker, B.B. and Rubin, J.Z. (Eds). *Conflict, Cooperation and Justice: A Tribute Volume to Morton Deutsch.* San Francisco: Jossey Bass, 1995.

Lewicki, R.J. and Bunker, B.B. (1996) "Developing, Maintaining and Repairing Trust in Work Relationships." In Kramer, R. and Tyler, T. *Trust In Organizations*. Thousand Oaks, CA: Sage Publications.

Lewicki, R. J., Stevenson, M. A. and Bunker, B.B. (1997) The Three Components of Interpersonal Trust: Instrument Development and Differences Across Relationships. Paper presented at the Annual meeting of the Conflict Management Division, Academy of Management.

Lewicki, R.J. & Stevenson, M. (1998) "Trust Development in Negotiation: Proposed Actions and a Research Agenda" *Journal of Business and Professional Ethics*, in press.

HOW TO IMPROVE TRUST IN NEGOTIATION

(PRESUMED TO START AT THE BEGINNING OF A NEGOTIATION):

1. DO THE PARTIES EXPECT A SHORT-TERM OR LONG-TERM RELATIONSHIP?

2. IF THE PARTIES ANTICIPATE A SHORT-TERM (TRANSACTIONAL) NEGOTIATION:

   A. ADDRESS CALCULUS-BASED TRUST:

   - Create and meet expectations

   - Convince others that the benefits of trust outweigh the costs of mistrust

   - Meet and keep short-term promises

   - Establish credibility

   - Establish a reputation for trustworthiness.

   B. PROPOSE SAFEGUARDS WHICH ANTICIPATE THE OTHER'S POSSIBLE MISTRUST, AND ASSURE SAFEGUARDS AGAINST TRUST ABUSE.

C. SEEK EVIDENCE OF THE OTHER'S TRUSTWORTHY BEHAVIOR:

- Does the other meet expectations?

- Is their evidence that trusting the other outweighs not trusting them?

- Does the other meet and keep promises?

- Is the other credible?

- Does the other have a reputation for trustworthiness?

3. IF THE PARTIES ANTICIPATE A LONG TERM RELATIONSHIP:

   A. PURSUE CALCULUS-BASED TRUST STEPS (SEE ABOVE).

   B. ESTABLISH KNOWLEDGE-BASED TRUST:

   - Frequent interactions

   - Establish familiarity

   - Be accurate in one's prediction of the other's actions and reactions

   - Consistently use information gained about the other to enhance the relationship.

   C. ESTABLISH IDENTIFICATION-BASED TRUST:

   - Establish/affirm similar interests

   - Establish/affirm similar goals & objectives

   - Establish/affirm common, coordinated actions.

APPENDIX

TRUST SCALE SCORING KEY

Calculus-Based Trust Items	**Knowledge-Based Trust Items**	**Identification-Based Trust Items**
1. _____	7. _____	10. _____
2. _____	8. _____	11. _____
3. _____	9. _____	12. _____
4. _____	Total _____	13. _____
5. _____		14. _____
6. _____		15. _____
Total _____		Total _____

NOTES

NOTES

NOTES

NOTES

NOTES

NOTES